## Praise for
## *Ghosts of Cape Sabine*

"*Ghosts of Cape Sabine* shares elements of the bestsellers *Into Thin Air* and *The Perfect Storm*. But this one trumps them both with its tales of not just death, but execution, suicide, and . . . cannibalism. Author Leonard F. Guttridge chillingly re-creates it all through recently uncovered journals, letters, and diaries."
                                                                    —*P.O.V*

"Cannibalism, near mutiny, bureaucratic wrangling, and the execution by firing squad of a private caught stealing from the ship's stores. The horrors of an arctic nightmare receive detailed . . . treatment."   —*The Boston Globe*

"Making the most of his material, Guttridge narrates fluidly and pointedly and will easily net the aficionados of adventure and disaster tales."
                                                                    —*Booklist*

"Guttridge's pursuit of records, letters, and diaries has enabled him to reconstruct the whole story, and it is as fascinating and exciting as any adventure novel."                                        — *The Atlantic Monthly*

"There's adventure aplenty here, not to mention execution, mutiny, starvation, suicide, and cannibalism. [*Ghosts of Cape Sabine*] deserves an honored place."                                                    —*salon.com*

*Turn the page for more praise...*

D0962785

# *Icebound:*
## The Jeannette *Expedition's Quest for the North Pole*

"On all levels, not least as a psychological tale of polar exploration, *Icebound* is a book well worth reading." —*The New York Times Book Review*

"Leonard Guttridge has performed a valuable service in setting the record straight. More to the point, however, he has told a gripping tale uncommonly well." —*The Washington Post*

"Meticulous, well-written, and truly exciting." —*The Atlantic Monthly*

"A beautifully executed narrative of sacrifice for science's sake. Guttridge has researched the story well and spices it up with the gossipy details that made life on the ship the stuff of Victorian soap opera." —*Kirkus Reviews*

"This is a dramatic story and Guttridge tells it well. He has uncovered some intriguing new information, including the reason the expedition's full story was never revealed." —*The Cleveland Plain Dealer*

"Uncommonly stirring . . . the kind of book about exploration that we feared had been banished by space travel." —*John Barkham Reviews*

"Guttridge unfolds a gripping story of suspense and adventure. He has ferreted out the facts about the *Jeannette* and the ship's company, and the colorful characters abound." —*Publishers Weekly*

"Guttridge does a fine job of re-creating the drama of the *Jeannette*. He is particularly adept at portraying the deteriorating relationships of men driven almost mad from frustration and disappointment." —*Sea History*

ALSO BY LEONARD F. GUTTRIDGE

*Mutiny: A History of Naval Insurrection*

*Icebound: The* Jeannette *Expedition's Quest for the North Pole*

*The Great Coalfield War* (with George S. McGovern)

*The Commodores: The U.S. Navy in the Age of Sail*
(with Jay D. Smith)

*Jack Teagarden: The Story of a Jazz Maverick* (with Jay D. Smith)

# GHOSTS OF
# CAPE SABINE

---

THE HARROWING
TRUE STORY
OF THE
GREELY EXPEDITION

---

# LEONARD F. GUTTRIDGE

BERKLEY BOOKS

NEW YORK

GHOSTS OF CAPE SABINE

A Berkley Book / published by arrangement with
the author

PRINTING HISTORY
G. P. Putnam's Sons  hardcover edition / January 2000
Berkley trade paperback edition / November 2000

All rights reserved.
Copyright © 2000 by Leonard F. Guttridge

This book, or parts thereof, may not be reproduced in
any form without permission.
For information address:
The Berkley Publishing Group, a division of Penguin Putnam Inc.,
375 Hudson Street, New York, New York 10014.

The Penguin Putnam Inc. World Wide Web site address is
http://www.penguinputnam.com

ISBN: 0-425-17654-1

BERKLEY®
Berkley Books are published by
The Berkley Publishing Group, a division of Penguin Putnam Inc.,
375 Hudson Street, New York, New York 10014.
BERKLEY and the "B" design are trademarks
belonging to Penguin Putnam Inc.

PRINTED IN THE UNITED STATES OF AMERICA

10  9  8  7  6  5  4  3

*For Jean*

WITH LOVE AND GRATITUDE

# CONTENTS

# PROLOGUE

"Most of us are out of our right minds. I fear for the future."
—LIEUTENANT ADOLPHUS GREELY

IT WAS 18 September, 1883. Twenty-five men huddled in their sleeping bags on an ice floe grinding erratically through the shifting ice and swirling currents of the Arctic's Kane Basin. They were the men of the Lady Franklin Bay Expedition, sent north to establish a base for scientific exploration and observation, and now engaged in a fight for their lives.

The expedition had had a turbulent birth, marked by scandal and political infighting in Washington, D.C., where the Secretary of War, Robert Todd Lincoln, son of the late president, had shown marked antipathy to the whole project. As a result, when the approval finally had come, the expedition had had to assemble in haste, and it showed, from the equipment to the ships to the personnel, a group composed primarily of Army Signal Corps soldiers with no experience in the Arctic.

Once up at Lady Franklin Bay, the personality differences had quickly made themselves known. One soldier drank too much. Another grew despondent. The second in command, Lieutenant Kislingbury, found the orders of his commander, Lieutenant Greely, objectionable, and Kislingbury was quickly relieved of duty. The expedition's doctor, Octave Pavy, clashed with the commander as well, and both wrote furiously of the other in the journals they kept. "If he could read my thoughts, he certainly must have read all the contempt I have for his person," wrote Pavy. "If he was anything but a doctor, I would deal with him summarily," wrote Greely.

Nevertheless, a degree of camaraderie developed, the scientific work went forward, and in a separate foray, the Americans jubilantly planted their flag at a point farther north than any human had ever attained—triumphantly surpassing 300 years of British polar record-breaking. For all its rocky beginnings, the expedition looked as though it would be a success after all . . . when the unexpected happened.

The ship that was supposed to resupply them after one year never came. The ship that was supposed to relieve them after two years never came. They were on their own.

Greely ordered a retreat to Smith Sound, 250 miles away, where more supplies were cached, but the gales blew, the ice thickened, their launch could make no headway. In desperation, Greely ordered the launch abandoned. If only ice floes could get through, they would ride them across Kane Basin to safety. Many of the men thought it was a bad idea, but they had no choice.

Now, more than five weeks since they had set out from their base, and after ten grueling days at the oars and drag ropes, the party had bivouacked on a paleocrystic floe one mile wide. They munched on seal meat before taking to their sleeping bags. No shelter was erected. The plan was to start off early the next morning. "I think land is within our grasp," Sergeant Brainard wrote. They were, in fact, some twenty miles from Cape Sabine, the pack having veered back north. Strong gales persisted, hurling ice-capped foam over the floe's rim. At the height of a blizzard, the floe broke in two. The segment with its half-frozen human cargo now whirled eastward across Kane Basin.

Powerful winds brought the party closer to the Greenland shore than to Ellesmere Island. When the storm abated, the party managed to erect a tent on the floe. It had space enough for only a few, Greely included. The others remained in their sleeping bags. But dulled senses revived enough to take in the words of the commander calling a council. To his people hunched in their snow-mantled bags, he declared that the Greenland coast about twenty miles to the east was now the only reasonable goal, "the only one where positive relief could be expected." Etah natives might be met there. The best course, Greely reasoned, was to "abandon everything but 2,000 pounds of selected baggage and with twenty days' rations start across the moving pack in the direction of Greenland." No one else agreed. Even Lieutenant Lockwood, while "hardly willing to give a decision, favored delay." Those were Greely's words, suggestive of Lockwood's characteristically neutral attitude. Sergeant Brainard's disagreement was stated with an outward show of respect. Within his bag that night, he scribbled a single word for the commander's proposal: "*Madness.*"

Confronted with unanimous opposition, Greely said he would wait another forty-eight hours, and unless there were "remarkable changes in our drift," he would order the move to Greenland. He confessed regret for being alone in his opinion. But, he wrote, "my duty to the expedition, the government and myself demands that I lose no time in such emergency." Unable to divine just how much weight this formal explanation could have among the men, he went further, disclosing a more nagging fear, calling attention to the "continued criticism of our movements which showed a mutinous disposition." Those who shared the tepee with him were excepted. His remark applied "to the other detachment. I heard mutinous talk through the canvas." Out of the commander's sight, Kislingbury scribbled his private view. It was heartfelt: "God knows there is not one here who had not done his level best to please him [Greely]. Great God, does he call it doing his duty to attempt his ridiculous plan of abandoning half our supplies and moving over floating ice because he has heard the men talking about him? Bah!"

More days passed. Snow, dense fog, and a steadily vanishing sun ruled out noontime observations. "It is terrible to float in this manner," wrote Pavy, "in the snow, fog and dark. This seems to me like a nightmare in one of Edgar Allan Poe's stories."

But the nightmare was only beginning.

In the months to come, the Lady Franklin Bay Expedition would engage in a battle of man against nature, and man against man, unlike any they had ever known: an epic of human achievement and human frailty, of heroism, hardship, bad luck, and worse judgment. Before it was done, their story, and those of their would-be rescuers, would encompass starvation, mutiny, suicide, shipwreck, execution—and cannibalism.

The facts have been only partly known until now and full of dark riddles, but freshly discovered journals, reports, and personal correspondence, as well as already public materials, have come together to provide, for the first time, the intimate, day-to-day details of the men's thoughts and feelings, and of the events of that ill-fated voyage, from controversial birth to bizarre and tragic finale.

So follow in the wake of men who left their homes or Army posts and who had no idea how cruelly the Arctic could play games with them. They would be tested in an environment that is to this day as forbidding as any on our planet: the bleak and convoluted shores of northern Ellesmere Island; the treacherous winds and currents of Kane Basin and Smith Sound; the ice-clad rocks of Bedford Pim Island; the inhospitable soil of Cape Sabine; the no-man's-land of the Lady Franklin Bay Expedition.

# I

# PRELUDE:
# "THE ARCTIC QUESTION"

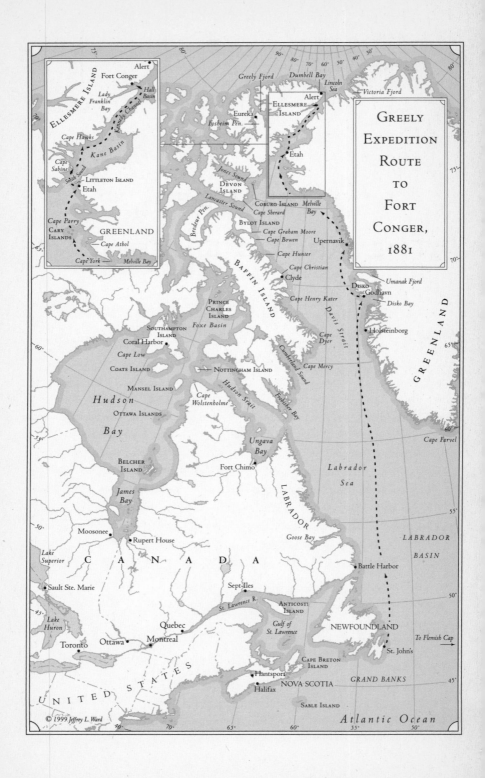

# 1

# THE CIRCUMPOLAR PLAN

ON 10 JULY, 1881, overloaded with a detachment of seasick American soldiers and a cargo ranging from 200 scientific instruments to 2,000 pounds of canned potatoes, the *Proteus*, which had left St. John's harbor only forty-eight hours before, was suddenly battered by heavy seas. Her departure had been tranquil. The American consul at that busy fishing port had boarded the steamer to wish her party Godspeed, and a few nearby tugs had blown whistles. Otherwise, Newfoundlanders had ignored the American expedition, except, noted its leader, "those who had a direct or prospective pecuniary interest in our movement."

What mostly concerned the citizens of St. John's, and its economy, was the seasonal come-and-go of whaling or sealing fleets. Not that anything could have stayed Lieutenant Adolphus Washington Greely at that moment. Not even news from Washington that James Garfield had succumbed to an assassin's bullet. On 4 July, Greely had telegraphed prayers for the president's recovery, adding that regardless of "further advice, the steamer will sail."

At nightfall on the sixth, a boat had drawn alongside the *Proteus* to deliver a last batch of mail and to await letters for home. Greely took to his bunk with five missives from his "darling wife." They gave him "great pain and happiness. Pain to reflect on our separation and mutual sufferings, happiness to know I am so dear to her." Sharing the stateroom with him, Greely's second in command, Lieutenant Frederick Kislingbury, penned equally impassioned words to a friend. He wrote of the four sons left behind: "How I miss my boys. Is there a man making more sacrifice than I?" How joyful their reunion would be on his triumphant return from the Arctic. "But," Kislingbury wrote, "I must not think of this until the end is gained." And Kislingbury pleaded for prayers that he would "go bravely through the long night."

Lieutenant Greely's spirits had revived with every fleeting minute. At midnight on the eighth he wrote, "The ship's two compound engines throbbing, our voyage commenced. We passed the majestic cliffs that form the narrows of St. John's, reached the open sea at 1:30 P.M. and discharged our pilot." The *New York Herald* correspondent who had clung to Greely's side was last to leave. He hurried ashore and inaccurately telegraphed his paper that Greely's northerly mission was twofold: to reach the North Pole and to rescue the men of the missing Arctic steamer *Jeannette* "from their glacial prison." In fact, Greely's purpose was to set up a scientific base camp, and he planned to take only a cursory look for the *Jeannette.*

Near midnight, a bright auroral arch had spanned the heavens like a nocturnal rainbow. The *Proteus* crew, seafarers all, were familiar with such phenomena and paid it no heed. For their part, the ship's passengers, Greely's landlubberly lot, had little inclination to marvel at new sights, thrust as they now were into the rigors and discomforts of shipboard life. The very morning after departure Greely himself was so seasick he failed to appear on deck until afternoon. The next day, Sergeant David L. Brainard managed an entry in his diary describing seas so powerful "our sleeping apartments are deluged, possessions floating in the flood," four of his Army comrades "ready to give up the ghost."

Prior to this expedition, Greely's seagoing experience had been limited to a two-way transatlantic crossing and the passage up from New York to St. John's. But he declared his faith in the *Proteus*; Newfoundland shipmasters had

assured him no better icebreaker cruised the northern waters. The commander's confidence was justified. Seven years old, the barkentine-rigged *Proteus* was
a strong ship, her frame of American white oak, her prow shielded with
wrought iron, and she was sheathed in ironwood from waterline to bilge level
and stem to stern. One hundred and ninety feet long, thirty feet wide, she
weighed 467 English tons. Her Dundee builders had, in Greely's words,
employed "the most approved methods of construction for use in heavy Arctic
ice." Hardy Newfoundland fishermen made up her crew, and their master,
Richard Pike, was a veteran ice navigator.

The American soldiers on board were Pike's passengers, and Greely, their
commander, intended to see that they behaved themselves. In his final dispatches to General William Hazen, the U.S. Army's Chief Signal officer and
his immediate superior, Greely reported that things now were in motion and
that "the men are behaving well—all but the party's engineer who keeps very
full of beer." He was referring to Sergeant William Cross, in charge of the expedition's motor launch. Otherwise, prospects were bright, and during those first
few days at sea, once recovered from his seasickness, the commander became a
conspicuous figure, striding fore and aft, his jet-black beard so profuse, albeit
neatly trimmed, as to mask any facial sign of emotion.

Entering Davis Strait, the ship battled more gales, and after the winds subsided, "vast bodies of ice necessitated navigating the ship from the crow's nest."
On 13 July, from his perch at the fore-topgallant masthead, a lookout sighted
Disko Island off Greenland's bewilderingly serrated west coast, its syenitic
slopes rearing blue-gray to 2,000 feet. Beneath them nestled Godhavn, a settlement whose royal inspector ordered a gunfire salute and paid the ship a wel-
coming visit. A kayak flotilla of local merchants came out, eager to trade. Here
the *Proteus* would stay a week, taking on the stores, dogs, and sledges that a doctor named Octave Pavy, who had gone before them, had assembled during his
long sojourn in the region. The doctor himself came on board, and Greely
placed him under contract as expedition surgeon, which required Pavy's swearing in as a member of the United States Army, a status he resented at the
outset.

The stay at Godhavn was highlighted by a ball in a decorated workshop.
Sergeant Brainard enjoyed "the giddy waltz with Eskimo ladies. Some with an
intermingling of Danish blood were really pretty, their hair coiled with a roll
on the head and tied by a ribbon, the hue of which denoted the wearer's social

and moral standard. Married ladies wear a ribbon of red, and those laying claim to virginity have a ribbon of white." Private Charles B. Henry, who had signed up with the *Chicago Times* to furnish copy on the expedition, reported a different color scheme: blue ribbons for wives, while "the soiled doves are compelled to promenade with green-covered boots." And the foreign visitors? "We 'cannibals' indeed look picturesque," he wrote, "not having shaved since our departure from St. John's."

A Danish brig left Godhavn with letters for America. Kislingbury had written continuously to his "darling boys," filling pages with descriptions of awesome sights on the passage up through Davis Strait, massive icebergs shimmering in a never-setting sun with exquisite hues of blue and green. And in a burst of sudden optimism, he told them he was brimming with self-confidence and perfect health: "I go hence most sanguine of success." Greely, meanwhile, addressed his wife with mingled emotions: "I wonder what you and the darling babes are doing. I am content in being here only in hope [that our] future may be made brighter. My love for you grows stronger and stronger even in these sorrowful days of separation." He added a reference to Octave Pavy: "The doctor talked considerably to me in French today, and we got along very nicely." It was a relationship that would not last long—soon they would be bitter enemies.

In fact, had he only known it, Greely had an early clue. Before leaving Disko, the expedition was joined by Henry Clay, grandson of the respected Kentucky statesman. Clay had wintered with Pavy at Disko, but they had grown to detest each other and even moved to widely separate parts of the island. Now they were again in close contact, fellow passengers on the *Proteus*. As Clay and Pavy made no secret of their mutual hatred, Greely realized that there could be no room in the party for both men and that he would have to do something about it. He had more immediate concerns, however.

Continuing north, the *Proteus* called at Upernavik. Here Greely learned that only ten sealskin suits were available, far fewer than he had anticipated. And the pair of Eskimo hunters and dog drivers he had expected were missing. Two others living nearby volunteered as replacements, and Lieutenant James Lockwood set out in the steam launch—the commander had christened it *Lady Greely*—to pick them up. He returned with two men named Jens Edward and Thorlip Frederick Christiansen, who was half Danish. They brought kayaks and hunting gear, but, wrote Greely, "unfortunately they speak no English." They, too, would play important roles in the tragedy to come.

While at Upernavik, Lieutenant Lockwood shot more than 100 guillemots, a narrow-billed seabird. With his specially designed Remington rifle, Lieutenant Kislingbury killed 420 more of them, and all were dried for preservation and added to the expedition's larder. Kislingbury proudly related this kill in a letter home that ended, "Do not worry the slightest about me, I know that all will go well."

That he and his commander expected to accomplish major scientific work in the Arctic says much for their self-confidence. Extensive polar exploration had traditionally been the province of naval personnel or other seagoers, and any landsmen with at least sledging experience. The Lady Franklin Bay Expedition, however, consisted of nineteen soldiers under U.S. Army Signal Corps authority; three civilians mustered into temporary military service; two Greenland natives; and the doctor, Octave Pavy, who also served as naturalist. Except for those latter three, not one could sail a boat, and few knew how to row. Only Sergeant Cross, already identified by Greely as a drunk, knew how to operate the party's steam launch, having worked in the Washington Navy Yard. For the most part, knowledge of dog-sledge driving and ice-field navigation, not to mention the terrible psychological strains imposed by the Arctic's long winter night, had been derived only from books. To most of the men, active service meant guerrilla skirmishes with the American Indian, not expeditions to the Arctic. It was not a recipe for success.

They were bound for a region of which civilized man knew next to nothing even while it exerted a grip upon his imagination. Concepts of the planet's unseen crown smacked of romance and fantasy, and not solely in the popular press. A former head of the U.S. Naval Observatory wrote of "a circle of mysteries. The desire to explore its untrodden wastes and sunset chambers has grown into a longing." A renowned British admiral marveled that 1,131,000 square miles of the globe's surface were "a sheer blank." Was it "a silent frozen solitude or an open sea teeming with life"?

Greely's voyage was expected to produce answers. To his general sailing orders was appended a formidable list of required scientific observations. They would begin at sea and continue at Lady Franklin Bay, on the eastern coast of Ellesmere Island, in conformity with existing instructions to Signal Corps observers "and those advised by the Hamburg Conference, which include observations on air and sea temperatures, air pressure, humidity, wind direction and velocities, precipitation, terrestrial magnetism, aurora and so on. Observations to be taken as specified by Karl Weyprecht."

Weyprecht was a bold and prescient Austro-Hungarian army officer, and what befell the Lady Franklin Bay Expedition was an unintentional consequence of his novel ideas. Weyprecht's vision extended beyond mere geographical discoveries, in the pursuit of which, he believed, men were more often motivated by chauvinism, commercial gain, or personal glory than by the pure quest for scientific truth. His dream had developed out of his own personal travels and a profound knowledge of the history of Arctic exploration. Born on 8 September, 1838, he had entered the Austrian War Marine Corps and had became a lieutenant at the age of twenty-three. He'd voyaged to the Orient, the West Indies, Mexico, and North America, charted the Dalmatian coastal waters of the Adriatic, and by the 1870s had set his sights on the mysterious and largely unknown realm above the Arctic Circle. His single exploring accomplishment, shared by fellow lieutenant Julian Payer, was the discovery of Franz Joseph Land. After a year in the ice, Weyprecht's party had abandoned their ships and were rescued finally by a Russian schooner. But it was during the long wintering in the Barents Sea that Weyprecht had contemplated the folly of nations engaged in polar rivalry through expeditions that too often came to grief. He envisioned instead a scientific bounty from something hitherto unthought of—international cooperation.

There had been nothing like this expedition in the history of Arctic voyaging, which had had a long and tortuous past. It had begun in earnest when eleventh-century Vikings penetrated to the northeastern shores of Greenland. By the late Middle Ages, commercial interests were sponsoring the first attempts to discover a northwest seaway across the top of the world in hopes of forming trade links between Europe and the Orient. With Queen Elizabeth's patronage, Martin Frobisher sought the Northwest Passage and felt he was on the right course, when rumors of gold nearby made him change direction. He found none. Another Elizabethan, John Davis, rediscovered Greenland after its abandonment by Norse colonists and entered the strait later named for him, but was turned back by ice.

In 1615, William Baffin did better, braving the perils of what became Melville Bay to reach a point 300 miles beyond Davis's farthest north, and in the process charted the great bay that bears his name. One after another, British naval expeditions set forth in search of the Northwest Passage. John Ross and Edward Parry took their ships across Melville Bay, too—a stretch of ice-clad water off the Greenland coast that whaling crews dreaded even half a century later. One of the Ross parties carried an astronomer who was not of the Royal Navy at all, but a British artillery captain named Edward Sabine. By the 1860s, Sabine was a general, and president of the Royal Society, and he gave his name to the bleak and rocky island in Smith Sound that would be the setting for the closing scene in the drama of the Lady Franklin Bay Expedition.

Parry charted the west coast of Baffin Bay. Finding the Northwest Passage still held priority, though, and in 1829 Ross set forth on what would be his last quest of it, only to be bottled up by ice for four winters before being rescued by a whaler. Undaunted, in 1845, Sir John Franklin set out with 129 officers and men on the *Erebus* and *Terror*, on the largest expedition yet to seek the fabled passage. It voyaged by way of Lancaster Sound—and promptly vanished, creating a Victorian exploration mystery that resonated deeply in the public consciousness.

At that point, the prime motive for probing the unknown changed. The goal became to discover the vanished Franklin expedition, and in the ensuing decade, no fewer than forty British and American expeditions were mounted for the search, many of them financed by Lady Jane Franklin, the explorer's wife. In 1853, however, finding Franklin's party was also the widely touted objective of a young Philadelphia surgeon named Elisha Kent Kane, who dreamed not only of finding the missing Britons but of planting the Stars and Stripes at the North Pole. He did neither, but was the first to pass through the northern exit of Smith Sound and into the 100-mile-wide basin that thereafter bore his name. Lionized upon his return to America, he died two years later, was mourned by the teenage spiritualist who loved him, and was given a funeral unequaled in splendor since that of Abraham Lincoln.

Isaac Israel Hayes followed. The ship's doctor under Kane, he crossed perilous Melville Bay in a record-breaking fifty-five hours aboard a fragile schooner, the *United States*, and explored the coasts of Greenland and Ellesmere, which was not yet known to be a vast island sprawling north. Hayes pushed farther, entering the narrow strait to which Kane had given a friend's name, Kennedy Channel. Its northern outlet, Hayes hoped, broke into an Open Polar Sea. When ice forced the *United States* to a halt, Hayes and a single companion left the ship for a daring overland dash, which he soon had to abandon. Obsessed by his notion of a prize, Hayes actually believed it within his grasp. He wrote of standing upon "these ice-girdled waters [that] might lash the shores of distant islands where dwell human beings of an unknown race."

Hayes sailed home reluctantly, convinced he had come close to discovering an Arctic paradise, and upon reaching Halifax, Nova Scotia, discovered two startling pieces of news. During his absence, the Civil War had broken out. And, more distressing for Hayes, word came that a rival in the polar stakes had sailed and was by then likely to have already reached the ice-cluttered wastes between northern Greenland and unexplored Ellesmere Island. Charles Francis Hall had sailed almost in Hayes's wake. An ill-educated printer from Cleveland, Ohio, he had left his business, a wife, and two children, determined to be the first American to score where the British had failed. To an unprecedented degree, Hall fraternized with Eskimos, emulated their dress, and immersed himself in their culture.

Twice he braved the Arctic, and then on his third expedition, in 1871, he took the *Polaris,* a refitted steamer originally named *Periwinkle,* into an ice-choked Smith Sound, leaving the vessel in a sheltered spot on the Greenland shore that he christened Thank God Harbor. Hall struck inland with a sledge and three companions, and returned to his polyglot and contentious crew boasting of having found a shoreline route clear to the Pole. Within two months, however, he was dead of a mysterious arsenic poisoning. Hall was buried on the shores of Thank God Harbor.

His shipmaster, Sidney Budington, had turned the *Polaris* toward home, but ice drove him ashore near the mouth of Kennedy Channel, and a gale swept the ship into the pack as the crew were unloading stores. Nineteen men, including George Tyson, chief navigation officer, were left marooned on the ice. What befell them made for an epic in itself. Tyson took command, and for six months the ice carried them southward. They drifted some 1,500 miles before a sealing steamer picked them up off Labrador.

Meanwhile, Budington had managed to steer the *Polaris* into Lifeboat Cove on the coast of Greenland, where ice crushed the ship to matchwood. Budington's party wintered in a hut built from the ship's timbers. They had saved two boats, however, and in the summer of 1873, they were seeking a landfall at Upernavik when they were rescued by a Dundee whaler.

Notwithstanding their travails and dark rumors about the true cause of

Captain Charles Hall's death—apoplexy was officially blamed—this expedition did have positive results, in both scientific observation and coastal survey. Hall's *Polaris* had voyaged even farther north than Kane Basin, into waters henceforth known as Hall Basin. Beyond lay Robeson Channel, closer yet to the North Pole, but ice blocked penetration through it. Also, by this time, superstitious fears had so affected the crew that Tyson wrote, "I believe some of them think we are going over the edge of the world."

Soon George Strong Nares, a veteran of the Franklin searches, embarked on what would be the British navy's first and last serious attempt to reach the North Pole. En route beyond Kennedy Channel, he left one of his two ships, the *Discovery*, at Lady Franklin Bay to winter. He carried on in the other, the *Alert*, and rounded the top of Ellesmere Island. As a disbeliever in the Open Polar Sea myth, he found his skepticism confirmed by icebergs so huge that his first mate, Albert H. Markham, described them as "a solid impenetrable mass no amount of imagination or theoretical belief could ever twist into an 'Open Polar Sea!' "

Nares had no faith in dogs. There were more than fifty, with Eskimo dog drivers, on his ships, but he sent out sledge parties man-hauled. First Mate Markham pushed farthest north, and on 12 May, 1876, planted the British flag at the highest latitude, 83° 20', yet attained by man. Scurvy struck a second sledge party, however, and on the grueling trudge south, two men died and were buried not far from Charles Hall's ice-gripped tomb in the vicinity of Thank God Harbor.

With thirty-six cases of scurvy on the *Alert* alone, Nares turned for home, blasting his way out of the ice with torpedoes. Supplies that the British had deposited on their way up—at Cape Sabine, Cary Island, and other points— would figure in Adolphus Greely's polar program.

For the British it was the end of an era. Besides that Farthest North record, Nares's people had brought home notes full of scientific data. Nares also had added a new adjective to the English dictionary: "paleocrystic," to describe the huge slabs of ancient ice his expedition had encountered north of Ellesmere Island. But it was the dread news of death from scurvy that dominated headlines. A naval court of inquiry censured Nares for failing to provide his sledge crew with fresh lime juice, which Nares had denigrated as a preventive. Much later, his expedition was reappraised, he was promoted to admiral, and in due course was knighted.

It was while the Nares expedition was struggling through Smith Sound that Karl Weyprecht, not long returned from his own sortie above the Arctic Circle, formulated plans for a new and revolutionary approach. To Weyprecht's thinking, such ordeals as the paralyzing cold, the crushing force of ice, the terror of scurvy, the peril of starvation, and the psychological tensions induced by long Arctic nights that could drive men mad were too formidable to be taken on by separate, often badly led or ill-organized groups of men in frail ships. The prizes sought were not worth the price paid. Searching for the Northwest Passage or a nonexistent Open Polar Sea, planting national flags in previously untrodden Arctic wastes, and racing to islands to see who could get farthest north or even reach the Pole itself—none of these, in Weyprecht's judgment, was anywhere near as important as the gathering of scientific data. Weyprecht believed that scientific research was the only justification for costly expeditions beyond the Arctic Circle and was better achieved by nations in concert rather than in rivalry.

On 17 September, 1873, Weyprecht had spelled out his ideas at the fourth annual meeting of the Association of German Naturalists and Physicists. Weyprecht argued that nations should join in building and maintaining a chain of observation posts encircling the North Pole and that the time for polar expeditions of individual nations was past. What Weyprecht proposed, reported the prestigious journal *Nature*, was a "girdle of stations around the entire Arctic region to record simultaneously observations relating to various branches of Physics and Meteorology, also Botany, Zoology and Geology."

Weyprecht's plan had won favorable notice: Prince Otto von Bismarck appointed a commission to study it, and the International Meteorological Congress gave strong support. An encouraged Weyprecht hoped to amplify his proposal for this group at its next meeting, scheduled for Rome in 1877, but Balkan wars intervened and the whole subject was shelved, much to Weyprecht's impatience. He was in frail health and knew how slim his chances were for recovery. Interest in his idea revived in 1879, however, when ethnic quarrels could no longer stay the more universal and popular absorption in science, fueled by well-publicized Darwinian theories, fresh astronomical discoveries, breakthroughs in the field of medicine, the spread of international telegraphy, and such inventions as the typewriter, the telephone, and electric light. When the Fifty-fourth International Meteorological Congress met in Rome in April 1879, Weyprecht was ready with his updated notions. They resulted in plans for an International Polar Conference to be held in Hamburg six months later, which Weyprecht anticipated would secure multinational agreement for a ring of stations on the roof of the world.

And he wanted American participation. He advised General Albert J. Myer in Washington that "this polar girth would show a large void if the United States excluded themselves." Myer was head of the Signal Corps, the Army branch specializing in meteorology, and he had just authorized the installation of a weather station at Point Barrow, the northern extremity of Alaska. But the Weyprecht plan stirred no great interest elsewhere in the War Department, and Americans in general suspected anything resembling foreign entanglements. On 13 September, the general told the Europeans that it was "not practicable" for the United States Signal Corps to be represented at the Hamburg meeting as requested.

At the same time, however, Myer wrote separately to Karl Weyprecht, asking for suggestions as to how the United States might still assist. When read before the conference, Myer's letter dismayed delegates who had hoped for more direct American involvement, but representing Denmark, Germany, France, the Netherlands, Norway, Austro-Hungary, Sweden, and Russia, they decided that their countries would go ahead without the Americans. Expeditionary forces would go north to make one year's simultaneous observations. The work would begin in July 1880 and continue for twelve months. Russia promised a station at the mouth of the Lena and another on New Siberian Islands, Norway one at North Cape, and Sweden one at Spitzbergen. Germany, Holland, and Denmark made similar pledges.

At first, action faltered. By 1880, only seven stations were under way, and a second International Polar Conference held at Berne that year had given up on the Americans. But the conference decided to press on, and optimistically designated 1881 to 1882 International Polar Year. More stations were added to the circumpolar ring. As an aid to those who would man them, Weyprecht published a bulky handbook titled *Metamorphosis of Polar Ice and Guide for Observation of Polar Lights and Magnetic Fields in Northern Regions*. He could at last see his vision approach reality. Countries never remotely acting in concert before had pledged contributions toward the success of the world's first International Polar Year. But Karl Weyprecht would not live to learn of the project's outcome—nor of the grim denouement to America's role in his long-cherished grand design.

# 2

# THE YOUNG GREELY

ADOLPHUS GREELY, LIEUTENANT, U.S. Army, was on an extended European furlough when he witnessed firsthand the sensation caused by the Nares expedition's premature return. He explained, "The Arctic squadron had reached the Irish coast and with all England I was absorbed in the story they had to tell." He hadn't been interested in Arctic exploration before. Now that changed: "When wandering through Westminster Abbey before the desire or intention of Arctic travels and exploration entered my mind, the epitaph to Sir John Franklin was the only one which so impressed itself on me that I carried it away in my memory."

Adolphus Washington Greely had been born 27 March, 1844, in Newburyport, Massachusetts, the son of a twice-married shoemaker named John Balch Greely. Adolphus's childhood had been spent in the shadow of a stepbrother, John, more than twenty years his senior. In Brown High School he had been an unambitious pupil, perhaps because of the family's inability to afford college. When war came in 1861, he'd enlisted in the Nineteenth Massachusetts Volunteer Infantry. Years later, he questioned the move: "Did I or did I not enter from patriotic motives? I am really uncertain."

But he took part in the siege of Yorktown; saw action at Ball's Bluff, Fair Oaks, and Savage Station; and was twice wounded at Antietam. Upon his recovery, he was commissioned second lieutenant in the Ninth Regiment, Corps d'Afrique (later the Eighty-first Colored Infantry), on garrison duty at Port Hudson, Louisiana. When his father fell ill, Greely tendered his resignation, "unconditional and immediate," and when it was turned down, he tried again the following year. He insisted, "I have served over three years, have been home only twelve days." Not until fall was Greely granted leave. He reached Newburyport only to learn of his father's death. "It quite overcame me to think that I had come so far and been too late to see him," he later wrote.

In 1865, Greely tried yet again to leave military service and failed. Still in command of black troops, he conscientiously looked to their welfare. Once, he wrote his stepbrother to get them a supply of mittens: "Some sewing society in Newburyport would be abolitionist enough to make 50 to 100 pairs for colored soldiers." Many of his men were owed back pay, and Greely wrote to Washington that "colored soldiers deserve as much as white soldiers, as they are fighting for the same cause."

Peace found Greely in New Orleans, where he thought seriously of setting up a cotton business with a workforce consisting of time-expired men from his regiment. All he needed was investments. Perhaps his mother could be persuaded to sell her house? He would do the rest. He wrote to her, "I am confident of getting along well, I have no vices and am able and willing to work hard. I have changed a good deal and am not as listless and inclined to laziness as when a schoolboy in the old Brown High." But in postwar Louisiana, a Northerner starting a business invited catcalls as a carpetbagger, and so he finally abandoned the idea, applied for a commission in the regular Army, and was posted as second lieutenant in the Thirty-sixth Infantry Regiment based at Camp Douglas, Utah territory.

There he served variously as quartermaster, commissary, and post adjutant, but it wasn't until he was detached to the Signal Corps that he found his true calling. He studied telegraphy under John C. Van Duzer, General Grant's wartime communications chief, and, soon a practiced telegrapher, he was sent to the Department of the Platte, Nebraska, to familiarize Army posts with the techniques of electrical transmission.

General Albert Myer had created a division within his Signal Corps devoted specifically to weather forecasting. By 1873, the Signal Corps issued seventy weather bulletins a day and almost as many weather maps. Other environmental benefits included river-level reports, frost alerts, and storm warnings. In extending those services far westward, Greely was aggressively active. He staffed offices coast to coast with trained observers whose job was to keep Signal Corps headquarters in Washington supplied with the meteorological data on which the Army's weathermen based their forecasts. Following transfer to the Fifth Cavalry Regiment in 1874, he was seldom in the same place for long, and his inspection tours within the spreading web of weather-observation posts soon identified him as the Army's top meteorologist.

At the end of that year, he was assigned to go to Texas to manage the telegraph lines and to build 1,100 more—his most challenging duty to date. His party would cross the state's southern half, then follow the Rio Grande northwest to El Paso, through country marauded by hostile Indians and outlaw bandits and with scant forestry for poles. But Greely went to work with what was now acknowledged in Washington as his characteristic zeal. Given three years with spare funds to finish the task, he did so in one. By early 1876, more than 1,000 lines were in operation, all working at locations of Greely's personal preference. On his say-so, timber was hauled from far-off woodlands, and junipers from the Great Dismal Swamp in Virginia went up as telegraph poles within sight of the Mexican border.

Erecting poles and stringing wire from Fort Concho to Fort Stockton was done by two detachments, each of thirty men, from the Eleventh (New York) Infantry Regiment. So energetic was the group's leader that in mid-January 1876, filing a report with Signal Corps headquarters, Greely singled him out for special commendation. And thus occurred the first link between Adolphus Greely and Frederick Kislingbury, the officer fated to burden his conscience in a region even more desolate and remote than the Texas plains they had strung with military telegraph wire.

Greely was no less proud of his own achievements. To his niece, Clarissa, he wrote, "It surprises me to think how much I have done. I have taken anything when it comes, decided on the moment and acted on that decision." And in another letter reflecting on how much he had personally gained from the experience, he wrote, "I feel this year has been prosperous and successful for me and has added to my standing and reputation. It too has given me increased confidence in my general ability."

Only a disastrous love affair, it seemed, could shake that confidence. In later years he would destroy revealing letters, leaving few details from which to sketch his early connections with women. One letter he left intact, however, except for the sender's full name, is simply marked "Miss M." It betrays a heart broken by age difference—and Greely was the younger.

He had said he loved her. She told him his love "belongs to an illusion really—to the woman whom you feel I ought to be—and of course, you are saddened and disappointed. My dear, learn to understand the difference between us. She, your illusion, is young in mind and soul. The real woman has put youth aside for ever—or rather, youth has deserted her. Were she young, and you unfettered, your expectations would encounter fewer disappointments. Always lovingly—" When, that same year, Greely applied for a furlough over-seas, he cited health reasons. To Clarissa, he expressed a desire to "get back into my old habits of general reading and thought." But it was also in hopes of some escape or relief from those emotional entanglements that, the lieutenant told his niece, he was "now in a mind to go to Europe."

It was during this visit that he was so much moved while contemplating the epitaph to Sir John Franklin in Westminster Abbey. The Nares affair filled newspapers. The expedition had not been expected home so soon. But if Greely's attention was captured by the Nares furor, he admitted, "Never in my wildest fancies did I picture myself as one of the *next* expedition which would sail northward between the 'Pillars of Hercules' into the Unknown Regions."

# 3

# Howgate's Colony

"Lieutenant Weyprecht's suggestions deserve the serious consideration of all civilized countries; were they adopted as a ground for action, a new era in polar exploration would be begun." *Nature*'s editorial words in 1876 were noted with interest by a United States Army captain named William Henry Howgate. Weyprecht and Howgate would never meet, but it was the independent efforts of these two men that would send so mismatched an American party as the Lady Franklin Bay Expedition north of the 78th parallel.

Strappingly handsome, a combination of ladies' man and hearty if incautious innovator, Howgate had immigrated to the United States from England at age twenty-one. First a newspaper reporter in Philadelphia, he moved to Detroit, and when the Civil War began, he joined the Twenty-second Michigan Volunteers as a senior lieutenant. He saw action at Chickamauga and Atlanta, and earned himself a brevet major's rank. Mustered out in the summer of

1866, Howgate was named postmaster of Romeo, a village north of Detroit, where he married Abigail Day, a farmer's daughter. And those immediate post-war years would prove the most tranquil of Howgate's odd career.

Tiring of the peaceful life, he secured a commission in the newly formed Signal Corps and soon enjoyed the wholehearted trust of its founder and first commander, General Albert Myer. When Myer fell ill, he appointed Howgate as the Corps's property and disbursement officer, and it wasn't long before Howgate's imagination became gripped by a formidable challenge, one that popular and technical journals alike described with awe as "The Arctic Question." The question did not refer simply to reaching the North Pole, but rather to the scope of discovery such accomplishment entailed, to the charting of temperate waters that many, Howgate included, believed surrounded the North Pole beyond the ice barrier, and to the prospects of discovering abundant game and vegetation and perhaps even making contact with a previously unknown tribal race. And by the 1870s, Howgate believed he had found the key.

It was colonization. With a permanent source of manpower in place at northernmost latitudes, regular advantage could be taken of the ice pack's seasonal crumbling. In 1875—the year Karl Weyprecht in far-off Graz enunciated his own plan for polar exploration—Howgate detailed his scheme in a forty-page pamphlet. It envisaged a party of some fifty men, mustered into military service for discipline's sake, shipped north with food, equipment, and prefabricated huts. Labor would be reinforced by Eskimos bribed or press-ganged on the passage north. Once installed, the station would be visited annually by a steamer bringing fresh supplies, news and letters from home, and additional personnel if needed.

Howgate had the colony's location mapped in his mind. He wrote, "The principal depot or post is to be located upon Lady Franklin Bay between lat. 81 and 82 [degrees]." Fuel would be no problem. Earlier expeditions had discovered coal seams along this stretch of the Ellesmere Island coast. Game was said to be plentiful. Howgate drew his information from reports of the Nares and Hall expeditions. The *Polaris*, Hall had said, had come excitingly close to "the crowning jewel of the Arctic dome." Howgate used less picturesque language. In one of his numerous petitions to the United States Congress for colonization funds, he quoted a member of Hall's party to the effect that had the *Polaris* beaten young ice formation "by a fraction of an hour they could have steamed unobstructed over a veritable 'open sea' to the Pole itself."

Howgate's principal champion in the popular press was James Gordon Bennett's *New York Herald*, whose circulation had gained from sensational coverage and promotion of geographic expeditions, the most memorable to date being that of Henry Morton Stanley's successful African search for the missionary David Livingstone in 1871. On the other hand, Howgate's plan was ridiculed by the *New York Times*, a losing rival to the *Herald* in New York's press circulation wars. On 29 December, 1876, it editorialized that the only "colonists" to be gotten would have to be handcuffed and hardened criminals, taken by force beyond the Arctic Circle and dumped there. When the relief ship arrived, the convicts could fib, saying they had reached the North Pole in the meantime. The men could hardly be expected to have abandoned their creature comforts, "warm huts, Bibles in large print, and all the facilities for poker, to make a long and difficult journey, when it would be much simpler for them to say they had done so." No, the best way to reach the Pole was by way of a succession of camps at half-mile intervals, each with "a lamp burning in the kitchen window." The explorer could warm his toes at one station, dine at the next, and sleep at a third, attaining the prize by easy stages. Tongue in cheek, the *New York Times* wondered why nobody had thought of this plan before.

Howgate refused to be nettled. For one thing, he remained high in the esteem of his boss, General Myer, whose declining health obliged him to leave matters increasingly in the hands of the Signal Corps property and disbursing officer. And Howgate had become so self-confident that he took little trouble to keep even extramarital activities a secret. His mistress, Nettie Burrill, a government worker from De Witt, Michigan, hosted Washington parties on a scale unusually lavish for anyone on a federal salary. But much of her money came from Captain Henry Howgate. He had begun drawing imprudently from Signal Corps coffers. In 1876, he built Nettie a large house on 13th Street only two blocks from the home of his wife and daughter. To questions raised about his seemingly inexhaustible funds, Howgate explained them as a legacy left to him by his father in England.

Few doubted Howgate's word, and his engaging personality, no less than the cogency of his arguments before learned bodies, won him significant support for his campaign to colonize the Arctic. The secretary of the Smithsonian Institution had pledged his cooperation "should Congress make the necessary appropriation." That was the sticking point. In Howgate's view, too many politicians opposed spending public money on what they sneered at as the chimerical pipe dream of men smitten with a polar virus.

Among Howgate's supporters, Admiral David Dixon Porter believed there was "an open polar sea for two hundred miles towards the Pole. Howgate's colony," he explained, "should consist of hardy men with cheerful dispositions, the best provisions and means of amusement. Nostalgia is the greatest enemy you would have to fear." Before the end of 1876, Howgate had won an opening round, getting a bill introduced in Congress for work on, in the official wording, "a plan known as 'Polar Colonization.' " At the same time, he gave thought to the colony's leadership. "The first in command," he declared, "should be a man able not only to gauge men but to control them." Zeal and energy were not enough. "Coolness of temper, firmness of rule, persistency of purpose, and a well-balanced mind, fertile in resources and expedients, are indispensable to success." It was asking a lot, but Howgate figured he had already found the ideal choice, that his words fit no one more aptly than Lieutenant Adolphus Greely.

Back from his European tour, Greely had become Howgate's closest friend, and whenever in the capital he lodged at the captain's home. Except during Howgate's absences on extramarital escapades, the two talked animatedly over dinner, the Arctic more often than not their topic. If Greely was not already prone to the polar virus, amity with Howgate would have ensured his infection.

Congress was considering the captain's bill "to authorize and equip an expedition to the Arctic Seas." Greely wanted its command. "I am extremely anxious to go," he wrote his stepbrother, "and think I can manage it if the bill passes."

Howgate's bill sailed through the House of Representatives, and on 9 February, 1877, was referred to the Senate committee on military affairs. There it stalled. General Myer had sought the opinion of General William Tecumseh Sherman, commander of the United States Army, and Sherman had no patience with harebrained notions for invading the Arctic. He announced via his aide that he "does not favor the scheme of Captain Howgate, especially if the army is to be charged the duty of establishing a colony to serve as a base for the searchers of the North Pole." Some in the Senate shared the general's views. Action on Howgate's bill was postponed until the next session of Congress.

Greely went back out in the field again, inspecting and supervising repairs to 1,500 miles of military telegraph lines from Santa Fe, New Mexico, to San Diego, California, and, undaunted, Howgate forged ahead with preparations for what he would publish as *The Preliminary Arctic Expedition of 1877*. Soliciting private contributions, he raised $10,000 to buy, or charter, and outfit a ship. It would enter the Arctic first, with someone to collect supplies and recruit Eskimos, thus laying the groundwork for the main colonizing party he hoped would sail in 1878. Lieutenant Greely could manage this preliminary venture, but Howgate was saving his friend for the principal event. Since Howgate counted on a sanction from the War Department, his plan was to keep the actual colonizing under Army auspices. The advance expedition would be more of a private affair, and the man Howgate found to lead it was George Tyson, the former whaler who had brought the *Polaris* survivors to safety. Tyson needed employment. He had a wife and son to support, and the book he had written of his *Polaris* experiences brought little income.

Anxious for the success of this initial voyage, Howgate personally supervised its outfitting, but it was more expensive than foreseen. "The total cost of the expedition must not exceed our estimate," he wrote Tyson, then seeking a vessel along the New England coast. "Will she require as large a crew and as expensive an outfit as estimated?" Even when Tyson found a fifty-six-ton whaleship, the *Florence*, at New London, Connecticut, a ship requiring no more than a thirteen-man crew, Howgate was on edge. "There should be no delay," he wrote Tyson in July. He insisted that Tyson keep him informed. He wrote, "Use the telegraph freely as time is becoming precious." Another message followed: "I must be there to see you off." He elaborated on sailing orders. The primary objective was "collection of material for use of the future colony on the shores of Lady Franklin Bay." The "material" included ten Eskimo families willing to leave home for distant colonization. Tyson's party would station itself on Disko Island until joined by the main expedition, a rendezvous scheduled hopefully for August of the following year.

So it was, in August of 1877, that the first part of Howgate's plan went into effect. The *Florence* hoisted anchor, and by late September had reached Baffin Land near the entrance to Davis Strait. Tyson's crew went into winter quarters, while Tyson set about soliciting Inuit families who would, if all went as planned, form the nucleus of Howgate's Arctic colony.

# 4

# HENRIETTA

OF ALL THESE events, meanwhile, Greely had no firsthand knowledge. His days had been spent in getting the telegraph line from San Diego to Santa Fe into working order. Punctilious to the extreme, he could be equally ruthless. He fired two operators for drunkenness and using "insulting language when referring to me." In the fall of 1877, he collected data to establish "danger lines" on the Sacramento and San Joaquin rivers, which would permit California merchants to telegraph flood warnings. On 6 November, Greely reported the line to Santa Fe completed and "open for business." And by that date, stationed mostly in San Diego, he had begun a love affair that, he said, "affects me quite differently from any I ever had before," and that would be of great significance to the Lady Franklin Bay expedition.

Henrietta Nesmith had been born in Thun, Switzerland, during a European tour by her well-off parents. The couple already had three boys, two of them twins. The new arrival was "a perfect little beauty." In 1860, when she was eleven, the family moved to San Antonio, Texas, where her father's pro-Union sentiment on the eve of the Civil War landed him briefly in jail. He sought refuge in Mexico, and only after more vicissitudes did the Nesmiths finally settle in San Diego, where, despite poor health, he soon established himself as a bank president and director of the Texas and Pacific Railroad Company. His wife died. And such was Nesmith's own physical condition that domestic burdens fell heavily upon his only daughter's shoulders.

Sturdy shoulders, according to a letter from Greely. He described Henrietta as "a woman of some years, twenty-seven I think. She is very tall, five feet, nine inches, and is not considered a beauty but certainly is not bad looking . . . fully fleshed . . . a commanding figure . . . black hair, dark gray eyes. Unusually graceful, considering her height." And she was strong-willed, "likes to have her own way." For Henrietta's part, it was not love at first sight. She told Greely, "You did not in any way attract me particularly. But when you tried, how soon you won me."

Winning Henrietta over took fewer weeks than she had expected. During autumn picnics in San Diego, she still was not swept off her feet, proposing to Greely that they wait until after his return to Washington, thus giving them time to gauge the depth of their affection. Separation only heightened their ardor. Near the year's end, Greely was at Red Bluff, inspecting the Sacramento River telegraph. He wrote, "You are the first woman to whom I have written a genuine love letter." She confessed in words that crossed his (as most did), "I am all yours. Not a shadow stands between us." Not until his return south to spend Christmas with the Nesmiths did Greely reveal his expectation that should Congress approve the Arctic colonization plan, he was in line to carry it out. Henrietta feigned interest, inwardly persuading herself that Washington's politicians would never consider such a crazy idea.

Believing their romance soundly on track, Greely took a circuitous route back to Washington, and reached the capital to find his friend Howgate anxiously awaiting word from Tyson on the *Florence.* Two days after checking in at Signal Corps headquarters, Greely wrote Henrietta, "I think now the Bill will pass on the coming session." Henrietta prayed otherwise. And although their correspondence grew ever more ardent, it was increasingly clouded by polar references.

Greely faced a dilemma. Henrietta told him frankly that although she had led him to think that she had no objection to his polar plans, "I hoped then as I hope still that the Bill will not pass." She would not want him to depart on such an enterprise until a year or two into their marriage, and only then "if you find no easier way to make a name for yourself." Why could not Captain Howgate lead the expedition himself, since it was his idea? To this question, Greely replied that there was no real cause for alarm, that were there the slightest possibility that she would suffer anything like Lady Franklin's ordeal, he would never go. But in this case, safety was assured. His party could not be lost or abandoned; it would be sustained by annual visits from relief ships. He told her, "Did I not believe the plan a feasible one, and that I am quite certain of returning to your arms safe and sound I should not desire to lead it." Still, Henrietta could not rest. Acknowledging her inability to change his mind— "I cannot tell or ask you to stay while your wish is so strong to go"—she reproached him for holding ambition and pride above all else: "I would rather be your wife as you are than your widow as the most revered man. . . . Oh, I love you so much, how can you leave me?" Greely told her to ignore the alarmist stories of San Diego friends and to bear in mind that "steam is in our favor, and coal abundant."

At least momentarily, Henrietta's apprehensions over Greely's polar plans were equaled by fears of a different sort. She knew her lover to be tall, slim, dark-complexioned, with a neat mustache and full side-whiskers, and that despite poor vision—"I have bought two pairs of eye-glasses, one for reading, the other for street wear"—he was attractive to ladies, among them Captain Howgate's daughter, Ida. Greely had known her eight years, and the Howgates considered him one of the family. This was his hasty explanation when, after inadvertently mentioning that he had kissed Ida on his return from the Far West, Henrietta had written, "If I tho't for an instant it was such a kiss as you give me, I would never write you another line."

Henry Howgate's latest move to win Congressional support for his project was a paper he wrote, and Greely read, before the American Geographical Society at Chickering Hall, New York, on 31 January, 1878. The colony he promoted would be at or near "the borders of the polar sea and for overcoming the physical obstacles in the pathway to the Pole." Lady Franklin Bay was the chosen site because of the coal seam found by the British in 1875. The colony's outfit would include miles of telegraph wire to maintain communication with subsidiary depots: "Copper wire is strong, light, flexible, and a good conductor, and can be worked while lying upon the dry snow or ice without support." Batteries would be left permanently at the bay station, where, given fuel, they wouldn't freeze. "And," he continued, "it is possible that the recently discovered telephone may be applied with advantage." They could erect observation balloons, using gas from the coal. Balloon experiments to aid Howgate's colony were already under way in Paris.

George Tyson's advance party of thirteen men was believed by this time to have gone into winter quarters at the head of Cumberland Gulf. Greely's expedition would join them at Disko in August—that is, if all went well, for no one knew what luck Tyson was having: "The loss or safety of the *Florence* must remain a closed book to us for many months to come."

Greely told Henrietta that Howgate was "a hard man in some ways . . . shows temper with everyone but me. I am more his confidant and friend than anyone else." All the same, Greely did not know how the captain, as Signal Corps purser, was using or misusing the public's money. These years of his promoting Arctic colonization were the precise period in which, according to future sworn testimony, Howgate embezzled some $200,000 of Signal Corps funds, half of it allegedly squandered on women of ill repute. With General Myer crippled by illness, Howgate was in effect chief of the Corps, approving vouchers in Myer's name and issuing checks without oversight.

Pushing for his Arctic colony and still a conspicuous figure on the Washington social scene, Howgate sensed trouble brewing. When the blow finally fell, he would stoutly defend his practices: "Every dollar I spent was for the good of the Signal Corps." The Corps engaged lobbyists who had to be paid off. Howgate would later testify, "I was instructed by our chief [Myer] to use the money as I saw fit, in fact lavishly." This attempted explanation lay in the future. But it was just two weeks after Greely had read Howgate's paper before the American Geographical Society that Secretary of War Alexander Ramsay questioned a request sent to him over General Myer's signature for an advance of $50,000 to be paid to Howgate out of public funds. Ramsay wondered whether it was proper to advance public money to "this officer, who is not bonded, and who is on disbursing duty by order of the Chief Signal Officer." At once began the first talk of an investigation into Signal Corps finances as managed by Captain Henry Howgate.

Greely gave Henrietta a revealing glimpse into the Howgates' domestic scene. One evening at the Howgates' home, Greely had studied Abigail Howgate, reflecting that she "had a pretty face and once I fancied I could have married such a yielding, clinging woman and been happy." But the more he had looked at her, the more there grew in his mind "the strangest sense of loathing, not against her personally, but I knew that a few minutes with me would [replace] flattered vanity with a strong active hatred." Some days later Greely squired Abigail Howgate to a White House reception "out of pity. Her husband will hardly ever go out with her nor will he remain at home."

Though Howgate may have spent some of the requested $50,000 on Nettie Burrill or other lovers, most was earmarked for his Arctic program. Tyson on the *Florence* was somewhere off the Greenland coast. If he reported success, Howgate would have to be ready to mount the principal expedition, complete with congressional approval.

In this area, Howgate had a formidable rival. James Gordon Bennett, publisher of the *New York Herald,* had long nursed ambitions for pulling off some Arctic version of his African scoop, Stanley's discovery of Livingstone. Already, one of Bennett's newsmen had accompanied the British sportsman-explorer Sir Allen Young aboard the Royal Navy steam bark *Pandora,* seeking a Northwest Passage and relics of the lost Franklin party. Colorful descriptions had filled the *Herald*'s columns. But Young's expedition had foundered, and by then Bennett was working on another, intending it to sail under U.S. Navy colors, the total expenses borne by himself. He had already selected a naval commander, Lieutenant George Washington De Long, who, at Bennett's instiga- tion, was in those early months of 1878 scouting at home and overseas for a suitable ship.

Notwithstanding a society scandal that had driven Bennett into European exile, his influence in Washington was still considerable. He soon had his ship, Allen Young's old steamer *Pandora,* which he bought, overhauled, and renamed *Jeannette.* But aware of Howgate's activity, he had to act fast. Within hours of the Senate Naval Affairs Committee's favorable report on what newspapers were calling the Howgate Bill, the press baron telegraphed De Long to hurry preparations. Howgate, he said, was "going ahead tooth and nail. He means business. However chimerical his plan, it is the only one before the public."

Greely's tone in correspondence was as optimistic as James Gordon Bennett's was anxious. He wrote Henrietta Nesmith that the Senate might pass the Howgate Bill at any moment. The House was less of a sure thing, but Howgate was "pulling wires" to keep the opposition silent. In this regard, Greely said, Howgate was "indefatigable." On a more personal level, Greely had a rival of his own. While duty confined him to the eastern United States, Henrietta had become the focus of admiration among Army officers stationed at San Diego. One had fallen so heavily in love with her that her failure to reciprocate had driven him' to the brink of suicide. Another suitor played on Henrietta's fears. "If Greely goes to the Pole," he told her, "it will kill him. Why don't you tell him?" Others warned her against marrying Greely before he left, while predicting also that if they didn't marry, she would tire of waiting for his return and sever the engagement.

Henrietta tried to convince her already far-off lover that she hadn't the stamina of some explorers' wives: "I am no Lady Franklin." Sometimes Henrietta ended her letters to Greely with a forlorn "I love you and want your goodnight kiss." Others she imbued with a passion so strong as to suggest a deliberate effort to seduce him into thinking twice about heading for the Arctic. She wrote to him that his recent love letters "affect me as much as your personal touch . . . give me a sensation of pleasure so exquisite it is absolutely painful . . . If you kissed me long enough you could make me do anything that you could conceive of, no matter how averse I might be to it at first." His total domination of her, she confessed, both gladdened and frightened her. She wrote to him, "I want you with me, and not a shadowy form in some dim distant regions. I am yours, body and heart and soul."

Some of Greely's responses implied that he was not quite sure of his reasons for heading into the Arctic at all. Going far north could not be guaranteed to bring him fame and fortune. He could, in fact, scarcely define his compulsion. But, he wrote, "neither you nor I believe that our place is to avoid everything that is dangerous, is hard, is difficult. That is not our idea of life." Even so, the very likelihood that Congress would pass the Howgate Bill had begun to worry him. Henrietta had suggested postponing their marriage until his return from the Arctic. Greely was only too well aware of those rival admirers in San Diego. "I could not think of going without you were my wife," he wrote. "I should suffer untold agony while gone." He would be affected by "all manner of doubts, I could not endure it." In another letter, he summed it all up: "My great love for you has put me in such a cruel position."

Engaged in an emotional transcontinental exchange, Greely was at first unaware of the headway gained by James Gordon Bennett in his own reach for congressional endorsement of a polar project. The Howgate Bill had gone down in defeat. On 18 March, 1878, Congress passed legislation to aid

Bennett, after his assurance that he would make good every penny spent. And this blow wasn't the only one to Howgate's and Greely's hopes. They heard that George Tyson, somewhere off Greenland's west coast, had made no progress at all in his effort to recruit Eskimos for the main expedition, the men as hunters and dog drivers, the women as "tailors and boot-makers." The *Florence* would return, Tyson unable to "induce the men to leave their native mountains (cheerless though they be) without their wives and children."

Hearing of Howgate's congressional setback, Henrietta wrote, "How can I help giving thanks?" But she failed to reckon on the captain's tenacity. He stepped up his lobbying and produced yet another booklet (forty-eight pages) entitled *Congress and the North Pole: An Abstract of Arctic Legislation in the Congress of the United States.* But Henrietta could now more confidently discuss marriage plans. Her letters became less expressive of fears relating to polar travel than apprehension about a new bride's marital duties. She winsomely claimed to have found the key. She wrote to Greely, "Make everything subservient to love and you can lead me where you please." And in another letter, "If you kiss me you must do it as by night."

# 5

# HAZEN AND LINCOLN

GREELY AND HENRIETTA were married in June 1878 at the Nesmiths' home in San Diego. They were denied much of a honeymoon. Congress was under pressure from settlers in the West demanding better protection against Indians. Need had grown for more communication between the military departments, and Greely, in New York a month after the wedding, recovering from "a very trying case of spinal rheumatism," was ordered to construct telegraph lines connecting the Bismarck signal office with Army posts in the Dakota badlands. Henrietta accompanied him on most of these travels, often helping in clerical work. But in early November she was pregnant. Greely arranged that she precede him to Washington; he would follow on completion of his duties.

Early in 1879, he was again settled in the nation's capital, where he heard of George Tyson's return on the *Florence* after fifteen months "in the regions of eternal ice"—Tyson's words to his wife. "Never before have I experienced such severe storms," he said. "I can hear the rushing of the wind and the roaring of the sea still." But Captain Howgate refused to consider Tyson's labors wasted and stubbornly insisted that they would "serve as a stepping-stone to the permanent work on which our hearts are fixed."

Meanwhile, Americans were reading about Bennett's *Jeannette*. Congress had given the Secretary of the Navy complete authority over the expedition's fitting out, but in the final weeks before the *Jeannette*'s sailing from San Francisco, the Navy Department lost interest, and Bennett, still dreaming of a Stanley-Livingstone scoop amid ice fields, dismayed Lieutenant De Long by directing him to forego an assault upon the North Pole in favor of a search for Baron Nils Adolf Erik Nordenskiöld, the Swedish explorer reported missing while probing a northeast passage in the *Vega*. Despite beflagged yachts and gunfire salutes, the *Jeannette*'s departure from San Francisco on 8 July, 1879, was a gloomy one for her commander, who felt his polar purpose thwarted by last-minute orders to seek the missing Swede. (As the world soon knew, Nordenskiöld was safe and sound, wintering on the Siberian coast.) And when newspapers could report nothing further about the *Jeannette*, swallowed by Arctic mists beyond the view of northern whalers, Captain Henry Howgate reentered the picture.

Early in 1880, he had yet another bill before Congress. It called for setting up "a temporary station on or near the shore of Lady Franklin Bay, for scientific observation and exploring, and to discover new whaling grounds." The captain's perspective was shifting from a romantic colonization to science and commercialism. He would even provide the ship, the *Gulnare*. All he wanted from the government were supplies needed to sustain twenty men at Lady Franklin Bay for two years. Where had he gotten the money to charter the vessel? Some were asking that question. Future evidence would suggest an answer, for it would show that Howgate was embezzling public funds to the tune of $60,000 per year.

Howgate's attention focused on the debate in the House of Representatives, where Washington C. Whitthorne, chairman of the Naval Affairs Committee, argued for the bill in fanciful terms while reminding his listeners of the now well-publicized circumpolar enterprise proposed by Karl Weyprecht: "Seven principal governments have agreed in what is called a polar congress to establish stations around the North Pole. In that region, according to the best information and most philosophical minds, lies the secret of human life." Whitthorne described Howgate as a "high-minded and noble-hearted" man who wanted the expedition to be under the protection of the United States flag and who "humbled himself [before Congress] and asked for this assistance." A skeptical congressman arose to wonder aloud, "What will you do with the North Pole when you find it?" No one replied. Howgate's second bill passed without further opposition; it was sent to the White House on I May, and Rutherford Hayes signed it.

Howgate had it all figured out. The *Gulnare* would be ready for sea within fourteen days. The Lady Franklin Bay detail would consist of an Army officer and fourteen enlisted men, who would report at the War Department no later than the tenth of the month. Howgate wanted Greely to lead the party, and Greely was willing, though he now had a ten-month-old daughter, Antoinette. General Myer recommended him especially as one "fitted to enforce that abstinence from alcoholic liquors which Arctic sojourners must avoid. He is considered by Captain Howgate, the originator of the scheme, as his right-hand man."

Two weeks after Greely's formal application, President Hayes authorized his appointment as expedition commander. Greely at once crossed the Potomac river to Alexandria, Virginia, where lay the *Gulnare*. He sent a note back to Henrietta: "Won't be home until seven, so please delay dinner until then." The Secretary of War and the Secretary of the Navy also paid the *Gulnare* a visit to ensure that she was "up to the standard of a naval vessel." Secretary of the Navy Richard Thompson ordered that a six-man board under Chief Engineer William Shock inspect her. Having given only grudging approval of the *Jeannette*'s fitness for Arctic service, Shock did not intend to let the *Gulnare* off easily.

Otherwise, Howgate's prospects looked bright. General Myer of the Signal Corps, physically frail and unaware of Howgate's misuse of finances, called him a generous donor who "has written much on polar colonization." True, the captain himself would not go north: "He lacks personal experience in the Arctic." Myer might have added that so did Lieutenant Greely, whom he instead described as "an officer of intensive Arctic research."

At the close of the month, Greely went to New York for supplies. He wrote Clarissa, "Expect we will sail 12 June. We have all necessary articles but no luxuries. The War Department compels us to fight for all we can get." But it was the Navy that upset plans. Even as thirteen enlisted men reported to Greely for loading duty, Secretary Thompson wrote Howgate that Chief Engineer Shock's inspection board at Alexandria deemed the *Gulnare* unsuitable. "Entering the ice in her present condition," declared Secretary Thompson, "the *Gulnare* would be crushed as easily as an egg-shell." With Thompson's condemnation of the ship in mind, Greely discreetly retreated from the *Gulnare* business.

Howgate, however, refused to admit defeat. For one thing, the *Gulnare's* master and first mate, both experienced whalers, wrote that they had never sailed a better ship. And Howgate rounded up a civilian party to replace the soldiers. "I have expended a large amount of money for the vessel," he told newspapermen. "I don't intend to let the expedition fall through."

The *Gulnare* was soon at sea, but on arrival at Disko, her machinery broke down. She limped home, leaving behind two of her party, Octave Pavy and Henry Clay, temporarily attached to the Signal Corps. The two were not yet at loggerheads. They would winter in Greenland, contract for goods and supplies, and study the coastal region and its people, all to benefit the main expedition they understood Captain Howgate would send out to create his Arctic colony.

Meanwhile, that summer, Greely continued to study all he could of Arctic literature. He contributed to the Signal Corps a list of auroras visible in American skies since 1874, and also an article, "Isothermic Lines of the United States." He was house-hunting in Washington while his wife and infant daughter stayed with friends near Norfolk. When the *Gulnare* returned from Greenland in ramshackle shape, he sent Henrietta his explanation for the ship's trouble: "The engineer neglected the fires and she had her iron fireboxes burned. It will take days to repair her." Henrietta couldn't have been less interested. She commented that he ought to be glad he had stayed at home. Her thoughts dwelled on the furlough she had successfully pressed him into applying for. For twenty days, they would be together. Never happy when they were separated, she wrote, "Won't it be lovely, dear, to be together again? You will appreciate me a little, won't you?"

A far longer separation loomed. The International Polar Conference had met in Berne. So far, definite commitments to help fulfill Karl Weyprecht's dream had come from only four countries: Austro-Hungary, Denmark, Norway, and Russia. The United States was conspicuous among the absentees. Actually, some scientific work was done by Signal Corps personnel at Point

Barrow, Alaska, but Greely, his own interest rekindling, thought a station should be established farther north "at some point in the archipelago of North America."

Late in September, Professor H. Wild, director of the Imperial Observatory at St. Petersburg, and president of the International Polar Conference, wrote to General Myer in Washington: "Allow me to implore that support *promised by you* for the *simultaneous observations* around the Pole. We only desire them for the period of one year." Before the letter could reach him, Myer had died. It was read by his successor, William Babcock Hazen.

The post of Chief Signal Officer had almost gone to Captain Howgate, but in November of that same year, 1880, James A. Garfield was elected president of the United States. Garfield and Hazen had gone to school together in Hiram, Ohio, and moreover, Hazen's wife was related to press lords who had supported Garfield's campaign. Howgate knew only too well that a Signal Corps chief other than himself was bound to order an audit of expenses. On 15 December, the outgoing Rutherford Hayes sent Hazen's nomination to the Senate. Three days later, Henry Howgate resigned from the United States Army and hurried out of town.

Alert to the possibility that Arctic enterprises might enhance the Signal Corps's prestige, General Hazen wrote a letter to the House Appropriations Committee that Lieutenant Greely delivered in person. "Greely, having immediate charge of polar planning," Hazen emphasized, "will lay before you certain papers showing the importance of continuing the work of the International Polar station approved May 1st." Hazen had read a lot into that legislation. His letter had edged away from Howgate's colonization theme, no real work had begun, and neither was there implied any firm alliance with the Europeans. But the papers Hazen sent before the committee—drafted mainly by Greely—carried an endorsement from the outgoing Secretary of War, who asked Congress to give "favorable consideration of this officer's estimate of $25,000 for continuation of the work in connection with the station at Lady Franklin Bay."

There was as yet no such station. And that there never would be seemed evident from the attitude of the new Secretary of War, Robert Todd Lincoln, son of the murdered president. He could not have cared less about the North Pole. He considered his main job to be the direction, as thriftily as possible, of ongoing military involvement in western expansion. Laden with reports from

Army officers in Indian country, neither Lincoln's mind nor his desk had room for schemes to girdle the roof of the world with stations manned by scientific snoops, certainly not if such foolhardy ideas cost money. Further compounding the difficulties confronting Greely was the new secretary's aversion to Hazen himself.

Hazen was already a controversial figure when he took over the Signal Corps. A West Point graduate in 1855, he had commanded troops in fights with Comanche war parties in Texas. With an Indian bullet in his body, he led an infantry brigade during the Civil War and took part in the battles of Shiloh, Chickamauga, Stone River, and Missionary Ridge. When peace came, he renewed a private war with General George A. Custer dating from their academic years. More recently, Hazen had criticized that headstrong cavalry officer for being too rough on Indian tribes. ("Custer is after Hazen's scalp," newsmen had gleefully reported.) In 1871, Hazen had married Mildred McClean, a newspaper magnate's daughter half his age, who accompanied him on at least one of two overseas assignments as American observer at the Franco-Prussian War, and six years later on the Russo-Turkish battlefront.

Between these foreign excursions, Hazen gave testimony before a congressional committee investigating a scandal of the Ulysses Grant administration, which helped drive Grant's Secretary of War from office. Hazen next had grappled with an Army colonel, David S. Stanley, who "has dogged me for five years . . . a drunken sot." Stanley accused Hazen of perjury before Congress and of hiding from enemy fire at Shiloh. Each demanded the other's court-martial. General William T. Sherman ordered that both be arraigned before the same military court. Each officer got off lightly, but, never noted for tact, Hazen clamored for more action, until Sherman threatened that "if General Hazen insists on reviving this controversy he will regret it to the last day of his life."

That Hazen had made foes in high places during a contentious career boded ill for Greely's polar aspirations. But with Howgate no longer on the scene, Hazen was Greely's main support. As for the ex-captain and old friend Howgate, Greely didn't know that the War Department under Lincoln was assembling evidence to accuse him of having systematically swindled the United States government. That such scandal would inevitably reflect upon the War Department as a whole went far to prejudice Lincoln against the Signal Corps at the outset. Congress, in March, 1881, passed a bill authorizing scientific work to proceed on or near the shore of Lady Franklin Bay. Upon General Hazen's recommendation, Greely was appointed by the president to its command. Yet more than a month followed before Robert Todd Lincoln bothered to notice papers brought before him for his signature. The press noted his delay. Secretary Lincoln, they reported, intended to critically review the whole plan. "So now," complained Greely, "it is pending whether the expedition shall be sent or not." Indeed, about the only response Lincoln made at first was an order to Hazen to inform him in detail of just how Lieutenant Greely had come to be in charge of things.

So Hazen and Greely were in the new secretary's bad books from the start. Neither did it help matters that Greely made no secret of his impatience with bureaucratic penny-pinching and delay. He raged at a congressional appropriation fixed at only $25,000. He wanted sole authority to order supplies and organize his men. The lieutenant's tone was too peremptory for Secretary Lincoln, who dallied even when reminded that prompt action was essential. The one person who had no problem with the secretary's uncooperative attitude—Greely called it "open hostility"—was Greely's wife. Henrietta was again pregnant and more than ever opposed to letting her husband sail off into the Arctic.

It was about this time that Greely heard from an officer whose name he may have forgotten since commending him for efficiency in the field, and who would play a large part in the story of the expedition. Clearly, the writer was distraught. Lieutenant Fred Kislingbury's compulsion to go north had less to do with polar exploration than escape from unbearable grief. He claimed no special reason why Greely should take him along: "How as to my scientific qualifications? I make no pretension even to anything in that direction." But he was willing to learn, and if Greely needed someone able to control troops, lead them through hardships, perform any task that demanded patience and endurance, "then I am your man. I can say no more, I think, to convince you of my eagerness to go."

Kislingbury had been born in the Berkshire, England, village of East Ilsley, and immigrated to the United States in the mid-1850s. He was in and out of the Army throughout the 1860s, and in 1866 married Agnes Struther Bullock, the twenty-one-year-old daughter of a retired British army officer in Windsor, Canada.

When his regiment, the Eleventh (New York) Infantry, moved to Fort Concho, Kislingbury was accompanied by his wife and two infant boys (two other children had not survived). A third son was born in 1874, and it was during the following year that Kislingbury assisted Greely in building a telegraphic network across the southwest plains. During the summer weeks of 1876, a fourth son arrived, and his parents christened him Wheeler Schofield, after Colonel George Wheeler Schofield, who had married Agnes Kislingbury's sister Alma. A Civil War veteran, Schofield had earned distinction in military circles as an ordnance expert who had redesigned the Smith and Wesson pistol for cavalry use. Fate would give Schofield a tragic, if minor, role in the sequence of events.

Kislingbury's regiment was next assigned garrison duty at Standing Rock in the Department of Dakota. But in April 1878, the first blow struck. His wife Agnes died. Kislingbury had her body taken to the family home at Windsor for burial, and while on two months' compassionate leave in Detroit, he first heard of the projected Arctic expedition, Lieutenant Greely commanding. As he later wrote, "This was my reason for wanting to go. I had just lost my first wife." By the time he penned those words, Lieutenant Kislingbury had lost his second.

She was Jessie Bullock, Agnes's sister, last of the three Bullock girls from Windsor—Alma Schofield, wife of the colonel and ordnance expert stationed at Fort Sill, had also died. Those sisters were an ill-fated trio. In May 1879, Jessie had accompanied Kislingbury and his four sons to Fort Custer with the lieutenant's regiment. The post stood on a bluff above the confluence of the Bighorn and Little Bighorn rivers, near the site of the disaster that had overtaken George Custer. On 30 October, 1880, Kislingbury rode out on a scouting mission north of the Musselshell River, heading a detachment of two sergeants and ten troopers of the Second Cavalry, which, with the Eleventh Infantry, manned Fort Custer. Five weeks later, on 4 December, word reached Kislingbury that his wife had suddenly taken ill and he had better get back to the fort. Fresh horses would be waiting for him at Terry's Landing and Ryan's, relay stations along the ride back. "I rode day and night through deep snow, reached home and found my poor wife dying. Great God! She had been dying a week." He raced upstairs to the hospital's isolation ward and knelt by the bedside, imploring her for some sign of recognition. It was too late. "She passed away the night of the eighth, after but barely recognizing me and unable to say a word. Her powers of speech had gone. I had just lost my first wife. Now my second, the last of three sisters, all taken within three years."

Kislingbury's grief-stricken words were in a letter to Greely. That wasn't all. An outbreak of scarlet fever at the fort threatened the lives of Kislingbury's two youngest boys. Their dangerous condition weighed on his mind even as he "placed my poor darling in her temporary resting place and prepared to return east for [her] burial with her sisters."

The children recovered, but a winter harsh even by Great Plains standards stalled travel and all but shut down communication. Snowdrifts cut off Fort Custer from the nearest railroad depot, not that trains were running. Kislingbury had, however, managed to receive a letter—"much detained by snow blockade"—from Greely, who, as yet unaware of the other's latest loss, invited him to join in polar plans should they mature. Kislingbury tried to get off a telegram: "Am grateful and hasten to say, yes, write me full particulars and details and what will be expected of me." He had applied for four months' leave and intended to depart for the east with his children and dead wife as soon as the weather relented. He wrote to Greely, "If it is decided that I go with you, I shall expect an order to report to Washington."

Weeks passed without further correspondence. Still snowed in at Fort Custer, Kislingbury wrote Greely again, thanking him once more "for your kind offer to take me with you. It is simply a godsend to me just now, a wonderful chance for me to wear out my terrible sorrow." He told Greely of Jessie's death, of how Greely's invitation had come "as a boon. The separation from my children will be as nothing compared to the prospect of having been with those who may accomplish some great and lasting good." Even if there were no such successes, "my children will love me better when I return and will be proud of the father who dared to brave the dangers we have read about of a sojourn in the Arctic regions." He would come back to them a new man. He was with Greely heart and soul. "You shall find no truer friend nor more devoted servant," he promised.

# 6

# A Turbulent Outfitting

As the weeks crawled by, however, Fred Kislingbury was still unable to leave Fort Custer on the mournful journey east with his boys and dead wife. "The snow and cold never seem to end," he wrote in mid-February 1881, words to which the Arctic experience ahead of him gave a touch of irony. "No sooner are roads open than they are blocked again."

For that matter, Kislingbury still did not really belong to Greely. Orders to the lieutenant had yet to be issued, despite Greely's and Hazen's petitions. The Secretary of War was influenced by General Sherman, whose opposition to Army involvement in Arctic schemes was as unshakable as in 1877, when he had vetoed that of Captain Howgate. Greely wanted Lieutenant Kislingbury ordered by telegraph to leave at once for Washington, but not even his pointed reminder that Congress had approved the expedition impressed the Secretary of War, and more likely it annoyed him. At any rate, Lincoln had basis for his refusal to act, in a ruling from Sherman that Kislingbury was needed with his regiment, "which is on exposed frontier duty." Bullheaded and undeterred, Hazen persisted: "It is very important that orders be issued [bringing Kislingbury east] without delay." And even Lincoln could not drag his feet indefinitely. He was hearing from congressmen who favored the expedition, and also from newspapers whose political support Lincoln routinely counted on. Some of the press already reported on the expedition as if it were a going concern, all credit to its command. The *New York Herald* described Greely as "peculiarly adapted by education and habits of study." *The New York Times* called him "one of the most trusted officers of the Signal Corps, an officer who had already made a creditable record as a scientific man."

During those early spring weeks of 1881, even as the fate of the Lady Franklin Bay Expedition hung in the balance, Greely acted as if confident that all was well. In the final weeks of Henrietta's pregnancy, he busied himself assembling men and procuring supplies. His brisk earnestness continued to irritate the Secretary of War, especially when he bolstered his requisitions with allusions to himself as the "officer selected by the President to command." On 17 March, he made his boldest request so far, that he be allowed full control of the $25,000 Congress had appropriated. Early action was necessary, if only to purchase the best pemmican, obtainable in far-off Manitoba or Saskatchewan.

And he volleyed more requests. He wanted permission to place Dr. Octave Pavy, already in Greenland collecting sledges and dogs, under contract with the U.S. Army as the expedition's official physician. He wanted the Army surgeon-general to be directed to ship to the Arctic via St. John's, Newfoundland, medical supplies for thirty men to last them two and a half years, the selection "carefully considered with reference to scurvy and such other complaints likely to prevail in such regions." And it was important that the enlisted men report to him no later than 10 May. Greely already knew several. All were highly recommended by their officers. He said that any change in the detail "will impair the efficiency of the command."

A week later, from his quarters at Riggs House, General Hazen wrote to the Secretary of War, "It is now twenty-seven days since the action was asked and I have twice written for it. Authorization to use the appropriation of $25,000 is imperatively necessary before any steps can be taken." A steamer for St. John's would leave New York within forty-eight hours, and letters for the

American consul had to go on board. "My great desire is to expedite this work, whose success depends on early action," Hazen stated further.

Henrietta Greely was likely to go into labor at any hour. She was unable to receive the husbandly attention she wanted and that Greely wished to give. So much for his expedition had to be secured and at the lowest possible prices. For the party's shelter, Greely wanted ventilating chimney blocks "of such size that the central opening will readily receive a large stove pipe." He was just as meticulous about ordering "a hand-atlas, well-bound with guards, so the maps while being of half-size when closed, will open smoothly and of full size." Harper and Brothers in New York would supply volumes on exploration, anthropology, medicine, and miscellaneous other subjects, besides a score of novels and some sixty magazines. Two hundred scientific instruments were listed in Greely's "Memorandum of Outfit": magnetometers, telephones, chronometers, anemometers, barometers, galvanometers, hygrometers, and "two pairs Conjugal Thermometers for Solar Radiation." To ensure the accuracy of the thermometers, the Winchester Observatory at Yale offered to examine and verify them. Greely had written that "heretofore there has been a lack of confidence in the low temperatures reported by Arctic explorers because of the imperfect nature of their thermometers." And his magnetometer had to be specially equipped with extra-light needles and mirror for auroral disturbances.

As for food, the *Army and Navy Register* reported that in compiling his dietary list, Greely was, in the main, guided by Professor Nordenskiöld's twenty-five years' experience as an Arctic explorer. The *Vega's* sixteen months above the Arctic Circle had produced among her crew not a single symptom of scurvy. Two thousand pounds of potatoes were ordered, packed in five-pound cans, and mixed vegetables in two-pound cans. "Preserved peaches can be sent in glass," he ordered. Greely gave detailed instructions for packing molasses and syrup. Canned meats would form only a small part of the supplies. Greely depended rather on "selected mess pork, the fattest that could be obtained." Antiscorbutics were of paramount importance. With this in mind, the commander ordered large quantities of cranberry sauce, dried fruits, damsons, and other sauces. He insisted also on onions, pickles, carrots, beets, and so much more of this and that, all to be carefully packed to prevent deterioration.

At the same time, since a suitable vessel had yet to be found, Greely was corresponding with shipowners. Most of their asking prices were too high. And his officers were not yet at hand. Summoned to Washington by the Secretary of War's belated order, Kislingbury had at last left Fort Custer with his dead wife, but in early April, melting snows and heavy rains flooded vast areas of the Great Plains. One newspaper reported that "the vast volume of water which has spread over Dakota Territory and the northwest is now creeping above the banks of the lower Mississippi. A tremendous overflow is apprehended." By the month's end, Kislingbury was again halted.

Still trying to push the Secretary of War into cooperating, Greely took a new tack. Public concern over the missing *Jeannette* had mounted. The Lady Franklin Bay project could be modified so as to allow a search. Greely asked the secretary whether, without seriously affecting the scientific objects of the mission, "you deem it of sufficient importance that I should send from the international polar station at Lady Franklin Bay a sledge party to Cape Joseph Henry to see if any vessel is in sight therefrom." In that locality, a mountain reared 2,300 feet, affording a wide view. Greely added, "The chances of any discovery are, of course, very remote. But it might be well to spare no pain even for this faint hope." When Robert Lincoln disregarded even that suggestion, Greely composed a brashly worded statement: "Although four weeks have elapsed since I was assigned to this duty, no paper, reports, estimate or plan has ever been returned to me, and excepting the detail of Lieutenant Kislingbury I am unaware that any action has been taken in this matter. Unless prompt and immediate action be taken, the expedition cannot sail, properly prepared and equipped, this year."

Those words were in Greely's copy. Whether he actually sent such a letter to the Secretary of War is uncertain. But at long last, the secretary moved. On 11 April, 1881, he ordered action on Greely's manifold requirements. These included authority for the lieutenant to draw up a contract with Dr. Pavy in Greenland. Much now proceeded on other fronts. Greely was at his busiest, spending hours at the signal office on G Street, dealing with matters that ranged from how safest to pack victuals to the continuing search for Arctic transport. He wanted two ships, one to carry the expeditionary force, a smaller vessel to take coal. At Greely's request, Secretary of the Navy William Chandler had sent a naval lieutenant, John F. Merry, to St. John's, where, aided by the American consul, he would inspect sealing steamers and make a selection. Just five blocks from where Greely wrestled with these problems, his wife braced herself for childbirth. A letter on its way to her from friends in San Francisco expressed the hope that "you will get through your trouble this month as you did when Antoinette arrived." As only Henrietta could know, this would be far from the case. She was mindful of the agony her mother had gone through at the birth of the male twins. Every passing hour, her emotions fluctuated between hope at each sign of a hitch in her husband's polar plans and nervous despair whenever it seemed that they advanced. That they most certainly had was evident on 12 April. The War Department sent Greely his first detailed instructions. He would command an Arctic expedition consisting of two other officers and twenty-one enlisted men. The force would have to assemble at Washington no later than 15 May and be at St. John's by 15 June.

Two days later, James Gordon Bennett's *New York Herald* announced that although the station at Lady Franklin Bay would be primarily for meteorologic study, "it has just transpired that it will also be an auxiliary expedition in search of the Arctic exploring steamer *Jeannette*." This news was unwelcome to Greely, and had an ironic touch, for he had himself proposed looking for Bennett's ship as a tactic toward galvanizing the Secretary of War into action. But he had other things to worry about. Most of the enlisted men assigned to his command were stationed with their regiments thousands of miles away in the West. They were now ordered to Washington, but the expected time of their arrival gave Greely scant opportunity to properly train, organize, and familiarize them with the expedition's purposes.

He had some causes for satisfaction. One was the assignment of Edward Israel to his command. A bright young meteorologist just graduated from the University of Michigan, Israel came with impressive credentials. He would serve as Greely's astronomer. Upon arrival in Washington, he was assured of a sergeant's rank with pay, as was George Rice, photographer. But Greely still had no second in command at his side. The Bismarck signal office, telegraphically monitoring Kislingbury's eastward journey, reported as late as mid-April that the lieutenant's whereabouts were unknown. Floods had washed away bridges. Train schedules might be delayed up to fifteen days. "Kislingbury is bringing his wife's remains east, I believe," ran a message dated 20 April, "and hence cannot come through with the mail which for the most part is carried on buckboard or horseback."

That same day, the Signal Corps weather bureau, which owed much of its existence to Greely, announced an imminent appearance of unusual meteor showers. The next morning was cloudy and cool. In the Greely's new home, 1413 K Street, Henrietta gave birth to a daughter at 7:00 A.M. It was the beginning of a day-long ordeal. As had her mother, she also carried twin boys. At five in the evening, both were stillborn. Her pain, and her husband's, can be only imagined. From the West Coast, a friend would write, perhaps unthinkingly, "It must have been sad to lose the little twins. Did they resemble each other exactly as your twin brothers?" And from a cousin: "Your suffering must have been terrible indeed. How comforting to you to have all this before Mr. Greely's departure, hard as it will be for you under any circumstances."

However traumatized by the triple births, Henrietta couldn't count on uninterrupted attention from her husband, pressured as he was by preparations to leave her. In those days following the birth of their second daughter, whom they named Adola, Greely had to ponder the advisability of repacking glass jars of peach preserves—the Army commissary sensed "a danger of the bottles exploding from cold"—and hurry the quartermaster-general into supplying keg nails, roofing felt, tarpaulin, small American flags, heating stoves, mittens, socks, and buffalo-hide sleeping bags. Some supplies were conveniently at hand, left over from the *Polaris* expedition. Others were not so readily available.

Greely wrote a New Bedford, Massachusetts, boat-builder asking a price estimate on a twenty-eight-foot whaleboat, five-oared with two spars, to be delivered at Boston by 1 June. In letters to private contractors, Greely was unable to guarantee prompt payment. He had to tell them with embarrassment that they would have to wait until July, "when funds can be drawn from the Treasury."

The prices of steamers at St. John's as quoted by Lieutenant Merry and Consul Thomas N. Molloy were too high. Deciding that Merry and Molloy needed a more experienced hand, Greely hired Hubbard Chester, who had been first mate on the *Polaris*. As Greely's personal agent, Chester had full powers to arrange the charter at St. John's and sign contracts for Greely to countersign on his arrival. In the same final week of April came word from Kislingbury, weatherbound in the Dakota badlands with his dead wife: "I cannot get away within ten days. Will not reach Washington before May 25th."

With the advent of spring, Henrietta Greely regained strength. Still seeing little of her husband, she persuaded other Army wives to donate for the expedition, as did she, clothes, books, games, cigars, and plum puddings. Greely contended with more vital problems. Samuel Pook, an officer at the Washington Navy Yard, where a steam launch for the party was under construction, warned about its boiler: "The steam engine will take up nearly all the length of the ship. It will be overloaded with the boiler. Better examine this matter yourself or you may not get what you want." And from an official at the Naval Observatory: "Sorry we have no portable transit instruments except those belonging to the Transit of Venus Commission." All would be required for the phenomenon's observation. "So we cannot spare any."

At Greely's request, the State Department had asked the British to provide copies of charts used by Nares in 1875, and a list of four depots he had left along the shores of Smith Sound and Kennedy Channel. The Admiralty in London generously complied. From St. John's, Consul Molloy, Lieutenant Merry, and Greely's agent, Chester, reported that of a number of steamers examined, the best was the *Proteus,* built in Dundee, Scotland, for the sealing trade. The owner, J. V. Stewart, would lease her for $400 in American gold per calendar month, assuming three months' employment, and would "guarantee to deliver up to 150 tons of coal at its cost price." Stewart also would provide ship's master and crew, all experienced Newfoundland seamen.

Added to expenses already incurred, the figure would leave Greely with less than a quarter of his appropriation, which, in any event, was not available until July. But with time pressing and word from St. John's that no sturdier vessel could be found, the deal had to be closed. Chester signed the contract in Greely's absence. The ship, it stated, "staunch and strong and in every way fitted for the voyage, shall be ready and at Lieutenant Greely's disposal from July the first." Three and a half months' employment was mutually guaranteed. Should the ship meet impassable ice, her captain, Richard Pike, would land the party at the most convenient point, "the act of God, the Queen's enemies, Fire and all and every other Dangers and Accidents of the Seas, Rivers, Navigation and whatever Nature and Kind, soever, during the said voyage, always excepted."

Greely later, and bitterly, wrote that charter of the *Proteus* left "less than $6000 [to be] spent economically, for our supply of coal, scientific instruments, boats, dogs, dog-food, woolen and fur clothing, pemmican, lime juice, spirits, special articles of diet, natural history supplies, table and household equipage, etc. Nothing was purchased except after most careful consideration as to its necessity and cost. Consequently, many very desirable articles were omitted and in all cases supply reduced to a minimum." Newspapers appealed to readers to donate games, mittens, books, and Christmas gifts. Certainly, with what he had left of government money, Greely could afford few luxuries.

Neither had he much chance for acquaintance with the men he would command. They all seemed willing enough, if of naïve expectations. Thirty-one-year-old Joseph Elison, volunteering for the duty, described himself as only five feet four inches tall but of robust health, and having spent ten years boning up on Arctic literature, he considered himself "fully aware of the different changes of climate to be endured." Others felt sure that winter months on snowbound Army posts on the western plains had ideally conditioned them for the rigors of the Far North.

Greely's cameraman, George Rice, raised on Cape Breton Island in the Canadian maritimes, eagerly anticipated creating a photographic Arctic record. Rice's brother, Moses, ran a studio in Washington that specialized in photographing politicians and other notables. Here Sergeant Rice gathered the expedition in front of the camera for a comradely group shot. The result shows them conservatively dressed in civilian suits, for the most part looking quietly proud, though Kislingbury—arrived at last—seated on the commander's right, wears a somewhat brooding expression. All are neatly mustached except for a clean-shaven Edward Israel, the young astronomer; a heavily-bearded Sergeant William Cross, machinist at the Washington Navy Yard selected as the party's engineer; and a more trimly bearded commander—he alone, of the twenty-one portrayed, with arms peremptorily folded.[1]

Problems of equipment and provisioning dominated Greely's thoughts. A Baltimore firm selling pemmican reported none on hand, because its evaporating machinery was closed down. If Greely ordered 2,000 pounds of the concentrated meat mixture, it could be ready for shipping in a fortnight, but anything less would not justify reassembling the machinery. This smacked of chicanery, but in any case Greely could not afford the cost. The renowned New York instrument firm of T. S. and J. D. Negus had promised delivery of four chronometers, but needed a delay of at least three weeks to "verify their rates in heat and cold."

On 26 May, the British steamer *Carmina*, carrying supplies from New York,

---

1. Subsequently, the photo had to be artificially altered, three faces cropped and replaced by those of genuine expedition members, because one man had quickly deserted and two others would take no part in the Arctic mission. Both photo versions circulate to this day, occasionally with identities miscaptioned.

had collided with a schooner at the entrance to St. John's harbor. She sank to her water-ways, with loss or damage to canned vegetables, damson preserves, lime juice, and other valuable antiscorbutics. Contemplating a vegetable garden at Lady Franklin Bay, Greely had asked the Department of Agriculture for advice on what seeds to take. He was told that since the department had no record of temperatures or amount of light in that region, nothing definite could be stated. It was suggested that turnips, cabbage, lettuce, radishes, and peas might be grown in the Arctic, but at this early date the department's seed stock was exhausted. Greely was advised to contact Landreth's Seed Warehouse, Philadelphia, which sent him some.

The thirty-foot steam launch contributed by the Navy Department was a problem. Could it be borne safely on the steamship *Nova Scotia*, bound for Liverpool via Newfoundland, with a large passenger list? Greely was told that the ship could take the launch at Baltimore, provided it weighed no more than five tons: "It will have to be carried at ship's davits for which ring bolts, properly secured, will be required." The launch had left Washington and reached Annapolis, but getting it to Baltimore was another problem, for the boiler wouldn't work with salt water, and the token crew for some reason couldn't rig a sail. The launch had to be towed.

It was June. Some volunteers were still delayed in Dakota territory, but Kislingbury had reached the east from Detroit. After reporting to Greely, he left for an overnight stay in New York. From the Astor House, he wrote to a close friend, wife of an Army comrade from his Fort Concho days. He sought prayers for his safety "through the long lonesome dreary night. My God! I cannot die now. I must come back." The next morning he left for St. John's, where he was to supervise the stowing of cargo on the *Proteus*.

Greely paid a farewell visit to his family in Newburyport. He was back in Washington in time for news that the photographic outfit was ready for shipping. By then the steam launch had been hauled on board the *Nova Scotia*, the local Army quartermaster nervously reporting that "it weighs nearer ten tons than five." But all freight and baggage were soon at sea, nothing left except the ammunition, which, it was belatedly found, couldn't be carried on a passenger steamer without breaking the law. The Baltimore quartermaster had it stowed in the magazine at Fort McHenry pending orders.

On 17 June, General Hazen issued Greely instructions. They enumerated the tasks to be undertaken at Lady Franklin Bay and promised relief ships scheduled for 1882 and 1883. Should the first fail to reach the station, it would cache supplies and dispatches on the east coast of Grinnell Land, northeast Ellesmere Island, and establish a small depot on Littleton Island, off the Greenland coast. If the 1883 ship was unable to clear Smith Sound, it would "land all her supplies and a party at Littleton Island, which party will be prepared for a winter's stay."

These ideas were actually Greely's and not subject to change. Greely had made that clear to Hazen "as forcibly as any man could"—the general's future words at a crucial moment. He was under "the absolute necessity of supporting him literally." The Hazen-Greely program was reported as exemplifying the purpose of the great international scheme for solving the riddle of that "Circle of Mysteries" at the top of the world.

Lieutenant Kislingbury was at St. John's, his mind still in a turmoil. He had written to his boys: "Poor little men! When I stop to think how I have torn myself from them . . . I almost give way. I can hardly realize that I am now separated from them, everything from Fort Custer to here was done with such a rush and now it is much like a dream." He had not yet "recovered from my terrible grief." By the middle of June, he had regained stability. He still dreaded the long Arctic night, and wrote that "were it not for my honor, my future, our future, at stake I would abandon all and come back." But in this letter to the friend of Fort Concho days, he declared that with the help of her prayers, "I may yet be my manly self again."

Soon he was not alone. The "rank and file of the Lady Franklin Bay colony," as the *New York Herald* put it, reached St. John's the morning of 22 June. The *Proteus* awaited them, fresh from ten days' overhaul in drydock. Locals greeted the Americans cordially, but some warned of rough conditions northward, quoting men of the whaling fleets coming in to tell of walls of ice and hundreds of icebergs. Greely was in New York, waiting to leave for Newfoundland on the steamer *Cortez*. Chances of getting under way from Newfoundland before 4 July faded. Greely telegraphed Baltimore about the gunpowder in storage at Fort McHenry. The quartermaster replied that he knew of "no means of transportation by which the powder can be delivered at St. John's by the third [of July] or at any other date."

The *Cortez* left New York on 21 June. She was off Halifax, Nova Scotia, four days later. Greely found a telegram from St. John's awaiting him. Expected stores had not yet arrived, were in fact crawling across New Brunswick by rail. Greely fumed: "The Quartermaster's Depot shipped the wrong way. Anything delayed as this should have come by steamer." He was still at Halifax when Kislingbury wired him more bad news. The sloop of war *Alliance,* bound for Baffin Bay in quest of the vanished *Jeannette,* had entered harbor. Her chief engineer examined the boiler in the steam launch that had so overloaded the *Nova Scotia* on her way up. He condemned it outright: "The boiler being a vertical tubular, it thoroughly fails by priming from salt water. Can have multitubular marine boiler guaranteed to take salt water made and ready by July 4th if you order today." The cost of replacement would be $400. Disgustedly, Greely telegraphed Kislingbury to get the job done. At the same time, he cabled General Hazen for permission to take some of the *Alliance*'s powder, replacing that locked up at Fort McHenry. In Washington, Hazen consulted with Secretary of the Navy William Chandler. No luck. Hazen advised Greely that the *Alliance* carried only a small quantity of powder for signal purposes. "You will have to purchase."

Greely boarded the *Proteus* at St. John's on 27 June. He found that what stores had arrived were "in endless confusion." If he felt his second in command, Kislingbury, was to blame, he kept his silence. In writing, he directed his wrath at "a policy which rendered it obligatory to perfect in two and a half months the outfitting of a party destined for over two years' separation from the rest of the world." The situation was not all discouraging. General Hazen had persuaded the Allan Line of Atlantic steamships to let the *Hibernian* carry up stores, photographic supplies, and ammunition. While Greely still seethed over "the failure of the quartermaster's depot to ship food via New York or Baltimore, delaying the whole expedition," the *Hibernian* was expected on 6 July. She arrived on schedule, and two days later, a hastily repaired *Carmina* staggered into harbor with what was salvaged of her cargo.

A last-minute telegram from Henry Howgate was more a growl than a Godspeed. Signal Corps headquarters had published a two-column spread in the *Army and Navy Register,* inspired by a letter to General Hazen from Professor Wild of the International Polar Conference, thanking him for having secured American involvement in the International Polar Year. Wild appointed Hazen "from this day a member of the Polar Conference." And the story asserted that the "Greely Arctic Colony" expedition owed its existence chiefly to the efforts of Karl Weyprecht. There was not the slightest reference to Henry Howgate. He wrote Greely of his surprise "at your failure to correct errors. I trust you will do so before sailing."

Greely had no time to compose a suitable response. The *Proteus* was about to hoist anchor. And Greely's embittered old friend was about to become a fugitive wanted for fraud and embezzlement. It was a strange downward turn in the career of one without whose pioneering energies Greely and his party might never have sailed. But equally true, it was Karl Weyprecht who almost single-handedly had established the International Polar Year, of which the Lady Franklin Bay Expedition was earmarked an important feature. Dearly would Weyprecht have wished to see his noble concept become reality. But on 29 March of that year, 1881—even as Lieutenant Greely was bending every muscle to forge an American link in Weyprecht's circumpolar chain—the Austrian, at age forty-three, died of pulmonary consumption.

## II

# THE STATION

# 7

# FORT CONGER

NEAR THE END of July, having sailed from St. John's to Upernavik and picked up its last supplies, as well as Jens Edward and Thorlip Christiansen, the two Eskimo dog drivers, the *Proteus* left Upernavik and crawled northward through dense fog. Such conditions were nothing new to Captain Pike's crew but had a depressing effect upon some of the American soldiers. There loomed the first signs of trouble. Lieutenant Kislingbury had sent his rifle to the men's quarters with a command that it be cleaned. When it failed to return, the lieutenant himself went forward and found that "no one seemed to know anything of the gun and they acted very indifferently about the matter." Sergeant Brainard retrieved the weapon, and Kislingbury found it still rusted. Brainard explained. Only one man, Private William Ellis, had volunteered to clean it; he had done a halfhearted job and growled that he would never do it again, that "it might as well be understood now that the men consider [cleaning officers' guns] menial work." Their interpretation of membership in the expedition ruled out such tasks. "Everybody, officers and men, would have to do their own chores."

Brainard's words took Kislingbury aback. He wondered aloud why the sergeant had not used his own authority to order the weapon cleaned. Brainard's response to this question went unrecorded. Kislingbury decided against telling the commander of the incident. For one thing, he had identified the leading malcontent in the forecastle as a corporal named Starr, who had joined the expedition with Greely's endorsement. Any report of Starr's misconduct might be taken by Greely as adverse reflection upon his judgment. Kislingbury had already noticed that the commander "does not favorably receive contrary opinions and I have consequently become cautious in this respect, not wishing him to think I oppose him." And, of course, by the time they reached Lady Franklin Bay, all the men might be in better humor.

Such was Lieutenant Kislingbury's hope. It was quickly dampened. At nine one evening, Greely ordered that after supper the men should be paraded on deck for a physical examination. Greely might more prudently have assigned this task to Dr. Pavy. Instead he gave it to his second in command. Sergeant Brainard privately noted what followed: "[Kislingbury] opened blouses and shirts, peering into the breasts of some. It was the most shameful affair that I ever saw. To submit tamely to such indignities is outrageous. It exposed us to the ridicule of the whole ship." Greely had blundered in ordering the inspection carried out in front of the *Proteus* crew, making the Americans a laughingstock. Otherwise there was no impropriety about it. Even when conducted by proper medical officers, physical inspections in the military were always apt to entail "indignities," as Brainard must have known. And Kislingbury was not a medical officer. All the same, Brainard attributed the lieutenant's behavior to "pure spite because we refused to clean the guns of the two junior officers and perform menial duties. This much is settled, they will have to look for themselves in future."

No serious ice had yet appeared. Greely decided after consulting Captain Pike that course could safely be set across Melville Bay to Cape York. There would be risks. That large and ever-turbulent stretch of water 300 miles wide was considered a graveyard of lost ships, "a mysterious region of terror," Elisha Kane had called it. In the English explorer Clements Markham's words, "Many a well-equipped ship has been caught in its fatal embrace. What tales of woe and disaster could its icy waters unfold." In one year alone, nineteen vessels were lost in Melville Bay, some crushed between massive icebergs, others hammered into the depths by frigid winds. Although confident in his own seamanship, Pike steered the *Proteus* into the dreaded waters with a sailor's apprehension. But good fortune rewarded him. Icebergs and floes were few and far between; the ship's crew could hardly believe their luck. At 4:00 P.M. on the last day of July, lookouts sighted Cape York. The crossing of Melville Bay had been accomplished in a record thirty-six hours. But the landsmen on board were unable to share in the seafarers' sense of relief. Kislingbury thought that his own people "show a disposition to complain. I have noticed a spirit prevailing that I fear will lead to insubordination."

Passing Cape York, the steamer next made for the southeast corner of the Cary Islands, some twenty miles off the Greenland coast. Kislingbury and Pavy went ashore. They found a cairn left by Captain Nares in 1875 and visited the following year by Sir Allen Young in the *Pandora*. Nares's depot of 3,600 rations was still intact, as was a whaleboat he had left there. Kislingbury thought Greely should take it, as did Lieutenant James Lockwood. The party already had a whaleboat, but the beached craft now before them was larger and obviously stronger. Greely refused to act on his lieutenants' advice, arguing that he would not feel right if he took the boat, that it might be of use to whalers. Kislingbury was baffled. Whalers seldom came this far north. He noted in his journal that "if the boat had been left there for humanitarian reasons it would perhaps be different." But the stores were there precisely for the use and accommodation of northern navigators. "As we need the boat, I am forced to say that Lieutenant Greely is making a mistake," he stated further. The commander said he would take another English boat known to be at Washington Irving Island. But who could tell in what condition it was? Wrote Kislingbury, "I go on the principle that a bird in hand is worth three in the bush."

August began with promising weather. An encouraged Greely decided not to stop at Cape Sabine, off the east coast of Ellesmere Island, where he might have examined the Nares expedition's sledging depot. Instead he had Captain Pike shape course directly for Cape Hawks. First, however, he sent parties ashore to Littleton Island and Lifeboat Cove, locations on the Greenland side almost opposite Cape Sabine. Here was the safest point from which to steam over to Ellesmere, a crossing of no more than twenty-five miles. Since its naming by the British thirty years earlier, Littleton Island, gateway to the relatively narrow Smith Sound, had been a useful stopover for explorers in search of either the Franklin party or the legendary Open Polar Sea—each expedition leaving its vestige in the form of a supplies cache or cairn with dispatches for subsequent visitors or for itself in the event of a retreat. It was here that the marooned *Polaris* people had spent a winter following the mysterious death of their commanding officer.

For possible use on the expedition's return passage, scheduled for September 1883, Lieutenant Lockwood led a party ashore at Littleton Island with six tons of coal. Lieutenant Kislingbury took the whaleboat to the mainland near Lifeboat Cove, scene of the *Polaris* wreck. Dr. Pavy, Clay, and the photographer Sergeant Rice accompanied him. Kislingbury scanned the site of the *Polaris* party's camp. Its cairn was demolished, emptied by nomadic Eskimos. But among the objects strewn around and about, Kislingbury found pages from a prayer book. He noted, "My eyes rested on a 'Prayer at the North Pole.' I shall retain it and should it be my fortune to reach the Pole I will offer the prayer with fervent zeal." Returning to the ship, the lieutenant sighted two walrus, a mother and her young. They bore down on the whaleboat head-on, and Kislingbury shot them at a twenty-foot range. The creatures sank at once. Kislingbury felt remorse, chiefly over the loss of game. "This is the provoking part of killing the poor things in water," he wrote in the *Proteus* stateroom that night. "I shall not do it again or allow it to be done, unless we are provided with harpoons. If you can fasten a harpoon into a walrus you can keep him from sinking."

North from Littleton Island, the sea appeared ice free. The *Proteus* reached Cape Hawks at 9:00 A.M. on 3 August. Greely took a party ashore and found the jolly boat left by the *Valorous*, one of Nares's ships, and it was launched and hauled on board the *Proteus*. Allen Young also had called here on the *Pandora* and had left 3,600 rations, mostly bread, stearin, preserved potatoes, pickles, and rum. Fog descended, slowing the *Proteus*'s passage, and on the fourth, with the ship's position at 81° 44' north, 1,100 miles above the Arctic Circle, the commander recorded, "We met an impenetrable icefield at 10 P.M. and the *Proteus* butted against it. We are at the entrance of Lady Franklin Bay."

Perverse fate took over. The very reason for the ship's trouble-free voyage of recent weeks revealed itself, denying the expedition a prompt landfall. Little ice had been met on the way up because a warm summer following a mild winter had kept it concentrated farther north than usual—but not north enough to have permitted ready access into Lady Franklin Bay. Only the previous day,

Lieutenant Kislingbury had written in his journal, "We can congratulate our-selves" on getting so far north so soon. Ever ready with an appropriate apho-rism, he noted, "Never count your chickens before they are hatched." Pike anchored his ship to the ice pack. Greely's expedition now lay off Cape Baird, a promontory of Bellot Island, which itself guards Lady Franklin Bay like a petrified sentinel.

Greely managed to get ashore and cache 280 pounds of bread and meat. Back on the *Proteus*, he was dismayed to hear from Captain Pike that the main ice pack to which the ship was tied had begun drifting south. Nothing could be done except vent frustration in writing letters. Greely told his wife, "I desire continually you, our home and its comforts." He could tolerate the present sit-uation only because of the future happiness he hoped would result: "There seems so little outside of you and the babes that is of any true value to me."

Kislingbury, sharing a stateroom with the commander, wrote long letters to each of his four sons. In one he said, "There will be so many matters of interest to tell my little men when I come home." He described how the ice extended "shore to shore across Robeson Channel and doubtless right through to the North Pole. I have seen Santa Claus up here." He told his sons that he had made arrangements with him to have Christmas gifts delivered from St. John's and Washington. "Papa has but one thing he dreads, and that is the long night . . . 130 days of darkness will be trying," he wrote to them, and said that this letter would be the last "until next year, when I trust the ship [carrying mail] will get to us."

Octave Pavy's pen was also busy, dripping spleen and disdain. Once, when a brief opening appeared in the ice pack, Greely happened to be sleeping. "If he had some idea of responsibility he would not sleep, as he has no provisions prepared for a nip," Pavy wrote. That three-letter word, in general use among whalers and polar explorers and most definitely an understatement, did not yet apply. The *Proteus* was in no immediate peril of being crushed by the ice. She was, however, being carried helplessly southward after having come within ten miles of her destination—Greely had selected as his campsite a spot along the shore of Discovery Harbor, an indentation of Lady Franklin Bay that drew its name from a British ship that once had sheltered there.

But luck had not deserted the American expedition. After seven days of enforced retreat, the ship was as much as forty miles south of Discovery Harbor when a westerly gale arose. The frozen expanse that had stretched clear across

Robeson Channel started to split along its western fringes. Great cracks spiderwebbed across it, and Captain Pike seized the advantage of as many of them as he could, pushing his ship at full speed through each new opening. The impenetrable body of the ice pack surged eastward. Its western edge continued to crumble. Her combined two engines at full pressure, the *Proteus* steamed through tossing floes, wildly zigzagging but again on a broad northerly course. On 10 August, she stood once more at the gateway to Lady Franklin Bay.

Pike anchored to an inshore floe. Greely went ashore to examine the cairn and records left by the British in 1875. Lieutenant Lockwood clambered across floes, then trod dry land and surveyed the coal seam. He returned to report it easily accessible. The frozen sea barrier, Kislingbury recorded in his journal, had so splintered that all the *Proteus* had finally to do was "cut through harbor ice. The proper thing to do tonight would be to give a hip! hip! hurrah!"

Unloading began at once. The men pitched camp in tents. On 13 August, they all were feverishly writing last letters home, for the *Proteus* was expected to get away the next day. No one knew just then that at the harbor mouth, ice had begun to resolidify. Fred Kislingbury found time for still more letter writing. He had appointed Colonel Wheeler Schofield, who, like himself, had married and lost a Bullock girl (Kislingbury two), trustee for his children should he not return. Kislingbury's final words to the boys were typically sentimental: "What a long time poor papa has to wait before he can hear from his pets again. I pray for my darlings morning and night. I am certain my little men are striving hard in their studies." And so deeply preoccupied was Kislingbury with his last letters home that he failed to notice his commander's growing irritation over the time he spent writing them.

Satisfaction with the speed of unloading—by 4:00 A.M. on 14 August, all general cargo was ashore—might have outweighed Greely's anxiety over personality conflicts. But even as his carpenters were hammering the first nails into the timbers brought north ready cut for house building, he knew he must somehow resolve the problem of Octave Pavy and Henry Clay. Pavy refused to stay with the expedition if Clay did. Of the two men, Greely vastly preferred Clay. More important, he could not, as commander, let himself be dictated to by a subordinate. But neither could he avoid the fact that Pavy was the least to be spared. "It gives great pain," Greely wrote in his journal, "to find Pavy such a man as to threaten to abandon the party. If he was anything but a doctor I would deal with him summarily."

Allowing him to remain a member of the expedition, Greely feared, guaranteed trouble ahead. But the party had to have its medical officer. Clay suggested a way out of the quandary by offering to return on the *Proteus.* Greely hated to lose him. "But our surgeon is indispensable and all honorable concession to retain him should be made." Less regrettable was the loss of Corporal Starr, now acknowledged by both Greely and his second in command as a subversive influence among the men, and he would also go home on the steamer. (Another returnee was Private Ryan, who had epilepsy.)

From the start, Octave Pavy was convinced that he knew more about the Arctic than the American Army officers would ever learn. He developed an early contempt for all of them. He himself could not boast a significant polar experience, but the Arctic had come to obsess him. Born in New Orleans to a French plantation owner, Pavy had studied medicine in Paris, where he also had affected the pose of painter and sculptor. He'd teamed up with a French explorer, Gustave Lambert, and was planning an assault upon the North Pole when the Franco-Prussian War intervened. Pavy served with some distinction in that conflict, but Lambert was killed.

Returning to the United States, Pavy had garnered publicity by having, off his own bat, equipped an expedition intended to search for the North Pole via the Bering Strait. Magazines had touted him as "a student-geographer and annotator of Arctic facts" with a physique "inured to Alpine work . . . a knowledge of navigation obtained personally on the high seas" and "an ardor not to be cooled by the rigors of an Arctic climate." Pavy's plan was to voyage northward from San Francisco and, in a final spurt, make for the Pole by raft, a contraption based on four twenty-five-foot India-rubber cylinders. "Pavy theorizes that an extension of the Kuro Siwo will carry him into the Polar Sea. He conjures that open water is continuous across the Pole itself," a magazine had reported.

Such were the myths then in circulation. Not that Pavy was first to overestimate the strength of the Kuro Siwo, the Black Stream of Japan that sweeps northward from the tropics to the Arctic Circle. Nor was he the last— Lieutenant George De Long had harbored similar hopes when he set forth on the *Jeannette.* At any rate, Pavy's "Expedition to the North Pole" never left port. On the eve of its planned departure in the summer of 1872, the expedition's financial backer either committed suicide or was murdered by his valet. Pavy had then withdrawn from public gaze to pursue a restless and often impoverished life, until he had the good fortune to attract a pair of Missouri physicians who helped him complete his medical studies.

In Paris lived a woman who would claim to be Pavy's abandoned wife, with a daughter also his. Even so, in the United States, Pavy had married a well-educated and well-to-do St. Louis girl. He had regained prominence among the scientifically inclined and lectured at the St. Louis Academy of Science. Learning of Henry Howgate's plans for an Arctic colony, Pavy had offered his services. He'd joined the second Howgate expedition, that of 1880, as its physician and naturalist, and when its ship, *Gulnare*, had returned damaged to the United States, he had stayed on in Greenland, as had Henry Clay, to prepare for future colonization ventures. Pavy had studied the Eskimo language, along with the region's flora and fauna, and had grown confident in himself as an Arctic expert. His self-esteem restored, it was a safe bet that once attached to a genuine polar exploration, one consisting of Army soldiers with no Arctic experience comparable to his, Octave Pavy would not agreeably submit to military discipline.

In those first few days at Discovery Harbor, how best to cope with the expedition's surgeon was only one of its commander's concerns. Actually, Greely had much to be thankful for. Unloading proceeded without a hitch, and that included 140 tons of coal. He was generally pleased with his noncommissioned officers, though still anxious about Sergeant William Cross, the former machinist now in charge of the steam launch and an inveterate tippler. And of the three dozen dogs taken on at Disko and Upernavik, more than half were found diseased and soon would die. But work on the house went rapidly ahead, the framework soon completed and flooring laid. Even Lieutenant Kislingbury noted that "Lieutenant Greely has a wonderful faculty for getting work out of the men, and under his supervision I can see that in a day or so we will be living inside."

But less than a week after the party landed, it was the second in command with whom Greely found most serious fault. On 15 August, he was "quite mortified" by Kislingbury's evident assumption that "he should have time for letters and not be required with his men at all times." Greely said nothing to him just then, but the hour approached when the commander could no longer keep his silence.

The wind had dropped. New ice closed up at the harbor entrance. Captain Pike chafed to start for home, but his ship was locked in. Besides three passengers, he had personal mail and important dispatches to take back with him, among them a lengthy missive from Greely addressed to General Hazen, outlining the relief program for 1882 and 1883. It was based largely on discussions Greely had conducted with the C.S.O. before leaving. The letter directed what had to be done should either of the relief parties encounter trouble at any point along the shores of Ellesmere Island or Greenland. With a dogmatism that he would have cause to regret, Greely ended his dispatch: "No deviation from these instructions should be permitted. Latitude of action should not be given to a party who on a known coast are searching for men who know their plans and orders." Hazen was to say that "there never was a more carefully elaborated, painstaking and conscientious plan of work than this drawn up by Mr. Greely and myself." But he would also in self-defense describe Greely's letter as "of a nature and character that I felt I was excluded from giving any orders that would in any manner conflict with his directions."

On the sixteenth, the house scantlings were in place. Another four days saw the structure all but roofed. Greely christened his little base Fort Conger, in honor of Omar D. Conger, a Michigan senator and tireless supporter of the Arctic project from its inception. Well before the end of the month, the station was close to planned operation. Shelter for twenty-five officers and men, the main hut measured sixty-five feet long, twenty-one feet wide, and stood fourteen feet high. Heavy tar paper coated its double walls, and a lighter layer covered the roof. Such pitch-black envelope would absorb the sun's rays in summer, trapping heat, and in winter, with the additional drifts of ice and snow, insulate against the cold. Canvas and tar-paper lean-tos were built at both ends of the hut for the magnetic instruments and general storage.

One entered the hut through a canvas alcove on its west side. A fifteen-by-seventeen-foot space at the hut's northern end served as the officers' quarters and was furnished with a table in the center and bunks for the three lieutenants and Dr. Pavy. Greely hung heavy drapes "so at night or whenever I desired privacy they could be drawn to cut off my corner from view." In addition to the bunk, set on a chest full of his clothing, Greely's "corner" included a small desk and rocking chair. Shelves above the desk held "the excellent Arctic library we are furnished with." The enlisted men's room, about double the size of the officers' and taking up most of the southern portion of the hut, contained twenty two-tiered bunks and four mess tables. The two areas were separated, near the hut's entrance, by a kitchen, common washroom, and a space for scientific study. The washroom had "an excellent bath-tub" and abutted against double chimneys, thus "was always comfortable for ablutions"—performed weekly, by Greely's orders.

The camp was conveniently situated on level ground within a hundred yards of the shore. Hills reared behind it, and a valley stretched northward, threaded by a creek and leading to the coal mine four miles distant. Visible southward from the camp was tiny Dutch Island, two miles offshore, and the eastern entrance to Discovery Bay, now almost totally covered by the ice that still immobilized the *Proteus*. Farther eastward, Hall Basin narrowed into Robeson Channel, on the opposite side of which lay the refuge where Captain Hall had raised the American flag and which he had named Thank God Harbor.

In those first days at Fort Conger, optimism and excited anticipation could be felt now and then, yet all was far from well. The commander continued to fret, often with good reason. As conscientious about plans for scientific work as for human shelter, he had arranged for construction of a wood hut, some 200 yards from the main quarters, to serve as the magnetic observatory. Banked to its eaves by earth and sod, it was still an uncomfortable place for the observer until, later on, a small fire grate was installed.

Greely was most dismayed by the consequences, only now discoverable, of the haste in which the expedition had been mounted. The scales of the solar and radiation thermometers were of such limited range that they would be useless at the most important season, from October to March. A dip circle had been specially made for the Lady Franklin Bay Expedition. The instrument, a magnetic needle balanced within a circular box and essential for estimating the direction of the earth's magnetic intensity, had been shipped erroneously to the United States Coast Survey. Greely had promptly remonstrated, securing a promise that the instrument would be sent to him at New York. Not until the day of departure from St. John's had it been found that the carefully boxed item shipped to him was "old . . . rusty . . . unreliable." There must have occurred, in Greely's later words, an "unwarranted and unauthorized substitution by some person [which] materially impaired, if not effectively destroyed, the value of our dip observations."

As August drew to a close, the *Proteus* remained bottled up in harbor, two miles offshore. In his freshly built quarters, Greely attended to business, first presenting his two lieutenants and Dr. Pavy with a paper formally stating each man's intention to return to the United States in 1883. Should any of the three wish to apply for command of the post, if continued under the international polar program, he should say as much in writing now, so that word could be sent back home for the War Department to make appropriate arrangements. Lieutenant Lockwood's response was cautious. Although "flattered" by Greely's request, he could not directly answer. "The year 1883 is too far in the future," there were "too many contingencies to be considered," making definite commitment inadvisable. The doctor tersely concurred with Lockwood's statement. But Kislingbury's reply was effusive. He was "devoted" to his duties, "greatly interested in the Arctic, eager to learn and discover everything pertaining hereabouts and as far north as possible." He felt physically fit to stay on in the Arctic beyond 1883 and "hold myself ready to remain here so long as my government desires me to do so."

All hands now lived within the hut. But any close camaraderie that developed was more conspicuous among the enlisted men than among the handful at the top. The expedition's second in command wrote letters "until my arm aches." Some betrayed homesickness. Mostly they registered optimism. Kislingbury wrote, "I feel that I shall successfully accomplish everything that I undertake and that I shall surely come back." Thus his pen ran on, the writer unaware of his commander's growing impatience. Near the close of the month, Greely noted that Kislingbury "rose to breakfast very late and went back to bed until dinner." It was bad enough that his other officer, Lockwood, had proved an insomniac and also slept in late.

Even on Sunday, arguably a day of rest, the two seemed to be overdoing it. Greely reprimanded each in turn. Lockwood humbly apologized, vowing to change his habits. Not so Kislingbury, who, Greely privately recorded, "complained that he felt in the way, that I inclined not to follow his advice." Kislingbury had referred to a recent "tramp over the hills" as work. Greely called it pleasure. Between the two officers, tension mounted with each passing hour. The *Proteus*, visible only through a spyglass, remained at anchor, still blocked by ice from leaving Lady Franklin Bay.

# 8

# THE DISBARRED
# LIEUTENANT

FOR THREE CONSECUTIVE days, breakfast had been delayed half an hour on Fred Kislingbury's account. He had received the commander's scolding with ill grace. He offered to miss the meal, let everyone go ahead and eat without him. Greely claimed that was not the point. Whether he skipped breakfast or not, he had to get up at the same time as his fellow officers and the men: 7:30 A.M. The commander's rationale at that moment was that when an officer could not show cheerful compliance with orders, his usefulness to the expedition was destroyed. He tried to point out this logic to Kislingbury, genuinely eager for the man to see things his way and thereby end the matter. Instead, Kislingbury argued that the officers need not be required to rise at the same time as the men. Losing patience with him, Greely snapped back that if he could not see fit to do as directed, he had better go. Without another word, Kislingbury stalked from the officers' quarters.

The second in command was now convinced that his services as a member of the expedition were no longer required. He withdrew to the stateroom on the *Proteus* and once more took up his pen. He wrote, "On various occasions Lieutenant Greely has shown a want of confidence in me . . . seen fit to find fault. I have for some time past felt that inwardly, for some reason best known to himself, he would be better pleased if I were not connected as the second officer of the expedition." Some disagreement or other was bound to have brought matters to a head. He continued, "The only thing I feel left for me to do is to be asked to be relieved from duty." Greely's blunt words that morning had left him no option. Kislingbury concluded, "It will doubtless be better if I go."

Kislingbury wrote these words to the commander that same forenoon. It was a letter far different from those profuse ones upon which, in Greely's view, he had spent too much time, but it was almost as long. Had the commander complained over something more serious, Kislingbury "would doubtless resist being relieved." But since he had spoken so forcefully over "a trivial matter," it was evident that "the comfort, peace and harmony, and even the success of the expedition, may be jeopardized if I remain." Leaving the party would entail a sacrifice. All of his year's salary and allowance, as paid in advance to the expedition's members, had been swallowed up in the settlement of personal debts. Kislingbury also had footed the bill for clothing, whose cost the War Department's allowance had not covered. He hoped the government would be "lenient" during the nine months left before he could resume drawing his regular pay.

Kislingbury asked that in the letter Greely had to compose for the Chief Signal Officer, reporting the circumstances of his return, attention be drawn to the state of his "pecuniary affairs." In case the *Proteus*, which would take him home, had to winter in the Arctic en route, he also would require "enough subsistence stores and antiscorbutics to last me until next season." He would leave the expedition in sorrow. "I have become fond of Arctic life," he admitted. "But I must be on my way and it would be better if I go before it becomes too late for me to do so. The *Proteus* is still within reaching distance." Kislingbury's final request was that two or three men be detailed to help him carry his gear to the ship. "I can reach her over the ice," he explained.

Kislingbury asked Dr. Pavy to deliver the letter. Shortly after dinner that same day, 26 August, Greely called the doctor, Lieutenant Lockwood, and Kislingbury himself outside the hut, beyond earshot of the men. He needed

Pavy and Lockwood as witnesses. He read Kislingbury's letter aloud, then denied having implied that he wanted the lieutenant off the expedition. He was not one to intimate or hint. "If I wanted a man or an officer to leave the party," he stated, "I would tell him so at once." Kislingbury replied that this was precisely what he had, in effect, done. "Very well," retorted Greely. "I will put it stronger. I will part with every officer under me and do the work myself with the help of my noncommissioned officers rather than have an officer unwilling to cheerfully agree to all my wishes." Did Kislingbury still wish to be relieved? The answer was yes; Kislingbury had no doubt that "it would be a relief to [Greely] to get rid of me."

Greely was convinced of the rectitude of his course. Kislingbury had made clear his "unwillingness to conform to post regulations he deemed obnoxious." What choice was left to his commander? The loss of Kislingbury might be regrettable, for he had a "peculiar fitness for field work," Greely wrote in his report earmarked for passage home on the *Proteus*. But, Greely insisted, "I cannot retain him." Regarding Kislingbury's financial concerns, the commander had no recommendations. His next step was to pen the official order: "First Lieutenant F. Kislingbury, 11th Infantry, acting signal officer, is at his own request relieved from duty as a member of this Expedition and returning by the steamship *Proteus* to St. John's, Newfoundland, will report without delay to the C.S.O. of the Army, Washington D.C."

Kislingbury returned to quarters and packed his belongings. Sergeant Brainard saw to his commissary rations. Accompanied by two other helpers, the lieutenant trudged rapidly across rocks and then ice. The *Proteus* was visible. But a plume of smoke drifted from her funnel. She was working up steam. She was getting enough to navigate a clear lead through the floes. And then she was running out of the pack. Kislingbury's anticipation gave way to alarm. Within minutes the ship, with full crew and two passengers, had escaped the ice, before Kislingbury had even reached the shoreline. Captain Pike had found a water lead and taken prompt advantage of it. Soon she was too far out for hailing. Kislingbury could do nothing but watch the *Proteus* turn her prow down Kennedy Channel. Letters to his sons, his account of the clash with Greely, the commander's own official report of the situation, all, like Kislingbury himself, had missed the ship. On the slopes behind Fort Conger, some of the expedition had gathered for a last glimpse of the homebound vessel. By 7:00 P.M., she had vanished.

Making his way back to camp in silence, Kislingbury pondered his "rather peculiar position." Should he ask that the commander's order be revoked? Seeing the new situation Greely might revoke it even without being asked. One thing Kislingbury felt sure of: "I could never endure remaining here doing nothing." Perhaps, he felt, he should "smother my feelings and go along, if allowed, as though the trouble had never occurred." He would wait a day or so to see what course the commander intended to pursue. "I expected that he would revoke the order and return me to duty," he wrote. That expectation was dashed within hours. The *Proteus*'s departure having rendered Greely's order impracticable, Greely "modified" it. Kislingbury had now to "proceed from this place to St. John's by the first visiting steamship. In the meantime he will be considered as on waiting orders."

Thus was Lieutenant Fred Kislingbury, United States Army, condemned to a mortifying state of limbo for at least a year. In Greely's official dictum, the officer was "not to be considered a member of this expeditionary force but as temporarily at this station awaiting transportation." He was forbidden any useful role in the scientific work, could not even, in Sergeant Brainard's words, "request a soldier to obey the simplest order." It was a situation unique in the annals of American military history. Not that the excommunicated lieutenant viewed his plight in such lofty terms. On a more immediate and emotional level, he felt that Greely's uncompromising stance only confirmed apprehensions that had so often disturbed him on the passage up. To Kislingbury, the truth was starkly plain. Totally out of touch though they now were with the rest of the world, his commander could hardly wait to see the back of him. "If not," asked Kislingbury, "why such haste in the issuance of this order?"

Though his dismissed lieutenant was not on board the *Proteus*, Greely was glad the ship had gone. Its departure "in a measure takes away my intense longing to get back to my wife and children." But he had resolved to carry out his mission, which he felt would be best achieved by continued discipline within the party and as faithful an adherence as possible to the customs of that civilized society from which they were so inexpressibly remote. On 28 August, a Sunday, he assembled all hands and told them that although separated from the rest of the world, they would observe the Sabbath. Games were forbidden, and all but those genuinely nonreligious were to assemble to hear him read the Psalms. Greely's choice on that first occasion was Psalm 133: "Behold, how good and how pleasant it is for brethren to dwell in unity." True enough. But those very restrictions on Sunday activity stirred resentment, and Sergeant Brainard wrote in his diary, "Arguments are plentiful."

But so were feelings that each man had a job to do. This mutual under-standing produced its own sense of unity. In a spirit of optimism, Greely found a placid charm in the camp's surrounds. "A large flock of eiderducks had settled in an open pool nearby," he wrote, "and to the northward some three-quarters of a mile, ten musk-oxen were quietly grazing. The adjacent brook-slopes and margins were clothed with vegetation . . . clusters of saxifrage, varied with sedges, grasses or the familiar buttercup. Higher up, countless Arctic pop-pies of luxuriant growth." And Greely wasted little time before starting the series of sledging trips by which he hoped to gain wider knowledge of the region and, most important, set up depots to victual the major research jour-neys he planned for the spring.

Fort Conger's location was about 1,100 miles above the Arctic Circle, and just inland from Lady Franklin Bay, which curves westward into Ellesmere Island. Looking east across Robeson Channel, on good days Greely could see the shore where the Hall expedition had come to grief. That was the Greenland side, and few explorers had pushed up the coast farther than Thank God Harbor. Not much exploration had been achieved on the Ellesmere Island side, either. Greely intended to rectify that, had planned trips not only across Robeson Channel into northern Greenland but within the interior of Ellesmere's upper region, called Grinnell Land.

On 30 August, Dr. Pavy and the photographer, Sergeant George Rice, set out under orders to strike directly overland for Cape Joseph Henry, along Grinnell Land's northern rim. They would seek traces of the missing *Jeannette* and at the same time assess the feasibility of sledge travel along the Grinnell Land coast. There being insufficient snow yet for sledging, Pavy's party had to carry their gear bodily. The morning after their departure, Sergeant Brainard and four companions also left northward in the whaleboat with 2,000 pounds of provisions, fuel, bedding, and other essentials.

Brainard was to creep around the Grinnell shore and establish a depot. He had to battle moving ice, only to find the ice foot—sea ice attached to the shore and unmoved by tidal action—too hummocky to land anything. "Our struggles northward had been in vain," Brainard wrote. "We could only turn about and head south again through the stubborn ice we had fought on the way up." After fifteen hours at the oars they were forced to land near the foot of Mount Beaufort, well short of Fort Conger. Here they tied up the whale-boat, made a cache of supplies, and pitched camp for a well-earned rest. They arrived back at the station on 3 September, having trudged over rough terrain for twelve hours.

That same day, Pavy and Rice got as far as Cape Union. From an elevation of 1,000 feet, the doctor saw a broad belt of open water, and beyond it solid ice all along the horizon, which would prevent further progress. Returning south, they halted at Lincoln Bay, where the Nares expedition in 1875 had left a supplies depot. It was broken down, its contents scattered, and the damp had spoiled bread, tea, sugar, salt, and tobacco. Defective bungs had emptied rum kegs. But some 1,200 pounds of canned meat were in good condition. Before the pair could continue, rheumatic pains and frostbitten feet slowed Rice, and after two days' travel, Pavy shouldering the other's load besides his own, Rice had to be half dragged. On 7 September, the doctor pitched a tent and ate cold roast beef and chocolate.

Rice watched without appetite. "He wants me to leave him and go," Pavy scribbled in his journal. "But tomorrow I will make him walk." And he did until, descending a valley, sometimes clinging to each other, the two men lost their way in a fog. Pavy realized that the sergeant-photographer could go no farther. Again he put up the tent, this time leaving Rice inside, and carried on alone, reaching Fort Conger at 4:00 A.M. on 9 September, almost as exhausted as the man he had left behind. A relief party of fourteen men under Sergeant Brainard set out at once with coffee, food, and wine. When they reached Rice, they found "his legs swollen to double size." Hauling him on a roughly built litter up and down steep rocky slopes, they were all pretty well done in by the time they stumbled into Fort Conger.

In the meantime, another preliminary foray had begun, with Greely in charge. The commander was accompanied by Lockwood, who had backslid into his old late-rising habits and drawn a letter of reprimand. Moreover, on a Sunday when games were forbidden, he had accepted an invitation from Lieutenant Kislingbury to play a game of cards. Since Kislingbury's official separation from the party, Lockwood was Greely's second in command, "successor in case of my death or permanent disability." Fred Kislingbury could well have lapsed into embittered idleness. Instead he tried to appear of use to the expedition. Greely made note of the lieutenant "bringing back from his walks mosquitoes and geological specimens." And his former second in command was "useful with a gun . . . targeted fourteen musk-cattle quietly graz-ing near the entrance to Black Rock Valley." But Kislingbury overdid it. Greely had ordered only eight musk cattle slaughtered. "This interesting species should not be exterminated, unless immediately needed for meat," he explained.

But now the commander was off on his first reconnaissance. He intended to survey a valley called the Bellows that led inland from the head of Discovery Harbor. Enough snow had fallen for sledge use, Greely alternately riding and running behind a nine-dog vehicle. After penetrating the valley some dozen miles, he decided to double the amount of exploration gained so far by order-ing Lockwood to take the sledge and return to Fort Conger by a separate route. The commander was not in the best of moods. Jumping a tidal crack, he had lost a pair of eyeglasses. When he returned to base, he found that Lockwood had preceded him. He had not gone as far as Greely felt he should have, "and can tell nothing of the country. He has ruined the sledge."

These early distractions drained some of the spirit that had so animated the party upon its arrival at Lady Franklin Bay. On 13 September, Sergeant Brainard wrote privately, "It is just five years ago today since I left home to make an ass of myself by joining the regulars." The version most often given of David Legge Brainard's enlistment would be that, following a visit to the Philadelphia Centennial Exposition of 1876, he found upon changing trains at New York City that he lacked sufficient funds to complete his journey home. He lived in the upstate town of Norway, his birthplace. Too proud to write to his family for money, he had taken the free ferry across to the Army post on Governor's Island and joined up. Square-jawed and ruggedly handsome, his sol-dierly appearance masking a dislike for regular Army life, Brainard had served his time in the Second Cavalry, seen action against the Sioux and Nez Percé Indians at age twenty, and been wounded in the face and hand at Little Muddy Creek, Montana Territory. In 1880, aged twenty-four, he had applied to join Howgate's Arctic colonization scheme. When this plan fell through because of the *Gulnare's* unseaworthiness, Brainard might have begun counting the hours to his return to civilian life. Instead, probably on impulse, he had volunteered from his post on the Montana plains for duty with the Lady Franklin Bay Expedition, and been accepted.

Despite his feelings about the Army, Brainard was in essence good soldier material. He believed that commands clearly issued should be obeyed. He had no patience with indecision at the top, which would sour his view of Lieutenant Greely as commander, even as Greely, unaware of Brainard's judgment, came to perceive him as "my mainstay in many things." He assigned him the duty of supply officer, responsible for the equitable issue of food, tobacco, clothes, and the like. Brainard's term of service formally expired the first week of September. "For the past five years," he wrote in secret, "I have looked forward to this date with the joyful anticipation of one who is to be delivered from bondage. But now I do not feel any more independent or happy." He passed Dr. Pavy's physical inspection and reenlisted on the spot.

Brainard's despondency those first weeks at Fort Conger resulted partly from a local exploration trip he had made with the commander and two others, Sergeant Maurice Connell and Private Jacob Bender. Each carried a forty-pound pack. Crossing a divide into a valley overlooking St. Patrick's Bay, just north of Fort Conger, Greely injured his knee and had to turn back. Brainard took over. He did not relish the position: "Nights were uncomfortable, we were three men in a sleeping bag intended for two. We tried to relieve our cramped bodies by cutting a slit in the bottom through which Bender put his head, resting his feet between the faces of Connell and myself. This experiment will not be tried again." And halfway up a mountain, a snowstorm drove them back. At the same time, Dr. Pavy, sergeants David Linn and Winfield Scott Jewell, with the two native dog drivers, were bound east for Cape Murchisan to cache supplies for spring travel. When ice became too thin to bear a sledge, they had to unload onto a paleocrystic floeberg (identified by its cubicle shape with regular lines of cleavage). Just in camp from his own unpleasant trip, Brainard left with Rice to complete the Pavy party's mission. They too had to retreat when a sledge runner broke in the ice foot. And that same month, a fire Greely blamed on carelessness destroyed one of the expedition's tents. Annoyed by these initial failures, Greely was all the more incensed to find "Lieutenant Lockwood playing cards with the enlisted men."

Greely's journal entries at this stage were not altogether cheerless. Sergeant Hampden Gardiner and Corporal Nicholas Salor, sent to discover practicable routes for loaded sledges in the vicinity of St. Patrick's Bay, found an eight-man sledge and a slightly damaged twelve-foot cedar boat with paddle, left by the British ship *Discovery* in 1876. Private Henry, with four others, repaired the boat the next day and brought in the sledge. Greely had the steam launch hauled higher up the beach for safety during high tides. And he found solace in the presumption that by this time, the *Proteus* had reached St. John's with personal correspondence and his report to General Hazen.

The ship indeed had, and Captain Pike made at once for the seaport's telegraph office. Word flashed to Washington. The expedition had arrived safely at Lady Franklin Bay "one month after leaving St. John's. Party all well." At Signal Corps headquarters, Lieutenant Louis V. Caziarc, acting chief officer in General Hazen's absence, sped the information to Henrietta Greely in San Diego and comfortingly described Pike's telegram as "cheerful . . . containing so much good news."

At Fort Conger, though the long night approached, tensions actually lessened. Set near the foot of steep gloomy cliffs and surrounded by rough treeless terrain and steadily hardening ice, the post brightened with an assortment of kerosene lamps and countless candles. Life acquired a sort of resigned serenity. Greely announced that birthdays would be honored with rum for the principal celebrant and freedom from duty for that day. There were novels to relax with, textbooks on Arctic exploration, chess, checkers, backgammon, playing cards, a sackful of amusement. And music—several of the men had fine voices, and instrumental accompaniment was at hand: violin, concertina, and what Greely described as "an orguinette with 50 yards of music," which so fascinated the Eskimos they "never wearied of grinding out one tune after another."

Responding to a request from the commander, Dr. Pavy, in the first week of October, submitted a detailed report on the party's physical health. It was generally good, but the medical officer foresaw dietary problems—for instance, a shortage of fresh vegetables. His stock of medicines was incomplete and "*absolutely deficient in essential* drugs." He recommended more suitable clothing for field work and such activity kept within limits, "in view of a retreat so far considered by you as certain." He wished to be kept informed of the commander's intentions on station "as well as your plans and means of escape . . . your plans will be in this emergency entirely my *guide* for the future." Greely was by this time all too aware of his medical officer's mordant state of mind. Even so, Pavy's unnerving choice of words—"retreat . . . escape . . . emergency"—left him shocked and apprehensive.

In the middle of the month, the sun appeared for the last time. Greely scaled a hill north of the station to bid it good-bye. He marveled at the heavens' coloration. Hues changed from pearly gray to shades of orange: "This magic touch of color blending with the snowy covering gave a new glory to our Arctic scenery which was further idealized by the rosy curly columns of vapor rising in the damp cold air from the few water spaces. Then the polar day gave way to the long reign of twilight and Arctic darkness."

Now the ice was strong enough for Greely's men to bring in musk-ox meat killed during the summer. A party sent out to mine coal hauled back three tons. Another under Lieutenant Lockwood took additional food supplies to make a depot at Cape Beechey and build a snow house there for use when serious sledging was under way. Greely meanwhile had sent Dr. Pavy off on another attempt to reach Cape Joseph Henry. His party took two sledges and fifteen dogs (one of the sledges, flying a small flag knitted by Henrietta Greely, was named *Antoinette*, for the commander's daughter). Sergeant David Ralston's birthday was celebrated. The men feasted on oyster soup, roast beef and gravy with assorted vegetables, and dessert of jelly cake, cherry pie, peach pie, and coffee. Greely's men knew next to nothing of one another's past lives, so, while they celebrated Ralston's birthday, no one knew of Matilde Ralston, who claimed that after marrying her for money left by a previous husband, Ralston had run off and joined the Army, leaving her penniless.

Next came Henrietta's birthday. "I sent the men a glass of sherry each," Greely noted. Lockwood proposed the toast to Mrs. Greely, and two days later was toasted on his own birthday, a celebration marred, in Greely's view, by the unexpected return of Pavy's party. The doctor explained that after they had cached bread and pemmican near Mount Parry, open water had stopped further advance. Pavy's written description was of "all the ice in motion, not as a pack but broken floes in contact as a terrible fight of Titans. With reluctance I decided to return home." That picturesque account failed to win over Greely, who recorded that "the doctor's explanation does not impress me. By his own admission he did not even await the turn of the tide to see what effect it would have."

Long before coming to the Arctic, the commander had demonstrated an ability to handle subordinates in a fair, prudent, and effective manner. That frustration had begun to erode this valuable talent became evident when Greely told the men they would be required to wash the officers' clothing. He asked for volunteers. None stepped forward. Greely told Sergeant Brainard to detail someone. That night, an uneasy Brainard wrote of Greely closing the episode with an unexpected warning: "A long talk was given to the crowd of angry and excited men. Lieutenant Greely said he was not a man to be trifled with and in case of mutiny he would not stop at the loss of human lives to restore order." This tense scene had played itself out in the men's living space, while outside the temperature fell below zero for the first time that season.

Most grudges and grievances thus far were short-lived. There was too much to occupy the mind. The program of fall sledging and hunting trips had drawn to its close. The hunters had been busy. Before darkness ended the season, they had shot twenty-six musk oxen, which, with more than a thousand birds killed off Greenland on the passage north, provided the party with some three tons of fresh meat. Duties were carried out daily, to the ceaseless din of floes in the bay "grumbling and growling against each other." November began with disappointing results. Lockwood set out with the open whaleboat to Thank God Harbor on the Greenland side, where he intended to check the condition of the Nares and Hall supply caches. His ferrying point, Cape Beechey, stood at the channel's narrowest width. A mass of swirling ice floes stopped him. He did, however, bring in the small twelve-foot English boat left by the *Discovery*.

At the same time, Greely told Dr. Pavy to lay out a depot for the exploration northward beyond Cape Henry in the coming spring. Pavy hauled stores to a depot already established at Wrangell Bay, but at such cost of dog weariness and sledge damage, besides exhaustion of the men in the party, that Greely wrote off the effort as a waste of time. He almost told Pavy so to his face. Only with difficulty could he head off another argument. Greely felt keenly that he had to guard his own tongue: "While free from mental depression, insomnia and feelings of lassitude which characterized some, yet at times I was affected by irritability, which it required a continued mental struggle to repress." Pavy remained the most persistent thorn in his side. Differences between the two, at first over relatively trivial matters, only thinly concealed a mutual antipathy. Greely informed the doctor that come spring, he could let him have a single dog team for sledging. As he did so, according to Pavy, he "leaned against the stove and avoided my eyes. If he could read my thoughts he certainly must have read all the contempt I have for his person."

Still, nothing of consequence hindered the steady pursuit of the expedition's scientific objectives. These included the observation and recording of aurora borealis. The phenomenon was visible about twice weekly. As with so many previous and subsequent penetrations of the polar regions, nothing that met the human eye was more guaranteed to inspire an eloquence bordering on the poetic. At first, such displays were, to Greely, of the familiar pattern, the sky crisscrossed by drapelike folds of assorted colors. As winter closed in, they struck Greely more like "lances of white light, perhaps tinged with gold or citrine, darting about the heavens in a pattern known as 'merry dancers.' " In the middle of November, the commander likened aurora to "a mass of freshly escaped steam brilliantly illuminated by reflected rays from a powerful calcium light." And later, "a beautiful and brilliant arch formed of convoluted bends of light similar to twisted ribbons."

These periodic and silent sky shows were a colorful backdrop to the activity of twenty-five men clustered together as if unrehearsed players in a drama of which none knew the outcome. They had duties to perform, specific tasks to undertake, an elaborate schedule to follow. Much of what they were to experience would be dictated by the inevitable interplay of their emotions—not to mention hapless decisions made in the homeland from which they were so ineffably remote. And if each of the men at Fort Conger had his private idiosyncrasies, the commander was no exception. Greely had a marked distaste for physical exercise and avoided insisting upon it by directing Sergeant Brainard to draw up enough work "of seeming value" so that the men had at least one hour's daily activity in the open air.

Of more definite value was the need to bank the hut for winter. A six-foot wall of ice had to be built around it at a distance of some three feet, which space would be filled by the expected dry snow to serve as insulation. Lockwood broke out the ice saws. Cutting blocks was a daunting task, so snow adobes were fashioned and left to freeze overnight. Brainard felt that the commander had designed this project as something to do "to keep us from thinking too much about the dullness of life in the Arctic. An ice-palace may serve as a nine-days' wonder. But what after that?"

So began the first winter. There were grounds for gratification. In readiness for the spring, four depots had been established northward along the Grinnell Land coast. Portions of the interior had been newly mapped. Attempts to cross Robeson Channel and check the stores at Thank God Harbor had failed, but the good outweighed the bad. It encouraged Greely, as conscientiously protective of his men's mental health as of their physical well-being, to take steps against the boredom so dangerous to morale. He initiated a school with regular classes in arithmetic, grammar, geography, and meteorology. Every other week he taught on the nature of storms, magnetism, and previous polar expeditions, and reminisced about the Civil War. Lectures were given by Dr. Pavy, who had wartime memories of his own to share but confined himself to medical topics.

Lieutenant Lockwood edited and hectographed a fortnightly news sheet, "Arctic Moon," which carried droll, sentimental, or sober features contributed by the literary minded, described in one of its issues as "the finest minds of the country." Another carried an advertisement intentionally humorous but in retrospect sadly ironic. "Information wanted of the Greely Arctic Expedition. It strayed away from home last July and was last heard from at Upernavik, Greenland. Address: Bereaved Parents."

With geographic exploration at a standstill, scientific observation doggedly continued. The magnetic observer's hut stood some 200 yards northeast of the main dwelling, and its magnetometer was mounted on a stout tripod whose legs were frozen into the earth for support. Ten readings were made hourly. The magnet hung on a silken fiber and swung readily in any direction, "to and fro," wrote Greely, "in a restless uneasy way which at times impressed me with an uncanny feeling." Another hut was built for such meteorological work as recording air pressure, temperature and dew point, wind speed and direction, the movement of clouds, and auroral visitations.

The superintendent of the United States Coast Guard had donated a pendulum to the expedition and instructed the young astronomer Edward Israel on its proper use. It was set up inside a lean-to built on the north side of the officers' room. Using brick and Portland cement bought for the purpose at St. John's, sergeants Gardiner and Connell made four strong piers for the pendulum's suspension. Slabs of ice girded the apparatus to ensure constant and uniform temperature. Greely had French plate glass set in front of this ice wall, and in the door leading into the officers' room, a quite clever arrangement completed by a set of reflectors throwing light on the pendulum, enabling an observer to remain comfortably in the officers' quarters while reading the oscillations through a telescope.

The party mounted a self-registering thermometer and an anemometer atop the 2,000-foot Mount Campbell on nearby Bellot Island. Another anemometer and a wind vane were perched on the ridgepole of the main building. Tidal observations were made hourly in a hole kept open in the lake ice. A snow house built immediately above it prevented the ice from freezing over too quickly and provided shelter for the observer. Distributing the workload as fairly as possible, Greely met no serious opposition from the men.

For one thing, they fed well in those first months. Shaping the expedition's dietary program, Greely had benefitted from the reports of the Englishman George Nares and Sweden's Nordenskiöld, whose experiences confirmed in him the belief that nothing was more important to the health and endurance of Arctic explorers than close attention to their nourishment. Part of this concern was the necessity of variety in their menus. As far as possible, Greely drew these up himself. He recorded: "No one knew a day beforehand (except in special cases) what the dinner would be. Every attempt was made to prevent the men from tiring of any food." Cooks were changed monthly. There was, for a considerable time, an abundance of victuals from which to choose. Thus one day's menu might read, for the two main meals, breakfast: musk-beef hash, oatmeal, fresh bread. Dinner: pea soup, roast musk beef, baked macaroni with cheese, rice pudding, fresh peaches. On another day, breakfast might be corned beef, oatmeal, and fresh bread, and for dinner, vegetable soup, baked pork and beans, corn bread, stewed peaches. Two snacks were served daily. And while Greely was aware of the use of lemon or lime juice to keep scurvy at bay— each man received one ounce daily—he felt just as sure that dampness, uncleanliness, mental ennui, excessive labor, and too much alcohol all contributed to the dread disease.

The officers dined not much differently from the men, their rank acknowledged only by extra dishes of peaches or pineapples, perhaps "a can of shrimp, crab, or other delicacy." All used silver-plated spoons and forks, and the table linen was changed twice a week. A room orderly, detailed daily, helped in setting the tables and washing dishes.

In mid-November, instead of giving a lecture, Greely read poems to his party, in his heart wistfully recalling the practice, when wooing Henrietta from afar, of sending her scraps of poetry. Thanksgiving Day was celebrated, in temperatures of thirty-three below zero, with snowshoe and sledge races and marksmanship contests in the dark. Punch was served twice. Private Henry described the target shooting arrangement, making sure to identify the victor: "A candle stood in a box marked by a bulls-eye. First prize was won by yours truly. There were three bulls-eyes, each could be covered with a silver dollar." Prizes distributed included preserved peaches, rum, tobacco, and towels. The mouthwatering dinner menu consisted of oyster soup, salmon, eiderduck, boiled ham, asparagus, deviled crab, lobster salad, peach and blueberry pie, raisin and jelly cake, vanilla ice cream, dates, nuts, figs, coffee—with a double ration of rum.

Still lurked the threat of low morale born of inaction. The skies put on their show. Lunar halos and mock moons were duly recorded, and, near the last day of the month, "very bright aurora, dazzling streamers." But other than the all-important duty of recording observations, and taking short walks, the men had little to perform. "Along such a wild coast," wrote Greely, "no satisfactory work can be done until the bitter cold of winter has bound fast into a secure and solid mass the sea-floes—the only true Arctic highway."

# 9

# THE FIRST WINTER

SOMETHING UNHINGED JENS Edward. The general gloom, perhaps. Greely blamed the continuing darkness, but the native dog driver would have been used to that. Homesickness, maybe—he had left a wife and three children in Greenland. At any rate, he wandered off. For weeks, the man had seemed depressed, and Greely had been unable to shake him out of it. When he had been missing for hours, Greely dispatched search parties. Two of them circled the station with lanterns, seeking tracks. Sergeant Rice fell, fracturing his left shoulder. Dr. Pavy bandaged it, and the search continued. They overtook Jens Edward ten miles from camp.

When he was brought back, Greely hadn't the heart to reprove him. And within forty-eight hours, the commander had the other dog driver, Thorlip Frederick Christiansen ("Eskimo Fred") to contend with. He had suddenly confronted the officers with a large wooden cross, protection against the men he cried were plotting to shoot him. Pavy pacified him, knowing more than the others of the man's language. Wrote Greely, whose own language was at times intemperate, "I am quite in despair as to how [Christiansen] and Jens are to be managed. It is not pleasant to be responsible for the lives and care of two savages."

But none of the party was unaffected by psychological stress. Even the sturdy Brainard confided in his journal, "One scarcely wonders that Hall died. I think the gloom would drive me to suicide in a week." Greely was himself not immune. Adding to his pile of unposted letters, he told Henrietta, "When I get back to you, have no fear that I shall ever be willing to leave you again. One such separation is enough for a lifetime." Only the promise of future fame and reward could justify the present ordeal. He continued: "I miss you so much, my darling, and want you so much, and yet with all my yearning for you I cannot bring myself to regret coming here. I shall at least have made my mark in the world."

Confidence regrew with the first glimmer of returning light. "The backbone of winter is broken," wrote Lockwood prematurely on 21 December. "Walking out at noon today I was just able to see the hands of my watch by holding it close to my eye." The surrounding silence awed him: "Standing still, one can almost hear his heart beat. The sense of solitude is sublime." The lieutenant wrote these words on Brainard's twenty-fifth birthday. The sergeant's own private notes had a different flavor. Looking back on a life "spent so far on pleasure-seeking and idleness, is it too late to begin anew?"

But he joined heartily in the festive celebration five days later, when once again rum flowed more freely, this time with eggnog washing down an abundance of rich food—mock-turtle soup and salmon, roast beef and potatoes, asparagus, green peas, coconut pies and jelly cake with a variety of fruit and ice cream. Christmas had fallen on a Sunday, so most merrymaking took place the next day. The last of Mrs. Greely's plum pudding was eaten with wine sauce. Some of the men put on a vaudeville show—Private Roderick Schneider cavorted as an Eskimo belle, Private Henry sang comic songs, and cigars were handed out by the displaced second in command, who also led in hymn singing. But dutifully alive to the dictates of his original disciplinary action, Greely could grant him no favors. Wrote Brainard during those Christmas hours, "The C.O. told me this evening to tell the men they were not to play card games with Lieutenant Kislingbury anymore—last night he played poker with the enlisted men." Greely had also informed the sergeant of the letter he had drawn up the previous year naming Lockwood in command should any misfortune befall himself. To Lieutenant Kislingbury, the men's quarters became all but off-limits. Brainard noted on 28 December that he "does not show in our room anymore."

The year ended with Greely lecturing on his Civil War experiences, privates Henry Biederbick and Schneider getting up a sack race across the ice to Dutch Island and back for a pint of rum—and with Dr. Pavy's increasing animus against his commander. Pavy's hero in Arctic exploration was the Englishman George Nares. Sometimes it appeared to the doctor that Greely spoke lightly of Nares's achievements, that he seemed unmindful of how much his party benefitted from caches the Englishman had placed. So while Greely greeted the new year in a relatively upbeat mood, exulting in his journal over the party's "excellent health, undiminished courage and strength," and preparing for a pendulum swing in the icehouse—"the arrangements thus far have been entirely of my own devising"—Pavy registered disgust: "Greely has no love for science. He is full of vanity." And the doctor had heard some of the men confess to having no interest in scientific discoveries, that they were there to make a stake. He commented, "What a comparison with the English—and to think Greely pretends the English are beaten."

In the middle of the month, a great storm struck Fort Conger. Greely sent six men to read the tidal gauges housed in a snowbuilt shelter only 100 feet from the main quarters lean-to. Though roped together, they lost sight of one another when wind gusts blew out their lantern. Brainard's booming voice alone kept them from blundering off in different directions and entangling the ropes. The gale wrenched the anemometer cups away and hurled them out to the sea ice. Yet two days later, bands of dark crimson and daffodil yellow suffused the southern horizon, giving promise of the sun's return. This appearance was followed by intense celestial activity, the sky at times erupting as if into heavenly forest fires. Fort Conger's meteorologist recorded twenty-two hours of auroral arches. One night in February, six mock moons were visible, three on each side of the real one. Kaleidoscopic patterns in the sky were matched below by mortal minds just as agitated. Repeatedly, Greely found cause to reproach his former second in command, late-rising again among the problems: "I twice had him called. He paid no attention, turned over and stayed in bed until noon. I have written him a letter on the subject." Lockwood also had returned to his old habit of sleeping in, but confessed himself "mortified" by it, and Greely, who could hardly risk losing another second in command, bore his apologies.

Left out of affairs, Fred Kislingbury had taken to long walks. He was not prone to the suicidal emotions that had apparently afflicted the dog drivers. But while upon these solitary jaunts, he was in no hurry to return to his limbo status at the camp. Once when Kislingbury had been gone seven hours, Pavy and Brainard went to look for him. They met him as he came back safe and sound. Greely was far from pleased: "As no object was gained by this trip of twenty-five miles in Arctic darkness, I requested that such a long absence should not be repeated until the return of the sun."

The light steadily improved. Tilting pages toward the south, Sergeant Brainard could read *Harper's Monthly*. Preparations for spring sledging began in earnest, further crowding the men's quarters. As described by Brainard, "We have the carpenter's shop, tinker's shop, tinsmith's, shoe and saddler's shop, meteorological observatory and office, magnetic and astronomical study, and photographic gallery." All this under the same roof with space yet found for dining and sleeping. Suitable lamps, according to Brainard, were "totally unprovided." The men had to do with inferior lanterns. The sergeant noted that "Private Jewell made his observations at noon from light furnished by the southern sky."

As dreamed of by the visionary Karl Weyprecht, the function of the circumpolar stations was, beyond all else, on-the-spot scientific observations. But Greely, Lieutenant Lockwood, and the doctor, too, thought at least as much of geographical attainments, of reaching higher latitudes than had the British, of perhaps getting to the Pole itself. On 19 February, Lockwood, Sergeant Brainard, and the driver Christiansen set out with a dog sledge on the season's first important trip. Their mission was to visit the depot near Cape Beechey to see whether Robeson Channel ice would permit a crossing to Thank God Harbor. The view was promising, level floes unmelted by the first weeks of sunshine stretching clear across to Greenland. Lockwood's report combined with the returning daylight to restore optimism among the men—symptomized by William Cross in furtive bouts of drinking. Greely suspected the sergeant of stealing alcohol from the lamps, and had told Brainard to keep an eye on him.

Even as the solar disk became visible on the last day of the month, the attitudes of his fellow officers dimmed Greely's pleasure. "At 7.30 breakfast comes to the table," he wrote Henrietta. "I am ready but no one else is." Pavy showed up five minutes late. Lieutenant Kislingbury, Greely wrote, "after being very deliberate in his dressing and brushing out his whiskers, etc., sits down *regularly* from ten to fifteen minutes late. His whiskers are his pride and I have known him to brush them six times in a single day." Lockwood's behavior was no better, but Greely knew of his trouble getting to sleep each night and tried to sympathize with the fellow. Kislingbury was the prime irritant.

Early in March, Lieutenant Lockwood, sergeants Brainard and Winfield S. Jewell, with Christiansen and a dog team, made again for Cape Beechey (Jewell had braved icy winds at a Signal Corps post on the summit of Mount Washington). Each man wore standard expedition clothing: a double suit of underclothing, a thick jacket lightly draped to keep snow from adhering to the wool, and three pairs of socks. The footwear of canvas boots or moccasins was of poor quality, further evidence, in Greely's view, of the limited time allowed him to outfit his party. But weather conditions gave promise, and Lockwood led his men at last across Robeson Channel.

The party reached Thank God Harbor within twenty-four hours. They found the graves of Captain Hall and two English scurvy victims intact. After making an inventory of the stores left by Hall's party, Lockwood struck south along the Greenland shore and came upon Hall's whaleboat. At the same time, a second party had set out to cross the channel, with Dr. Pavy in command. Its object was to establish a depot at a coastal break called The Gap, some twenty miles north of Thank God Harbor. Pavy's party returned to Fort Conger first, in good spirits, which quickly evaporated during an argument with Greely over his having employed two dog teams instead of one. Pavy had assumed that both teams would be in his charge during the whole trip north. Not so, Greely retorted: "Lieutenant Lockwood's work being the most important it must not suffer."

Pavy's medical reports, which Greely expected regularly, had slipped behind schedule. Greely wrote in his journal, "I must say my stock of patience is nearly exhausted with him." Just three days later, he told the doctor "very sharply, that I would tolerate no insubordination." The argument might have dragged on had not Lockwood's return focused attention on other matters. During his party's ten days' absence, they had covered at least 135 miles in temperatures well below zero. Brainard's journal supplied details. One night, while sheltering in a hastily built snow house, they had found their last few matches too damp for use. "I tried lighting the waterproof matches and wax matches. Both refused to burn," Brainard reported. The party needed fire for cooking and for melting ice into drinking water. Sergeant Jewell saved the day. From inside his shirt he tugged an old love letter. He struck the last match, the paper caught, and with it he lit the alcohol lamp, "which won't be allowed to go out again while we remain in our snow-house."

After returning to Fort Conger, Sergeant Brainard set off once more, with an eight-man party, to deposit the small *Discovery* boat on the Greenland side, at the depot Pavy had just established near The Gap. The boat would be useful if the ice broke up in the channel and left a springtime sledge party stranded. On the return, Brainard crossed paths with Dr. Pavy leading a party north. Pavy had theorized that travel could be made north of Grinnell Land and across the frozen Polar Ocean to eventually strike new land. Greely disagreed, but, he said, "I considered that no chance of geographical success should be neglected, so assigned one of my dog-teams to Pavy for this work." Greely had given the doctor "the smallest flag we have. I hoped he would be able to display it further north than Albert H. Markham had done the English standard"—thus did Greely show the sort of chauvinistic enterprise Karl Weyprecht had deplored. Pavy pleaded a headache. Greely told him not to leave until he felt fit.

Pavy set forth on 19 March, with Greely's reminder to look out for any signs of the *Jeannette* and with a written Godspeed, "trusting that your earnest enthusiasm for polar exploration, united with your practical experience, will insure all success." Although aware of how necessary were Pavy's services as physician, Greely was glad to see the back of him. But he could not overlook Pavy's value to the expedition. "He has deceived me in so many ways," Greely wrote Henrietta. "He has, I understand, been sowing the seeds of dissension and discontent among the men" and had plotted "to destroy Lockwood's chances [for northerly exploration]." The physician-explorer was "eaten up with jealousy." But he was out now on "important work. While despising the man and his methods I most heartily wish him all luck and a safe and speedy return."

Pavy's directions from Greely were to follow the Grinnell coast and discover whether land existed beyond Cape Joseph Henry. He was accompanied by Sergeant George Rice and the driver Jens. A two-man support party saw them off as far as Lincoln Bay. To better the English record of Farthest North was now understood by all members of the expedition as a principal reason for their being in the Arctic. As Private Henry put it in his journal, Pavy's party "had left for the Frozen Polar Sea to explore the mystic north and (if possible) beat Commander Markham's claim of the highest latitude ever reached by a human being." From Lincoln Bay, after the support party had turned back for base, Pavy pressed on. Near Cape Union, a sledge runner broke. Rice and Jens set off on foot back to base for a replacement. It was attached five days later, and the men continued north.

They reached Cape Joseph Henry on 17 April. A storm kept them under canvas forty-eight hours, and when they sought to push on, it was only to confront an expanse of ice-littered water. Pavy would write, for Greely's edification, that viewed from Cape Joseph Henry, "the Polar Sea was of such rough appearance that no sledge, even lightly loaded, could have made any progress over that inextricable maze of huge bergs and enormous hummocks. If such was the ice over which the British dragged heavy loads and cumbersome boats, I admire their perseverance and applaud their pluck and gallantry." Pavy could travel no farther. He had to turn back. In the meantime, floes behind him had separated, making a channel almost a mile wide. Fearful of being marooned, the party waited, encamped on a paleocrystic floe. It grounded against land ice. The men scrambled ashore, leaving their tent, stores, and supplies inadequately cached or scattered.

Ignoring Pavy's praise for the English explorers, Greely confided to his journal that the doctor had erred in his choice of a departure point for crossing ice. He should have pushed on some six miles northwest of Cape Joseph Henry to Cape Hecla, the northernmost point of Grinnell Land. Pavy's decision "eventually proved fatal to his success." Had he quit land at Cape Hecla, "the party would probably have avoided their polar drift, which resulted in the loss of the greater part of their stores and the complete abandonment of their expedition." The fact was that Greely had no wish for a civilian, especially one he disliked, to represent the Lady Franklin Bay Expedition in beating the English record of Farthest North. Pavy had come close to doing so. As Private Henry wrote, "If open water had not interfered with their plans they would have beaten Markham." But Greely wanted this achievement to be made by the United States Army. Moreover, he considered it less likely to occur on the Ellesmere Island side than in northern Greenland.

So while Pavy was still absent, Greely had sent forth a large party under Lockwood, giving him "command of the Greenland coast exploration towards which all our recent exertions have been directed." Those words were

Brainard's—he was in Lockwood's party. Lieutenant Greely charged Lockwood with "full control of the most important sledging and geographical work of the expedition," and that was "the extension of knowledge regarding lands beyond the Arctic Circle." To the accompanying cheers of those remaining behind, the party had left Fort Conger on 3 April with one dog sledge and three other fully loaded sledges weighing a total of 2,000 pounds and hauled by seven men.

Lockwood's party had not gone far before coming across fresh footprints leading toward Fort Conger. They were those of Sergeant Rice and Jens, returning to get the new sledge runner for Pavy, at that time stalled near Cape Union. Lockwood's own group was soon slowed by deep snow, and they had yet to cross Robeson Channel when Private Henry complained of rheumatism. Lockwood ordered him back to the station. As the crossing began, Sergeant Maurice Connell's feet froze. He, too, returned to Fort Conger, borne halfway on a sledge, with the lieutenant himself in the drag ropes. When Lockwood rejoined his men, they were struggling across an only partly frozen channel, fragmented floes overturning sledges, the dogs having to be unharnessed each time while a sledge was set right and its load relashed. Camping on snow-covered floes was sheer misery, Brainard's sleeping bag "hard and cold as iron." For much of the second week of April, blizzards kept the men in their bags. When they were able to continue, fresh snow had piled on the floes, forming hillocks down which sledges slid, spilling loads and entangling dog traces. The animals leaped and howled. The men cursed.

Once on the Greenland side, the party marched all night to reach the *Polaris* boat camp. They set up tents, which violent snow squalls struck down. Again the men could only snatch rest, in minus-thirty-degree cold, by squeezing themselves deep inside frozen sleeping bags, which their body heat converted into soaking straitjackets. A violent wind gust swept a loaded sledge into midair, and as it fell, a runner gashed Sergeant David Ralston's scalp. Bandaged, he remained with the party, but Private William Whisler, with severe chest pain and spitting blood, started back on foot across Robeson Channel. Private Biederbick, wetting himself because of a weakened bladder, staggered after him. Reduced to five in number, the party fought new gales to put up their tents, mittened hands clutching ice-coated poles. When able to eat, they munched hungrily on hard bread and frozen meat, much of which the dogs pilfered.

Lockwood crossed Newman Bay toward Gap Valley. Sometimes a hard snow crust permitted speedy travel, but more often the snow was fine as sand, clogging the runners. The largest sledge was so heavily burdened, it took all five men to haul it. On 22 April, they reached the vicinity of Repulse Harbor and, noted Sergeant Rice, "groped their way down the dry gorge to the bay with little knowledge of their whereabouts or surroundings." Pitching camp in the thunderous wind was a battle. "For more than two hours," wrote Brainard, "we struggled with the tent before we could get it fastened down, covered with an intricate network of lariats and lashing-lines to prevent it from ballooning and taking flight." While the men tried to sleep, the dogs ate the remaining bacon and ten pounds of English beef. Sergeant Linn was the party's cook. He tried his hand at making a pemmican stew. So tart was the taste of the limes in the pemmican, it made the stew unpalatable, and the pemmican had to be eaten raw. Wrote one of the party, "This has made several mouths too sore to gnaw hardtack, so we break it in tea."

They pushed on northeastward, a mountain range to the south of them, the frozen sea to the west. Eskimo Fred fell sick and was relieved of his place behind the traces and attached to the load of his own sledge, from which perch he wielded the whip across the straining dogs. On the twenty-sixth, they came across a cache of provisions left by Lieutenant Lewis Beaumont of the Nares expedition—forty rations in good condition, with well-preserved rum. And the following day, they camped at Cape Bryant after eleven grueling hours in the drag ropes.

With Pavy still absent and Lockwood also gone, Greely had been left with only one commissioned officer, Lieutenant Kislingbury, "my only companion. I hardly exchange more than fifty words a day with him. I have tried to make his stay here endurable." But Kislingbury "has low tastes, has for months spent hours playing cards with the enlisted men, whom he treats as equals, putting himself exactly on their footing." Greely escaped the gloomy atmosphere early on the twenty-seventh. While Lockwood and company were pitching camp on the other side of Robeson Channel, Greely set out on a sortie of his own, taking three enlisted men to drag sledges. Before leaving, he wrote a letter designating Lockwood as commanding officer "in the event of my decease." Kislingbury was at Fort Conger only "casually." With Lockwood away, Greely left Sergeant Israel in charge of the station, thus intensifying the humiliation to which Lieutenant Kislingbury had by no means become inured.

Greely's party headed for the interior of Grinnell Land, stopping at depots that Sergeant Cross and Private Bender earlier had laid partway along the route. On the fourth day out, they discovered a scenic fjord. Greely named it Ida Bay, after Howgate's daughter, unaware that back home his old friend and mentor was a fugitive sought by lawmen in several states (in due course, there would be also a Mount Howgate). In the same spirit of honoring those whose efforts had helped launch the Lady Franklin Bay Expedition, the commander tagged General Hazen's name to a 500-square-mile frozen lake, "its snowy covering reflecting diamond dust from the midnight sun." He named a fjord for the Secretary of the Navy, William Chandler, but nothing for the Secretary of War. And from the Garfield Mountains (after the president he knew had been shot but did not know had died) descended a spectacular river of ice which on Greely's map promptly became Henrietta Nesmith Glacier. The party was back at Fort Conger early in May.

Pavy's little force had returned five days earlier. His story of failure at Cape Joseph Henry fueled Greely's distaste for him, which at times came close to pathological. "He is a tricky, double-faced man, idle, unfit for any Arctic work except doctoring and sledge travel and not first-class in the latter. He is an excellent doctor," Greely assured Henrietta in the correspondence he was building for the relief ship. "So you may rest easy on that score. He is too much of a Frenchman to be uncivil or impolite to his commanding officer. He and Lieutenant K. consort entirely together—when not with the enlisted men— united by the common wish and desire to break down the commander but not daring to openly act." Greely did not amplify on these alarming words.

Lieutenant James B. Lockwood's party was about to make history. On 29 April, his support group, two of them snowblind, had turned back for the *Polaris* boat camp. Lockwood, Brainard, and the indispensable "Eskimo Fred" Christiansen, with a single dog sledge and twenty-five days' rations, plunged on alone. They approached Cape May, where Lieutenant Lewis Beaumont, after charting miles of the Greenland coast, had planted the British Union Jack. They read Beaumont's pitiful message, left in its cairn by his scurvy-ridden party. "All have done their best. We will go on as far as we can and live as long as we can. God help us." The snow grew deeper. Sometimes Lockwood's sledge had to be lifted bodily onto firmer crust. He decided to bypass Cape May and make directly for Cape Britannia, reaching it on 4 May after six marches. On the 2,700-foot-high promontory, jutting out into the frozen sea, "we unfurled

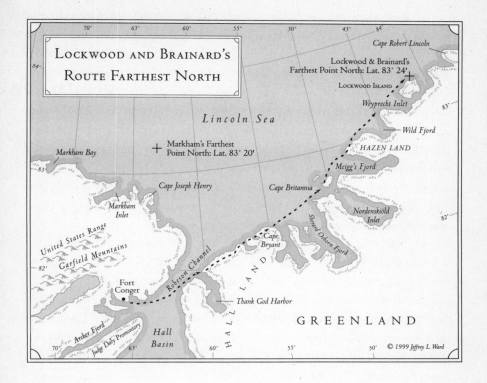

our small American flag. The British have seen Cape Britannia but we are the first to set foot on it."

They camped in a tent on bare ice before pushing on to the next cape, forced by huge hummocks to a sinuous route and crossing tidal cracks whose treacherous ice seesawed and splintered under the dogs and sledge. Their advance along the shoreline that no explorer before had seen lasted five days. A snowstorm halted progress. "When it ceased," wrote Brainard, "a pale sun appeared like a grease spot in the sky." Each time the three men cast eyes northward, it was to peer through murk obscuring the horizon. That fabled Polar Ocean beckoned, but not a trace of land. They continued northeastward, passing capes and fjords, to reach their northernmost point on 15 May. Lockwood's observation showed 83° 24', the closest yet to the North Pole, and four miles beyond Albert Markham's highest latitude.

They marked the new Farthest North with another flag and a rock pyramid nine feet high enclosing a self-recording spirit thermometer and a tin cylinder that contained expedition records. Then they turned back, conscious, despite physical pain and bouts of snowblindness, of having set a new record, of having surpassed 300 years of British polar record-breaking (their own record would last just thirteen years). With occasional halts for rest, sketchings and the deposit of small supply caches for "next year's work," a final five marches brought the triumphant trio to the boat camp, where a support party had waited three and a half weeks. Three days later, all hands were across Robeson Channel, to be greeted personally by Lieutenant Greely. Lockwood and Brainard had been absent from Fort Conger sixty days, and traveled almost a thousand miles in more than forty marches, mostly in temperatures of well below zero.

A gratified commander wrote to his wife, "Lieutenant Lockwood reached a point about 70 miles northeast of Cape Britannia. He beat the latitude of Markham (and of the world) *on land* by two miles or more. I am of course delighted beyond measure. The men all come in with excellent health. Three lives paid for the English discoveries. We beat them and lose none." Just as exultant was Private Charles Henry, with no inkling of the dreadful fate his commander would ordain for him as he wrote, "The Greenland party arrived 1 June in good health, not a single instance of scurvy, but two men totally snowblind. Lieutenant Lockwood, Sergeant Brainard, and one native traveled 75 miles beyond Cape Britannia, and placed the Stars and Stripes at the most northern point ever reached by mortal man."

During the following summer weeks, short journeys were made westward across Grinnell Land. New lakes were discovered, new glaciers, rivers, and mountains. In the tradition of nineteenth-century polar explorers, geographical features were named after previous explorers, prominent national figures, the discoverers themselves, or comrades and even relatives. (Very few such names would endure. Most of those Greely marked on his map were changed and changed yet again by successive expeditions.) Greely led a party late in June complete with a four-wheeled cart carrying telescopes, sextants, a prismatic compass, and other instruments. The cart was used because the snow was all but gone. The party reached Lake Hazen on the twentieth, and closely examined the terrain beyond.

The weather was warm, the air often alive with birds, bees, butterflies, and mosquitoes. On the eve of the Fourth of July, celebrated with a half gill of rum and lime juice to wash down pemmican and hard bread, the wheels fell off the cart and all gear had henceforth to be shouldered by Greely and four enlisted men with him. Their efforts included modest excavation, which yielded a number of Eskimo artifacts. But added to labor was risk and discomfort, especially at river crossings. Temperatures fell, freezing the water through which the men waded holding their precious instruments aloft at arm's length. By the time the party had returned to Fort Conger, overland marching in waterlogged boots had worn out most of their footwear. "But," Greely recorded, "the area of newly discovered land which fell under my observation closely coincides with that of the entire land discovered by the British expedition of 1875–76."

Life at the fort continued much as before. Musk oxen straying within rifle range were shot, except for calves Greely intended to send south on the first relief ship. Meteorological observations were dutifully recorded. Magnetic readings, Greely reported, were conducted "conformable as far as one instrument would permit to the Hamburg International Polar Conference program, observations timed as recommended by Weyprecht." There were disappointments. "The garden, I regret to say, proved a total failure, despite all care," Greely reported. But the command's physical health remained excellent, with morale now buoyed by anticipation of a visiting vessel from home.

Some of the party had taken to scaling nearby slopes for a better view of the channel southward. The ship would bring news and letters as well as fresh food supplies, and would depart with return mail and the party's proud announcement of having reached the Farthest North. It would also take away Lieutenant Kislingbury, to his own immeasurable relief, and to Greely's as well, freeing him as it would from the discomforting presence of the fellow officer he had made to feel an outsider. "We may see the relief boat steaming north," wrote Sergeant Brainard eagerly. "A few more weeks of thawing might give a clear path." An optimistic Private Henry wrote, "The chances of a ship coming are better every day." Her arrival could surely not be delayed, given the *Proteus*'s easy passage through Kane Basin on the way north the previous year. The harbor ice was rapidly breaking up. Sergeant Cross raised steam on the launch Greely had named *Lady Greely,* and took her for a trial run. On 22 July, walrus were seen off Distant Cape. All these events were taken to mean that Kane Basin must be at least partly ice free. On the twenty-eighth, Sergeant Rice and Corporal Joseph Elison, descending from Cairn Hill, just behind the station, spoke of a "golden opportunity" for a vessel to enter Lady Franklin Bay.

# 10

# PRIVATE BEEBE
# AND THE *NEPTUNE*

IN WASHINGTON, PREPARATIONS for the first relief expedition to
Lady Franklin Bay would have earned no merits for zeal. In November 1881,
five months after Greely's expedition sailed, General Hazen had placed before
the Secretary of War the commander's request (among the instructions brought
home on the *Proteus*) that a Signal Corps sergeant and seven other Army men
be sent him in 1882. Two weeks later, Hazen was informed that the secretary
opposed the employment of any additional soldiers. Aware that he could
expect little cooperation from Robert Lincoln, the Chief Signal Officer had
then taken the initiative. For one thing, he assigned some of his own personnel to a self-taught crash course on the Arctic and placed a Sixteenth Infantry
officer named William H. Clapp in charge.

Studious as well as effective in combat, Clapp had earned encomiums from
his superiors during the Civil War. Now he proceeded to look up everything
written about the Arctic that he could lay his hands on. A mass of papers

related to the Lady Franklin Bay Expedition fell upon his desk. Hazen wanted the captain to be so familiarized with the subject that he would be able to render expert assistance when the relief expedition was fitted out. Beyond reading, Clapp could not do much yet other than obtain from the proper bureaus the stores Greely had requested.

Had Henry Howgate remained with the United States Army, he would have controlled what was now Captain Clapp's function. But Howgate was a fugitive from justice. Since his resignation from the Army shortly before Greely's departure, he had secured land in Florida known as the "Howgate Grant, given by the King of Spain to a loyal officer." Citing Florida's salubrious climate and potential for profitable agriculture, Howgate had offered real estate for sale in ten-acre lots at low prices and on easy terms. The Greelys may have had some stake in this venture. A fortnight before Greely's sailing from St. John's, Howgate had written Henrietta a letter. She was nursing the new baby, suffering from vertigo and exhaustion, and preparing to return to San Diego, where she and the two infants would live with her ailing father. Howgate first referred to the article in the *Army and Navy Register* that had so infuriated him. "After reading it," he told Henrietta, "you will understand my feelings." Then he had added, "Of course, I will look after the Florida land and any other business or personal matter you want attended to. Advise me when you expect to start for California."

But then it had become unsafe to have any contact with the former Signal Corps captain. Confronted with evidence of Howgate's malfeasance while in charge of finances, General Hazen had ordered his arrest. Howgate's wife continued to live at the home on H Street and received the usual monthly allowance from her errant spouse, posted each time from a different town. Howgate and his paramour Nettie Burrill were seized first in a remote corner of Michigan and returned to Washington. He was accused of embezzling $40,000 worth of government funds. Some reported the figure much higher, incurred partly while he was fitting out the *Gulnare*.

Released on bail, Howgate fled town. He was recaptured and jailed, but still had enough influential friends to arrange prison visits by his wife, his mistress, and his daughter, Ida. After criticizing prison toilet facilities, he was permitted to go home for twice-weekly baths. On one such visit, the loyal Ida entertained her father's guard with a piano recital long enough for Howgate to escape out the back door with Nettie. The couple stole aboard a yacht that took them down the Potomac River and into Chesapeake Bay. After a stopover in the bridal suite of a secluded coastal hotel, they plunged inland and made their way west under assumed names. Federal pursuers lost Howgate's trail somewhere in Nebraska. But he remained the object of a manhunt that would outlast the Arctic expedition that he, more than any other American, had done so much to promote.

As for Henrietta Greely, she now knew what it was to be an Arctic explorer's wife. Early in March 1882, she had received a letter from another, Emma De Long, whose husband was missing. Greely had carried letters from Emma to the lost lieutenant in the event he should find him. Emma's words to Henrietta were bravely comforting: "I think you will reap all the benefits from your sacrifice that have passed by me and left me stranded. Your husband will return to you having reached the Pole or come nearer to it than any living man." His party would be succored and victualed annually. "Their greatest danger," she wrote, "will come when they are sledging, and men rarely lose their lives that way." Two months later, Emma De Long learned that the *Jeannette* was wrecked off the Siberian coast and that her husband had perished.

News of the *Jeannette* tragedy helped stir action toward communicating with the two North American stations, one at Point Barrow and Greely's on Ellesmere Island. On 6 May (the day newspapers headlined De Long's fate), General Hazen's Arctic Division convened to make plans. Two days later, Hazen asked that an agent with a naval officer be sent to St. John's to charter a steamer. The agent he sent was William M. Beebe, Jr., a private in the regular Army. Beebe had been acting as Hazen's secretary. He was in fact the general's protégé and had served as a young first lieutenant on Hazen's staff in the Civil War. In 1878, when Hazen was denying charges of cowardice under fire, Beebe had sprung to his defense. Later, when Beebe sought reinstatement in the regular Army while stigmatized as a drunkard, Hazen had assured him, "I will always be glad to speak a good word for you."

The general was about to do so now, inadvertently saddling Beebe with a hapless role in the history of the Lady Franklin Bay Expedition. As before, plans met resistance from the Secretary of War. Hazen urged that it was "of the utmost importance" that a ship be hired "before ice blocks passage." Secretary Lincoln replied that first he wanted a statement showing how the previous year's appropriation of $25,000 for Greely's expedition had been spent.

Hazen left for St. Louis on other business. In his absence, Captain James

W. Powell of the Sixteenth Infantry, acting Chief Signal Officer, told Lincoln that fresh funds would have to be appropriated no later than 1 June if a relief ship for the Greely party was to sail that year. Powell did not mince words: "The safety of the officers and men who have voluntarily gone to inhospitable and inaccessible regions may be jeopardized by delay." In that same missive, Powell referred to "an understanding" that Greely's people would be visited yearly until finally recalled. Sending Powell's request over to President Chester Arthur for approval, the Secretary of War weakened it by adding, "I know of no understanding." But Robert Lincoln was no fool. He knew that should disaster befall the Greely party, he would have to share responsibility for it. He sent the White House another note, this one asserting that because of the manner in which General Hazen had handled the past year's appropriation, "every penny was used up." So it was important that provision be made at once for an expedition either to reinforce the men at Lady Franklin Bay or bring them home.

Hazen returned to the capital. He was shown a copy of Secretary Lincoln's statement that he knew of "no understanding" about annual relief visits to Fort Conger, and he at once shot off two letters to Lincoln in the last week of May. One reminded the secretary that when passing the original bill on which the expedition was founded, Congress had certainly understood it. So had President Garfield, who had signed it. And subsequent legislation for continuing the work meant exactly what it said: The government was obliged to send a supply expedition to Lady Franklin Bay annually until its work was completed. Hazen added, "As the mentor of the International Polar Conference under whose immediate charge the United States' part was placed, I suppose the secretary of war fully understood this."

Hazen's next letter contained a detailed outline of what the Greely expedition was all about. It ended with: "The obligation rests upon the Govt to send a supply expedition each year." Hazen asked that these letters, addressed to Secretary Lincoln, be forwarded to the president. But they were not, and Hazen sent yet another, telling the secretary that "the lives of the Lady Franklin Bay party depend solely on timely action here. The ship must sail from St. John's by 1 July to insure the fullest chance of reaching the party. Every day after 1 July the vessel is delayed lessens the chances of reaching these men at all."

It was now up to Congress. Captain Powell had telegraphed his absent chief that "the Secretary of War is emphatic that no contracts be made for the relief expedition until the appropriations bill has passed." At the same time, Powell told Private Beebe that "arrangements must go on. The need to aid Greely is above all technicalities." Hazen had given Beebe the task of securing a suitable ship at St. John's, his only guidance to come from Consul Thomas Molloy and Commander Dana Green, a naval officer detailed to help him.

Burdened with tasks for which he had no previous experience, Beebe did his best. "Everything I need in the way of information attainable has been furnished me," he asserted. But he feared time running out. No ship could get him from the United States to St. John's before 24 May. "The last steamer of which I have information sails [from St. John's] for Disko on 29th," he informed Hazen. "I feel my time in St. John's is all too brief for the work I have there." Commander Green shared Beebe's anxiety. Still more ominous was a report from Consul Molloy. Sealing steamers were coming into St. John's disabled by boisterous weather and ice so thick they had been unable to penetrate the usual sealing grounds. "All the fleet will have to undergo repairs. I fear there will be some difficulty in chartering this season," Molloy reported. Beebe sailed from Baltimore on 17 May. En route at last, he hoped for success while beset by misgivings. For much of the voyage to the Canadian maritimes, he was confined to his cabin by seasickness—in his own words he was "the most uncomfortable wretch alive."

On arrival at St. John's, he and Commander Green called at Consul Molloy's office. They were unable to see him before ten the next morning, the twenty-fourth. Gone were Beebe's hopes of getting away before the end of the month. Ships were available. Molloy took the two Americans to inspect *Proteus*, *Bear*, and *Neptune*. *Proteus* was the superior vessel, but her owners wanted $26,000 payable by two drafts before sailing. Beebe and Green chose *Neptune*, at a cost of $6,000 per month. Their hands still were tied. Congress in Washington had yet to approve any appropriation. By telegraph, Hazen tried to comfort Henrietta Greely: "I hope you are not worried. Our bill is sure to pass." And as Louis V. Caziarc, friend of the Greelys and a lieutenant on Hazen's staff, told Henrietta, the general was not waiting for politicians to make up their minds. Stores were assembled, and, Caziarc assured Henrietta, Greely would "get everything he has asked for [including] a cartload of reading matter." By 10 June, all would be ready in New York for shipment. As for the ship, Caziarc stated that "if Congress makes no appropriation, General

Hazen says he will hire a vessel on his own personal responsibility and I am assured the country will back him."

In this same letter, dated 28 May, Caziarc wrote that the officer to command the relief expedition had yet to be selected. Caziarc did not know of Beebe's deepening involvement. That soldier had understood that all he was to do at St. John's was secure a ship and supplies and send them forthwith to Greenland, with a naval officer on board in charge of the relief party.

Beebe in St. John's could see his time running out. Final word had not yet arrived from the *Neptune's* owners in England concerning their agent's arrangement with the Americans, whose Congress had still to act. No officer to command, nor other personnel, had been named. Seeing failure on all sides, Beebe admitted, "[I] felt that I should return [from St. John's] in disgrace." He was still quaking with apprehension when, on 4 June, Hazen cabled him to "turn over the Newfoundland business" to Commander Green and proceed himself with the ship to Greenland.

Even then, Hazen did not intend to send the bewildered Beebe farther than Disko and nearby points, where he was to secure additional stores. Yet Hazen heaped still greater responsibility on him, in the form of an order to use his own discretion. If possible, he had to take the ship himself with provisions and an Army sergeant into Kane Basin and beyond. Beebe's assumption now was that he had to "prepare the way, so far as I can, for the caches designated by [Greely]." This mission was "so entirely different from any former experience of mine," he wrote the general, "I would have given five years of my life if at any time after you left Washington I could have backed out."

Now it was too late for that; Beebe pronounced himself glad to go. But only "*as your immediate representative*. Unless I have some especial assignment, my position as a *private*, general service—with a sergeant on board—will be embarrassing. I should either be made a sergeant or better still, made a lieutenant." But it appeared too late for that as well. Beebe remained a private—not, of course, in command of the ship, which had a competent captain named Sopp and a chief mate, James Norman, who had been ice pilot on the *Proteus*.

Beebe's position was ambiguous, to put it mildly. Lieutenant Caziarc sought to clarify things, without much success, in a letter he sent him. Although a sergeant was indeed included in the relief party, the others being privates, Caziarc hoped that Beebe would "have no difficulty in securing compliance by use of your personal influence, supported by your official connection as disclosed by this letter." Later, Captain Clapp, on Hazen's staff as chief of the Arctic Division, would testify that "it would be difficult to speak of any one as having been in command. Mr. Beebe was set up, more in charge than command, I would say. He was, at that time, a general service clerk on duty in General Hazen's office. I do not know the exact term to be applied in regard to him." At that same future date, Hazen would be criticized for having appointed a man "he knew to be an habitual drunkard."

In response to a plea from Beebe, the general added eight soldiers to his relief force. Four deserted almost immediately. Neither Hazen nor Beebe was then aware that had the commanding general of the Army, General William T. Sherman, had his way, Beebe would have had no party or not gone at all. An inveterate opponent of polar ventures, Sherman told the Secretary of War, "I regard the whole thing as a waste of money and a waste of precious life—the scientific advantages are less than nothing." But the Greely relief expedition was about to get under way. On 7 June, Captain Sopp came on board the *Neptune*, and Beebe was favorably impressed. "He will have good discipline," Beebe believed. Also, Beebe asked General Hazen if he could purchase pigs, cows, and sheep to take north so that Greely's party would have fresh meat. He had just finished this letter to Hazen when the *Neptune's* first mate reminded him of something that produced a postscript: "Norman says that with the exception of the pigs, which can be penned in the hold or lower deck, livestock is impracticable on account of the dogs."

Beebe's desperate hope was to reach Lady Franklin Bay. After reporting to Lieutenant Greely at Fort Conger, he was to return on the *Neptune*, bringing back dispatches, mail, and whatever (or whoever) Greely wished. If unable to reach the party, Beebe was to establish depots at points designated A and B in Greely's memorandum of instructions—Cape Hawks on the Ellesmere side, and Littleton Island off the Greenland shore. After making these depots, Beebe would, if possible, leave a record of his proceedings at Cape Sabine.

But all of these plans were contingent upon Beebe's early departure. On 19 June, in the United States Senate, the bill appropriating $33,000 for continuing the work of two Arctic stations (Point Barrow included) was referred to the commerce committee. Secretary of War Lincoln saw trouble looming. "Time is getting short," he wrote the chairman, "and I suggest the advisability of pressing the passage if it *can be done.*" It was done five days later. Carrying eight tons of provisions, the *Neptune* sailed from St. John's on 8 July in blinding rain. Fourteen hundred miles to the north, Lieutenant Greely had just completed his proud report claiming Farthest North for his country. Lieutenant Kislingbury was anticipating an end to his ordeal of professional exclusion and eager for a reunion with his sons. All hands were as one in expectation of news from home, their hopes sustained by the continuance of sunlit open water in Lady Franklin Bay.

Private Beebe on the *Neptune* was seasick. "I did not care whether we floated or sank," he groaned. His only comforter was the chief mate, Norman. When he was Greely's ice pilot on the *Proteus*, Norman had accompanied Greely ashore each time to examine caches. Norman had a master's certificate, and ambitions to go to New York or Baltimore the next season and secure command of a vessel. Beebe told him that if he succeeded in piloting the *Neptune* to Discovery Harbor and back in reasonable time, he, Beebe, would get General Hazen to put in a good word for him. Norman told Beebe, who was relieved to have someone close upon whom he could rely, that the *Neptune* would make as good a trip as had the *Proteus*. She was faster under steam, her boiler was new, and she was a more powerful iceboat.

This statement seemed true enough when, approaching Disko, the ship met an extensive ice field. "Our progress did not exceed three miles an hour," said Beebe, a landsman who did not deal in knots. "[We] worked our way northward painfully slow [but] breaking with ease and pushing aside the solid ice-pans." This early display of the *Neptune*'s ice-cutting strength was particularly welcome to Beebe when the Danish inspector at Disko warned him that he could hardly hope to reach his destination, that the previous winter was "unusually severe."

After some delay awaiting the arrival of sealskin pants and sleeping bags, the *Neptune* left Disko on 20 July. Crossing Melville Bay, she met thicker ice, driving sleet changed to snow, and, on the twenty-sixth, the *Neptune* "remained helplessly drifting with the tides, within plain view of Cape York with its numerous glaciers." Littleton Island came in view three days later, but Captain Sopp told Beebe in his cabin that they could go no farther. Beebe went on deck and "found an unbroken ice barrier 12 to 20 feet thick extending across the head of Smith Sound. The ship was therefore turned southward and a comfortable anchorage was at last found in Pandora Harbor." Named by Allen Young for his ship (later the ill-fated *Jeannette*), shut in by the Crystal Palace Cliffs on the south and Cape Kenrick to the north, this coldly scenic bay twenty-five miles south of Littleton Island was most times a safe shelter. But now it was battered by a succession of southwesterly gales, and riding them out a whole week was, for Beebe, an unnerving experience, "our anchor being lost and two heavy hawsers, warping the stern of the ship to the rocks, were parted."

Once the *Neptune* had managed to clear Pandora Harbor, she ran into more ice. It kept her twelve miles short of Cape Hawks, where Beebe intended to establish a depot and leave a whaleboat, as specified in Greely's instructions. The season was still young. Most of Sopp's crew regarded the accumulation of ice as a temporary phenomenon and were sanguine that it would move soon enough before a northerly wind. But luck was against them. With "eight miles of impassable ice between us and land," the *Neptune* would not venture any farther north.

The floes closed in more heavily. They piled to the bulwarks. At midnight on 12 August, Beebe stood on deck with the first mate "when a gentle crackling of the young ice attracted our attention and by the bright sunlight we could see the water slowly trickling through." Captain Sopp forced his ship into the opening lead. But the struggle against that frozen barrier had taken its toll. "The boiler overstrained and sprang a leak," reported Beebe. "This added greatly to our anxiety." At Beebe's urging, Captain Sopp turned the ship about and steamed back south to Payer Harbor, an inlet on the Ellesmere side sandwiched between Cape Sabine and Brevoort Island.

Here the Nares expedition had left a depot in 1875. Beebe repacked the cache more securely, but left none of the stores he had himself brought north. He marked the cache with two oars, then early on the twenty-third told Captain Sopp they had better move out. Beebe left a message for Greely recounting events, mostly a chronicle of woe. But, "determined to turn all my efforts to land supplies and whaleboat as far north as possible," he spoke with Captain Sopp, and again the *Neptune* labored northward. Ice and gales buffeted her into a futile zigzagging. Once more, Captain Sopp sought shelter in Pandora Harbor. On the twenty-sixth, the heavy floes, "crushing together with every change of wind and tide, were thrown up into huge irregular drifts impassable even by the trained seal-hunters who composed our crew. The idea of landing the stores by means of a sledge or boats was therefore abandoned."

Still, Beebe had not given up. "Pushed the ship into every channel leading towards Cape Hawks. But the western shore above Cape Sabine was unattainable," he wrote. Fearful that Littleton Island also would soon be blocked off,

Beebe decided to place a depot there without delay. Floes ruled out a landfall above Cape Sabine—"new ice is forming every night faster than it disappears during the day." He was determined on landing stores at Littleton Island. But still hopeful of obeying Greely's wishes to the letter, he would then wait until compelled by the lateness of the season to fall back. He wrote in a letter to Greely that he was "establishing depots and whaleboats where they will be of value to you. I cannot express my regret at the failure of all my efforts to reach you or to carry out fully your instructions." And in another message, he promised to "earnestly urge that next year's relief ship leave St. John's as early as mid-June."

Beebe's messages were cached as part of two small depots he left, 250 rations at Cape Sabine (enough to feed Greely's party ten days) and an equal amount opposite on Littleton Island. These were his depots A and B. At Cape Sabine, he also had left a whaleboat. From Littleton Island, the *Neptune* recrossed Smith Sound to Cape Isabella, where Beebe put ashore his remaining whaleboat. Ice was thickening, the *Neptune* starting to leak. He wrote Greely a final note: "I leave the whaleboat here as a last resort, in hopes you will be able to reach this point and use it for crossing to Littleton Island." In the opinion of Captain Sopp, First Mate Norman, and the ship's engineer, any further delay would imperil the vessel and all on board. "I cannot hold the ship any longer," Sopp cautioned. At 11:40 A.M., Tuesday, 5 September, Private Beebe gave a reluctant assent and the homeward voyage began.

After forty days steaming to and fro in Smith Sound and lower Kane Basin, the *Neptune* had left a total of 500 rations, half on either shore. She steamed steadily away with at least 2,000 rations on board. However unhappily, Private Beebe was obeying orders. His instructions specified that if the *Neptune* failed to reach Fort Conger, he was to bring all his stores back home—enough to have fed Greely's party for at least three months.

Reaction in the United States to the news of the *Neptune*'s return to St. John's laden with food intended for Greely was mixed, some of it sympathetic. Commander Winfield Scott Schley, a naval officer unaware of his own destined connection to the Greely expedition, thought that Beebe's failure to reach Lady Franklin Bay could have made no serious difference to Greely, who had to stay only one more year and was understood still to have a two-year food supply. "In placing his stores, Beebe had carried out his instructions except that one of the depots had been made at Cape Sabine," Schley remarked. Commander

Frank Wildes, another naval officer earmarked for a significant role in events, felt that a commissioned officer should have been in charge of the relief party rather than a lowly private. Someone of higher rank might well have stretched Greely's mandate enough to have left all stores in the north instead of bringing most of them home. Wildes did not know that before sailing, Beebe had sought in vain the promotion he deemed necessary.

General Hazen withheld comment until Beebe submitted his report. But he wired the mournful news to Henrietta Greely. Lieutenant Louis Caziarc followed up with a letter. The *Neptune*'s return was regretted, "but not unforeseen and was provided for by the ample provisioning of the station." It was a pity Henrietta had to wait longer for news, but there was no cause for uneasiness. The past winter was supposed to have been a wild one (as suggested by reports from Lieutenant Patrick Ray at Point Barrow), "and the loss of the dogs we know [via the *Proteus* in 1881] to have taken place will prevent any rash exploring expeditions." The *Neptune* had placed depots at three (sic) points. He assured her, "The northernmost depot established was at Cape Sabine. That is all we know at present."

# 11

# THE SECOND WINTER

BY THE EVENING of 27 August, 1882, while the *Neptune* steamed this way and that amid the floes of Smith Sound, anticipation of relief at Fort Conger turned to despair. "I have quite given up the ship," wrote Greely, "as have most of the men." Dr. Pavy reminded him, "I told you some time ago I did not think the ship would come." His antipathy toward Greely festered. The tenor of his private notes was increasingly contemptuous. Yet though he failed to keep records as comprehensive and orderly as Greely wished, Pavy's concern for the party's health was self-evident. He encouraged the cooks to vary their menus. Bread, meat, molasses, fruit, vegetables, and preserves were still in good supply. Thirty-three musk oxen were killed that month, and scores of ducks, ptarmigan, and dovekies. Pavy conducted regular physical examinations of the men and made sure their beds were kept dry.

So everything seemed in good order as the party faced a second winter. But morale had ebbed. On the last day of the month, Greely sent Lieutenant

Lockwood to beach the steam launch *Lady Greely* on Dutch Island. He had delayed laying it up until the last moment. The move seemed symbolic of a realization that the relief ship would not appear that year. "The life we are leading now is like that of a prisoner of the Bastille," wrote Lockwood. His "Arctic Moon" had long been abandoned, for lack of interest. Yet despite fading spirits, Lockwood in the officers' quarters wrote of "hilarity in the other room, in marked contrast to the gloom in this." Laughter rose, even bursts of song, and Private Schneider—German-born, as were seven of his comrades—played the violin. Greely entered the men's room for an occasional game of chess, and in an atmosphere brighter than that next door.

In his October medical report Pavy reiterated that his stock of medicines was inadequate in "*essential* drugs." Greely challenged him to say what these were, and at his corner desk that night, he recorded that "cod liver oil and digitalis were the only medicines ever specially mentioned as needed." On the twentieth of the month, Pavy wrote to Greely, asking information on "our future stay in the Arctic, as well as your plans and means of escape." The request could have been made verbally, but the doctor wanted everything in writing. Octave Pavy had genuine concerns, not the least of which resulted from his "scanty . . . ill-chosen medical stores." He had been in Greenland when preparations were under way in Washington, thus had had no say in the selection of medical stores or the consulting library. And now, he wrote, "since the ship is not coming, and the fall work cannot be changed, it is necessary to decide on our future spring work. Hence, as surgeon of the expedition, I wish to be officially informed of your plans."

Greely replied that "while holding in high estimation your medical skill, I cannot bring myself to concur in your opinion that our prospects are gloomy." Diet; warm, dry quarters; absence of scurvy; and, in the past year, "our success in the field" gave promise that the coming winter would be trouble free. This response, Pavy thought with deepening rancor, exemplified the commander's lack of respect for his surgeon's duty to safeguard "the health and lives of the men placed in my medical charge by the United States government."

Needing a break from the tensions at Fort Conger, the doctor secured Greely's permission to journey southward along the Grinnell Land coast in search of caches or signs of a visiting ship. He took Brainard and Eskimo Fred. It was no picnic for the sergeant. The dog-skin sleeping bag given to him by Pavy, too small for stretching, ruined his sleep. But beyond Cape Baird,

Brainard noted that "the incessant trotting of the dogs, the bright moonlight, and the exhilarating air [at temperatures of ten below] tended to elevate our spirits." The party was away two weeks. They saw nothing more significant than water clouds over Kane Basin and, farther south, a clear iceblink.

Greely clung to discipline. When bear tracks were sighted, triggering thoughts of a hunt, he forbade any venture beyond 200 yards without his permission. Ignoring the edict, Sergeant David Linn set off after the bear. When Linn returned with no game, Greely demoted him to the rank of private. He did so in front of the entire company. Linn's duties were assigned to Sergeant Maurice Connell, Irish-born and, Greely thought, "one of our best men"— an opinion not long to prevail.

Thoughts of a retreat from Fort Conger nagged Greely more and more. If no vessel were to come by the next August, he would have to abandon the station, traveling by boats along the west coast of Kennedy Channel and Smith Sound. He mulled the possibility that a relief vessel had managed to reach Littleton Island and would be waiting there. Pavy scoffed at such reasoning. How would the party reach Littleton Island? The steam launch could not be counted on to pierce ice fields, and, he said, "we have a whaleboat but no one who knows how to manage it." Pavy concluded, "This lack of nautical experience bears greatly upon our security."

Pavy drew no comfort from the demeanor of any of the Army officers. Lockwood was generally silent and noncommittal before the "absolutism of Greely," and Kislingbury, by virtue of his ostracism, seldom spoke. Any suggestion Pavy put before the commander in person was instinctively disregarded. "If Greely exercised his mind in the proper direction, with the same avidity with which he exercises to oppose me, we might accomplish some good things." How woeful, thought Pavy, was this expedition when compared with those of the Englishman Nares, the Swedish Nordenskiöld, the Austrian Weyprecht. Pavy likened Greely's criticism of the Nares expedition to "heroes attacked by a pygmy." The doctor chose to forget that in the eyes of many of Nares's countrymen, that expedition had been a scurvy-ridden fiasco.

Fall advanced. Greely had kept three musk oxen to send home for study or breeding. Now one died, and Greely decided against keeping the others. Sergeant Francis Long took them across the ice to Bellows Island. Once untied, one animal died immediately. The other would not stay, and ran after the sledge, "following Long like a dog." Perhaps the young creatures, no less than the humans who had adopted them, feared abandonment. Back at the station, the animal continued to trail Sergeant Long, until it was "finally carried into his old pen where he died next day, from what cause we could not ascertain."

Birthdays were celebrated—in October, that of William Ellis, who, at forty-two, was the oldest member of the party. And the commander began a new series of lectures, starting in November with one on his hometown, Newburyport. For the scientific observers, the celestial elements did their share toward defeating boredom. At times, auroral streamers leaped across the heavens, trailing fiery patterns of changing shapes, brilliant pencils of light, graceful folds, arches or patches of vivid and varied color. One awestruck member of the party likened what he saw in the sky to "the coiling and twisting convulsions of a gigantic serpent."

Sergeant Ralston recorded, "A magnetic storm is raging. The needle is on the jump all the time." Private Henry carefully penned in his notebook that the display defied description. He attempted it anyway, marveling at the spectacle's shades of greens, "from the softest apple to the dark invisible green of the hemlock pine." Greely wrote of "intricate garlands . . . gleaming lances . . . shining spears." Dr. Pavy found the phenomena too overpowering for description and labeled it "Dante's Inferno."

The aurora gave Greely fresh inspiration for lecture topics. Astronomy became a favorite. Also, he told himself that the men's spirits were reviving. Their appetites had improved; they fed well. On Thanksgiving Day, Greely proclaimed "special cause for gratitude for our exemption from sickness and death, and success in scientific and geographic work." Brainard, his number-one sergeant, did not share in this optimistic outlook. He still bore an ill-definable grudge against military service. As Christmas approached, he wrote, "The men grow more captious. The celebration becomes nothing more than a mockery." But Brainard's choleric view of things was more an expression of private emotions than a faithful portrayal of events. There was again plenty to eat on Christmas Day, and a party atmosphere enlivened by Eskimo Fred dancing a hornpipe. The following week, Private Schneider placed on the game rack an illuminated placard wishing everyone a happy new year. And shortly afterward, on Sergeant Cross's birthday, Greely was relieved to notice that "he refrained from drinking any spirits, a reform I trust he will continue."

The festive spirit had its limitations. Greely brooded over Lieutenant Kislingbury's "habitually consorting with the enlisted men, playing cards with

them, at first in the observers' room, out of view." Then he did so more openly:
"I did not wish to interfere with him . . . wished to give him no pretext for
claiming this command, which I firmly believe would be most unfortunate, in
case of fatal disability to myself." Recalling that happier time when he read
poetry to Henrietta or sent her poetical fragments through the mail, Greely
read verses to his men. He also, noted a disgusted Dr. Pavy, "tells them that
all the work of the English is considered a failure." Little did Greely know, Pavy
thought, with what disrespect the men spoke of him behind his back.

The doctor recorded an incident indicative of his commander's obstinacy.
It occurred the night of 23 January, when Pavy "noticed the moon just disappearing behind the mountains of Musk Ox Bay, leaving behind a light which
formed a parhelion." Greely entered the observer's room and told Private
Henry, then on duty, that an aurora was sighted. Henry went outside and then
returned, saying all he could see was a mock moon. Greely said he had studied
astronomy long enough to know what he was talking about. And even after
Sergeant Ralston had checked in the magnetic hut and found no signs of auroral activity, Greely ordered him to record in his journal, for that date, an aurora
"which never existed."

Octave Pavy's disdain for Greely now knew no bounds. "What friendship
and regard can a commander inspire who is completely unfit for command?"
he wrote. While Pavy privately indulged himself, Greely engaged in equally
quiet self-examination. Was he too lenient? He had thought it best to avoid
squabbles. He wrote in his own journal, "I deem the work and the success and
lives of this party too valuable to endanger by harsh, violent or unjust words
or measures. Naturally of a somewhat irritable disposition I have carefully
restrained myself." That same week, he issued orders confining the enlisted men
to within a 500-yard radius of the fort, relaxing his earlier restriction. Sergeant
Brainard still chafed: "What was the intention of the order in the first place
except to gratify personal vanity?" It was not out of concern lest somebody
might freeze if wandering too far. "Do enlisted men freeze sooner than officers? The whole affair is a miserable farce and only for the excellent disposition of the men mutiny might have been declared."

Greely looked forward to spring sledging before the arrival of the 1883
relieving vessel or, assuming the worst, the necessity of proceeding south on
their own. Brainard and others made periodic trips to Cape Baird to establish
a supply depot usable in that event. Too much activity in the meantime did not

sit well with Dr. Pavy. Early in March, he advised against further explorations because they might weaken the men for the retreat. He suggested that they spend no more than a night or two in the field. Greely's reaction was predictable. In his journal, he wrote that since Pavy's medical report showed the party in good health, "I should feel I was doing an unsoldierly and unmanly act in abandoning the work. It has been all retreat [with Pavy] ever since last autumn." And confronting the doctor, he stressed that early spring expeditions were "planned and fitted out solely for the purpose of increasing our knowledge of the Arctic regions. While I have the honor to command, and as long as I am fit for duty, I shall continue to pursue the object in view."

Increasing scientific knowledge instead of expanding mere geography was largely forgotten. Both Greely and Lieutenant Lockwood were impatient to break the Farthest North record they themselves had recently set. On 10 March, Sergeant Rice headed across frozen Robeson Channel for Thank God Harbor to bring back the twenty-foot British iceboat. That day, Lieutenant Lockwood led a party across that same expanse of ice, but their mission was to lay depots on the Greenland side for a projected thrust northward to the 84th parallel. This preliminary fieldwork was performed with little trouble, although the dogs had devoured their harness and whip, leaving only, as Sergeant Jewell wryly reported, "a few pieces of ivory and the whip-stock, these being spared by them on account of their indigestible qualities."

Near the end of the month, Lockwood's sledging party set out on the main assault. But the pack was breaking up early. Thin ice gave way. Men, dogs, and sledges all but sank. Open water along the base of 1,300-foot-high cliffs forced the party to detour through an ice-choked valley. A brave attempt to cut steps across a glacier failed. There were too many obstacles, even for the impetuous Lockwood, and he took his group back to Conger. Greely was surprised and less than pleased by their unexpected return, and Lockwood himself was chagrined. He wrote in his journal, "Do I take up my pen to write the humiliating word *failed*? I do, and bitter is the taste." He clamored to be off again. A new Farthest North was still achievable, but in a different direction.

Greely assented. The British had been beaten on the Greenland side. Now, Greely's hope was that the highest latitude would be attained on the Ellesmere Island side. With Sergeant Brainard, Eskimo Fred Christiansen, and a team of the ten best dogs, Lockwood left the station on 25 April. Wrote Greely as they disappeared among the hummocks of Archer Fjord, "This will be the last extended field expedition during the remainder of our stay in the Arctic, which should end when the relief ship arrives in July or August."

IN WASHINGTON THE previous fall, when General Hazen had submitted William Beebe's report of failure to the Secretary of War, he had added, "There is not the slightest reason to suppose that Lieutenant Greely's party is suffering, and no apprehension for its safety need be entertained." He drew Robert Lincoln's attention to the amount of subsistence Greely had taken north with him, the abundance of game and coal said to be in the neighborhood of Lady Franklin Bay, and the fact that the party would be "comfortably and warmly housed and well supplied with Arctic clothing." This sort of thing was pleasing to the secretary's ears. When an infantry officer volunteered to lead a relief expedition to Greely the next season, Lincoln replied, "I know of no such expedition"—a response that Hazen later was quick to publicly recall as typifying the secretary's parlous indifference.

The Chief Signal Officer was intent upon avoiding a second failure in the Arctic, aware that he appeared in many eyes responsible for the first. Henrietta Greely blamed the *Neptune's* troubles on that ship's late departure from St. John's. Hazen responded that the problem in Smith Sound was not that of moving fields of ice but of a vast ice barrier that had defied seasonal influences. He wrote, "I don't think there would have been any difference if Beebe had got away earlier. . . . At the northernmost point that Beebe reached he found himself on the leading edge of the winter ice which had not in the least broke up. So his arrival earlier would have availed nothing."

All the same, Hazen set things in motion for the next year's relief expedition and for it to sail earlier in the season than had the *Neptune*. In the beginning of November, scarcely a month after his reassuring words to the Secretary of War, he sent Lincoln a copy of Greely's instructions relating to relief ships. He told him that Greely's plans ought to be followed. Hazen could do no other, having endorsed them and, indeed, having portrayed himself as their co-author. But the *Neptune* experience had taught him that unforeseen events in those northern waters might compel a departure from the rigid Greely scenario. The day would approach when Hazen conceded that things might have turned out better "if Beebe had been instructed to cache all his stores at Cape Sabine or on Littleton Island, or in that neighborhood, rather than bringing them back to St. John's." But to have pointed that out now to Secretary Lincoln would have amounted to self-indictment. All he could bring himself to say was that "every possible contingency must be provided for."

In that same November week, Hazen had addressed a letter via the adjutant general's office to the commander of the Department of Dakota, asking for a suitable officer and men to compose the next year's relief party. His letter never got beyond Washington. It was returned, and Hazen was told that he should have addressed it solely to the adjutant general. It went off again, reworded and readdressed. Such attitudes on mere technicalities were, in Hazen's view, more than bureaucratic pinpricks but characteristic of a decided apathy on Secretary Lincoln's part toward Arctic exploration.

Lincoln once had told him flatly that no additional Army men would be authorized for the Lady Franklin Bay enterprise. The secretary thought that instead of soldiers, "it would be much more desirable to get people from the Navy as they would have the instructions necessary for carrying out C.S.O.'s special requirements." An exasperated Hazen had shot back that "to change the full control of this duty now would be swapping horses while crossing the stream." His other communications to Robert Todd Lincoln were so worded as to indicate that while Greely's party, despite the *Neptune*'s vain attempt to reach it, was not in any present danger, results might be catastrophic should relief not reach them in time the following year.

Secretary Lincoln knew that if such events occurred, he would not escape accountability. It was true that blame for Beebe's hapless performance could be dumped with little effort on General Hazen's shoulders, which also could be said of the odor of scandal left at the Signal Corps by the still fugitive Henry Howgate. Moreover, news filtering in of the *Jeannette* disaster was more of an embarrassment to the Navy Department than to the War Department. Even so, it was obvious how avidly the national press feasted upon anything that resembled official blundering. Robert Lincoln was not one to court bad publicity. His unconcealed opinion now was that the object of an expedition to go after Greely should be not just to relieve him but to finish an Arctic project that never should have concerned Americans in the first place.

Lincoln's views on polar jaunts were in accord with those of General Sherman, chief of the U.S. Army, who wrote on 23 November that "the expedition of Lieutenant Greely to Lady Franklin Bay is in no manner, shape or form military duty under the laws or usages of the United States." That soldiers volunteered for such Arctic stunts was beside the point. "I know the more desperate an enterprise the more ready are men to volunteer. This does not alter the fact that those who order are alone responsible for consequences." He believed that a chartered steamer the following summer should bring Greely's party home and be done with it. "We know enough already of the North Pole and its surroundings, and can find profitable employment for our army inside our natural boundaries."

So Sherman officially opposed sending any more soldiers to augment the Lady Franklin Bay Expedition. But other influences were at work. Newspapers reported the terrible suffering of parties marooned in far northern regions as described by survivors of Lieutenant George De Long's *Jeannette* expedition. A naval court of inquiry had left questions of blame unanswered, and relatives of some who had died in Siberia demanded a congressional investigation. Certainly, no one in the War Department wanted an Army repetition of the Navy's frozen tragedy. On a more personal level, Henrietta Greely and Lieutenant Lockwood's family had already been lobbying for action. While Hazen wanted "the station maintained at least one year longer to realize the full purposes for which it was originally established," Henrietta found herself in agreement with General Sherman that her husband be brought home as speedily as possible.

The American station at Point Barrow, under Lieutenant Patrick Henry Ray, was functioning without problems. Numbering a dozen men, half of them Signal Corps personnel, the party had sailed from San Francisco on the schooner *Golden Fleece* in summer 1881, two weeks after the departure of the *Proteus* from Newfoundland. Its assigned program was considerably less ambitious than that of the Lady Franklin Bay Expedition, consisting chiefly of mapping and minor exploration, and its location was much closer to home. Eight or nine other countries had stations in the Arctic under the Weyprecht plan. But none was farther north or more remote than the Greely party. And few at home felt America's prestige in the slightest at risk. This domestic decline in enthusiasm for Arctic exploration was all it took. Even as Greely at Fort Conger wrote of his party's "work and success," Washington politicians sought ways to pull the country out of any current or future international programs for unlocking the Arctic's secrets. The result was an act of 3 March, 1883, requiring that the station at Lady Franklin Bay be abandoned, that Lieutenant Greely and his full detail be brought home.

This job still would be the Army's. William E. Chandler, Secretary of the Navy, wanted no part of it, having enough to contend with from the awkward questions swirling around the loss of the *Jeannette*. And of course, in his instructions for the first relief visit, Greely had asked that an Army sergeant and seven other soldiers be detailed. So Robert Lincoln had no option other than to deploy another military unit for the Arctic, the source for volunteers, as before, U.S. Army posts on the Great Northern Plains. The high latitudes of some posts were presumed to have conditioned the troops to extreme Arctic cold. The official summons was telegraphed 23 November, 1882, significantly italicized, directing a detail "from those who *may offer their services* . . . who *volunteer*." A fortnight later, Lieutenant Ernest A. Garlington, Troop L, Seventh Cavalry, stationed at Fort Buford, submitted the names of seven soldiers who did just that, including that of a sergeant—and his own.

Before the end of the year, Hazen was looking for a ship. Again he enlisted the aid of the U.S. Consul at St. John's. In Washington, he had to depend on what cooperation he could wrest from Robert Lincoln, with whom he was at loggerheads on another issue. A dispute had flared over whether the Weather Bureau, pioneered and run by the Signal Corps, should be separated from the Army. In his latest annual War Department report, Lincoln asserted that it should. Holding the opposite view, Hazen had persuaded some of his officers to sign a circular so critical of the secretary that Lincoln partisans thought Hazen should be court-martialed for disrespect.

When House Representative Frank E. Beltzhoover of Pennsylvania painted the Signal Corps under Hazen as corrupt and mismanaged, the C.S.O. tried to badger Lincoln into an investigation of the congressman. Lincoln refused, scolding the general for having spread word of his action before he, Lincoln, had any chance to respond. Beltzhoover had stepped up his attack. Hazen's efforts to involve Congress were "ludicrous effrontery," and his letter to the secretary "a piece of stupid audacity." These well-publicized clashes disturbed even Hazen's friends, one of whom warned him, "I beg of you, act with more deliberation. You utterly lack tact and show it by consistently going into print over your signature. You give the Secretary of War all opportunity to snub you. I advise you most urgently to keep quiet, hold your tongue."

This friend was asking the near-impossible of William Babcock Hazen, who, however, did his best to avoid ruffling too many feathers while pressing for compliance with his needs for the Lady Franklin Bay Expedition. His patience was sorely tested. At far-off Fort Snelling, Montana Territory, the process of selection from among volunteers was in the hands of General Alfred Terry, who for some unexplained reason was unable to start on this selection until the second week of January 1883. Only then did Terry choose a lieutenant, a corporal, and two enlisted men. The lieutenant was Ernest Garlington.

Hazen was told that it was still too early in the season to bring this detail east. Hoping Lincoln would decide otherwise, he laid before him, on the eighteenth, a summary of facts. He said that Garlington ought to be at hand in Washington because "the preparations for the expedition should be left very largely to his judgment." The idea was to reach Greely at Discovery Harbor in Lady Franklin Bay. If unable to get that far north, Garlington's relief party would go ashore on Littleton Island and establish a depot, with shelters built, to await Lieutenant Greely, "who in September of this year will march to the south expecting to find the party there." Sledge teams would go out from the island to meet the retreating men.

Lieutenant Garlington would need all the time he could get to properly arrange his expedition. Thus Hazen asked Lincoln to "reconsider the decision to delay sending him [Garlington] here. It is not too early to commence the necessary preparation." This proposal got results. By the end of the month, Lieutenant Garlington and his little party were en route to Washington. Hazen, meanwhile, had notified Henrietta Greely of the choice for command, "a first lieutenant of the Seventh Cavalry, a man who of all others in the army I would submit. Sober, persistent and able." Henrietta wrote back, "I am glad you have found an officer of whom you approve so thoroughly."

The Arctic Division at Signal Corps headquarters still consisted of one man, Captain William Clapp, and a small clerical staff. Clapp was caught up in the latest relief expedition more than he had been with Beebe's, so much so that he had officially asked General Hazen if he might go north himself as its leader. His hopes of being chosen for the command were high, only to be dashed by Garlington's appointment. Clapp would later complain that his request had been deliberately ignored. Not so, Hazen responded, it must have slipped the captain's mind that "I informed him verbally and delicately that I was not prepared to send him out." Captain Clapp took his duties seriously. Having studied hard the reports of Hall, Hayes, Nares, and Markham, and consulted Chief Engineer George Melville and other *Jeannette* survivors, he was confident that he had "as good a knowledge of [Arctic exploration] as was possible for one who had not actually been there."

During the initial phase of planning, Clapp submitted proposals that, for the most part, met with General Hazen's approval. There were significant exceptions. For instance, Clapp recommended that the stores and house for winter quarters be placed at Cape Sabine or higher, on the west coast of Smith Sound or Kennedy Channel, rather than on the east coast at Littleton Island. Sledge journeys by previous explorers generally were made along the western shore, which, Clapp had no doubt, would be Greely's course if he had to retreat. Clapp also thought that "as a measure of safety" the relief ship should land its supplies and winter hut somewhere on the way up, before getting too dangerously far into the ice field.

Hazen brushed these suggestions aside as contrary to Lieutenant Greely's stated wishes. Clapp persisted as much as he dared, working on his superior in private conversations. Greely's requirements, as written by him in August 1881, had reflected a confidence born of the *Proteus*'s bringing his party safely to Lady Franklin Bay "through practically an open sea." In Captain Clapp's view, they did not cover everything and should not be considered wholly binding upon those in Washington who, after all, were responsible for organizing Greely's relief.

Changing the location for the supply depot and winter hut might save the party from attempting the admittedly short-distanced but uncertain crossing from Cape Sabine to Littleton Island, Clapp argued. And unloading that vital cargo on the relief ship's upward passage would be a wise precaution should the vessel become icebound farther north. Still, General Hazen refused to budge. He insisted that Greely's plan "ought to be inviolate." Greely's own words forbade any "deviation from these instructions." And, Hazen added, his judgment had not rested solely on the ease of that northward voyage on the *Proteus*. Greely, he said, "knew more about what would be best to do than any other man in the world. He had studied the subject."

So had Clapp. But conceivably with a shrug, the captain gave up. And when Clapp was directed to prepare a "rough" of instructions prior to Lieutenant Garlington's arrival in Washington, it conformed absolutely with Lieutenant Greely's original blueprint for relief.

Once Garlington was on the scene (he reported at Signal Corps headquarters the day after his thirtieth birthday), Clapp was shunted aside. After

all his study and devotion as head of the Arctic Division, he had now to surrender control of affairs and was left with only the task of seeing to the procurement of sledges and tents. "I thought this was an injustice to me." Clapp
made one last attempt to have the Greely program modified. But he was virtually alone in his arguments. People within earshot of them included Garlington who, as newly appointed relief commander, had been furnished a desk
in the captain's office. It was not a felicitous proximity. Clapp's hurt feelings
were on constant display, so much so "that it caused [Garlington] to feel
aggrieved towards me." What the new arrival most likely thought he recognized
at Signal Corps headquarters was some bureaucratic infighting in which he had
no desire to become embroiled.

Ernest Albert Garlington was born in Newberry, South Carolina, the son
of a planter, lawyer, and brigadier-general in the Confederate army. He'd
attended private schools in his youth and had expected to inherit the plantation with his father's law practice, prospects that were ended by the South's
defeat. For a time thereafter, he'd held a clerical post with a railroad company,
but at age nineteen entered West Point, where his Southern background and
manner did not endear him to fellow cadets. There were frequent brawls. As
second lieutenant, Garlington was assigned to the Seventh Cavalry Regiment.
He was enjoying graduation leave in Georgia, where his parents had moved,
when news broke of the defeat of his unit under General Custer at Little
Bighorn. Although only ten days of Garlington's furlough had expired, he
packed his trunks and left for Washington, where he sought orders to join the
regiment at once. So many officers had been killed with Custer that Garlington
quickly became first lieutenant.

Garlington was in the field with the celebrated Seventh Cavalry on numerous occasions during the next five years. For a time, he served as regimental
adjutant. In 1877, he took part in operations against Nez Percé warriors in
Montana, and the following year commanded an improvised detachment fighting the northern Cheyenne in Nebraska. It would be at the height of a fierce
engagement with Native Americans that Ernest Garlington's gallantry would
earn him his country's highest military award. But that came in much later years.
Long before then, his professional honor would be tarnished in consequence
of his having volunteered to face challenges altogether different from any he
had faced on frontier service.

During those spring weeks of 1883, General Hazen wrestled with questions of costs and appropriations and conducted a varied correspondence—letters to the Army's commissary general in New York, the U.S. Consul in St. John's, the Danish legation in Washington, and sundry others. Much of his mail had to do with the charter of a suitable ship and the procurement of material for the hut to be erected on Littleton Island. Hazen wanted to make sure that nothing went wrong with this latest relief effort. The general had come to feel that he alone was identified with American polar forays and thus blameable for ensuing failures, which was evident in a memorandum he placed before the Secretary of War on 1 April.

Hazen declared that the expedition to Lady Franklin Bay ought not to be considered exclusively a Signal Corps enterprise: "The station makes important observations in connection with the international meteorological scheme, but it has also for its purpose, under the original act approved 1 May 1880, other observations and explorations which are in no way beneficial to the Signal Service and might have been done by any other branch of the Army, Navy, or the public services." But Robert Lincoln wouldn't let Hazen off the hook that easily. He returned the memorandum with a significant endorsement: "The Arctic expeditions originated in the Signal Office, and no other Bureau seems to have taken the slightest interest in them. It was solely upon the urging of the Chief Signal Officer that the Secretary of War, not without reluctance, took the steps which have placed these expeditions on foot." This exchange bespoke an inclination on both sides to foreswear responsibility. It hardly boded well for the twenty-five waiting men at Lady Franklin Bay.

# 12

# FATAL AMBIGUITY

AFTER CLEARING ARCHER Fjord in late April, Lockwood's party had swung west, penetrating deeper into Grinnell Land. They reached another fjord, to which Lockwood gave Greely's name. Traveling along its shore, at times slowed by blizzards, they viewed two headlands, north and south, at the mouth of the fjord. On the party's maps, these features became Cape Brainard and Cape Lockwood. The men did not secure a new Farthest North but did establish an Arctic Farthest West record, in the process charting large areas of Grinnell Land. They came to an immense ice cap (subsequently the Agassiz Glacier, named for the nineteenth century's great Swiss-American naturalist). Lockwood decided to turn back. As they plodded wearily through deep snow, their food ran low. The dogs howled hungrily. A reluctant Lockwood, always appreciative of their loyalty, permitted one to be shot and fed to the others. Another dog weakened, one of the best, named Disko King. It was abandoned within sight of Fort Conger, into which on 26 May the men staggered, half-conscious from sheer exhaustion.

Lockwood's mini-expedition had returned to a company riven by personal conflict, especially at the top. Lieutenant Kislingbury had suggested that a party be formed to head south for Littleton Island and await a relief vessel. The commander rejected the idea. Dr. Pavy had handed in a belated medical report for the previous year. Greely termed it "discreditable . . . lacking in interest." He felt "humiliated that such a report should come from a surgeon connected with an Arctic expedition." Pavy heatedly declared the expedition's physical health as good, but Greely could not bring himself to applaud. Indeed, he fancied that given the doctor's dire prophecies of the party's future, it must have distressed him to find the men in tip-top shape.

Greely next ordered the doctor to submit, by the month's end, a report on natural history, with a description of all the specimens on hand and appropriate notes, and, earlier still, "six complete sets of botanical specimens so arranged that they could be securely stored and transported." Before either of the deadlines were met, Pavy asked something for himself: a certified copy of all his correspondence with the commander. Greely refused. His feuding with the doctor had reached the point where he was inclined to blame him even for some of the men's improprieties, which included cutting up hospital blankets for underclothing. There were, Greely had insisted, enough flannel shirts to go around.

And so it went. When the results of Pavy's natural-history work came before the commander, Greely deemed them "exceedingly poor." Stuffed birds were crudely wrapped in paper, insects dust-covered and stuck haphazardly to cork or in matchboxes. Eskimo relics were mixed in with shells, musk-ox skins were sprawled as if forgotten on the house roof, animal skeletons hung unlabeled on rough tripods, and the botanical specimens were a mess. The whole collection was badly in need of organization, classification, and inventory. That, at any rate, was Greely's judgment. Such was his animus against the doctor that he found it easy to feel betrayed, misled into believing that Pavy, all along, had conscientiously discharged his officially appointed role of naturalist as well as surgeon. On 1 June, Greely appointed Lieutenant Lockwood as naturalist in Pavy's place.

Greely knew that Lockwood's credentials in natural history were minimal at best. He implied as much in his journal. "Dr. P. is, of course, better suited for the duty than Lieutenant Lockwood. But prompt action and obedience are particularly required at this time." The relief ship's expected arrival left only nine weeks to get records and specimens in good order. To Private Roderick Schneider, Greely's acting clerk, went the immediate task of labeling and listing the rocks, fossils, pressed flowers, animal skins, and stuffed birds gathered by the Lady Franklin Bay Expedition thus far.

The officers' room at Fort Conger those polar summer hours presented a dismal scene. According to Pavy, all four occupants, himself included, ate their meals in silence. There were "no conversations, we look upon our plates as the dogs in their platter. What a situation in the Arctic regions, and the cause of it all—Greely!" Without assigning blame, Lockwood also wrote of "the happy quartet. We often sit silent during a whole day. A charming prospect for four months of darkness, penned up as we are." Instead of sarcasm, Lockwood might have contemplated the fact that as veteran soldiers of the American prairies, most of the party, the commander included, never should have been there in the first place.

Pavy's contract with the United States War Department formally expired 20 July. He had determined not to renew it. "My work has been made painful by the opposition, attacks, and difficulties put in my way by the C.O.," Pavy wrote. Greely told him directly that "the surgeon general [of the Army] never would have sanctioned had he surmised even the possibility of your quitting, under any circumstances, a command situated without the confines of the civilized world." But Pavy knew his moral obligations, the Hippocratic oath weighing upon him. He would continue to bear responsibility for the party's physical health, "was devoted to the welfare and success of our undertaking," and would maintain full control of the medical stores and instruments.

Notwithstanding ongoing tension in the officers' quarters and a simmering uneasiness among the men, all hands acknowledged the Fourth of July. Lieutenant Kislingbury, who seemed to have an unlimited stock of cigars, gave some out as prizes in a target-shooting match. Both Greely and Kislingbury took part in a baseball game. They were, sneered Sergeant Brainard, "as usual on the losing side." Someone's cursing drew a stern rebuke from the commander. Still more disturbing, according to Brainard's penciled notes, was an announcement made by Greely that four cans of plum pudding had mysteriously vanished. "He said they had been stolen." Brainard added startling words: "If he had accused a *man* there would have been a general uprising of the party to obtain satisfaction."

On the nineteenth of that troubled month, the commander ordered Pavy to surrender his official papers and diary. The doctor protested that the diary was private, "destitute of any official value, a mere record of events, hypotheses and reminiscences, closely mingled with personal and intimate thoughts, detached notes, with letters of entirely private character, for the only use of my family." The doctor's refusal was all the incentive Greely required to place him under instant arrest. The moment contained a fleeting threat of violence. Dinner was just over, the commander seated at his corner desk. He had sent Private Schneider to summon Brainard, who reached the commander's side to find "the doctor standing over him in a threatening attitude." Pavy had just exclaimed, "I accept the arrest physically but not morally." Greely turned to Brainard, telling him to inform the men that their medical officer faced eventual court-martial for disobedience of orders. "The future discipline of similarly situated parties," Greely justified to himself, "will suffer if this officer be not tried."

Greely was tempted to summon a guard and place the doctor under close arrest. Saner thoughts prevailed. Pavy had expressed willingness to continue as the expedition's doctor. Better for Pavy to continue unimpeded, seeing to the commander's own health needs as well as those of the others, even while technically under arrest. But if Lieutenant Kislingbury was thus far the Lady Franklin Bay Expedition's odd man out, so in somewhat different fashion had become the party's physician. Kislingbury commented on the commander's latest move: "Putting Doctor Pavy, the most sensible and hardest-working man we have, in arrest is another of his silly acts. It was a put-up job, as will be proven as soon as this miserable farce can be investigated." Kislingbury, nevertheless, continued his attempts to be a working member of the expedition. Greely dutifully noted: "He turned over to me, as a personal contribution for the expedition, two large tea cans full of lichens. He has devoted much of his time during two years seeking lichens and mosses, tending to them carefully."

Expectation of a ship's arrival again gathered momentum. Unlike the previous year, it was accompanied by serious thoughts of the alternative. Should no vessel appear by 9 August, the station would be abandoned and a retreat begun southward by boats to Littleton Island. At the end of July, the launch

*Lady Greely* was tried under steam and reported serviceable. Stores and supplies were carried piecemeal to Dutch Island to make departure, if found necessary, less of a toil. But hilltop observation reports of ice disappearing, Kislingbury wrote, "cause our hopes for a relief vessel to mount."

Greely thought it an appropriate moment for thoughtful review. The monotony of Arctic life, the depression of months of cold and dark, the restricted diet, and the privations of winter and good spring sledging all had passed without a single case of scurvy or loss of limb, or even serious frost-bite. When the sun returned each time after nine months' darkness, "from one to three sledge parties had been in the field on journeys entailing from two to sixty days' absence and 3000 miles of travel." The North had been conquered as never before on land or sea. For the first time in three centuries, England had to yield the crown of Farthest North to another nation. Westward, the Polar Ocean had been discovered by crossing Grinnell Land (actually, this was no polar ocean but Greely Fjord, which led to the islands skirting Ellesmere's western coast). Weyprecht's scientific program had gone ahead "as far as instruments and means permitted and in two years over 500 observations were made and recorded daily."

Such was the formal accounting. Greely kept personal worries to himself. "The unfavorable experiences of other expeditions, the forebodings of my surgeon, and the knowledge that not any party had ever passed a second winter in such high latitudes, all combined caused me great uneasiness, a great mental trial," he wrote. Spring had brought encouragement, much of it derived from knowledge that the men were in good health. But "perfect ease of mind cannot come until a ship is again seen."

IN THE MATTER of Greely's relief, General William Hazen intended that other branches of government service, especially the Navy Department, should bear some of the weight. Moreover, following the *Neptune* experience, the C.S.O. was less inflexible in adhering to the Greely format. It might be usefully supplemented with an extra safety measure. On 14 May (three weeks after Lieutenant Lockwood left Fort Conger on what Greely decided was the last exploration before the relief ship's arrival "expected in July or August"), Hazen proposed to Secretary Lincoln that a naval vessel escort Lieutenant Garling-ton's relief ship into Baffin Bay. At this point, Lincoln likewise thought it prudent to share the burden and possible future blame. He passed Hazen's proposal to his cabinet colleague, Navy Secretary Chandler, with a favorable annotation. The tender would be able to "bring back information, render assistance, and take such steps as might be necessary in case of unforeseen circumstances."

On 18 May, with no response so far to his request, Hazen left Washington for Newfoundland to select, at St. John's, the "best vessel available." He was accompanied by Lieutenant Commander Bowman H. McCalla as naval adviser. During the chief's absence, Captain James W. Powell again served as acting C.S.O. Soon after Hazen's departure, Chandler sent for Powell and asked if the tender, should he approve its use, might have to enter ice. He also wanted to know if it would be required to carry supplies for Garlington's party. Answering no to both questions, Powell backed off further discussion, pleading that he had not had enough time to study the subject and that anyway Hazen would return shortly to handle affairs himself. But Chandler wanted information right away. He told the captain to prepare a memorandum of instructions.

Powell assigned this task to Lieutenant Louis Caziarc, "who I thought would be conversant with General Hazen's views." Caziarc's duties in the Signal Corps office at this time were wholly clerical, such as editing office regulations and organizing correspondence files. The C.S.O.'s views, as Caziarc was able to recall them, entailed a slight deviation from Greely's instructions, namely that the relief expedition would land its stores at Littleton Island on the passage north. Actually, this modification was not so much Hazen's original idea but largely inspired by William Clapp, the captain no longer directly involved.

At any rate, it was with this departure from the Greely program in mind that Caziarc made some rough notes. He showed them to Lieutenant Garlington, who made no comment other than to ask what would become of him if, having left stores behind, the ship froze in farther north, forcing him to go into winter quarters. Caziarc replied that perhaps he could leave just half his stores on Littleton Island. Throughout this exchange, Garlington viewed Caziarc as a small cog in the expedition machinery. So although Caziarc thought his ideas were getting a favorable hearing, Garlington "studiously avoided giving any official expression of opinion. I inferred he was drawing up that paper of his own accord, to have it ready if called for, more his private opinion than anything else."

This was, in fact, Caziarc's own conception of his role. He had familiarized himself with previous orders to the extent of presuming his views of some small value. But that was all. "I prepared, by way of advice, this instruction as to what I thought the best scheme the office could give the Secretary of the Navy for cooperation between the two ships—to be accepted or rejected as the C.S.O. or acting C.S.O. thought fit." They were his personal views. "I had been asked to draw the memorandum. I wrote it." It was not intended as an order for Lieutenant Garlington, "but merely as a memo. During the general's absence I had to be very careful that I said nothing that he would, on return, disapprove. But that did not prevent me from declaring my opinion."

The next day, Garlington was unavailable for further consultation, having left for New York to supervise the packing of the expedition's stores. Also, General Hazen was still out of the capital and unaware of Caziarc's memorandum, which was duly handed Captain Powell for placing before Secretary Chandler. The memorandum was brief. The naval tender, if there was to be one, would join the main relief vessel at St. John's and accompany her to the vicinity of Littleton Island. Here all the relief ship's stores would be landed except enough to deposit small depots farther up en route to Discovery Harbor. Placing these more northerly caches was in accordance with Greely's instructions. They would serve his party should it have to abandon Fort Conger and retreat south other than by ship.

Greely's program said nothing of leaving stores at Littleton Island. In that regard, Caziarc's memorandum differed from it. As for the tender, it would remain at Littleton Island until Garlington's relief ship returned, with or without Greely's party. Following this rendezvous, all would return home. One of the questions left unanswered was how a slower naval tender could keep up with the relief vessel after leaving St. John's if, as the memo's concluding paragraph stated, "nothing in the northward movement must be allowed to retard the [relief vessel's] progress." It was of "the utmost importance that she take advantage of every lead, to get up to Lady Franklin Bay." But by and large, the memorandum did not conflict with Greely's scenario—except for its stipulation that stores be landed at Littleton Island on the passage north.

Caziarc assumed that on this point he was correctly reflecting Hazen's opinion. After all, Greely's letter of instructions was drafted August 1881 in the general belief that the Fort Conger station would be maintained for years if regularly visited by a relief ship. "He had no idea of breaking up the station," Caziarc stated. The government had now decided to do just that, recalling Greely and his party even though that would mean severing America's principal link with the International Polar Conference. Therefore, Caziarc reasoned (as had Clapp before him) that Greely's outline for relief need not be regarded as binding in every particular. Caziarc saw no purpose in carrying stores north of Littleton Island to "be exposed to risk of destruction in the heavier ice."

For Lieutenant Caziarc to have any say at all in these matters did not please Captain Clapp, charged at the outset with authority in Arctic planning. But Clapp's duties at this stage concerned the procurement of stores. And while he had learned, to his annoyance, that Caziarc was brought into the picture, he did not know of the lieutenant's "memorandum of instructions."

That it made sense to land stores at Cape Sabine was publicly stated by Henry Clay, Dr. Pavy's erstwhile companion in the north until their mutual abhorrence and Clay's return on the *Proteus*. Clay had read of the direction that Signal Corps plans for Greely's rescue or relief seemed to be taking. Almost the same day on which Caziarc was composing his memorandum, the *Louisville Courier-Journal* published a letter from Clay stating that "if a ship does not reach Greely's party by next September, they must set out on their long journey of at least 300 miles from Fort Conger to Cape Sabine." Supposing they made five miles a day, it would take them till near the first of November to reach their destination. "Well before then the long Arctic night will have settled down upon them. Their condition will be truly pitiable."

Clay went on that "as Fort Conger is situated on the western shore of the channel leading north from Smith Sound, and the retreat of Lieutenant Greely's will be down the coast of Grinnell Land, why should the landing [of stores] be made, as proposed, on the eastern side of the sound opposite Cape Sabine? The party to be saved is on the western side. No unbroken line of ice, in the fall or early winter, will extend from Lifeboat Cove [on the mainland near Littleton Island] to Cape Sabine. There is no certainty that Smith Sound can be crossed at all. The comfortable quarters of Lifeboat Cove, though almost in sight, will be inaccessible to them." They could not return to Fort Conger, would be unsheltered at Cape Sabine, and once their small amount of supplies ran out, "they will be past all earthly succor. Like poor De Long, they will then lie down on the cold ground, under the quiet stars."

What Lieutenant Caziarc had written in his memorandum resulted from earlier discussions General Hazen had initiated at Signal Corps headquarters.

But Caziarc did not know that Hazen was now in the process of revising his own thoughts. In St. John's selecting a relief steamer, he had received a telegram from Captain Powell on Secretary Chandler's behalf, asking how far north the naval tender might have to voyage. Fearing that unless he reassured Chandler on this point the tender would not be granted at all, Hazen telegraphed back that it would go no farther north than the southern edge of the ice pack. He added that he would return to Washington on 2 June and to "hold all instructions until I come." Hazen's views on what those instructions should consist of had changed back to the original. Confident that the tender would be his, he was "determined to revert strictly to the Greely memoranda." The tender, he envisioned, would itself be a depot, thus there would be no need to land any stores on Littleton Island during the passage north.

As for the ship itself, Hazen, on Commander McCalla's recommendation, had already made his choice. She would be the *Proteus*, the same 467-ton steamer that had taken Greely's party to Lady Franklin Bay. And as on that earlier voyage, the master would be Captain Pike, aged fifty and a mariner since boyhood. Pike had commanded the *Proteus* for nine years, had prospered as a Baffin Bay sealer, and would take his son aboard as first mate. Otherwise there was some element of doubt about the caliber of the ship's company. Not that Hazen expressed dissatisfaction. Visiting the ship with Commander McCalla to inspect the boilers, he met a dozen of the crew, and "they impressed me very well." Captain Pike also thought his crew generally acceptable. But the ship had been secured for the relief mission so late that most experienced sailors were already engaged for the cod fisheries. "Of course," Pike would say, "you cannot expect to get the same sort of men always. They were not as good a crew as in the year before."

In Washington at Signal Corps headquarters on Sunday afternoon, 4 June, Lieutenant Caziarc had his duty clerk type two copies of his "rough draft" memorandum, which surprised Captain Powell "because it was not official." Even so, the captain put it in the same envelope with the detailed instructions for Lieutenant Garlington, which were based on the original Greely relief program. Early the following morning, Hazen was back in Washington. He called at once upon the Secretary of the Navy to personally announce the chartering of the *Proteus* and to tell him "what we wanted done in the Arctic seas . . . the tender to go as far as Littleton Island and do escort duty." Secretary Chandler had by this time agreed to place a naval vessel at the relief party's disposal, on condition that it should not be required to enter the ice field and that it should stay in company with the *Proteus* only as far north as was safe.

Hazen was next given the package of Garlington's instructions, with a respectful request from Lieutenant Caziarc that he examine and return them "as rapidly as possible in order to have them hectographed. We had to make quite a number, some for the press as well as the officers." They came back to Caziarc soon enough and with the general's endorsement, "as if it was his intention that the memorandum should accompany the instructions, that it was part and parcel of them." Those were Caziarc's later words when called upon to explain. He had not acted on his own "personal wish and desire," but thought he had "a warrant for putting [the memorandum] in with Lieutenant Garlington's instructions."

That memorandum was fated to trigger a controversy marked by confusing testimony and suspicious memory lapses. Secretary Chandler, to whom a copy was supposed to have been sent, denied he ever saw it, claiming that if he had, he would have acted on its recommendation that Garlington leave a depot at Littleton Island on the northward voyage. Hazen would also deny seeing the memorandum at the crucial time. Lieutenant Caziarc's explanation was that when the packet of instructions went before the general for his signature, he could not have carefully studied them. It would have been inconsistent of Hazen to have consciously approved the recommendation because, in his own words, "it having been arranged to send a U.S. ship with the *Proteus*, the absolute necessity of first stopping to unload at Littleton was obviated."

The general most certainly saw that memorandum the day after his return. Lieutenant Garlington was also back in Washington, and he made straight for Signal Corps headquarters, where, in Lieutenant Caziarc's office, he was handed the envelope containing his sailing orders. For the most part, they were in accordance with Greely's original instructions. The 1882 relief expedition having failed in its mission, Garlington was to make for Lady Franklin Bay with ten men, "eight of whom should have practical sea exposure," and three whaleboats and ample provisions for forty persons for fifteen months. Should this 1883 expedition also fail to get through, it was to leave supply depots with whaleboats at intervals along the Ellesmere coast to aid in the retreat that Greely, given the absence of relief by September, was under orders to begin.

Garlington's relief party, having by this hypothesis failed to reach Fort

Conger, was to set up a winter station at Lifeboat Cove (Littleton Island), where its main duty would be to keep telescopes trained westward across Smith Sound and from which, when practicable, "a party of six with dogs, sledges and a native driver should make for Cape Sabine." To Greely's insistence that his relief plan be strictly adhered to, General Hazen added his own emphasis. Garlington was to make every effort to reach Lady Franklin Bay, allowing nothing to delay him on the way up. So it was with great bafflement that Garlington found, in the same envelope with his instructions, an unsigned memorandum to the effect that he must stop en route and leave stores at Littleton Island.

The lieutenant gathered up the papers at once and headed for General Hazen's office. Garlington read him the memorandum aloud, pointing out the conflict: "By stopping I might lose opportunity, if I found clear weather and open water, of getting through." To the lieutenant's surprise, Hazen said he had not seen the memorandum before and had no idea of how it found its way in with the instructions. But neither did he disclaim all responsibility for it. Indeed, he was himself "anxious" to order a stop at Littleton on the way up. "However, the Greely letter was law to me and the orders were founded upon it." The memorandum? The work of a well-intentioned staff officer. All the same, although Greely had directed inflexible compliance with his plan, "you may be governed," Hazen told Lieutenant Garlington, "to a great extent by your own judgment on the spot."

As the general would later testify, he thought it not a bad idea to suggest a stop at Littleton on the way up. But he wished to leave Garlington "with his mind unbiased and unclouded. I said nothing further about [the memorandum], thought it best to leave it to him to exercise his entire discretion as far as he could while carrying out also Greely's letter and the instructions based on it." It was an odd exchange in Hazen's office on G Street, Washington, that Monday afternoon, 5 June, 1883, and, coupled with the incompatible documents, would prove yet another exercise in fatal ambiguity.

# 13

# YANTIC AND *PROTEUS*

ONCE HAZEN HAD convinced William Chandler that the tender would not be required to enter ice, the secretary had telegraphed Rear Admiral George H. Cooper, commander of the North Atlantic Squadron, ordering a naval vessel to be detached for the Lady Franklin Bay Expedition. The closest ship at hand was the *Yantic*, in commission on the North Atlantic station and anchored in Hampton Roads. Chandler directed that she be sent to the Brooklyn Navy Yard for speedy preparation. Through Admiral John C. Walker, of the Bureau of Navigation, he also ordered that the *Yantic* be lightened to increase her coal capacity. And when Walker visited the vessel in drydock, he had all but one of her six guns removed.

The *Yantic* was a bark-rigged steam frigate launched at Philadelphia in 1864 and had seen extensive Civil War service, providing landing parties and gunfire support for Union amphibious attacks. Since then, she had been stationed in the Far East and had patrolled South American waters. While the

Signal Corps office was handling the fuzzy paperwork, Admiral Cooper reminded Frank Wildes, the *Yantic*'s captain, that "your vessel may be absent a long time from port and supply depots and she may encounter stormy weather and ice." Placed in drydock, the *Yantic* was sheathed from bow to abaft the foremast with six-inch oak planking spiked on the outside of her copper. The North Atlantic Fleet engineers had examined the ship and reported her boilers "in good condition, except in back connections and some leaky tubes." The boilers were three years old.

Lieutenant Garlington meanwhile had spent only a few hours in Washington before again leaving for New York. He checked into the Grand Hotel and was promptly visited by Commander Wildes, who told him that the *Yantic* was still confined to the Brooklyn Navy Yard and would take at least seven days to reach St. John's. Garlington had been directed to sail with his men on the *Yantic*. But he was anxious to get to the *Proteus* quickly "so as to handle stowing cargo as I wanted." He cabled Hazen in Washington, asking that he and his men be permitted to go on a faster vessel, the cargo steamer *Alhambra*, which was to carry the expedition's stores as far as Newfoundland.

Garlington's cable reached General Hazen at Fort Myer, near Washington, on the afternoon of 6 June, 1883. Hazen decided to refuse the lieutenant's request, afraid that from the *Alhambra*, a merchant vessel, some of Garlington's "volunteers" might desert. "Facilities for discipline" were better on the naval ship. One of three sergeants attached to Garlington's party had already disappeared. Another, George Wall, praised by Hazen as "an excellent soldier," was in fact a bad choice, recently married and reluctant to leave his new bride. Hazen telegraphed the refusal to Garlington's request on the seventh. By that time, it was irrelevant—the *Alhambra* had already sailed.

Not until 13 June did the *Yantic* leave New York. She proceeded through Hell Gate at 4:00 P.M. and into Vineyard Sound, her passengers Lieutenant Garlington and his small party of a surgeon and eight enlisted men, her captain regretting that he had not had sufficient time to absorb crucial details of his assignment. The *Yantic* still had been in drydock when he received his sailing orders from the Navy Department, and like those from Hazen to Garlington, they were hardly a model of clarity and precision. The *Proteus* was chartered to fetch Lieutenant Greely's party from Lady Franklin Bay, and "in view of [her] possible destruction it is desirable that you should proceed as far north as practicable in order to offer succor. Under no circumstances, however, will you proceed beyond Littleton Island, and you are not to enter the ice pack."

Before leaving St. John's, the *Yantic* would take on all the coal she safely could, and at the same time Wildes was to confer with Garlington on what to do if, before landfall at Littleton Island, the ships had to separate. Wildes was told that throughout the voyage, "details must be left to your judgment, and the Department considers it only necessary to call your attention to the desirability of cordially cooperating with Lieutenant Garlington, affording him all the assistance in your power." Wildes had received these orders from Secretary of the Navy Chandler only three days before sailing, and until then he hadn't even known that his ship would go north of Upernavik, other than what he had read in newspapers.

Neither did he think that the *Yantic* was in perfect shape for what might lie ahead. General Hazen would say that it was believed the ship "was in all respects thoroughly equipped for that special service." Commander Wildes, a forty-year-old Bostonian, was less confident. The oak sheathing was to prevent sharp ice from cutting the ship's side, but "it added nothing to her strength to resist a crushing strain." While it was all very well to be told that the *Yantic* would not be required to enter ice fields, Wildes believed that "to say that she was thoroughly equipped is not accurate."

She had left New York with unreliable boilers. Repairs had been pushed night and day to hasten departure. They were not finished on the sailing date, material to complete the work still stacked on deck. "She is provisioned for barely nine months," reported *Frank Leslie's Weekly*. "And she is not strong enough to grapple with heavy circumpolar ice." There were no plans to do any such thing, but the vessel and crew were deficient in other ways, some of which could have compelled Commander Wildes to respectfully protest. With so little time before sailing, he had thought better of it. His crew was larger than customary. "Fifty men would have been enough," Wildes would say. And his people would suffer from the cold. The *Yantic* had only recently cruised in the Caribbean. Unaware of his new destination until the last moment, Wildes hadn't applied for warmer clothing. The *Yantic*'s preparation for polar waters being a naval matter, General Hazen wasn't briefed on every detail, as he defensively stated later when bemoaning the fact that "never before did a commander start on an Arctic cruise with his men equipped for the tropics."

Meanwhile, the *Alhambra* had put in at Halifax on her way to St. John's. What Hazen feared about desertion had occurred. A telegram from that Nova Scotian seaport informed him that the newly wedded Sergeant Wall had fallen down a hatchway and injured himself. Angrily, Hazen cabled back that the sergeant's duties were so important that he had to continue on to St. John's. Somehow eluding this directive Wall made his way back to Washington, where an Army surgeon certified that he had feigned injury to get home (Wall was subsequently court-martialed). When the *Alhambra* reached St. John's and discharged her stores, no member of the expedition was at hand to transfer them methodically to the *Proteus*. This task had to proceed under Captain Pike's supervision. Slowed by fog, the *Yantic*, with Lieutenant Garlington fretting over delay, didn't reach St. John's until 21 June. Garlington found that loading the *Proteus* in his absence had certainly been slipshod. He had to break out many of his stores to get at meteorological instruments. Guns were missing. Other than three rifles, a shotgun, and two pistols, the relief expedition was without firearms.

Garlington was also lacking in sergeants. But on the way up, he had made friends with John C. Colwell, a lieutenant on the *Yantic* and "a very pleasant fellow," who wished to join the expedition. Garlington telegraphed Hazen, asking if this appointment could be arranged. Hazen applied to the Navy Department, which at first said no, whereupon the general turned to his Secretary of War. This method worked. Secretary Lincoln told Chandler, "I am anxious that the relief expedition should not fail in bringing Lieutenant Greely's party home." Commander Wildes of the *Yantic* regarded Colwell as an energetic and zealous subordinate and didn't look kindly at what was afoot. "Losing Colwell weakens the vessel in a department which should be strong," he argued. But on 23 June, the Navy lieutenant was officially transferred from the *Yantic*'s wardroom to Garlington's Army party and billeted on board the *Proteus*.

Closeted in his cabin on the *Yantic* during the passage up from New York, Wildes had discussed almost daily with Garlington on how best the two ships should cooperate. The officers agreed that the *Yantic* wasn't to be considered part of the expedition but as a tender or transport to take on the *Proteus* crew should that ship run into trouble. In Garlington's private view, the *Yantic* couldn't be "of any particular service." He suspected that selecting a naval vessel as escort for the relief steamer was merely a sop to public opinion, certain influential newspapers having urged such a move. And he didn't anticipate that the two ships would remain in close company for long.

As for that confusing memorandum tucked in with his formal instructions, Garlington paid no more attention to it. He declared, "My duty was not to wait for the *Yantic*, not to land stores at Littleton Island, but push forward, take advantage of every favorable lead." Should the *Yantic* meet heavy ice, she would have to be left behind, the *Proteus* carrying on alone. Once at Discovery Harbor, Garlington would get no argument from Greely, for he carried with him a letter from the Chief Signal Officer stating that "owing to congressional action, probably controlled somewhat by misfortunes to other Arctic expeditions, it is necessary to discontinue the work at Lady Franklin Bay and to direct the return of your party."

Should Garlington fail to reach his destination, only then would he deposit his men and stores at or near Littleton Island. His understanding was that he must get all he had as soon as he could to Lady Franklin Bay. "I always understood that Lieutenant Greely's supplies would be exhausted at the end of August 1883," he stated. Garlington had gained this impression from General Hazen's dire warnings of starvation at Fort Conger. Hazen couldn't have forgotten, even if he didn't convey as much to the lieutenant (or to Secretary Lincoln), that Greely had set out in 1881 with provisions calculated as ample for a three years' stay.

In a St. John's hotel room, Garlington and Commander Wildes conferred again and composed a memorandum of agreement, which Wildes's clerk handwrote and the two officers signed. It stipulated that once at sea, the *Yantic* would remain in company with the *Proteus* as long as possible. Garlington was determined that "the *Yantic* was not to interfere in any way with my progress north. If she could get along with me, well and good, if not I was to leave her." The *Yantic* would proceed to Disko Island under sail, saving coal, then steam to Upernavik. Farther north, she would leave small cairns with messages at Cape York, southeast Cary Islands, Pandora Harbor, and Littleton Island, assuming she got that far up. Pandora Harbor would be regarded as the main base. But the *Yantic* was not to stay there later than 25 August, before which date the *Proteus* would try to communicate with her. "Should the *Proteus* be lost we would push a boat or party south to the *Yantic*," they agreed. This arrangement for the ships' movements was the best that Garlington, given the circumstances, felt he could make. And there was always the chance that Commander Wildes would indeed get his ship as far north as Littleton Island.

Many hopes were pinned on the success of this expedition. Anna Lockwood, the lieutenant's mother, had written Henrietta Greely, "God grant we may hear cheering news when the relief ship returns. It is a terrible ordeal that we are called upon to undergo, this suspense, this ignorance of all that may have befallen. My dear boy is ever in my thoughts. The harrowing details of De Long's party and all they underwent I know you have read with painful interest." Henrietta had written to Lieutenant Garlington that "on every hand I hear such praise bestowed on you that I feel the relief of my husband's party is in very earnest hands." General Hazen was all reassurance. "Everything shall be done," he wrote Henrietta, "and everything shall succeed. . . . I am confident everything will go right." Everything devised by study had been attended to. And Henrietta wrote to Greely's niece, Clarissa, "I feel very well satisfied now and think the only thing left to do is await as calmly as possible."

Fortunately for their peace of mind, none was aware of Lieutenant Colwell's misgivings after his transfer to the *Proteus*. "None of her boats were seaworthy. Two were stowed up on the gallows frame, and standing under them one could see daylight through the seams. Her rigging was old, her compasses untrustworthy," he observed. Neither was Colwell happy about the fact that the ship's first mate, Captain Pike's twenty-one-year-old son, had never been in the Arctic (the second mate, also young, was Pike's cousin).

But Colwell, the thirty-two-year-old son of an Army captain killed leading his company at Antietam, wrote optimistically to his mother, "I will land with Garlington and his party of ten men and a doctor at the highest point possible, and after building a house and arranging the stores the Greely party will be reached by sledges during the late fall or early winter and be brought down to the station we have established. The house [purchased, unassembled, at St. John's] has only to be set up when we go ashore." The expedition was thoroughly provisioned, even to abundant cigars and tobacco "and enough clothing for a small army. There isn't much chance for me to get cold. I have always wanted to take a trip to the Arctic regions and I couldn't possibly go under more comfortable and favorable circumstances. It suits me exactly."

Although the *Yantic* was designated as escort or tender for the *Proteus*— "the two ships," Hazen would say, "tied together by the mandate of their instructions"—no knowledgeable person expected they would stay that close for long. Colwell wrote on 29 June that "we sail in about half an hour in company with the *Yantic* but will probably separate outside as the *Yantic* has to economize coal and we will sail as fast as possible for Disko and Godhavn." Lieutenant Garlington described the two ships' departure from St. John's in pleasant terms—the day was beautiful, a breeze blowing gently offshore. He then noted, "After clearing the Narrows, the *Proteus* set her course close into shore. The *Yantic* set sail and went more to the eastward. We lost sight of her at 7:30 P.M." Convinced that the two ships could not possibly stay together, Garlington expected to see the escort next at Godhavn, the harbor for Disko Island, and even there, he "intended to wait for the *Yantic* but not indefinitely. This was the understanding between us."

Final letters were written to be taken ashore. Garlington wrote encouragingly to Henrietta Greely. Every possible effort would be made to bring her husband out this season. If the *Proteus* did not get through to Lady Franklin Bay, Garlington promised her, "I most assuredly will by means of sledges. I am quite sanguine of success. I have good determined men who have their hearts in their work." (Garlington also had a Newfoundland dog, which he had adopted at St. John's and named Rover.) He sent General Hazen a last letter. The *Yantic* was not expected to accompany him far, "as she will have to depend upon her sails alone, on account of her limited capacity for carrying coal." Garlington didn't deem it wise to link his own progress to the unpredictable winds of the season "and consequently will not allow myself to be retarded on my way north. All that can be done will be done to get the ship to Fort Conger."

# 14

# SHIPWRECK

THE *PROTEUS* AND the *Yantic* had soon separated. At top speed the *Proteus* made nine knots, the *Yantic* only four. But Lieutenant Garlington on the *Proteus* thought Captain Pike's crew ominously troublesome. Pike knew they were sub-standard: "They might not be as smart and quick as I wanted." As for Pike himself, Garlington had no personal knowledge of his expertise with nautical instruments. The soldier relied more upon his naval lieutenant, Colwell. He still fretted over "the arms and other stores I had sought at St. John's." They were not found during a second search through the ship's cargo at Godhavn, 6 July. And he was forced to wait longer in harbor than he wished in order to obtain skin clothing, dogs, and two Eskimo dog drivers. Still there was no sign of the *Yantic*. "She is probably cruising under sail," wrote Colwell, "to save her coal." He added optimistically that "the signs up here all point to a very open season north. We may be able to steam straight up to Lady Franklin Bay, get the party there on board and return this season."

Not until 17 July did the *Yantic* reach Disko Island. She had run into a gale five days earlier that had carried away a main topsail sheet. She anchored in Godhavn harbor at about 6:30 P.M., and Garlington went on board. Commander Wildes told him that since the continuing voyage would be mainly under steam, he intended to have work done on the boilers before departure. Also his ship would take on more coal. The *Proteus* steamed northward alone, leaving the *Yantic* with her boilers stripped. Garlington felt he had little choice: "The time necessary for repairing the *Yantic*'s boilers and additional delay in procuring coal was longer than I deemed justified in further delaying my progress north."

Two hours out of Godhavn, the *Proteus* ran aground. She was cleared by putting the engines alternately ahead and astern at full speed. Still, Garlington worried: "The careless manner in which the ship was being navigated was brought forcibly to my mind." Crossing Melville Bay on the eighteenth, the *Proteus* shook violently, tumbling Garlington from his bunk. He got to his feet, peered through the porthole, and saw ice clear to the horizon. He raced up on deck, figuring that Pike must have taken the ship straight into the pack; it was "unbroken in all directions except to the southward." With an artificial horizon placed on a floe, Lieutenant Colwell obtained a reading that convinced Garlington the captain of the *Proteus* had committed a navigational error.

The ship was forced back southward, then westward, Pike looking for open leads. Progress was made rounding Cape York, where the ice was looser, and early on the twenty-first, a party landed at one of the Cary Islands to examine the Nares cache—a boat in good condition and 60 percent of the stores still usable. Garlington left a message for Wildes when he came up: "Will steer for Hakluyt Island [near the Carys] then Littleton. All well and in excellent spirits."

The next day, the *Proteus* steamed into Pandora Harbor. Garlington left further word for Wildes, reporting that even from the ship's crow's nest with a high-powered spyglass, no ice was visible. He decided to take advantage of what he concluded were favorable conditions and pass Littleton Island without stopping. The *Proteus* did so on 22 July. Then ice reappeared, nudging the ship westward.

At 3:30 P.M. that day, Pike anchored in Payer Harbor, near Cape Sabine. Garlington went ashore to examine the depot Private Beebe had left the previous year. It was in fair condition, and the whaleboat only scarred by bear claws.

In the same proximity of Sabine was a second cairn, left by the Nares expedition in 1875 on Stalnecht, a rocky islet connected with the mainland at low tide. If Greely carried out his intention to retreat down the Ellesmere Island coast along Smith Sound, he could be at Cape Sabine within two or three months. Garlington only briefly thought of landing part of his stores there— they totaled four depots of provisions, each of 250 rations. Uppermost in the Army officer's mind were General Hazen's instructions that nothing be done that would retard his passage to Lady Franklin Bay. After peering northward through his glass and "satisfying myself that there could be no mistake about the presence of a favorable lead, I started back and reached the ship at 6:30 P.M."

He hurried to Pike's stateroom. The captain was resting on his bed. At the doorway, Garlington called that open lanes were visible northward toward Cape Hawks. Pike sat up and said he was not yet ready to leave Payer Harbor. He wanted fresh water and to fill his bunkers from the ship's extra coal cargo. Pike, in fact, intended to remain in harbor "several days" or until the ice had entirely passed out of Smith Sound. Two of Garlington's own men, ashore taking magnetic observations, returned on board to report that contrary to their commander's impression, the sound appeared completely blocked. Pike thought that even a week's delay at Payer Harbor would not be detrimental to the expedition's relief effort. But Garlington was eager to get moving. He offered Pike the use of his detail in filling the bunkers, and so peremptory did Garlington's tone strike the captain that, Pike asserted, "I felt if I did not proceed and the expedition failed, my lingering at that point might be blamed. So I went against my better judgment." He grumbled to the American that he was "just as anxious as anyone to get north." Then Pike climbed on deck and ordered the *Proteus* under way.

She started at 8:00 P.M. Garlington sent Colwell up into the crow's nest to join the first mate, Pike's son, in keeping lookout. At about midnight, with the sun at this time of the season just barely above the horizon, the loose pack through which the ship had steamed began to solidify. Pike decided to ram, "trying to wedge two floes apart," in Lieutenant Colwell's words. A man carefully lowered to the ice followed along the crack to see if it extended into open water. He came back and said it did. Pike put the ship's bow against the crack and worked the engines at full speed. The strong ship of oak and cedar and copper and iron clove through the widening pans of ice until, rewarded by so many open lanes, Pike was at a loss which to enter. But options were quickly denied him. Ice floes drifting down Smith Sound the night before had returned larger than ever on the shifting tide. Four miles off Cape Albert, they closed about the ship and halted her. She lay inert, positioned east to west, tightly gripped—and within tantalizing sight of a polynia whose open branches threaded clear to the northern horizon.

Pike heard the timbers of his ship strain and split. Floes seven feet thick rafted to the rails. Garlington summoned his party and ordered the stores made ready for throwing on the ice. A weaker ship would already have been crushed to matchwood. Garlington and three men hurried into the main hold to break out provisions earmarked for Greely at Lady Franklin Bay. They felt the ship shudder under the impact of ice ripping away the entire starboard main rail abreast the boiler and engine room. Lieutenant Colwell came racing down the hatchway. Garlington told him he had better get the boats clear at once. As Colwell dashed back on deck to do so, the *Proteus* shook again. Bulwarks gave way, and ice crashed through the ship's side and into the starboard coal bunker.

Its pressure had squeezed deck plates; seams gaped wide. Leaving the fast-flooding hold, Garlington was back topside. One of his noncoms rushed up to report that his detail had cleared the forepeak of its stowage of food depots. At that moment, Garlington ordered everything thrown overboard. Disgustedly, he noticed that with the exception of the boatswain and chief engineer, the *Proteus* crew had already abandoned their posts, were concerned with saving only their own effects, disregarding the stores intended for Greely's relief. It was every man for himself. Garlington's efforts were of little avail. Besides what he was forced to leave in the flooded hold, many of his boxes going over the shattered starboard side were missing the ice and vanishing under water. Garlington sent two men on the floes to rescue crates as they fell and shove them across to firmer ice. "This they could not do rapidly enough," he said, "and about thirty per cent of the stores thrown over went under."

Lieutenant Colwell had gotten a dinghy and the ship's starboard whaleboat safely on ice. Floes crunched the port whaleboat against the ship's side until a few of Pike's seamen and Garlington's soldiers hacked it free. Pike ordered the men to abandon ship. The din of grinding ice, splintering timbers, and men shouting was compounded by the barking and yelping of twenty-two huskies hurled overboard and scattering in all directions. The dogs did not include Garlington's Rover, who, a soldier would say, "never got in anyone's way."

By evening of what was another nightless day, all hands were stranded on separate ice floes and still within sight of Cape Sabine. Colwell had been the last of Garlington's relief party to leave the ship. She steadily filled. Sergeant William Lamar, who had seen to the rescue of the chronometer, sextants, and records, shouldered a camera. He hastily set it up and focused on the *Proteus* as she sank. She went down faster as the tide turned and ice pressure slackened, taking to the bottom much of her cargo of supplies and mail. Members of Garlington's party thought Pike's crew "acted like pirates, stealing all they could—soldiers' clothing, buffalo overcoats and robes. We could not stop them, they had all the guns." This scenario was not strictly true. Colwell had a shotgun, Private Moritz (his artificer) a repeating rifle, and another private a Winchester. Garlington had a Hotchkiss rifle and a Navy and Army revolver, with ammunition. But the *Proteus* crew had five shotguns and six rifles. And as Pike admitted to Colwell, with few exceptions his men were "a worthless lot, but I can do nothing with them." Garlington saw them steal whatever they fancied.

It would be pointed out—by General Hazen, no less, though to save his own skin—that "by law and custom in those waters the fact of the shipwreck discharges all hands." Their shipping articles were no longer in force, "there is no longer pay nor officers." Whatever the crew's misconduct after the sinking, it was "not from a spirit of mutiny but because the captain had no authority over them." Perhaps so. At any rate, men, boats, and salvaged stores now floated on different floes. In the deepening gloom, Garlington and Pike worked to assemble everybody and everything on the same floe. They would next, Garlington figured, make for solid ground. Lieutenant Colwell was particularly active. Around midnight, he led a party in a loaded whaleboat to the island whose eastern promontory was Cape Sabine. There he set up a cache of tea, bacon, canned goods, tobacco, and sleeping bags. He returned to the floes at 2:00 A.M. Ice closing the approaches prevented another trip until 5:00. By that time, an ebbing tide had carried the whole party closer to shore.

Colwell and four men crossed to the island a second time, accompanied by a boatload of Pike's crew. Minutes later, the ice pan carrying the other shipwrecked men started drifting out to open sea. Garlington quickened his efforts to land stores. He hoped to leave provisions amounting to 500 rations, enough to last Greely's party three weeks if they got this far south. He felt he could do no better. He and Captain Pike set out in their separate boats. Only two men in Garlington's party knew how to row. After a rough passage, during which the lieutenant's boat was nearly swamped, they landed at Cape Sabine and hurriedly unloaded. They struck out for the floe again, only to find all leads closed.

Colwell, meanwhile, was back on his floe, supervising the haulage of supplies, equipment, and instruments across the ice and into his whaleboat. There was no room for everything, and Colwell had ten men of his own party to consider and eight of Pike's, these now in a mutinous mood after watching their captain pull away from the floes. They were convinced that he had deliberately abandoned them. Colwell heard them loudly cursing. "They all seemed much demoralized," he noted.

Some were in a spirit to seize Colwell's whaleboat and go looking for the *Yantic* on their own. The lieutenant did the safest thing. He took aboard all eighteen men, throwing back on the ice virtually all the supplies that he had labored to stow in the boat. Even the loaded dinghy Colwell had hoped to tow ashore was cut free—to be saved, however, by Sergeant John Kinney, who plugged a leak with his thumb for four hours, while the artificer Moritz, alone at the oars, brought it safely to shore. All of Colwell's and Moritz's skills were needed to navigate the overloaded boats among floes steadily congealing and closing leads. And once on dry land, some of Captain Pike's men were still growling, a few to the effect that for deserting his men on the ice they would never let him get back to St. John's alive.

Thus it was that at midday on 25 July, as the Greely party more than 200 miles to the north prayed for signs of a ship or, should none arrive by the first weeks of August, a meeting with her somewhere along the retreat south, the *Proteus* lay shattered and out of sight beneath the frozen sea. With boats hauled up and made secure, her exhausted people sprawled upon the rocky shore. Garlington tried to take inventory. He estimated that his party's provisions would last about forty days. Captain Pike checked his supplies and figured he had salvaged the same amount. Their old floe, cluttered with abandoned stores, was still in view but receding eastward with each passing minute.

Pike told Garlington he would like to take one of his two whaleboats for a last dash to the floe in hopes of retrieving more of its precious burden. Colwell, now increasingly a source of advice to the Army lieutenant, thought it unwise to let any of Pike's men get their hands on a naval whaleboat. Pike finally pulled away with the *Proteus* boats containing six of his New-foundlanders and six American soldiers. They brought back some supplies, but a great deal remained piled on the floe, as it merged with the general pack and vanished in the spray-laden dusk. That was not all. Before mists and disappearing sun ruled out long-distance observation, a mortified Garlington saw clear water tracks open to the northern horizon. Captain Pike had anticipated as much. He had figured on staying one day longer in Payer Harbor, before allowing himself to be overruled by the officer in command of the American relief party.

Fog closed upon the shipwrecked men. Garlington told them to get what rest they could. The next morning, he crossed to nearby Brevoort Island and left a woeful record of events, beginning with the *Proteus* saga: "Nipped . . . she stood the enormous pressure nobly for a time, but had to finally succumb to this measureless force." Few provisions were saved. "The United States steamer *Yantic* is on her way to Littleton Island with orders not to enter the ice. Swedish steamer will try to reach Cape York during this month. I will endeavor to communicate with these vessels at once, and everything within the power of man will be done to rescue the brave men at Fort Conger from their perilous position," he wrote. He pinpointed the location of caches—500 rations of bread with tea and sleeping bags three miles from Cape Sabine facing Buchanan Strait, 250 rations in the same vicinity left by the *Neptune* in 1882, a cache of clothing at the cape, and the small Nares depot on nearby tiny Stalnecht Island. And over at Littleton, the other 250 left by Beebe. Garlington ended on a contrite note: "It is not within my power to express one tithe of my sorrow and regret at this fatal blow to my efforts to reach Lieutenant Greely. I will leave for the eastern shore just as soon as possible and endeavor to open communications."

Sunlight had burned off the fog. Garlington's mind wrestled with options. The drift of his thoughts and instincts, the assessments he pondered, his concepts of duty all would emerge in future testimony and correspondence. Much depended upon the extent to which he could rely on or anticipate the *Yantic*'s movements. The principal object was to establish contact with her. He knew of Commander Wildes's orders to take his ship as far as Littleton Island, if he could accomplish that without encountering serious ice. Should Wildes be successful, Garlington would get from the *Yantic* all the stores she could spare, set up a manned station on Littleton to look out for the retreating Greely party, and send everybody else to St. John's for additional help. "A sealer could then be secured and sent north," he reasoned.

But could he count on the *Yantic* reaching Littleton Island? "This was the point I had to mentally settle," he wrote. Commander Wildes had a large crew, 140 men or more, with limited provisions and a vessel in no way adapted for ice navigation. Could she force passage across perilous Melville Bay, which the reinforced *Proteus* had required three days to accomplish? The questions were obvious enough. Garlington's answers were painfully inconsistent: "I did not believe [Wildes] would succeed in getting through Melville Bay where we had met so much ice." At the same time, mindful of orders for the ships to rendezvous at Littleton Island, Garlington "always had in view the chance of her getting through."

It was possible to sympathize with Garlington in his quandary. As recalled by a naval commander destined for his own pivotal role in the Arctic drama, "It was a cruel situation in which this young officer of cavalry was placed, taken from his station in Dakota, after six years of service with his regiment, and suddenly finding himself [marooned] in the middle of Kane Sea, with the whole responsibility of a most important expedition on his shoulders. That he had voluntarily assumed this responsibility did not make his position any the less distressing."

Garlington could feel thankful that he had a United States naval officer at his side. Yet he didn't act automatically upon Colwell's advice. At a consultation between the two Americans and Pike that forenoon, Colwell proposed that he cross Smith Sound immediately with a picked crew and lightly equipped boat, and proceed due south from Littleton Island in hopes of intercepting the *Yantic*. In the meantime, Garlington could establish the Littleton Island winter station in accordance with his orders, leaving a small party at Sabine to greet the retreating Greely expedition. Pike, for one, thought this idea was good. Garlington rejected it. Pike proposed that the whole party cross Smith Sound to Littleton Island and await the *Yantic*'s arrival. Garlington turned this option down, too.

He worried over provision for himself as well as for Adolphus Greely. He knew that in about five weeks, with no relief in sight, Greely's party would begin its retreat south, along the east coast of Ellesmere. The distance from Discovery Harbor to Cape Sabine was about 200 miles. Garlington concluded that waiting at Sabine for Greely to come down would be foolish. "It would have been necessary to draw on the supplies already deposited for Greely's party, and if he should arrive he would find his own supplies diminished and the addition of another body of men no better off than his."

Garlington's orders were that if he could not reach Lady Franklin Bay, "you will retreat and land your party at or near Lifeboat Cove [effectively Littleton Island] and prepare for remaining until relieved next year." And Greely's own directions were that if unable to get through Smith Sound, the relief party should establish a station at Lifeboat Cove, "where its main duty would be to keep telescopes [trained] on Cape Sabine and land to the northward."

But the sinking of the *Proteus* and the loss of supplies had denied Garlington hopes of compliance. Nor could he afford to wait for the *Yantic*'s arrival. If he tarried at Littleton for as long as a fortnight on the chance that the consort would show up, his "supplies would have dwindled to a dangerous degree." By that time, too, the season would be closing, and to then head south in search of the *Yantic*, with small craft their only transport, would mean having to "force our way through much young ice [which] would have delayed the boats' progress, preventing any communication of the disaster."

As for leaving provisions, he had none with which to sustain a Littleton Island depot. The 500 rations he had just cached at Cape Sabine, with what the Nares expedition and the *Neptune* had left, were little enough for Greely but would have to suffice. For his own use, those forty days' rations salvaged for his thirteen-man party included 600 pounds of hard bread, much of it found wet and thrown away; 300 pounds of bacon; pemmican, mostly spoiled; and 400 pounds of canned meat, fruit, and vegetables—hardly of banquet proportions. And Garlington saw no signs of much game. It would be said that he should have left at Cape Sabine or Littleton Island two-thirds of the supplies he had saved from the wreck, some 2,100 individual rations. "But," he argued, "I could not foretell how long our journey would take. If I had left my small stock of provisions at Littleton, I would have severely endangered the safety of my men to no purpose."

That same evening, in three lifeboats and two Navy whaleboats, one towing a dinghy, Pike's twenty-one-man crew and Garlington's dozen, with his large pet dog, crossed to the Greenland side. It surprised no one that the *Yantic* was not there. Sodden by rain and snow, the men camped on the shore near Lifeboat

Cove, and the next morning they were on their way south, having left nothing on Littleton Island but a record reporting the subsistence caches on the other side and outlining Garlington's intentions: "I am making for the south to communicate with the *Yantic*, which is endeavoring to come up. Every effort will be made to come north at once for the Greely party." But since the *Yantic* was overloaded and forbidden to enter ice, they would "have to get another ship." The record contained no message for anyone in particular, and no advice at all for Commander Wildes should he get through to Littleton Island.

Reaching his goal of communication with the *Yantic* meant that Lieutenant Garlington would have to visit points of contact agreed upon at St. John's, sort of Arctic "post offices" where each party would leave messages indicating future movements. Regardless of how far north the *Yantic* steamed beyond Melville Bay, assuming a safe passage across that formidable stretch of water, it did not appear likely that the southbound boats and the northbound naval frigate could miss each other. After Littleton Island, the next potential rendezvous was Pandora Harbor.

Garlington's and Pike's boats separated in the night but reached the harbor within five hours of each other Thursday evening, 26 July. They found no *Yantic* there, nor a message. Unable to push on because of fog, Garlington penned a note: "Will go south, keeping close inshore as possible, and calling at Cary Island, to Cape York, or until I meet some vessel. Hope to meet *Yantic* or the Swedish steamer *Sofia*, which should be about Cape York."

When the journey continued, Garlington had the *Proteus* boatswain transferred to his whaleboat because only two of the dozen soldiers in it could row. Thus, counting Lieutenant Colwell and himself, there were seldom more than four or five men at the oars. The boat flotilla arrived at Northumberland Island on 29 July. Again, anxious eyes sought the *Yantic*, but in vain.

Unbeknownst to Garlington's and Pike's hard-pressed crews, that ship was more than 500 miles away. It had not yet crossed Melville Bay but was fogged in at Upernavik and taking on coal—"a detention," in Commander Wildes's words, "such as any prudent mariner, under like circumstances, would have considered necessary." His *Yantic* had in fact not left even the first stop, at Godhavn, until 26 July, having been delayed two weeks by boiler repair, coaling, and bad weather. She had arrived at Upernavik late on the twenty-seventh, at about the time Garlington's boat party, far to the north, were encamped at Pandora

Harbor (and, farther still, Greely's party had begun preparations to leave Fort Conger). When coming up with Garlington, the *Proteus* had not called at Upernavik. Why, then, had Frank Wildes? "To obtain information as to what the weather had been during the past season, what kind of a winter they had, what knowledge of ice movements which would influence me in my choice of routes across Melville Bay." Local opinion was favorable, ice conditions promising a safe passage. But fog had closed in again, and it was the end of the month before the *Yantic* next took to sea.

Holding steadily on course, after a rare trouble-free crossing of Melville Bay, the *Yantic* came within sight of Cape York. The date was early 2 August. Land ice stretching fifteen miles offshore forced Wildes to bypass the cape and continue northward for the next prearranged "post office," the Cary Islands. This also being Garlington's destination, the course his boats took and that of the *Yantic* should have converged. But a blizzard that kept his and Pike's parties under canvas on Northumberland Island showed no sign of slackening. The Army lieutenant turned to the Navy's Colwell for advice. It was disturbing. A crossing to those outer islands would be "extremely hazardous with heavily laden boats in rough seas," especially with so few experienced men at the oars. Garlington agreed. They would not stop at the Cary Islands. And when the weather lifted, they made directly south for Cape York.

Skirting the Carys was not in accord with the St. John's agreement between himself and Commander Wildes, but relying on the judgment of his nautical subordinate, Garlington felt he had little choice. Still hugging the coast as closely as ice allowed, the shipwrecked men pulled hard for Saunders Island. They landed at 9:30 P.M., 2 August. The island lay some forty miles east of the Cary Islands, which the *Yantic*, having sighted Cape York but not stopped there, was steadily approaching. And on her northward course, some time during the not quite dark but mist-cloaked hours of the same night, the *Yantic* actually brushed by Saunders Island, where Pike's and Garlington's boats were drawn up, the weary soldiers, mariners, a single naval officer, and two Eskimos sleeping uneasily in wind-buffeted tents.

When the *Yantic* reached Cary Islands, her captain went ashore. He found the message Garlington had left there 21 July on the way up, but no record of any subsequent visit. At 10:30 A.M., Friday the third, after leaving his own record, Wildes got under way again, still northbound and steaming up the

Greenland coast ever farther from the five shipwrecked boatloads. The next day, from the *Yantic's* crow's nest, Littleton Island came in view. At the same moment, 200 miles south, Garlington's and Pike's parties were again on the move, pulling doggedly for Cape York, where no message from Commander Wildes awaited them because the *Yantic* had not stopped there.

On Littleton Island, Wildes found Garlington's startling report, penned just one week earlier. The *Proteus* had sunk. Garlington and his relief party had left for the south in boats, hoping to meet up with the *Yantic*. Beyond realizing that he must somehow have passed them on the way up, Wildes felt himself at a loss. Now had come his turn for anxious deliberation. Garlington had left no sign of where Pike's crew were or what they were doing and not a clue as to what he desired the *Yantic* to do if or when she reached Littleton Island. It may have dawned on the *Yantic's* commander that Garlington had doubted that the ship would get that far north. At any rate, Wildes had his Navy Department orders not to proceed above Littleton Island. But neither would he station any of his men there with a depot for the Greely party. "I had no Arctic outfit, only flannel shirts, cloth trousers, and the ordinary seaman's outfit furnished to every man of war for service in a temperate and tropical climate." He had only a sail for shelter, coal but no stove to burn it, no matches to start a fire. "A party under those circumstances could not have lived through the winter."

Thus had Wildes to revise his strategy. Instead of heading north for Lady Franklin Bay on board ship, Garlington was one of a shipwrecked party not north but south of him. The *Yantic* and the boat parties were looking for each other in the wrong places. Wildes could see only one sensible course to pursue, and that was to forget Lady Franklin Bay and make all speed back south. He had decided that his "first and paramount duty" was to pick up the boats containing Garlington's and Pike's men. He "hoped to find them at Cary Islands or somewhere between Cape Parry and Cape Athol." The *Proteus* was no more, but the St. John's agreement still could apply. So it made sense to expect that Garlington would try to communicate with the *Yantic* at one of the prearranged points of contact.

And what of Greely's party? Wildes satisfied himself on that score. It would be inhumane to leave ill-clad and inadequately equipped men on Littleton Island to look out for Greely and most likely perish before they could set eyes on him. Neither could Wildes bring himself to leave a cairn of provisions. For one thing, he had not been asked by Garlington or Hazen or anybody else to contribute supplies of his own in furtherance of their mission's object. True, the *Yantic* was by no means short of sustenance. She had sailed from New York with eight months' provisions, "every available space utilized for their storage," and, that amount being deemed insufficient, still more rations were taken on board at St. John's. At Littleton Island, the *Yantic's* hold contained 7,000 pounds of bread, 5,500 pounds of salt beef, 6,000 pounds of pork, flour, rice, and other comestibles—enough rations to last her large complement four months.

Wildes might have tarried at Littleton Island, as would be suggested, long enough "to cache a portion of his surplus provisions and stores to welcome the arrival of Lieutenant Greely and party on that inhospitable shore." But no. Wildes decided that his immediate duty was to go after the relief party's boats and try to reach them before they were exposed to the hazards of Melville Bay. He believed he might overtake them in the neighborhood of the Cary Islands, in which case there would be an additional three dozen mouths to feed. The *Yantic* herself would have to hurry south to avoid being trapped in Melville Bay ice, for Wildes "knew we would [then] be helpless and our imprisonment of indefinite duration."

The Greely party would have to fend for itself. Wildes had no fear for their safety—they were living in a region "reported well stocked with game." And during the course of a retreat, not only would they find caches on the Cape Sabine side of Smith Sound but, should they cross to Littleton Island, they would discover that the waters between the island and the shore "abound in walrus," while on the mainland "reindeer are plentiful." Frank Wildes's assumptions didn't conform with the impression Garlington would purport to have had concerning game in the region. In fact, all Greely's people could be sure to find on Littleton Island was the small cache left by Beebe in 1882, enough to last ten days.

But the next cache southward, although more than 200 miles distant, contained substantial provisions for twenty men. Greely would know of it, having landed there on his way north. And hadn't Elisha Kane, during prolonged and frequent forays above the Arctic Circle, coped and survived, likewise the cavalry lieutenant Frederick Schwatka while seeking relics of the lost Franklin party? The Greely people, Wildes told himself, "would have to live Eskimo fashion, but Kane and Lieutenant Schwatka did that." So in the first week of August, as the Greely party at Fort Conger poised to begin its own journey south, Commander Frank Wildes took his *Yantic* from Littleton Island, leaving neither supplies nor a message. And he, too, shaped course for the south.

# III

# THE RETREAT

# 15

# MUTINOUS RETREAT

UNAWARE OF EVENTS in far-off Washington and their consequences in the lower Arctic, the men at Fort Conger had again looked out for a relief ship. Greely's eagerness was as intense as anybody's, but in deference to his command position, he kept his emotions hidden. He anticipated letters from Henrietta and dispatched his own proud news of Farthest North. Greely decided that some members of his party ought to go back on the ship. Greely had his private choices. Sergeant Cross, for one. Drunk from stolen spirit lamp fuel, he fell from the launch and might have drowned had not Brainard hauled him out of the freezing water. Greely would have welcomed a replacement for Cross. But as things stood, he could not be sent home; he was indispensable, "a skilled mechanic," wrote Greely, "from whom I had expected better things."

The commander looked forward to getting rid of Lieutenant Kislingbury. His status, with the expedition but not of it, was a perpetual embarrassment to both officers. As for Kislingbury, he fed on the prospect of escape from the prolonged mortification of being less than a supernumerary "on temporary station," in Greely's cold words. And the lieutenant yearned to see his sons. So hopes had remained high as the months advanced. They dwindled when August arrived with still no sign of a ship. Gales had swept enough floes from the bay to enable Greely to set off in the steam launch and check ice conditions farther south. He landed beyond Cape Baird and, from a vantage point, could see much of Kennedy Channel. It was ice free. Conditions appeared perfect for a visiting steamer. None appeared.

Greely had set 8 August as a deadline. Should no relief ship arrive by then, he decided, "this station will be abandoned and a retreat southward by boats to Littleton Island will be attempted." The stipulated departure date in Greely's instructions was I September. Sensing a dangerous decline in the mood of his men, he was anxious for an earlier getaway. His orders alerting the party had not been received with uniformly good grace. When he personally notified his former executive officer, Kislingbury "gave no notice, turned his back again, and left the room. I should have reprimanded him," Greely wrote, "but do not wish to do anything which would cause anyone bitterness."

Greely should not have allowed the other's apparent rudeness to bother him. It was hardly the first churlish display on Kislingbury's part, and Greely could guess how soundly rooted the lieutenant's feelings must be. To prove himself of use to the expedition while officially cut out of it, Kislingbury had hunted game—he was an excellent marksman—and had aided Sergeant Israel in astronomical observation. He had ventured ideas of his own to the commander, sometimes with pathetic earnestness. Greely ignored or belittled them, fueling that very resentment that he claimed, in his journal, he was anxious to avoid.

But Greely now had other things to think about. Resigned to the second nonappearance of a relief ship in Lady Franklin Bay, he expected at least to meet it somewhere along the retreat down the Ellesmere coastline. He believed that supplies en route would not present a problem. He had already established a depot at Cape Baird, on the other side of Archer Fjord, within view of the station. "That point being well supplied, we would be able to leave there fully rationed and equipped," he thought. Farther south, Greely could count on more ration caches and cairns, those he had deposited along the Ellesmere shore while coming north on the *Proteus*. So the retreat would not be slowed by boats overloaded with supplies. All would go well, provided, in Brainard's words, "nothing upset the scheme [Greely] had meticulously worked out for an independent retreat southwards."

In his original directions, the commander had set a condition that should the relief vessel fail to get through Kennedy Channel, it must not only deposit supplies on the Ellesmere coast as far north as possible but, on the Greenland side, leave a manned winter station in place on Littleton Island. So even if his retreating party remained confined to the Ellesmere side, supplies were expected to be borne from Littleton Island, just twenty-three miles across Smith Sound, to the lonely headland known as Cape Sabine.

The party stepped up its preparations for retreat. "Most men," Greely was pleased to note, "turned in their private diaries, which, with forty-eight photographic negatives, were carefully packed in a stout watertight box." Dr. Pavy made up his own shipment with the help of Private Henry Biederbick, a young pharmacist in his native Germany who was the expedition's hospital steward. Volumes of records were stuffed into three tin boxes, including original and letterpress copies of magnetical and meteorological papers. This quantity weighed more than fifty pounds. The pendulum was boxed twice, total weight exceeding 100 pounds. The precious chronometers, thermometers, and other instruments were carefully crated. The party would take four rifles, 1,000 rounds of cartridges, and two shotguns, with sufficient ammunition. The enlisted men each would be allowed to carry eight pounds of personal baggage, the officers sixteen. In addition, Greely took his dress uniform with epaulets, sword, and scabbard as, he told Lockwood, an "emblem of authority." He also carried, at Lockwood's request, that lieutenant's favorite revolver. Lockwood owned two, and wore the other constantly.

Essential to a safe retreat was sufficient sturdy footwear. That for the spring sledging had consisted of only eleven pairs of boots and six pairs of moccasins. "A poor showing," Brainard had written, "for 25 men with several months of field work ahead." Private Julius Frederick, a native German of short stature who had fought Sioux braves on the American plains, had to "do his best as shoemaker." Outwardly, Sergeant Brainard continued to perform as a dutiful, respectful, and highly competent noncommissioned officer. Only in his private journal would the twenty-six-year-old noncom vent his true feelings.

Words written by certain others might have been expected. For instance, when Greely criticized Sergeant Jewell's proficiency as an observer in front of the men, Dr. Pavy wrote that the commander "killed enthusiasm as Macbeth killed sleep." And when loading of the boat was under way, Sergeant Cross, in charge of the steam launch, took a decidedly jaundiced view: "There is not a ghost of a chance of getting out. We have got enough stuff to load six boats and not a mouthful of food. All our food is at Cape Baird. We have got a load of trash, etc. Everything is piled up." The commanding officer had "characteristically dithered." But David Brainard's vituperative jottings in a notebook he took pains to conceal would have read strangely indeed. Once, he had heard the commander express scorn for Army deserters. Brainard wrote, "This is not the first time that we have been compelled to listen to his unwelcome prejudicial views. This man (I cannot call him a gentleman) comes among us like a serpent in Eden and creates eternal hatred towards himself."

Not until 9 August was there any chance of crossing Archer Fjord from Dutch Island. Greely formally ordered the station abandoned. The party had spent 721 days at Fort Conger, 268 marked by a total absence of sun. Two hundred and sixty-two days were devoted to sledge travel, aggregating a distance exceeding 3,000 miles. The expedition had attained an unequaled latitude in the north, charted a hundred miles of Greenland coastline, and had penetrated Ellesmere Island deeper than any previous exploration. "The program of international observations had been carried out as fully as instruments and circumstances would permit," Greely recorded, "and during the two years there had, on average, been made and recorded daily fully five hundred observations."

Now it was ended. Greely sent word to Dutch Island, where a portion of his crew stood by the launch, to start a fire under its boilers. Five thousand pounds of coal had been bagged and stacked there for the retreat. Brainard described the scene at departure time: "Dishes, cutlery, were left unwashed on the table, the beds as we had crawled out of them this morning." He had then nailed the door shut.

The expedition's dogs would be left behind. Five of the eldest had been killed much earlier because they consumed too much food. A younger white dog had produced a litter of pups. When it was time to leave, the canine complement at Fort Conger consisted of twenty-one dogs and two puppies. They would be needed in the event of a return to the station. So ten barrels of seafood were opened, six barrels of pork, and a barrel of hard bread, enough to keep the animals alive an estimated couple of months. Material abandoned as unnecessary to the retreat included sealskin coats, ten musical instruments, boxes of botanical specimens, stuffed birds, "fine collections of fossils" and other natural history sets, neatly assembled and labeled since Pavy's replacement as the expedition's naturalist. Neither was room found for the lichens picked and canned by Lieutenant Kislingbury. Had a ship arrived, Greely would bitterly recall, all of this "could have been placed on board in short order."

Brainard and Francis Long were last to leave. At half past two in the afternoon, Greely, on Dutch Island awaiting a favorable opening in the ice, signaled the sergeants to join him. They quickly did so, and except for a small pack of barking voracious dogs, Fort Conger stood silent and deserted.

Greely knew that even with wholly loyal and respectful subordinates, he would have had his work cut out for him. The journey to Smith Sound from Robeson Channel entailed 250 miles of southwesterly voyaging in a season of unpredictable weather and ice conditions. How long it would take was beyond reliable calculation. Thus although his party could expect to collect about sixty days' provision from depots along the way, victualing could still become a touch-and-go situation. Repeatedly, the lives of twenty-five men, his own included, would depend on the accuracy of his judgment. Success at each exigency would hinge on his party's full cooperation. He thought he had long identified the slackers and malcontents, and could have argued silently that some were useless freight, of less value along the retreat than the load of scientific instruments and records he was determined to take home. What Greely could have no foreknowledge of was the contempt with which his leadership would be regarded not only by Dr. Pavy, Lieutenant Kislingbury, and an uncharitable handful of the enlisted men, but also by three or four of the eight sergeants and two corporals whose fealty he hoped could be taken for granted.

"Everything is piled up on the beach from the station to Dutch Island," recorded Sergeant Cross. "None of the men know what to do, what boat to go in. Things look more like a mob than anything else." But with Cross in control of the steam launch *Lady Greely*, the party started off in an organized fashion at three o'clock, the launch towing the whaleboat, the English jolly boat *Valorous*, the iceboat Lieutenant Beaumont of the Royal Navy had left at Thank God Harbor, and a small Eskimo dinghy laden with reserve supplies. At this point, the expedition's most valuable member was Sergeant William Cross, who knew more about steam-craft engines than any of his comrades. The launch he controlled was strongly built, oak-framed and planked with cedar, thirty feet long, and fitted with three keels for use as runners should her ten tons, not counting cargo, have to be dragged over ice. No sledge could bear that weight. Canvas roofed the cockpit, Cross's post of duty. Cross had already proven himself likely to cause Greely trouble, owing to his love of liquor. At the same time, Cross knew of his importance to the party, a confidence that compounded scorn for his superiors, Greely above all, which would fill page after page of the engineer's private journal.

The first delay occurred soon enough, when, shortly after midnight, ice nipped the launch. The craft came near to capsizing, water sloshed over the rail, and, in Cross's words, "it was fun to see them skedaddle out of her." His caustic reference was to the alacrity with which, understandably, the officers leaped from the launch to make sure that the towed boats would not be crushed. As it was, the nip had carried away the whaleboat's rudder. The party was among floes along the shore of Archer Fjord. "Here we camp without tents or food," Cross grumbled. Some picnic, he thought, naturally blaming the officers—Lieutenant Kislingbury excepted. "Our two worthies" were less adept "than a twelve-year-old boy," he wrote. Greely was a sight to behold, "in government boots, a pair of sealskin pants to within two inches of the boot tops, a heavy white shirt, a revolver outside of all and only half in its holster."

The officers were among six men occupying the launch. The others crowded the towed boats. Sleeping bags spread over oars laid lengthwise provided shelter, but there were bags enough for only half the expedition to occupy. The rest were at Cape Baird. When the men on the first ice watch were relieved, they crawled gratefully into bags just vacated by the new ice watchers. Snow fell heavily. Sergeant Brainard noted, "Our start does not appear auspicious."

GREELY'S PARTY HAD no sooner gotten away again at eight on the morning of 10 August when, to the men's astonishment, the commander called a halt. He sent Lieutenant Lockwood and Sergeant Connell to the floe near which they had just camped to see if open water existed all the way across the fjord. Lieutenant Kislingbury thought this unnecessary, that "the condition of the lead was plainly visible." Sergeant Cross heard Greely declare that he had not been in his sleeping bag all night. "No," wrote the engineer, "but he stretched himself out in the fire-room of the steam launch and discommoded my fireman [Private Linn]." A clear lead having been reported, Greely took to his bag, from which, noted Kislingbury, "he issued directions to everybody at once, and off we started again." But the sea had risen before anybody managed to close the stern hatch, and for hours Sergeant Cross was up to his knees in water. Even so, left to himself at the launch controls, Cross felt very much in charge. "Thanks to the old man turning in and Linn at the helm, we had a good run of it to our camp at Baird," he noted.

Here the supplies cached earlier were brought aboard the boats, and a note was left in a cairn. Greely ordered another halt until the wind died down. Kislingbury, in the launch with its crew and the commander, said he thought that once the wind fell, the ice would be back down the channel. Greely said nothing to this observation and snapped at the men. "He gets very excited," wrote Sergeant Brainard, "and loses control over his tongue. Never at any time does he show the dignity due his rank."

Brainard made no sympathetic allowances for his leader's dilemma. Adolphus Greely was groping his way through a crisis wholly alien to him. He had successfully commanded men on Western prairies of the United States. He had so far managed, at times precariously, to maintain discipline in an Arctic environment. But what those classes of duty had in common was their stationary nature. Now he had to lead a five-boat party hundreds of miles by water and over ice, painfully aware of the men's knowledge that he could not guarantee the expedition's reaching safety any more than they could. His capacity for command would be tested as never before.

The expedition had left Lady Franklin Bay with forty days' rations. Greely calculated that caches still ahead would provide another twenty, more than enough to last as far as Cape Hawks on the western shore of Kane Basin. But could they reach that point? All five craft shipped heavy seas, cakes of ice riding the wave crests. Sergeant Cross silently cursed at his waterlogged post and ridiculed the commander: "He is on the bow giving directions how to steer . . . ran the boat in circles, wasting coal. After fooling around for two hours looking for Carl Ritter Bay, he gave it up at 8 P.M. and turned in. Most of us knew we had passed it in the fog." On their convoluted course, they had indeed brushed by Carl Ritter Bay, but "Old Stubbornness" had insisted otherwise.

The launch took its little entourage into another blind lead. As ice bore down on them, Greely "gave orders to back hard," wrote Cross. "The painter [towline] of one of the boats got foul of the launch's screw and we came near to losing the launch. The C.O. lost his head and began abusing me again."

Lieutenant Kislingbury, excluded from authority, was among those alarmed by the ill-concealed uncertainty of their commanding officer at crucial moments. Low ranking members of the party had to seize the initiative with shouts of "Axes, let's do something!" Kislingbury, in the launch with Greely, had suggested following a route he presumed relatively safe along the coastline to reach Carl Ritter Bay. Greely pointedly ignored the advice. "That we saved several miles and touched only one piece of ice" confirmed his presumption that habitually disregarding the comments of his former second in command was not only militarily proper, given Kislingbury's official removal from the expedition, but demonstrably in its best interests.

Thus were things going when the party touched land above Carl Ritter Bay. Greely had the boats unloaded, then managed to get two hours' sleep in his bag before awaking to find that the steam launch, tied up at a grounded floe, was also embedded in mud, "having been allowed," wrote an exasperated commander, "to touch on a falling tide." Without pausing for breakfast, he set the party working to free her. The task took only half an hour, the men working frantically to lighten the launch, reloading when it was freed. Sergeant Cross stumbled from under the canvas launch cover, clearly drunk. He had been at the fuel alcohol while the others slept. In a fury, Greely blamed him for the grounding, which could have cost the party still more vital time had the craft not been freed. "With the ebbing tide we would have been detained nine hours," he recorded.

Sergeant Cross had a different version. After discovering the launch aground, "we were getting her off nicely, I was blowing the surplus water out of the boiler to lighten her. Our illustrious C.O. heard the noise and turned out." Under the sergeant's directions, the men were pulling the launch higher when someone told Greely that there was plenty of water under the bow. "The C.O. answered, 'I don't care.' After he harassed the men for half an hour and had her stern embedded in the bottom, he cried out for me to come forward. My duties were required in the engine room. I heard him raging. . . ."

Rage Greely did, fuming at Cross to man the bow and keep the launch's head straight. Two minutes' delayed response snapped the commander's self-control. "With profane language I ordered him out and threatened to shoot him if he refused"—words soberly admitted to in Greely's own journal. The diaries of other men gave a more frightening picture. Corporal Joseph Elison heard the commander shout, "God damn your soul! Come out where I can see you when I want you." Cross had begun to argue, until Greely all but screamed, "Shut up, or I'll put a bullet through you!" Cross tossed back, "Do as you please."

Shaking with anger, there was little more Greely could do. He had all the rum transferred from the launch to another boat and the alcohol on it limited to that needed for cooking. Greely wrote, "It is difficult to know what to do with such a man who thus tampers with the safety of the Arctic party." Cross took "malicious pleasure in doing anything but what he was ordered to." The engineer's addiction to liquor was cause enough for serious disciplinary action. Greely knew he would have been justified in breaking him from sergeant to private, as he had already done to David Linn for a relatively minor offense. But he had to overlook Cross's misdeeds, the price paid for his services in the launch's engine compartment. Threats and sharp reprimands were about all Greely could employ, for the present, to control his intractable sergeant. "I can do nothing more than shoot him, which I would not do except for direct disobedience of orders in an emergency."

They stopped at Carl Ritter Bay long enough to load three barrels of food, hard bread and pemmican, left by the expedition two years before on the passage north. Greely could now rely upon fifty days' total rations, with 5,500 pounds of coal. The flotilla set off again and made a fine run for six hours. Around midday, with heavy ice ahead, they reached the southern shore of Carl Ritter Bay and made fast to foot ice. All but Greely and the watch took to their bags. Greely was unable to sleep. "By 2 P.M. the ice was closing in on us. I stationed Whisler on the hill with orders to advise me the moment he saw any sign of the pack loosen," Greely wrote. Private William Whisler reported a lead in sight, but soon more ice had gathered. Greely ordered the boats to move. Amid the ice floes, they struggled out of the bay. "During this run," Greely noted, "Cross was repeatedly guilty of mutinous language. He seemed to make everything go wrong with the engine. All I could do was reprimand him severely."

That afternoon, a massive berg blocked progress down Kennedy Channel. It split, leaving a narrow passage no more than twelve feet wide and more than a hundred yards long. The opaque ice walls towered to more than fifty feet above, permitting only a sliver of visible sky. To the awed men in the roped line of boats, it was as if they glided slowly through a deathly cold, blue-green tunnel. They emerged into open choppy seas, but after a good three hours' run, ice gathered again, and so did discontent among the men. "Our boats," wrote Sergeant Brainard, "are gradually being imprisoned by the ice-cakes coming together." The party now averaged only two miles a day, using coal "unnecessarily," in Sergeant Hampden Gardiner's opinion, "and [we are] in a worse position than before."

The following day they lay alongside the ice foot, keeping an anxious eye on conditions in the channel. Twice, Lieutenant Kislingbury plodded ashore—"I try to help whenever I can"—climbing a hill to survey the ice, then waiting for low tide before he could cross the broken floes and rejoin his companions. Each time he reported no change, no promising water breaks in the vast gray-white expanse. And each time his information, delivered personally to the commander, was received with barely a nod of the head. Kislingbury expected no more. Indeed, he had come to derive some slight solace from his peculiar circumstance as an officer *sans* authority—with the expedition yet not of it. That state of separation, that freedom from responsibility, enabled him to view and perhaps more accurately assess things from a detached vantage point. He might thus have become a source of reliable counsel, leading even to restoration of his position as second in command. But Greely solicited no advice from him and spurned any offered.

The ironies were not lost on Fred Kislingbury. Now and then a tone of cheerful resignation lightened his journal entries. Yet in the freezing blackness of his sleeping bag, only with anguish could he contemplate a safe return to civilization, imagine the bewilderment on the faces of his loved ones, the four motherless sons in particular, as he strove to explain why he had been summarily cut off from the expedition before it truly had begun. And it said something for his innate amiability that after describing the commander's warm berth on the launch, "alongside the boiler, covered by canvas and comfortable," and contrasting this with the plight of those in the open boats, shivering in sleeping bags caked with frozen slush, Kislingbury was still able to add, "But why complain, as we are all jolly and good-natured in spite of everything." The lieutenant particularly admired Sergeant George Rice, whose duty was to keep a sharp lookout in all weathers for suitable leads in the ice. His perch was a slippery one on the stern of the English boat *Valorous*. Kislingbury had extra footgear and drawers, which he let Rice wear. "I would willingly strip myself and crawl into my sleeping bag than have him do so because he is without doubt the most indispensable man we have."

While most of the party slept in boats, as many as could moved ashore when opportunity arose. Some slumbered on hard ice, as Lieutenant Lockwood was apt to do, bedding down on a small berg, "laying my sleeping bag on top of the spare sheepskin one and thus slept comfortably." All the same, Lockwood predicted "this young ice is going to be a serious obstacle." On the night of 14 August, Greely had noted it steadily thicken. "Greatly uneasy," he wrote, "I slept little." The next morning the ice moved rapidly south before a northerly gale. Lanes opened invitingly, only to close quickly. Sergeant Cross, who usually remained on the launch, thrust his head from under the canvas roof of his combined engine space and bunk. He saw the commander cocooned in his sleeping bag on an ice-fringed strip of beach, and the bag appeared agitated, looked "as if erupting." Greely was flexing his limbs, as Cross well knew, to maintain blood flow, but so lacking in respect was the sergeant for his chief that he professed to find this comical.

Worry, no less than physical effort to keep his feet warm, accounted for Greely's sleepless nights. He had been under a growing compulsion to break beyond the ice-locked shore into the channel. The wind still was pushing the ice fast southward, and no good leads were in sight, but against the likelihood of the launch getting permanently frozen in if they stayed where they were, Greely preferred the risks of mid-channel. If only they could get the launch over to one of several grounded bergs about a mile offshore, the boats following and hauled across floes when not under oars, they would be in a more promising position—further navigation would, of course, still have to await the right conditions. Such was the commander's reasoning, and virtually nobody shared it. Lieutenant Lockwood offered no alternative, but then he seldom did, having few original ideas of his own bearing on general strategy. Kislingbury's views were not sought, his private journal alone revealing his thoughts: "Confound the man, cannot he keep still and wait for the ice to move? He has no idea of the seriousness of running into the pack, in fact seems to want to do so." If Greely's purpose was to escape entrapment, why leave a sheltered ice foot for bergs or large floes about which the young ice steadily coalesced? But there was nothing Kislingbury could say because he had "no particular post or duty." The once second in command had not been given charge of even one of the boats.

Greely possessed tenacity and resolve in great measure. But they were combined with an irascibility born of indecision—all in all, an ominous mix.

Noting the doubtful expressions of his noncoms, not to mention the sullen-ness of the lower ranks, when he announced his intentions only stiffened his determination. "We started out at nine," wrote Lockwood, "employed all hands and managed to get the launch out with a great deal of labor." While getting her out, Cross flung insolent remarks from the engine room. Twice Greely had to castigate him. "Everything went wrong at the time steam was wanted," he complained. "Several orders to 'go ahead' received no attention." The reason was soon clear: Sergeant Brainard ducked into the engine room and emerged to report the engineer drunk again.

Greely despaired, for it was "utterly impossible to watch the alcohol cans every minute." But this time something had to be done. He yelled at Cross to get off the launch and into the whaleboat under Sergeant Rice. Private Julius "Shorty" Frederick, who had assisted Cross as fireman, was assigned control of the engine. By the middle of the afternoon, following much effort, the launch stood in the lee of a grounded berg 300 yards offshore, secured to it by ice anchors. But how safely? Young ice steadily congealed all around as Lieutenant Lockwood and a team brought the boats up from the ice foot. They had to be unloaded and reloaded three times, cargo passed from floe to floe. Before this exhausting task was completed, the floes sandwiching the launch had cemented together. "We three boats are cut off from the launch," wrote Kislingbury, who had accompanied Lockwood. And while Greely scribbled futilely that "we are where I can get out readily unless the ice changes," Kislingbury noted that to leave the sheltered ice foot now was "the most insane movement of all."

Kislingbury never felt more isolated. Lieutenant Lockwood was his replacement as second in command, thus by definition a confidant of Greely's and not a fellow officer with whom he, Kislingbury, could share plans and con-cerns. Neither could he converse in any friendly fashion with the men. Since Greely's stern injunction back at Fort Conger, effectively placing the men's quarters off limits to him, he had been careful to avoid anything resembling indiscreet fraternization with the lower ranks. Yet while he could not consider himself even a subordinate within the expedition, the lieutenant had several sympathetic friends among the men. The same could hardly be said of the com-mander.

Greely had persuaded himself that had he abandoned the *Lady Greely* ear-lier and placed the boats and supplies on the drifting ice, floating them southward, the party would by this time have reached south of Cape Lawrence. Now the idea appealed to him all the more. When he proposed it to his people, their reaction was acute dismay. Not that they were all that surprised. They had guessed for some time what he had in mind. Private Jacob Bender thought that "taking to the floes" would be "simple suicide." Sergeant Brainard scribbled in his notebook that ever since leaving Fort Conger, Greely had "kept the men in a state of great anxiety owing to his desire to abandon the launch and put the boats on the floe and drift south to Littleton Island."

Greely's top sergeant thought such an act would be little short of lunacy. Everybody except Greely knew the perils of such a course. Brainard wrote that rather than pursue this "insanity, a cache of provisions should be made here and the whole party retreat to Fort Conger." They would have thirty days there to secure game and coal before winter set in. "Next spring our excellent line of retreat may be conducted down to Littleton Island, with sledges and the provisions cached here used to advantage." Besides, what if the relief ship had not pushed through the Melville Bay pack to that island? "What would we shivering wretches do on arrival at the beginning of winter with nothing to subsist on?" Floating willy-nilly south in hopes of touching Littleton Island was, Brainard repeated in his notebook, "insanity, and if my opinion is ever asked I shall tell what I think."

During the night of the fifteenth, Greely slept fitfully in the launch. Lockwood, as was his custom, fought insomnia in a sleeping bag on an ice floe. Dr. Pavy and Sergeant Rice huddled some yards off in the whaleboat with Sergeant Brainard. And here, Pavy, keeping his voice low, submitted a grave proposal. If the commander made the attempt to abandon the launch and drift on floes, he would pronounce him of unsound mind, therefore incapable of further leadership. It would not be difficult, Pavy emphasized. Lieutenant Greely's "frequent outbursts of passion evinced insanity." The doctor declared his ability to prove the legitimacy of such action before any court of inquiry. Lieutenant Kislingbury would replace Greely as commander and lead the expedition back to Fort Conger. Come next spring, they would retreat along the Ellesmere coast to meet the relief vessel at Littleton Island, and if ice prevented a crossing, they would wait at Cape Sabine. Should Lieutenant Lockwood refuse to acknowledge Kislingbury's authority or otherwise oppose the idea, he would be placed under arrest. Sergeant Rice sided with the plan and turned to Brainard, urging his agreement because, Brainard wrote, "the men would all go with me and it was the only means of saving the party." The solemn step would be taken if Greely determined to go through with his foolhardy idea.

Nothing in Brainard's notes at the time reveals his reaction to Pavy's proposal. But the withering tone of his other diary entries indicates assent. As senior noncommissioned officer, he was duty bound to have reported the conversation to Greely. "But I knew his obstinate nature," Brainard wrote, "and feared he would immediately put into execution the plan we all wished to prevent, that of drifting helplessly in the polar pack."

Neither was Lockwood told anything of a contemplated mutiny. He had no inkling of it, judging from his words, which, in any case, were generally few and noncommittal. The *Valorous*, the other English boat, and the whaleboat now lay penned together in a little harbor formed by three icebergs. With Greely in the launch and Lockwood on his floe, five men occupied the whaleboat, six in each of the others. Kislingbury wrote, "The sleeping bags are arranged on the masts and sides somehow and we manage to make out." But the expedition was immobilized. Brainard volunteered to strike across the floes and overland to Cape Lawrence and check on ice conditions. Greely said no, opposing any separation of the party. But so long as the air stayed motionless, they would remain iced in. Wrote Lockwood, "Oh, for a southwest wind." And Sergeant Gardiner, concerned over Greely's seeming lack of forethought—"the pemmican, our most valuable food, is the first thing he issues"—added, "We have 38 days' rations in all."

They had been locked in for five days. On 18 August, after a breakfast of corned beef and beans in a snowstorm, Greely thought he saw an opening in the pack wide enough for his flotilla. Kislingbury felt nothing could be done pending a favorable wind, "and every man in the expedition sees this but the commander." Greely ordered the attempt made anyway. Two hours of grueling work maneuvering the boats among the floes left the party farther north than where it had started, with an ax lost and the men discouraged. All told, they were more than 100 miles from Fort Conger, but had perforce followed a tortuous course of twice that distance. They still were some 100 miles from Littleton Island and Cape Sabine. Greely sensed his party's despondency, and Sergeant Rice, "who has excellent judgment, said on my asking him that he thought the route impracticable. But while eating supper I decided to get out of the ice, launch or no launch, in twelve hours."

He sent Brainard and Linn across the floes in search of a suitable lead.

They returned having seen none. Undeterred, Greely ordered movement. After an hour, the boats managed to reunite with the launch, but it took another ninety minutes to get the launch to open water. Not until midnight did the *Lady Greely* start off with the smaller craft in tow. "We are out in the open boats," wrote Cross, "snow-filled clothes and sleeping bags wet while C.O. housed in alongside the launch boiler toasting his chin."

Greely accidentally fell overboard. His fellow lieutenants Kislingbury and Lockwood hauled him out of the frigid water. "I hope it will cool him off for a few days," wrote Cross. "Whisler says he should have drowned. The way things look, if C.O. has his way, we will wind up like Franklin." The deposed engineer thought Pavy and Kislingbury of most value "to get the party out of the scrape our ignorant commander has got us into."

Adolphus Greely could never have divined how lonely and unloved he had become. Cross's derisive jottings would not have surprised him, nor Lieutenant Kislingbury's "Confound the man, why can't he be sensible and do things right?" The commander might only have shrugged at Corporal Joseph Elison's characterization of him as "a fraud or humbug . . . the lunatic gets us into one scrape after another." His informal clerk, Private Schneider, termed him "a miserable fool." Greely might have foreseen that respect for him as commander, never high, would sink with every freezing and back-breaking mile of the retreat. But he could never have suspected (nor would he ever know) what the one enlisted soldier he felt he could trust and rely upon, even admired, thought of him at this stage. Sergeant Brainard wrote in the second half of August, "All that ignorance, stupidity, and an egotistical mind without judgment can do in the injury of our cause is being done. Why will the United States government persist in sending a fool in command of Arctic expeditions?"

# 16

# GARLINGTON AND WILDES

AFTER LEAVING LITTLETON Island on 3 August, one week before the Greely party left Fort Conger, the *Yantic* had put into Pandora Harbor, along the eastern shores of Smith Sound. Here, Commander Wildes found Garlington's and Pike's records, to the effect that their boats were keeping as close inshore as possible and aiming for the Cary Islands, then Cape York, at either place where Garlington hoped to meet the *Yantic* or the Swedish ship *Sofia*. Encouraged by these messages as to the propriety of his decision to forgo the Greely expedition in favor of the shipwrecked party, but now aware that he must have passed those boats on his way up, Wildes resumed his southward passage in pursuit.

What had developed would be variously described as a cat-and-mouse chase, a game of tag in icebound waters, an exercise in cross-purposes, and sad errors. It could have been lamented equally as a round of misjudgments and mistimings. If charted on a map of Kennedy Channel, Kane Basin, Smith

Sound, and upper Baffin Bay, the tracks of all relief vessels employed so far, Beebe's *Neptune* and the late *Proteus* included, would have presented a geometrical nightmare. From Pandora Harbor, the *Yantic* ran down close inshore, a seaman in the crow's nest on lookout for cairns, boats, or men. Late on 4 August, the ship stood seven miles off Cape Parry and touched at Northumberland Island. Here some of the *Yantic's* people found boot tracks, empty cans, scraps of clothing—the remains of the camp Garlington had occupied less than forty-eight hours earlier.

The boat parties were right then making a brief halt at Saunders Island, just twenty miles south of the *Yantic,* which could have reached them in four hours' steaming. But ice had thickened. The *Yantic* remained at her anchorage for three days, Wildes having decided to "await the moving offshore of the ice or a loosening up of the pack." Perhaps the Garlington-Pike flotilla had called at Cary Islands and left a record, or might be even now at that prearranged "post office." Thus figured Wildes as he took the *Yantic* across to the islands in the teeth of a gale. This call there was his second within a week. With the *Yantic* in close, he fired a gun. It drew no response, nor was any new message found on land. A baffled Wildes ordered full steam ahead for Cape York, the final rendezvous as dictated by his and Garlington's agreement at St. John's. Along the way, he passed Saunders Island, where, had he landed, he would have found the record left by Lieutenant Garlington—again, only two or three days before.

The Garlington-Pike parties were blocked in by ice along the Greenland shore about fourteen miles above Cape York. On 9 August, fierce winds blew the floes away from in front of the camp and the boats were launched immediately, Colwell's party strengthened by the addition of an engineer and two firemen from Pike's crew. All hands were weary after days of seemingly endless rowing between floes or man-hauling boats across them until drag ropes skinned freezing fingers. The Americans had also to contend with simmering threats of violence from the Newfoundlanders. Coming down the coast, a sergeant had told Lieutenant Colwell that some of Pike's men were overheard muttering plans to steal the relief party's whaleboats, superior craft to that of the *Proteus.* Many were in a dangerous mood. Once when their captain called upon them to haul boats up, all but his son and the ship's firemen ignored him.

The boat parties reached Cape York early on the tenth. Etah natives confirmed that no vessel had been seen, and they knew nothing of the steamer *Sofia.* Garlington at once drew a wrong conclusion. He had never felt sure that the *Yantic* would risk the crossing of Melville Bay. "If the *Sofia* had not been able to get through the Melville pack, I thought the *Yantic* certainly had not." The *Yantic* most certainly had, and gone on to Littleton Island, and turned back in the Garlington-Pike party's wake. She was approaching Cape York even as the shipwrecked soldiers and seafarers beached their boats at that headland, the agreed-upon final point of communication. A reunion at last seemed inevitable.

Then, not for the first time, Frank Wildes changed his mind. On the way up eight days before, he had passed Cape York without stopping. Now he would do so again. The *Yantic*'s fuel was running low, and a southerly gale had sprung up. That his ship had safely crossed Melville Bay once with an over-loaded crew was no guarantee, thought Frank Wildes, of a southbound encore. An ensign on the *Yantic*, one of three voluntary naturalists, observed that by this time Wildes felt his responsibilities had become greater than were appropriate. He had not found the boat parties; he was hopeful for their safety but his purpose now was to hasten south for help. "It was expected," recorded the ensign, "that on getting in cable communication with the [Navy] Department, a relief expedition would be quickly organized from the North Atlantic Fleet." Chartering sealers at St. John's would enable a new party to get as far north as Pandora Harbor before meeting heavy ice. "Practically everybody in the steerage expected that the Navy would hustle and start something before winter."

In this light, Wildes's decision to bypass Cape York and hurry on south was understandable. The commander himself would declare that with dwindling fuel, ice forming on all sides, and "the land being unapproachable, the imprudence of remaining in this vicinity became sufficiently obvious and I bore up for Upernavik."

Were it not for poor visibility, the men at Cape York might have seen the *Yantic* beyond the shore ice and joyfully hailed. Instead, that same afternoon, Lieutenant Colwell "sat on a rock in the hillside in a snowstorm, looked at the ice solid far out to sea and thought what a cheerful thing was a birthday anyway." Rain or snow fell for another five days. Garlington now suspected that the *Yantic* had gotten no farther north than Upernavik, had perhaps turned back for Godhavn, thence for home. It was imperative that he catch up with her. The question was how best to do so. He consulted with Colwell, and they settled on a daring plan. Colwell's boat would be lightened as much as possible, and he would attempt a direct crossing of Melville Bay before following the Greenland coast down to Godhavn at Disko Island. Pike and Garlington meanwhile would creep all the way around to Upernavik, as close inshore as ice permitted, stopping at islets en route. Upon arrival at Upernavik, unless the *Yantic* was there, they would wait for whatever came first, a ship or word from Colwell, who by that time, if all went well, would have crossed Melville Bay and reached Godhavn. If necessary, Garlington and Pike would winter at Upernavik. Unless a ship appeared at Godhavn, Colwell's party would do the same there, quartering themselves among Eskimo hamlets.

"Winter the best you can," Garlington told the Navy lieutenant, "taking advantage at the first opportunity to communicate with me." The plan was extremely dangerous to Lieutenant Colwell and his crew, "a somewhat motley collection—three soldiers, two civilians, an Eskimo who did not understand English, and myself." Bad weather at Cape York delayed the departure of both parties until 16 August. Garlington left a message telling of Colwell's intended thrust across Melville Bay to Upernavik, "as probably the *Yantic* is in that vicinity, ice having prevented her progress north." The message told also of his own and Pike's determination. "With God's help we all hope to reach port in safety in good time." The record contained no useful reference to the Greely expedition, nothing that might have informed a visiting ship of that party's certain attempt to make south from Fort Conger. Not that much in the way of guidance could have been said just then—at least not by Lieutenant Garlington.

The approach of winter weighed heavily upon his mind. Greely's known destination, Cape Sabine or Littleton Island, lay more than 200 miles above Cape York. Contact with that party before the season ended was now a hopelessly diminished prospect. Thus ran the Army officer's thinking. But by no means would everybody share his estimate of how much time remained before winter fell. Many were to agree with General Hazen's brusque assessment of that August record which Lieutenant Garlington left at Cape York as nothing but a declared "termination of the relief expedition at least sixty days before [the navigable] season came to a close and [which] gave not the slightest intimation of any further effort to rescue Lieutenant Greely."

It was impossible for Garlington to figure every aspect of his predicament. John Colwell had no time at all for such mental exercise or he would have thought twice before agreeing to so crazy a mission. Once under way, try as he might to keep near the broken edge of the Melville Bay pack, gale-force winds flung the whaleboat repeatedly off course. Seasickness collapsed three of his men; the language barrier limited the Eskimo's assistance. Often Colwell found himself navigating with an effective crew of two.

Winds subsided on the second morning out. Colwell handed over the tiller, made a pot of tea, and warmed canned meat over burning alcohol. After breakfast, the wind veered to southward. Colwell shook out his reef and set the mainsail. Another gale arose, and the whaleboat ran rapidly before booming gusts until, after struggling to take in the mainsail, the lieutenant sought safe shelter among drifting icebergs, to one of which he made fast. This tethering afforded precious little safety. The bergs kept cannoning into one another, breaking asunder each time with a roar and a barrage of ice that pelted the already snow-soaked men. With the boat grapneled to a berg, the bow oarsman had to stand by each time with an ax, ready to cut the painter should the berg disintegrate.

Unaware of the boatloads coming south, one directly braving Melville Bay and three others creeping around the Greenland shore, Commander Wildes on the *Yantic* had arrived at Upernavik. Here, the sense of haste faded. Wildes hauled fires, intent on remaining "as long as prudent" before steaming farther south for the coal mines near Godhavn. He had learned from the Danish governor that the Swedish vessel *Sofia*, in the Arctic for meteorological study, had called at Upernavik two weeks earlier. Wildes felt there was little enough for him to do while lingering there. Some days he sent his men ashore with rifles for target practice. On the seventeenth, he invited the wardroom to a champagne dinner. Icebergs drifting into harbor became a nuisance; all hands were repeatedly called to tow them away.

Wildes chartered a whaleboat and sent it north with an Eskimo crew and fifteen days' supplies for thirty-seven men. It was to go as far as the native settlement at Tasiussaq, some fifty miles up the coast, where arrangements could be made to look out for the retreating shipwrecked parties. Then Wildes prepared for the *Yantic*'s departure. The date was 22 August. Ten days had elapsed since his arrival at Upernavik. In most elaborate terms, he would explain his reasoning: "The short summer of this high latitude being at an end, the weather having changed, vegetation having become brown and withered, the birds having departed with their young, ice and frost forming each night, the autumn gales being liable to set in at any time, and knowing that the first one of any severity would put the ship on the rocks, [with] great risk increasing daily, I got under way."

At five the next morning, Lieutenant Colwell's "motley crew" in their bat-tered open whaleboat were under sail just eight miles from Upernavik. By leav-ing Garlington at Cape York and crossing Melville Bay, they had accomplished one of the most remarkable feats in the history of Arctic navigation. Now the wind had died. They manned all oars to reach shore, not certain of where they were. The bleak landscape was empty, "not even a dog being visible." They fired shots to attract attention. Colwell had his Eskimo reconnoiter. He returned, gesticulating wildly. They had indeed reached Upernavik. Eagerly, now, the lit-tle party straining at the oars rounded to the settlement, where Colwell was "met at the landing with the information that the *Yantic* had left at nine the previous evening for the south. This was," added Colwell, "a very great disap-pointment to us all."

No time was spent in hand-wringing. Wildes had left a note saying he was bound for the coal mines at Godhavn, where he would remain no later than 15 September, then would take the *Yantic* on to St. John's. "There was nothing for it but to keep on after her," Colwell wrote. Colwell knew he would have to reach Wildes in time to have him come back north for Garlington's and Pike's peo-ple, who, for all anybody knew, were trapped somewhere along the Melville Bay ice foot. "I proposed starting at once in my boat." The ever-helpful Danish authorities at Upernavik insisted that he abandon the weatherbeaten whale-boat and take the governor's own sturdy launch, well provisioned. To the cheers of the settlement's entire population and a farewell gun salute from the gover-nor's small battery, Colwell left at 3:00 P.M. that same day. "The weather was calm, so we pulled all night and all next day." And behind them, at Upernavik, excitement soon stirred anew. The *Proteus* boat parties, having made good progress hugging the coast through lump ice, arrived safely in harbor. Gar-lington was told that he had missed the *Yantic* by two days and Colwell's little crew by just one.

Some forty-eight hours out, Colwell had the company of friendly natives in kayaks. Early on the last day of August, they ran under sail before strong winds to the southeastern point of Disko Island. Colwell sent a man up the hill overlooking Godhavn harbor. To the lieutenant's huge relief, he reported back that the *Yantic* was sighted at anchor. Colwell was soon on board in Commander Wildes's cabin, telling him all. By 6:30 P.M., the *Yantic* was steam-ing out of Godhavn, this time course set north back to Upernavik, the gover-nor's launch in tow. And at Upernavik on 2 September, after some forty days

of peril, hardship, hapless near-misses, and blind maneuvering about the northern waters of Baffin Bay and beyond, all the Americans were reunited—with
the conspicuous absence of the Lady Franklin Bay Expedition.

BY EARLY 19 AUGUST, the retreating party under Greely accomplished
a further ten miles until the tide changed, closing their water lane. They drifted
rearward again. In the evening, to much surprise, Lieutenant Greely ordered
that steam be raised. Once more the boats moved dizzily among the floes, until
forced to halt yet again and anchor to a grounded berg. Kislingbury thought
that if Greely would only wait for a favorable wind, saving precious coal in the
meantime, "we would probably get a paying run." Greely himself conceded that
the ice had not opened up as he had expected, and he, too, lamented the wastage
of coal.

The next morning, the party lay in Rawlings Bay, close to shore. Forced
repeatedly to zigzag or backtrack, they still were scarcely more than 100 miles
from their starting point. Sergeant Brainard and "Eskimo Fred" Christiansen
set out wearily over ice, then ashore through deep snow, to scale a ridge and
survey Smith Sound. All they saw was ice, unbroken and impenetrable. "With
heavy hearts, we turned back." At 4:00 P.M., the launch grounded. "She lies
alongside a precipice of ice," wrote Lockwood. It took five hours to get her off.
"Because of the moving ice and rise and fall of the tides, it is as difficult to
find a suitable place for the launch as it would be for a large ship."

At Cape Collinson early on the twenty-second, a shore party brought
aboard 240 rations left by Nares's people. Foxes had eaten much of the bread
and gnawed at the bung of a keg of rum, emptying its contents. Private
Schneider heard the commander "grumbling because the English didn't leave
more of a cache." The following morning, Greely ordered another departure.
"No one but a fool would have done so," in Private Bender's opinion. But Greely
was anxious to reach Cape Hawks, where Nares had left another cache and
where there might be a relief vessel. Sergeant Jewell had returned from a survey of his own ashore and reported ice closing in only 500 yards ahead. Still
Greely ordered the move.

Almost at once, he was obliged to scatter the boats. "For a time," he wrote,
"we were jammed against the icefoot by the pack." The boats were all nipped,
wrote Kislingbury, between ponderous floes that were held apart simply by

young ice. "We broke through this slowly, and not a moment too soon, for the boats managed to squeeze through two floes when they came together like a steel trap." Greely had the boats cut adrift from the launch and run up to shore. Ice pressure almost overturned the launch; she "groaned and shrieked, was finally pulled along the ice foot and got up into a nook, where she was made fast. During all the excitement the men behaved splendidly." Kislingbury added, "The whole strait is one moving mass of ice, frightful to look at." Some of the whaleboat's timbers had cracked. All this because of Greely. "If he would take the advice and heed the reasoning of those who understand there would be some encouragement." But as things stood, the party faced ruination. "There is serious dissatisfaction among the men. Poor fellows, they cannot be blamed."

When motion was again possible, the party pushed into Kane Basin. Still keeping to the Ellesmere side, they halted near Cape Wilkes in a small natural harbor. Greely had the English jolly boat chopped for firewood. Badly stove in, it had leaked and had to be dragged. Little had occurred to improve the men's feelings about their commander. Cross lengthened his private scurrility by referring to him as "our shirt-tail navigator," or STN. Private Schneider wondered why "our foolish commander leaves no cairns or records along the coast." Sergeant Brainard feared the expedition would result in "another Franklin disaster." And when they got under way again and Brainard sighted a good lead half a mile wide, Greely wouldn't take it and instead "ran into every little open space he saw. We ran 18 miles when 6 would have done."

Still keeping as close as they dared to shore, the party crossed Scoresby Bay and paused at the foot of one of Ellesmere Island's countless capes. "God help us," prayed Kislingbury, but his journal entry that evening struck an optimistic note. "Another day's run like this will take us to Cape Hawks, where surely we must meet the ship." The wind had sprung up in their favor. "Go to it, dear wind, you have helped us more than any other of the elements and will get us out of this scrape yet."

Of late, only minor disturbances had occurred among the men. Roderick Schneider, who served as duty cook as well as the commander's private secretary, tired of the double duty and asked to be relieved from cooking. Greely told him no, whereupon the private shouted a protest, pitched to his sleeping bag, and sobbed. Greely knew the man's nerves were cracking, and he feared that others must soon show the same signs. Lieutenant Lockwood took over as temporary cook, preparing and issuing bacon. The party and its string of

boats were some twenty miles north of Cape Hawks. Greely sent the dog drivers ashore to hunt game. They returned empty-handed.

The ice field split into a promising lead. The tortuous passage resumed.
The lead proved a blind one, and the boats were soon beset by "ice of the worst
kind," wrote Greely, "nearly all slush with occasional pancakes." He was not
talking of breakfast. Private Bender noted "the old boy looking blue at present." Assuredly, Greely's thoughts were troubled. "I cannot understand why no
ship is sighted. We shall be in an unenviable position if we reach [Cape] Hawks
and find none, the season late, coal gone, future entirely uncertain." He had the
launch grapneled to a floe forty feet wide and the boats strung upon it. The
commander spent all his time on the launch, now, "hugging the boiler," in
Cross's savage words, "whining orders, while we are jumping up and down on
a floe hardly big enough to hold 25 men, much less three boats, provisions,
and gear. We are half-clad, some barefoot."

Even Lieutenant Lockwood, taciturn while usually supporting the commander, described the outlook as "gloomy. Thick sludge all around, no open
water in sight. Steam is kept up all the time, about 80 pounds of coal needed
daily for banking." The chopped-up small boat, the launch's ripped-out lock-
ers, old barrel staves, had provided fuel now nearly all gone. Trapped by sluggish ice, the launch and three boats clustered with it drifted aimlessly. Corporal
Elison noted the fear with which he and his comrades studied the drift. Greely
was not conspicuous among them. "Our noble commander has turned in his
sleeping bag as usual—he gets us from one scrape into another."

At midnight on 23 August, Lieutenant Lockwood had the watch.
Mournfully, he gazed at the ice, which moved only slightly, with its continuous sounds of groaning and grinding. Beneath the launch's turtleback, Greely
slept. The amount of time he spent in his sleeping bag was becoming a scandal, at least among those who had given up on him as a competent leader. Some
were actually timing him, calculating the hours during which he remained
almost totally hidden. On the twenty-fourth, the drift was steadily southward.
Private Julius Frederick shot a seal and got him before he sank. Some of the
men found the blood an invigorating drink. "Our noble STN," wrote the irre-
pressibly caustic Cross, "grabbed the liver and had the blubber put on the
launch to burn in the boiler." This was lunacy, in the former engineer's view,
"for the way things look at present we will have to winter somewhere on the
coast and every pound of blubber will be worth its weight in gold." It was of

little use as fuel, would give but a few minutes' fire, "all the grease will run through the grate bars before burning." It seemed to Cross that whenever anybody did anything without Greely's direct orders, he—the commander—feared he was losing control. "He has once or twice tried to regulate our bowels, but I think I have him there."

While Greely might have been better served had he consulted with his men, he had not lost control over them, nor did he intend to. Late on 25 August, he sensed a weakening in the ice pack's clutch. He ordered the launch into motion and wrote later, "With great difficulty we bored our way through the moving pack." Dense fog and a restrengthening of the ice drove them ashore at Cape Louis Napoleon. Here they were at the threshold of Dobbin Bay, across which lay Cape Hawks. Some thought a ship might be anchored there. After four hours' steaming, sideswiped by tossing floes, the boats had crossed the bay and reached the cape. No vessel appeared. Greely hopefully rigged a tripod on a floe, topped by a fifteen-foot flag. But no ship could have seen it in the fog rolling over the bay, so Private Schneider, in the *Valorous* whaleboat, fashioned a large tin horn, which he blew at two-minute intervals. None of the party could have dreamed that men sent by their government into the Arctic to bring them home were just then assembled no farther north than Upernavik, exchanging tales of failure, uncertain what next to do.

Sergeant George Rice took a companion across the restless pack to nearby Washington Irving Island and scaled its summit. They found provisions left by the English explorers—five boxes of moldering bread, potatoes, pickles, stearin, and a keg of rum. But there was no record of any visitation since the Lady Franklin Bay Expedition itself had called there two years earlier while passing up Kane Basin on the *Proteus*.

Rice brought Greely the dismaying news. Greely wrote, "We are now in a critical situation, not knowing what can be depended on. Since no vessel reached this point in 1882–3, we must all feel uneasy as to the relief party being at Littleton Island." His people had struggled for well more than 300 miles to reach this hoped-for rendezvous in Kane Basin, battling through "constant ice of such size as must be seen to be believed." He forced himself to detect a bright side. After hundreds of narrow escapes, he wrote, "we had reached a secure harbor from which we looked southwest a scant fifty miles to the bluffs of Cape Sabine."

All hoped now for a ship at Littleton Island. At least that place had a coal depot; they had left one on the passage north, enough fuel to carry them southward to Cary Islands "where we could live on the English rations until spring," wrote Greely. But that would be a gamble. "Failing to find stores or a ship at Littleton Island, our position would be deplorable in the extreme." They still were confined to the Ellesmere coast, which meant making a stop facing Littleton Island. Sergeant Rice had also reported that the water southeast was navigable as far as the eye could see. And that was enough for Greely. He decided to abandon his shore-hugging course. He would make a straight short-cut fifty-three-mile dash from Cape Hawks across Hayes Sound and Buchanan Strait to that essential landfall, Cape Sabine.

It proved to be no dash. When only a few hours out, the party shivered in suddenly plummeting temperatures, and new ice slowed the boats. In Sergeant Brainard's view, escape from the pack had now become, to say the least, "a matter for conjecture." He asked Lieutenant Greely to consider reducing food rations so they could be extended. Fearing a depressing effect on the party, Greely said no. He waited for the ice to break up. Once more, his men groused. Sergeant Cross, as usual, found comfort in taunts. Yet, he scribbled, it was not "just animosity against our commander" that made him write in this vein. "If I should live to get out of this mess he has put us in, I will face the world and can bring twenty others to prove more than I have written here."

Surrounded by a vast wasteland of ice and snow broken on the west by rocky cliffs and snowclad mountains, all four boats were firmly frozen in and thickly coated with frost. In the launch, Lockwood crouched beside the engine, while Greely and others in their bags filled the stern sheets. Private Jacob Bender wrote, "We have about 40 days' rations and don't know if we can get any more. Under present circumstances the boats are useless and the new ice is not strong enough to bear sledging." The men spent most of the time trying to sleep. Lockwood thought the daily inaction more exhausting than sleeplessness, and the riskiest of movements. Addressing men in the boats and on the ice, Greely strove to impart cheer. Kislingbury deemed his words "bosh, buncome," yet himself remained hopeful. "I have an inward feeling that we will get out of our troubles all right." After dinner, the men sometimes sang familiar old songs. "We are, under the circumstances, a jolly set of fellows." Both the lieutenant and Sergeant Brainard remarked on the party's occasional high spirits, without giving their commander the slightest credit for them.

Greely ordered an inventory of rations. They amounted to 1,140 pounds of meat, mostly pemmican, and 1,100 pounds of bread. With luck, these would last up to sixty days (contrary to Private Bender's estimate). The cooks used stearin lamps for the first time. These worked satisfactorily, and the time taken to cook meals was no longer than with alcohol, but they emitted acrid smoke. Each man meanwhile had his private thoughts. Elison felt that the commander "made a mistake when he entered this pack. He apparently thought we would drift south steady, he never calculated that we would drift north, east, and in all directions." Kislingbury presumed that there was "nothing left us probably now but to make sledges out of one of the boats to haul the others and the rest of our stuff from floe to floe to the land." They had a twelve-man sledge for the best boat, and the English iceboat brought from Polaris Harbor. "The launch of course must be abandoned."

On the last day of August, as their would-be rescuers reassembled far to the south with little or no unified purpose, the ice-trapped men drifted three miles. Greely declared that ten days was all the time they could afford to spend waiting for the winds to break up the pack and permit boat travel. Lockwood complained of a lack of reading matter. He had brought from Fort Conger pamphleteered bits of Shakespeare and old copies of the *Nineteenth Century Magazine*. "Also, we have Kane, Hayes, and Nares on the launch." Bender, in the launch's stern with the commander and Private Biederbick, noted that "the old man is like a turtle attached to his house, he only goes up sometimes to see out of the flakes and goes back again. I think he is getting bed sores from laying down so much." Either Greely saw those words or Bender uttered some aloud, for he charged the private with disrespect and ordered him off the launch into one of the boats.

But others, too, complained about Greely's apparent preference for crammed confinement within his sleeping bag over more open and encouraging contact with his men. In Kislingbury's opinion, Greely had "lost all activity." Cross typically scoffed that "he don't know what to do himself and is too stubborn to ask them that does." Greely would have been shocked by the violence of Sergeant Brainard's words: "The C.O. is seldom out of his bag. His appearance indicates the most abject cowardice. Inspiring the men with hope, his miserable sneaking actions excite feelings of contempt."

On 1 September, the expedition's young meteorologist, Sergeant Edward Israel, determined its latitude position as 78° 91'. Here Kane Basin narrowed into Smith Sound. The Eskimos brought in a small seal from two miles across the ice, and had no sooner done so when the ice convulsed. A wall of old floes charged upon the expedition's floating prison, and in a thunderous turmoil, the pancaked ice surrounding it heaved asunder. As enormous slabs crashed against the boats, the men fought to get each craft on more stable surfaces. But ice pressure had forced the launch upward until she appeared as if to capsize. "Our brave STN," according to Cross, "yelled, 'Save the steam launch everybody.' What good is the steam launch when we have not five hours of hard steaming coal? But he wanted to save the launch and let the small boats go to the devil." Cross went on cruelly that the commander worried most about the launch because it offered a warm place to stow away in.

The launch survived. It rose beautifully until the pressure slackened with a falling tide. But the commotion had left the party badly shaken. Some advised hastening on through leads left by the crashing of the floes. Greely said no— a dense fog had come on; to continue would be a recipe for danger. So the men crouched within or against boats perched and teetering on separate floes. And stronger grew the conviction that the chief peril to the party was a lack of sound leadership.

Karl Weyprecht, architect of the International
Polar Year *(Heeresgeschichtliches Museum, Vienna,
courtesy Austrian Embassy)*

Adolphus Greely, Lieutenant, U.S. Army,
during the Civil War *(NARA, College Park)*

Frederick Kislingbury, the Lady Franklin
Bay Expedition's second in command,
fated for a prolonged and tragic humiliation *(Linda Kislingbury Cain)*

William Henry Howgate, the Signal Corps' disbursing officer, before the scandal (*NARA, Washington, D.C.*)

William Babcock Hazen, contentious Chief Signal Officer (*The Hudson Library and Historical Society*)

Henrietta Greely with baby Rose (*Library of Congress*)

Secretary of War Robert Todd Lincoln, son of the late president and an expedition opponent (*Illinois State Historical Library*)

The expedition studio photograph, before and after. Following the first photo (above), Corporal Grimm deserted, Corporal Starr was sent home as a malcontent, and Private Ryan was found to be epileptic. Greely had the picture doctored (below) to remove their faces and to replace them with those of Private Ellis (second from left, back), Private Biederbick (seventh from left, back), and Sergeant Ralston (fourth from right, back). Octave Pavy's face (third from right, back) was pasted in as well. (*Naval Historical Center*)

The *Proteus* unloading at Discovery Harbor, where Greely would establish his base, naming it Fort Conger (*U.S. Army Military History Institute*)

The *Proteus* in Lady Franklin Bay, the expedition's hut visible in the background (*NARA, College Park*)

Building the expedition's home at Fort Conger (*U.S. Army Military History Institute*)

Greely's corner, officers' quarters, Fort Conger. He hung a curtain for privacy while sharing a room with two fellow officers and the party's surgeon. (*NARA, College Park*)

Lieutenant Lockwood's sledging party about to leave for North Greenland, 1883 (*U.S. Army Military History Institute*)

Lieutenant Lockwood, Sergeant Brainard, and "Eskimo Fred" Christiansen return from Farthest North journey, which broke a record the British had held for 300 years. (*NARA, College Park*)

Expedition's steam launch, *Lady Greely*, in Discovery Harbor, Lady Franklin Bay *(U.S. Army Military History Institute)*

*USS Yantic,* escort to the second relief expedition. Unsuited for ice navigation and with crew clad for the tropics *(Naval Historical Center)*

Private William Beebe, ill-suited leader of the first expedition (*The Hudson Library and Historical Society*)

Frank Wildes, captain of the *USS Yantic* (*Naval Historical Center*)

Ernest Garlington, cadet, who would lead the ill-fated second relief expedition (*U.S. Military Academy*)

Lieutenant John C. Colwell, U.S. Navy (*Joshua Colwell*)

*Proteus* crushed in ice, morning 23 July, 1883 (*NARA, College Park*)

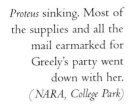

*Proteus* sinking. Most of the supplies and all the mail earmarked for Greely's party went down with her. (*NARA, College Park*)

Aerial view of Bedford Pim Island. Lower prominence is Cape Sabine.
(*Natural Resources, Canada*)

Left to right: *USS Alert*, *USS Bear*, and *USS Thetis* in Godhavn harbor during relief operation, May 1884 (*Naval Historical Center*)

Bow of *Thetis.* Eskimos with dogs and sledges and seal during relief expedition, May–June 1884 (*Naval Historical Center*)

*Thetis* nipped off Greenland. *Bear* astern (*Naval Historical Center*)

Collapsed tent where the starving survivors were discovered (*NARA, College Park*)

The man who rescued Greely, Winfield Scott Schley (*Naval Historical Center*)

The six survivors on *Thetis*: Brainard and Greely, front row. Back row, left to right: Long, Frederick, Connell, and Biederbick (*NARA, College Park*)

Adolphus Greely, shortly after his rescue
(*U.S. Army Military History Institute*)

Greely as Chief Signal Officer (*NARA, College Park*)

Scraps of tent clinging to the rocks (1987) mark the site of Greely's last camp. *(Peter Schledermann, Arctic Institute of North America)*

Rocks and barrel staves among the relics *(Karen McCullough, Arctic Institute of North America)*

Configuration of Greely's stone hut at Camp Clay still visible from the air *(Peter Schledermann, Arctic Institute of North America)*

At the stone hut *(Peter Schledermann, Arctic Institute of North America)*

The burial ridge, Camp Clay. The ground still faintly reveals the shallow graves, a large stone (left side, middle two, top) at the head of each. *(Karen McCullough, Arctic Institute of North America)*

# LINCOLN VETOES RELIEF

FOR GARLINGTON'S PARTY, Pike's people, and the *Yantic's* oversized complement, reunited at Upernavik, the location of the Lady Franklin Bay Expedition was a matter of guesswork. The question at that Greenland settlement was whether the season was too far advanced for Commander Wildes to take the *Yantic* north yet again in search. Wildes thought it was. Attempting to cross Melville Bay "with its imminent ice-pack which must have begun to move and spread looked like an unjustifiable risk." Garlington agreed, favoring St. John's as base for fresh initiative. Relief might yet get to Greely by sealers if prompt action was taken at that Newfoundland seaport once the *Yantic* arrived with her shipwrecked passengers. But all this was speculation. Neither Garlington nor Wildes had the necessary Arctic experience to assess and plan. As for the veteran sealing skipper Richard Pike, nothing would show that his opinion was invited.

Could Pike have cared? He may well have had enough of American explorers. If asked, his answer might have been that navigation from Upernavik would stay open until the end of September. So testified General Hazen after talking with Newfoundlanders. "But Lieutenant Garlington made no demands on Commander Wildes to return with him and his party in search of Greely," declared the C.S.O. "Had he made such demand, Wildes could have refused at the manifold hazard of being cashiered." But that risk did not arise. Lieutenant Garlington was in agreement with the *Yantic's* captain. So with its extra passengers on board—one, Garlington's surgeon, "totally disabled, had to be carried like a child"—the American frigate had swung her stern to the upper Arctic and her bows southward.

She anchored in St. John's harbor on Thursday, 13 September. Garlington's harrowing report flashed via telegraph across Canada into the United States. His first message was to Hazen: "It is my painful duty to report total failure of the expedition." The *Proteus* was crushed. The lieutenant said afterward that sending this telegram "was the saddest duty I have ever been called upon to perform." Lieutenant Colwell of the Navy, writing to his family, unapologetically conceded that all hands had failed in "the main object of the expedition—the getting those twenty-two [sic] foolish people out of the trap they have been in for two years."

Garlington's cable was received by Captain Samuel M. Mills, who had replaced Powell as acting Chief Signal Officer while Hazen toured the Far West inspecting signal posts. Mills telegraphed him at once, his grim news, ironically enough, speeding part of the way over lines set up under Lieutenant Greely's supervision. Commander Frank Wildes's first message was to the Secretary of the Navy, William E. Chandler. The *Yantic* had reached Littleton Island without much difficulty and, returning south, "searched coast and islands thoroughly. Ice-pack then closed in, could neither get around or through and was obliged to retreat." Secretary of War Lincoln got the word from an Associated Press dispatch. The *Yantic* had arrived at St. John's, and "her tidings are lamentable." And what particularly disturbed the nation were follow-up telegrams from Garlington revealing that at Cape Sabine, the *Proteus* party had cached only 500 rations, enough to last Greely, now surely on his way south, no more than twenty days.

Throughout the remainder of that Thursday and into the weekend, the Navy and War departments, which shared space with the State Department on premises just west of the White House, bustled with activity. Corridors echoed with dark theorizing over what must have gone wrong in those distant polar seas. Reporters crowded the signal office for detail of Garlington's sailing orders, especially those dealing with the landing of stores. Lieutenant Louis Caziarc, routinely in charge of Signal Corps paperwork and now in the role of spokesman, "answered rather quickly and without proper care and told my clerk to get me a copy [of Garlington's orders]." Too harassed to check its contents, which would have revealed that confusing memorandum, he handed it to newsmen, who were soon telling the nation that Garlington had been directed to land stores at Littleton Island on his passage north.

Newfoundland newspapers meanwhile were having a field day, especially with the disclosure that too few supplies were left for the Lady Franklin Bay Expedition should it have begun its retreat. *The Evening Mercury* deemed Lieutenant Garlington undoubtedly a gallant officer but no Arctic boatman, had "never seen a floe" before boarding the *Proteus*. Now the Greely party would be on its way south "to meet that aid which is not there for them. Let us hope they will survive the winter." And they could so, with Littleton Island still reachable by supply vessel, "if the United States authorities will only act at once."

Garlington had little time to read local newspapers. He was busy responding to telegrams from Washington, where boldly headlined newspaper accounts by writers seeking scapegoats had compelled the government to show concern and effort. Within forty-eight hours of Garlington's bad news, Secretary Lincoln made known that if any possibility existed of reaching Greely before winter set in, he would act at once. Telegrams crisscrossed land and water. The Americans in St. John's were asked if a steam sealer could be chartered to take them, fully provisioned, back up to Upernavik and beyond. Three first-class sealers with coal in their bunkers lay at St. John's. Garlington cabled Washington that "there is a bare chance of success" if a sealer manned with volunteers from crews of the *Yantic* and *Powhatan*, another American warship at St. John's, set forth with Lieutenant Colwell in command. "The ship must be under U.S. law and subject to military discipline. Nothing can be done with foreign officers and crew. If anything is to be done, it must be done at once."

Considering what his proposal would entail, especially the time required by congressional action, Lieutenant Garlington was asking the impossible and doubtless knew it. Commander Wildes's response was unmistakably negative: "To charter another foreign ship with foreign crew on this duty at this late season would simply invite fresh disaster." The *Proteus* was badly handled, her crew a disobedient mob. "Ship must be American-manned and officered by Navy and thoroughly equipped." Anyway, winter quarters would have to be established so far north that "the attempt would be useless. Melville Bay will be impassable by October 1st at latest. Ship cannot winter at Upernavik." Neither did Wildes regard sledging from Upernavik a practicable option.

From far-off Washington Territory, the Chief Signal Officer urged otherwise in a series of desperately worded telegrams. Well-provisioned sledging parties could be arranged at Upernavik "to meet Greely, who is now probably at Littleton Island on his way south." If it was too early for sledging from Upernavik, small coastal craft would have to be used. At any rate, U.S. Consul Molloy in St. John's would have to be telegraphed at once to send men north by small steamer that would "cost but a few thousand dollars." The Danish legation in Canada, if asked, might get Greenland-bound nationals to give maximum assistance. Hazen sent at least six transcontinental messages from the New Takoma signal post. Immediate word to St. John's might make all the difference.

The general's telegrams were directed to his second in command, Captain Mills. He wrote: "Do all in your power to prevent delay of preparation. What I want done requires no preparation." Hazen reiterated his belief that if a steam sealer left St. John's even as late as 20 September, almost a month of safe navigating season would remain for it to reach either Littleton Island or Cape Sabine. Everything depended on rapid decision at the War Department. "Time is more valuable than all else," Hazen asserted. This message, Hazen's last from the Far West, was never sent. Before it could be transmitted, incoming wires from the nation's capital informed the general that the matter was already settled.

Throughout that weekend, secretaries Lincoln and Chandler had been under pressure to make a move. They also knew of urgent personal entreaties. Henrietta Greely, at home in San Diego recovering from an unspecified "critical illness," wrote worried letters, particularly to Captain Mills. Could not a steamer, if started immediately with stores, reach Godhavn or Upernavik and winter, sending sledging parties north? "Garlington says we have a chance of success." She added pointedly that "Mr. Greely expressed to me complete faith in the government's care for its own expeditions."

Letters to Henrietta from well-meaning friends and relatives were not always felicitously worded. Greely's mother wrote from Newburyport that the suspense was dreadful. "Everyone here is feeling bad. You know how hard I tried to keep him at home." Greely's niece, Clarissa, wrote that "it seems to me that if Lieutenant Garlington had left the stores at Littleton Island there would have been some chance for Adolph to obtain food when he reached there." But what would befall him now? "I cannot sleep, and I know that you must be in agony all the time."

Then Henrietta received the authoritative and chilling intelligence. Hazen was the first notified, in the telegram from Captain Mills that had stopped him from sending yet another appeal. The War Department had reached its conclusion. Expeditions that year were "not considered advisable." The statement was issued on the Saturday following the *Yantic's* return to St. John's. A disgusted General Hazen wondered why Robert Lincoln "at most gave one day to consideration." Captain Mills, as acting C.S.O., sent Henrietta the information in words phrased hopefully to soften its blow. "The Secretaries of War and Navy have carefully considered with kindly disposition and indifferent to expense the feasibility of sending another vessel. They concur that nothing further can be done this year. Every effort will be made in the spring and summer of next year to reach the party at the earliest possible moment." And the bulk mail written to the expedition's members by their loved ones at home? "We regret," said the War Department, "that it all went down with the *Proteus.*"

Angered by the decision of the War and Navy departments after little more than twenty-four hours' study of options, both Greely's wife and, in Washington, Lieutenant Lockwood's military veteran father vented protests. But it soon became clear that neither William E. Chandler's nor Robert Todd Lincoln's mind could be changed. By Tuesday evening, Captain Mills had telegraphed Henrietta that the secretaries' decision had been made only "after a most laborious and patient consultation with Arctic explorers of eminence." There was simply no time to help Greely that year. Still, not to worry. En route for Cape Sabine, the commander would "wisely" realize that "there is now not the remotest chance of reaching him either by boat or sledge." And if not trying to push on to Upernavik, he would likely "retrace his steps to Lady Franklin Bay. His case is viewed hopefully."

More personally, because of his friendship with Henrietta's husband, Lieutenant Louis Caziarc wrote to Henrietta, distancing himself somewhat from the decision of his higher-ups. Garlington's and Wildes's dispatches from

St. John's had aided in the decision against further action that year, "but you should know that every word said [in Washington] has been for the sending of a party. But the prospects of accomplishing anything in a region where light is fast disappearing, and the fact that an expedition cannot be started without delays in provisioning, fitting, coaling, etc., have led those who must decide to decide unfavorably."

Caziarc spoke of the "supplemental instructions"—the memorandum he had composed and that was already a source of bewilderment in the national press. It had been given to Garlington "to be acted on according to his discretion. Though indecisive at best, it allowed Garlington leeway to land at Littleton on the passage north all the stores not needed for more northerly depots." As it was, "when the ship went down, everything went with her." Not that Garlington should be condemned before he had a chance to defend himself. After all, he was only complying with the instructions dictated by Henrietta's husband, whose own voyage north on the *Proteus*, Caziarc gently reminded her, was "so short that I fear he could not quite realize that the two following ones should prove so impossible."

There was little more that Henrietta could do, especially when her most influential ally, General Lockwood, father of Lieutenant James B. Lockwood, appeared to capitulate. After repeatedly calling on both cabinet ministers to fit out a relief expedition without delay, Lockwood felt sure they had arrived at an honest conclusion. The relief expedition dispatched would be put in greater peril than those it was sent to relieve. Indeed, Mr. Lincoln would not admit that the Greely party was in extreme peril. An expedition now was vetoed "only after experts had pronounced it impracticable and [better] deferred till next spring. I am compelled however reluctantly to acquiesce in this decision." And that reluctance was short-lived, for each time he called at the War Department to "review the situation with those who have dispassionately studied it I return in better spirits."

General Lockwood's bouts of optimism reflected the success of the government's efforts to allay popular anxiety. In a memorandum dated 19 September, the Secretary of War described Greely's situation as "by no means hopeless." If his party had left their station no later than 1 September as ordered, "he has the advantage of daylight." Arriving at Cape Sabine, he would have learned of Garlington's disaster and made plans for the winter. He had rations at Sabine, more caches elsewhere in the neighborhood, and 240 across at Littleton Island. Even if he decided to journey back to Lady Franklin Bay, there was "more than a year's supply of the best assorted food" on which to subsist. All things considered, the expedition, the secretary insisted, must be in pretty good shape. Captain Mills wrote to Henrietta Greely in similar vein, concluding with "[Greely] cannot fail to know that the most earnest efforts will be made to relieve him next year."

Throughout those final September weeks, Henrietta Greely was far from silenced by the War Department's excuses. "If the *Proteus* could reach Upernavik in eight days from St. John's," she wrote Lieutenant Caziarc, "another vessel could do the same." A ship could have started from St. John's since the *Yantic*'s return, and before fall yielded to winter could have reached far above Upernavik. "I have great faith in Mr. Greely's ability to cope with the situation. If any man could escape the dangers that beset his party I believe that he will. All the same, I feel that the government has not kept faith."

Lieutenant Caziarc had little he could usefully add to what he already had written to Greely's wife. But wishing that he could be in San Diego to console her, he began writing with less regard for the constraints of his office. He was puzzled by Garlington's conduct after the shipwreck. Why had that officer not remained at Littleton Island or Pandora Harbor until the *Yantic* reached either place? "I assume he had no confidence in the *Yantic* coming up," he wrote. Caziarc tried to use comforting words to describe the belief of "those most familiar with Arctic work" in the Greely party's ultimate safety. Even so, it struck him as deplorable that an expedition "so carefully fitted out [as Garlington's] should have been brought to utter failure by a series of calamities and as yet unexplained neglects. I am writing to you," he confided, "without a bridle to my tongue."

In the same spirit of candor, after referring to "the half-mutinous crew of the *Proteus*," Caziarc touched on Commander Wildes's conduct as strange: "His failure to put stores off at Littleton Island or at Pandora Harbor passes my comprehension." On arrival at those places, Wildes had learned of the *Proteus* wreck and the loss of her provisions. "I cannot understand why he did not put off everything from his ship's stores which he could foresee would be necessary to Greely's safety," he continued. In these letters to Henrietta Greely, the lieutenant gave no sign of concern that he himself might have some explaining to do about those "supplemental instructions" and their recommendation that stores be landed by Garlington on the passage north. But in the light of the *Proteus* wreck, that idea might be recalled as a wise one. As for now, although the *New York Herald* had just published the *Yantic's* log, Caziarc wrote, "We are still so much in the dark."

Captain Mills tried reassurance. No effort would be spared to set on foot "another expedition at the earliest moment possible. Great diligence is being used to determine the proper course of action." This determination would involve analysis of advice from knowledgeable persons more conveniently at hand than in Newfoundland. Some recommendations were not solicited—for instance, that of Chief Engineer George W. Melville, one of the principal *Jeannette* survivors. Melville told the Secretary of the Navy that "Greely without doubt is now at Littleton Island." (The party had, just then, come to within thirty miles of it, looking out for Cape Sabine and huddled on a floe drifting to and fro at the whim of winds and tide.) Convinced that whalemen were known to cruise as far north as Cape York as late as 20 October, Melville volunteered to lead a party of his own to Greely's and "encourage them to hold on." A ship sent without delay from St. John's to Cape York could land a rescue crew with supplies, boats, and sledges before ice blocked further progress.

The chief engineer's bold proposal was not unconnected with personal and professional worries. He had a too-talkative wife to silence for his own peace of mind with respect to the *Jeannette* disaster, and had to produce a persuasive explanation for the failure to save his own captain, George De Long—problems compelling Melville to brace for accusations of, in his own words, "murder." At any rate, his scheme for Greely's relief was criticized by Captain James A. Greer of the Navy, who had voyaged to Littleton Island on the *Tigress* in 1873 in search of the missing *Polaris* crew. Greer thought a vessel might reach Upernavik but could go no farther north this late in the season. "Another night begins about mid-October," Greer argued, "and the best a new relief expedition could then do would be to go part of the way and wait for next summer to resume the journey." He didn't think sledging from Upernavik possible.

George Tyson also voiced his opinion. This most notable survivor of the *Polaris* expedition was undergoing hard times, a book about his Arctic adventures having sold poorly, and he now worked as a low-paid security guard at the War Department. Tyson offered to take command of a schooner and bring Greely home the following spring. The Secretary of War replied that plans were not that far advanced. Lieutenant John Danenhower, the only other officer to come back from the *Jeannette* (and George Melville's *bête noire*), professed himself "ready to go at any time and on any expedition that may be organized." But as Danenhower knew, his controversial semiblindness would have precluded such action.

Commander Frank Wildes's initial report had left the Secretary of the Navy far from satisfied. Chandler might have been in a more acquiescent mood were he not under compulsion to steer his department through currents of ongoing scandal in the wake of the *Jeannette* disaster. It was less than a year since he had been obliged to engage in a "compact of silence" between certain of that tragedy's survivors quietly at one another's throats. In the process, he had found it necessary to suppress charges the late commander George De Long had drawn up in the Arctic before the *Jeannette* foundered. The Navy's court of inquiry was so handled as to paper over dark facts relating to the *Jeannette,* her officers, and the crew. All this as Chandler sought congressional approval of a naval expansion program that would place the United States on equal footing with European powers by the dawn of the twentieth century. He knew how eagerly the Navy's political foes would jump at any chance to exploit whatever event tended to cast his department in a bad light.

During those very same days after the *Yantic's* return, and while questions pelted both Navy and War departments, Emma De Long, the *Jeannette* captain's widow, published a scrupulously sanitized version of her husband's journals. Chief Engineer Melville, referring to the *Jeannette* affair, wrote her confidentially that "there is a good deal we both might say that has not been said." Secretary Chandler knew so as well and intended to avert any further risk of scandal. So he bore down heavily on the *Yantic* commander's failure to keep company with the *Proteus* as far as Littleton Island. "You and the *Proteus* were at Disko on July 15th when the *Proteus* sailed north, but you were still there on July 26th." By that time the *Proteus* had passed Littleton Island and sank. The *Yantic* was not at the island until 3 August. Had she not been fully eleven days behind the *Proteus,* "Garlington's relief party would have stayed [at Littleton] with stores, and telescopes trained on Cape Sabine." Greely "would not have found awaiting him, as is now the case, neither house nor provisions but only the record of complete failure."

So it would seem that the *Yantic* did not properly fulfill her duty as tender to the *Proteus* and thereby "defeated the object of the expedition." Even when Wildes knew of the disaster to the *Proteus* and Garlington's southward turnabout, Wildes "could have landed provisions [at Littleton] but did not."

In advance of his formal report, Wildes responded to Chandler's letter as forthrightly as he dared. After leaving St. John's, the *Proteus* had steamed on ahead at top speed. To conserve coal, the *Yantic* had followed under sail. But even had she run with all six of her fires burning, she couldn't have kept pace with the *Proteus*. It would, indeed, have been better for all had orders been the other way around, had the *Proteus* been told to keep company with the *Yantic*. Also, the *Yantic* was hurried out to sea before completion of repairs to her boilers, a task that took six days at Godhavn. The *Yantic* could not arrive at Littleton Island with a dwindling coal supply and boilers leaking. Furthermore, to get there in the first place meant crossing Melville Bay, itself an intimidating challenge. From all Wildes had read and learned of the dangers, he "felt justified in delaying the attempt to cross, or even making the attempt to cross at all." But he did cross, and on reaching Littleton Island and learning of the *Proteus* loss, he had considered his "first and paramount duty" to pick up the shipwrecked boat parties. He believed Greely's people were in no danger—they were in a region reportedly stocked with game, and should they retreat south, they would find provisions on Littleton Island, besides more on the west coast of Smith Sound.

That was Wildes's only mention of his neglecting to leave any of his own foodstocks on Littleton. Showing how determined he was to get at the truth, the secretary had demanded of him a "schedule of provisions" carried on his ship. Wildes enclosed one without comment. On 3 August, when off Littleton Island, the *Yantic* had on board 30,000 pounds of provisions. At New York upon her arrival home, she still had 20,780 pounds in her holds. Since this surplus could not be easily explained away, Wildes hurried along with other details. Ice or fear of besetment had hindered his attempts to overtake the boat parties. Only after prolonged and fruitless pursuit did he make for Upernavik. Throughout all, he had acted in accord with his best judgment. "I did not intend to run the vessel under my command in the haphazard happy-go-lucky fashion which finally brought the *Proteus* to grief," he insisted. Ready to shoulder any blame rightfully his, he requested a court of inquiry. "I do not wish to rest under the imputation that I have needlessly left Lieutenant Greely's party to the possibility of perishing by starvation."

Such arguments had left Chandler unmoved. He believed that the Navy commander and the Army lieutenant should never have contemplated, as they had evidently done four days before leaving St. John's, separation of their ships on the passage north. The vessels should have left Disko together. The call at Upernavik just to ask Danes how the ice was moving was unnecessary. Instead of those six days' delay, the *Yantic* could have reached Littleton Island before the shipwrecked *Proteus* people left for the south. Finally, Chandler stated that the department "condemns your failure, when you found that the demoralized party had gone south, to land materials for a habitation, clothing and some food for the forgotten Greely party." Further action in the case, Chandler had added ominously, would be determined.

Lieutenant Garlington was still at St. John's, preparing responses to the ugly stories he knew were circulating. They included the question of his disagreement with Captain Pike, which apparently had sealed the *Proteus's* fate. To settle this one on the spot, Garlington arranged an interview with the Newfoundlander in the office of John Syme, agent for the ship's owners. With Syme as witness and Lieutenant Colwell also present, Garlington asked Pike if he had proceeded under pressure against his own judgment. Pike replied that he had seen open water north from Sabine as plainly as had Garlington. But he had felt that two or three days more spent filling the ship's bunkers would be valuable, inasmuch as the delay would allow still more ice to be worked "well out of the sound. You, Lieutenant Garlington, in a peremptory manner reiterated [otherwise] in such a way I felt that if the expedition failed, my lingering at that point might be blamed." But Pike conceded that he had not made his feelings perfectly clear to Garlington at the time.

What most incensed the lieutenant were American newspaper accounts published within forty-eight hours of his return on the *Yantic* and based mainly on the Caziarc press releases in Washington. The *New York Herald* for 15 September stated that Garlington would immediately ask for a court of inquiry into his conduct. Among his first telegrams from St. John's, he had made clear that no supply depot was left at Littleton Island on the way up because "it was not in my program to do so." The *New York Herald* had reported that a memorandum of "supplemental instructions" now published for the first time showed that it certainly was. It stated further, "It seems to be generally conceded by those who have given most attention to the subject that the complete and disastrous failure of the relief expedition was mainly due to the omission of Lieutenant Garlington to land his stores and house at Littleton Island, or some other accessible point near the mouth of Smith's Sound, before attempting the hazardous mission beyond." Had he done so, the *Proteus's* sinking would have been far less consequential. Garlington's party could have retreated to their secure base of supplies and organized a sledge expedition up the Ellesmere Island coast. "As it is now, there is no party at the mouth of Smith's Sound to cooperate with Lieutenant Greely and no considerable supply of food there for him to retreat upon."

Interviewed by a newsman that same weekend, General Hazen appeared to confirm that "supplemental orders" to land stores at Littleton on the way north were indeed added to the main body of Garlington's instructions. At the same time, a perplexed Secretary Lincoln secured a copy of that troublesome memorandum and discussed it with his cabinet colleague Chandler behind closed doors. They supposed it to be "an authentic copy of Hazen's instructions to Lieutenant Garlington." Evidently, then, Garlington had disobeyed an order. This inference was rapidly gaining ground when Lieutenant Caziarc learned for the first time that Garlington, on the eve of his departure from Washington for the north, had shown the memorandum to General Hazen and been told not to regard it as binding.

Caziarc was in an awkward position. For that matter, so were General Hazen and the rest of his signal office, which overnight had become a hive of confusion and distress. Someone contacted the *New York Herald*, which thereupon gave the story a different spin. Disturbing questions were still headlined. Who was responsible? Was there a blunder? On the one hand, the signal office touted the memorandum as evidence of its foresight in guarding against the kind of misfortune that did, in fact, befall the *Proteus*. But Lieutenant Garlington had been encouraged to ignore the memorandum and adhere strictly to the original instructions as composed by Greely. It seemed that those supplemental orders were not orders at all, but merely suggestions that Garlington might act upon if he thought proper. So, in fairness, Caziarc believed that further criticism of that officer should be suspended "until he can be heard in person."

That moment arrived at the close of the month. The *Yantic* was in drydock in New York on the twentieth. Garlington alighted from the train in Washington the next day. (It was the week when Greely's people, so long frustrated in their efforts to reach land, still drifted without control from Kane Basin into Smith Sound. They were appreciably closer than any of them realized to a landfall at Cape Sabine.) At the Washington railroad depot, Lieutenant Garlington was not alone. Besides his small band of soldiers, he had Rover with him, the Newfoundland dog that had accompanied him throughout his arduous experiences, presumably without a complaining bark. In terms of public relations, this move was hardly sensible. The press made sure of mentioning it, but solemnly added that on the lieutenant's word, the canine had consumed not a morsel of food earmarked for the Lady Franklin Bay Expedition.

# 18

# THE LONELY COMMANDER

KNOWING HIS JUDGMENT was suspect, Greely was not averse to venting a gibe of his own. On one night there were promising leads, and some of the party urged that he take advantage of them. He refused to do so, the fog too thick. The next morning he felt entitled to boast of the "prudence of my decision. Those who last night were clamorous to go on had nothing to say this morning when not a pool of water could be seen." Later that day, hunched down in his sleeping bag on the launch, he heard Lieutenant Kislingbury, twenty yards away in the whaleboat, "discussing our situation" with the enlisted men. Kislingbury was emphasizing, contrary to the commander's view, that an attempt should be made to reach shore.

Greely struggled half out of the bag. He shouted across the ice that Kislingbury should hold his tongue, that his words fomented discontent and were but one step short of mutiny. Kislingbury called back that he hadn't intended his remarks to reflect upon the commander. Greely's response was that they could do no other, and he said further, "If you have any suggestions they should be made to me." Kislingbury retorted that he was tired of doing so, that they were invariably ignored. "Because of no account," rapped Greely. The melancholy exchange across uneven sheets of ice petered out. But after an hour's deep thought, Greely decided upon a council composed of himself, the other lieutenants, Dr. Pavy, and the sergeants Brainard and Rice, in whose judgment, he wrote with no inkling of the former's contemptuous references to him and the latter's role in a mutinous conspiracy, he had "always placed instant reliance."

He gathered all five in the launch with him. According to Kislingbury, he began by saying that there was no reason why he had to defend or explain his entering the pack instead of keeping to the shore, that he had stated his reasons on previous occasions. As indicated by the notes of all three lieutenants, the conversation went this way: Greely commended Sergeant Rice upon his skill in navigating the ice because he (Greely) lacked the necessary expertise besides "having the disadvantage of poor eyesight." Nobody, Greely continued, could value life or have more to live for than himself. Had he not a wife and two children? But in the present situation he had no right to act alone, hence his invitation to a meeting. "I am not infallible," he said.

He expressed himself in no doubt that a party and provisions "and I believe a ship" would be at Lifeboat Cove (adjacent to Littleton Island). Regarding Cape Sabine, Greely stated, "I don't think we should calculate on anything but the 240 rations known to be on the south side of Payer Harbor." Unexpectedly, he turned to Kislingbury. "You are next in seniority; let us hear your general views." Kislingbury didn't hesitate. He was all for abandoning the launch and the *Valorous* jolly boat and making for Cape Sabine with the stronger sledge and two remaining boats. Greely asked: "Have you considered the weight of a heavy twelve-man sledge, two boats, and over 5000 pounds of baggage?" Kislingbury said it was better than waiting where they were for the chance of perhaps one day's steaming by launch. "We could move everything piecemeal from floe to floe."

Consulting a map, Greely reminded Kislingbury that north of Cape Sabine, the shore receded too deeply for keeping anywhere close to it. Dr. Pavy chimed in that they should abandon all but one boat. He agreed with Kislingbury that they should start right away. "We could make four miles a day and reach Sabine within a month." Lieutenant Lockwood, who appeared not to have given the matter much thought, first recommended starting "in a day or two," then sided vaguely with Greely, "favoring the status quo, leaving circumstances to shape our course. It is extremely difficult to make up one's mind."

Later in his journal, Lockwood wrote what he had refrained from saying to Greely at the council. The commander evidently hoped either that young ice would soon cement the floes together enough to allow sledge travel or that leads would open up to permit passage by the launch and its tow, "in which case he thinks of going directly for Littleton Island. I doubt if we are able to do this. I think the ice will always be broken up and in motion."

Greely had heard the others out in silence. He repeated his opinion that the best course was to await some change in the ice conditions before making any positive move. Brainard also leaned in favor of doing nothing yet. So did Rice, who thought that they "were not losing ground but gaining gradually by drift." Thus the two sergeants tended to agree with their commander, who made no secret of his gratitude for their support. Mercifully for Greely, he didn't know that on this same day, Brainard wrote that "the men don't lose sight of the gross ignorance and incapacity of the man who brought them to the present strait."

Greely acknowledged the importance of reaching land but still believed that riding the drift would do no harm. The party had enough rations—bread, meat, and potatoes—and fuel to last until 1 November. And that was how Greely's council wound up. Leave things as they are. Watch for any opening, even if only half a mile long, pointing in the right direction. If none, wait for the ice to congeal fast enough to bear the expedition's weight. What immediately followed this meeting was hard labor, based on Sergeant Rice's recommendation that canvas sails be fashioned into a tent and the launch seats torn out to make two additional sledges. Cross and Elison were put to work on this project. Slats for the sledges were made from old barrel staves and the thwarts of the English *Valorous* boat. Shelter was a sudden problem. In that first September week, the temperature plunged far below zero. Greely had the launch sail and jib, the whaleboat sail, and the dinghy's small one cut up for the sides of a tent. Supported by oars and masts, it resembled, when finished, "an Indian lodge" and could accommodate seventeen men. The other eight found shelter in the iceboat, which itself was converted into a pup tent with canvas housing.

They were not in that makeshift home very long. The ice opened tempt-ingly. But the launch and boats had not advanced more than a mile when it closed again. Wearily, the men hauled the boats on a floe some 200 yards across and again set up the tent. They were now beset off Bache Island, still in Kane Basin but less than thirty miles above Cape Sabine, and on the Greenland side of the Basin some forty miles north of Littleton Island. And a rising wind accelerated their drift. Languid spirits revived. Snatches of song and laughter echoed across the ice, slabs of which held a pole upright from which fluttered the American flag. Once, the party's frozen platform was joined by a massive berg that loomed paternally, or threateningly, 100 feet above them. And when Greely wrote one day that Sergeant Connell had been heard making demoral-izing comments, he added, "But this is no place for discipline."

On 8 September, the commander decided to abandon the policy of wait-ing patiently. Thus they would abandon the launch as well, and also the *Valorous* boat. He would take the two remaining boats, the twelve-man sledge, and one of the two just improvised, and try to land at Cocked Hat Island, a barren holm in Buchanan Strait hard against the jut of land that peaked at Cape Sabine. With Lockwood and Rice, he had scaled the berg that continued to hover near, and from its summit could see that the ice was in good condition for travel in that direction. Greely called another council and announced his plan. They would take two boats, all provisions, instruments, and records. "We would have 6500 pounds or more to haul, must travel three times over the same ice." The pendulum alone, with its case, weighed 100 pounds. Greely was relieved, and proud, that not one of his men voiced any objection to taking it. "Once at Cocked Hat Island I intend leaving everything except sleeping bags, cooking gear, and a few days' rations, and move thence rapidly to Sabine."

Preparations began for departure. Snow fell heavily, as the men disman-tled the *Valorous* and ripped at the steam launch Greely had so proudly named for his wife. The final indignity to the launch was the wrenching away of its turtleback, which, cut to pieces, would serve as boards to go under the sleep-ing bags in the tepee. Greely bade a silent farewell to the launch, placed a terse record in what remained of it, and from the *Valorous*'s masthead left a signal flag flying in hopes of its sighting by the longed-for relief ship.

The party moved off around noon on 10 September. Sergeant Brainard forged ahead to select the best route. The first load consisted of the English boat *Beaumont* and the big sledge bearing 700 pounds of freight, dragged by fourteen men over two miles of hummocky ice, followed by two small sledges, each with five men at the drag ropes. A sledge runner broke through the ice. Precious time was lost man-hauling the load back on track. Once on more stable ice, Greely ordered the tent set up. He returned to direct the second load: 2,000 pounds of cargo and the thirty-foot-long whaleboat. It took six miles of dogged travel to make good less than two. One of the small sledges broke down and was left behind. After the third and final load, Greely issued rum to the exhausted men, twelve of whom slept in the tepee that night, the rest in boats under tattered sails. At daybreak, the weather cleared. And from the highest point of their latest ice floe base, the men could see the coast of Cape Sabine.

How to get there via Cocked Hat Island started an argument. Directly facing the party was a wide expanse of broken floes glued together by frozen slush. Lieutenant Lockwood favored striking east in hopes of skirting this unnavigable patch. Sergeant Rice opted for a course westward. Pavy and Sergeant Brainard advised against altering their present position, other than to move to the southern edge of the floe they occupied and await spring tides, expected in a few days. Brainard reasoned that the tides might break the ice enough to allow boat travel. None of these ideas satisfied Greely, who proposed heading southeast by a series of floes he assumed extended for miles in that direction.

The next day, the twelfth, Rice and four others, including Lieutenant Kislingbury, plodded across the ice to determine travel conditions. They returned separately but with the same report. There was little likelihood of safely leaving the floe they were on. Even so, however much of a gamble, it had to be taken. The party's floe was a component of the restless pack and sometimes veered northward, opposite to their intended course. Now the whaleboat had to be abandoned. Twice, its weight had broken the big sledge, without which, Brainard noted, "we are helpless." Lockwood expected that boats would be found at Cape Sabine. Leaving the whaleboat with a signal flag flying from an upright oar, the men moved on again, the first stage being to haul everything to the edge of the floe. They had to pull loads five times, each forward struggle taking an hour and a half. Greely worried about the effect of all this effort upon morale. Even "the absence of sufficient light to cast a shadow had very unfortunate results." Men were bruised, their muscles overstrained. "When no shadows form, and the light is feeble, there is the same uncertainty about one's walk as if the deepest darkness prevailed."

A southwest gale sprang up. Greely wrote, "We are drifting northeast, losing all the ground gained. We go back as fast as we advance," while Kislingbury wrote, "We are completely at the mercy of the wind now and God alone knows what is in store for us." They camped on the edge of the floe, a shivering group looking to their leader for some sign of hope. Greely decided they would bypass Cocked Hat Island and make directly for Cape Sabine. While in the crude tepee, Greely and the doctor argued fiercely, Pavy declaring that had his suggestions been heeded, the party would be safe at Fort Conger instead of helplessly adrift in Kane Basin. Greely denied having received such advice. In any event, staying on at Fort Conger beyond 1 September when no ship came would have been against orders. Grumbling that the men were not pushed hard enough, Pavy left the tent. Greely directed Lockwood to note down every word that had passed, and in his own journal wrote that Pavy's "insinuations regarding the men are as base as his other statements are mutinous."

At the close of that miserable day, Greely compared the figures handed to him by Sergeant Rice, who regularly recorded their position, with those of the past twenty-four hours. "Yesterday's observations at noon placed us at lat. 78 degrees 55 minutes. Today, lat. 79 degrees 01 minutes North, a loss of seven miles of our dearly earned ground." The commander and Rice agreed not to let the others know.

"We are nineteen miles from Sabine," wrote Lieutenant Lockwood on 16 September. Greely estimated that the party had forty days' rations. But he had again changed his mind, and now intended to make east for the Greenland coast. "Situation very critical," wrote Lockwood. "Both coasts visible." Greenland on the left hand, Ellesmere the right, neither seemingly accessible. At another council, which Lieutenant Lockwood recorded in shorthand, Dr. Pavy insisted that the only escape was to push across the broken pack toward Sabine at once. The heavy pendulum again came under review. Greely told the men that he wanted to save it but did not wish to lessen the party's chances by carrying it any further. Again to his relief, all seemed to agree that it should be kept as long as possible. The general consensus was that the party remain where they were and wait until the spring tides, now at their height, had passed. "By that time," thought Greely, "the drift will have developed itself and we can tell better what to do."

Greely strove to assure the party of his anxiety to reach shore as soon as practicable. But his uncertainty was disturbingly evident. It gave his erstwhile engineer, Cross, fresh excuse to scoff. Cross wrote, "The old villain is such a liar we can't put any confidence in anything he says." But the consistent revision of hopes and ideas could not be helped, given the perversity of the winds and currents that governed the floe to which the party clung. Sometimes it drifted southeast, at others southwest, occasionally even rotated so the men found themselves facing in the direction opposite to one they had the previous night.

The elements mocked and toyed with them, undermining their calculations. By noon on the seventeenth, the drift was more westerly, making Cape Sabine again the objective. Cocked Hat Island looked like a promising first stop, but within forty-eight hours the pack had suddenly decided to veer southeast. The party had to race frantically across a sea of broken floes that carried them off at different angles. They crossed five lanes by boat, and between each one had to transfer their 6,000-pound load to the sledge for passage over the rough ice. Each change from sledge to boat and back to sledge threatened to tear apart the expedition. "There was," wrote Greely, "a constant danger of floes splitting and drifting away with parts of gear and even men stranded on them." In all this turmoil, a comforting rite was not forgotten. On Private Whisler's birthday, Greely directed that he be issued cranberries, and extra sugar for his coffee.

It was the next day that Lieutenant Greely initially decided they should abandon most of their baggage and start across the pack to Greenland, that Sergeant Brainard wrote "Madness" in his journal, that Octave Pavy compared their situation to a nightmare out of Edgar Allan Poe.

The tepee was once more set up, and cause for satisfaction was provided by Eskimo Fred, who, despite poor visibility, shot a 600-pound seal. Both native dog drivers, Kislingbury thought, were "worth their weight in gold." Meals were prepared in the tepee, with stearin used in one of the cooking lamps to save alcohol. It was over the stearin lamp that they cooked the seal blood, the nutritional value of which had been remarked upon by past explorers. Greely thought the stuff tasted like raw eggs. And the fumes from the heated stearin caused coughing fits that convulsed Bender. Greely told him to change places with Sergeant Connell, who had slept under tarpaulin in the iceboat. Connell joined the tepee detachment. Greely had come to identify Connell as one of the expedition's prime troublemakers, and he detailed Sergeant Ralston to keep a special eye on him. Kislingbury learned of this and called it spying.

What if the men did growl? He wrote, "Only a saint could endure these circumstances without complaint."

Indicative of how bewilderingly erratic was the party's recent course, the abandoned whaleboat popped into sight only two miles off, signal flag still flying. Greely sent eight men in the iceboat to retrieve it, but manhandling it back over sludge ice proved too taxing an effort and they left it where it was. On the twenty-third, more snow fell. The beleaguered men gnawed on hard bread and corned beef mixed with seal meat. The doctor dealt with a lengthening sick list—the commander had an inflamed cut finger, Lieutenant Kislingbury a painful rupture, Sergeant Cross a frostbitten foot, Schneider and others diarrhea aggravated by the constant seesaw motion of the floe. The whaleboat reappeared. Lockwood and seven companions made another attempt to reach it, on foot across skittish ice. After a mile, separating floes threatened to cut them off. They scrambled back for safety. The whaleboat vanished.

By now, the drift had carried the party once more westward, to within sight of Cocked Hat Island. In addition to the English cache of 240 rations believed to be at nearby Cape Sabine, Fred Kislingbury thought it not unlikely that the relief ship had gotten up as far as Cape Isabella, at the southern entrance to Smith Sound, if not Sabine itself. The lieutenant's constant worry was for his motherless brood, "my dear little fellows at home. I am powerless to help them." Should the relief ship return home with none of the party, how great would be their sorrow. "Oh, that some whispering angels could give you the comforting news that we are still safe and our prospects not altogether hopeless."

# 19

# COURT OF INQUIRY

LIEUTENANT ERNEST GARLINGTON spent the first days in Washington working on his report to the Chief Signal Officer. It was a recital of bad luck, redeemed by the survival of the shipwrecked men. In no way had his misfortunes added to the perils confronting Greely, who, should he reach Littleton Island, "will divide his people among the different Eskimo settlements on the mainland. And the stores he will find on his line of retreat, supplemented by the game of that region, will be sufficient food for his party during the coming winter." Alternatively, and this Garlington thought most likely, Greely would have remained at Fort Conger, where he had good shelter, abundant provisions, "with what game the country affords," to carry him through.

Garlington's report concluded with reference to "the manifest injury" done him through published assertions that he had been given a "memorandum of instructions" to land stores at Littleton Island before sailing and had disobeyed them. "The paper was not addressed nor signed, indeed bore no official mark whatever," he insisted. He had found it among his rightful instructions. He reminded General Hazen sharply that "you said, in substance, you did not know how it had gotten in there. I did not then, nor have I at any time since, regard it as an order."

Dated 2 October, the lieutenant's report to Hazen was not seen by Secretary Lincoln until fourteen days later. It had been filed at Signal Corps headquarters awaiting the C.S.O.'s return from the Far West. While in San Francisco, at the Palace Hotel, Hazen had written to Henrietta Greely, telling of his intention to ask why the *Yantic* had left Disko Island a fortnight later than she was supposed to. And why hadn't the *Yantic*'s captain left stores for Greely? Since Frank Wildes was a naval officer, not from the Army, these questions were more properly put by Secretary Chandler, who certainly did so once he had absorbed the details of Wildes's full and official report, much of which repeated what Wildes had asserted in his earlier sharp correspondence with the secretary. Boiler repair, coaling, and fog had delayed the ship at Disko more than two weeks. But neither fogs, snowstorms, nor drifting icebergs had prevented the *Yantic* from crossing Melville Bay, to reach Littleton Island safely.

Wildes was prone to wax lyrical even in formal communications. Once, at Littleton, he had climbed to the island's crest and gazed northward. He wrote, "No words of mine can describe the stern and rugged grandeur of this gateway to the pole as seen on a bright and beautiful day. The great northern pack, rough surfaced and of a yellow *mer de glace* color, stretched in a huge semicircle from Cape Ingersoll to Cape Sabine." Discovering Garlington's note about the shipwreck, Wildes, "immediately got under way." And then had ensued the erratic pursuit of the boat parties. On Northumberland Island, traces of their camp were discovered. "Long tongues of ice ran out several miles," preventing a halt at Cape York. Weather worsened. Wildes had shaped course for Upernavik, where his crew passed the time ashore at target practice and, Wildes blandly implied, dalliance with Eskimo girls. Disko's Godhavn was the next stop, then the return to Upernavik and at last the gathering of the relief parties.

There were times during the *Yantic*'s desultory passage north when, Wildes continued, "we began to think that Arctic cruising had been somewhat exaggerated, but the terrible news which met us on our arrival [at Littleton Island], the obstacles to our progress southward, and the absolute necessity for giving

up the search, convinced me that this frozen region is not to be trifled with."
The *Yantic* was inadequate for its assigned mission. Wildes advised that never
again should the department send a ship north of Newfoundland unless it was
built and equipped to meet heavy ice, and with a crew provisioned and clothed
for an Arctic winter. Such was not the case with the *Yantic.* Wildes stressed, however, that he had "made every effort to carry out both the spirit and letter of
my orders." Except for a single passing reference to Garlington's men as the
"Greely relief party," Commander Frank Wildes's report to the Secretary of
the Navy made no mention at all of the Lady Franklin Bay Expedition.

Freshly returned from the West, General Hazen had submitted Lieutenant
Garlington's report to the Secretary of War with a letter intended to absolve
himself of any culpability arising from the matter of that "memorandum of
instructions." This action required some sophistry on Hazen's part, for it hardly
suited his interest to appear as if shifting blame to Garlington, Caziarc, or
Greely, three soldiers for whose discharge of duty he was, as their military superior, ultimately responsible. Greely's words at the outset forbidding any deviation from his program had made "delicate any change-making." But in the
expedition's absence, Congress had intervened to mandate that the Lady
Franklin Bay station be shut down and the men brought home. This decision
legitimized the instructions that stores be landed at Littleton Island on the
passage north. But then the Secretary of the Navy had agreed to send a naval
vessel with the *Proteus* as convoy. "The convoy itself being a depot," wrote
Hazen, "it was thought best that Greely's program remain as Garlington's
guide." So the injunction to stop first at Littleton and land stores became
"merely a suggestion."

Strictly speaking, then, Garlington had not disobeyed orders. All the same,
matters remained that the lieutenant would have to clarify. After the loss of the
*Proteus*, why had he not set up some sort of depot on Littleton Island with what
stores were saved? He had started back south in boats with forty days' supply,
which he could expect to increase with game along the way. And when south
of Cape York he was in friendly Eskimo country, "fairly supplied with the
necessities of life," why, out of six boats, had he left none for Greely? To all
these questions, Hazen promised Secretary Lincoln satisfactory answers. And
Greely? Hazen insisted, "I do not consider [his situation] desperate and fully
look forward to his rescue next season, preparation for which must be timely
and complete." Hazen's cabled messages from the western plains following

Garlington's return had told Secretary Lincoln that Greely's situation might be critical. But the C.S.O.'s latest communication, enclosed with Garlington's report, contained no echo of those desperate telegrams, which, he was to recall much later in self-defense, the Secretary of War had criminally ignored.

Those final autumn weeks of 1883 saw little in the way of firm plans for the relief of the Lady Franklin Bay Expedition, but preparation for a court of inquiry was designed, it was formally announced, "to investigate all matters relating to the *Proteus* relief expedition including, particularly, the failure of the *Proteus* to keep in company with the *Yantic* up to Littleton Island or in that neighborhood." Not only had Navy and Army personnel to brace themselves, but testimony would likely be expected from the two departmental heads. Lincoln's note to Hazen acknowledging receipt of the letter accompanying Garlington's report gave some hint of how his and Secretary Chandler's stories would concur. Lincoln told the C.S.O. that since he and Mr. Chandler had first seen that "memorandum of instructions" only recently, they "formed an opinion as to [Garlington's] having disobeyed an order." It appeared otherwise. "It is now clear that it never was an order. But," the secretary added tartly, "it is equally clear that having seen it and having under your orders a discretion," Garlington could not have acted more wisely than to follow the suggestion of landing stores on Littleton Island.

Lieutenant Garlington, meanwhile, had too much on his mind to have noticed that his predecessor as commander of a failed Greely relief expedition had come to an untimely end. Early in the year, before Garlington's appointment to command of the second attempt, Private William Beebe had been expected to be given some role in it. But reports of his drinking habits had reached General Hazen who, if he had seriously considered sending Beebe on a second voyage into the Arctic, most certainly dropped the idea. Following upon his failure to reach Greely, to be thus ignored was a humiliation that doubtless preyed on Beebe's mind. He was unmarried and lived alone. Early on 6 August, two months after the Garlington party had sailed, he was seen at the National Hotel in Washington persuading someone to get him two ounces of laudanum. He had, it was reported, "the appearance of a man who had been drinking hard." Later that day, the benighted Army private who had never truly relished scouring polar regions for lost explorers, was found dead at his home. The cause of death: a drug overdose.

The four-man court of inquiry into the loss of the *Proteus* convened in a hearing room at the War Department on 8 November. Brigadier General Stephen Vincent Benet, the Army's chief of ordnance (and grandfather of the poet), presided. The judge advocate and court recorder Major Henry Goodfellow had already secured copies of all available reports and correspondence on the history of the Lady Franklin Bay Expedition and of the two failed relief expeditions. Though not a court-martial, the process would inevitably carry an implication that Garlington was on trial, so he had obtained permission to have a prominent Washington lawyer, Linden Kent, serve as his counsel.

He needed one, for he faced the most searching questions. His idea from the outset of the expedition was that the *Yantic* should not impede in any way his passage north. Major Goodfellow then asked Garlington if "any dependence upon the *Yantic* being of any assistance to you was entirely problematical."

"Yes, sir," the lieutenant answered.

"Then of what use was the *Yantic* to your expedition?"

"Practically none. She was sent up there, I thought, simply to satisfy public opinion."

Garlington was asked if it would not have been a wise measure to land, say, half or even one-third of his supplies on the way up.

"I think if stores had been landed at all, they should have been landed on the other coast."

"But Greely expected to regard Littleton Island or Lifeboat Cove as his objective point?"

"He had to pass by the other point to get there. He planned to come by [way of] Cape Sabine."

Whole days were spent in discussion of the mysterious memorandum, from which Kent sought at the outset to separate his client. Had anything occurred in the signal office that contemplated leaving any stores at Littleton Island on the way up? "None whatever," replied Garlington. "The only time [the memorandum] was referred to was when I called General Hazen's attention to it."

The document had been drawn up first by Lieutenant Caziarc under orders of Captain Powell, who, when his turn came to testify, admitted as much, but added that office command had been abruptly thrust upon him when Hazen left town, and he knew little of what was going on.

The general himself, under questioning, also distanced himself from the memorandum, convincingly enough, since he was on the other side of the country when it was written. He explained, "It seems some such information was given out by the officer in charge of instructions, Mr. Caziarc. I would say he was never charged with the work of the Arctic expedition. He was merely called in to compile this little memorandum. That was perhaps the only original work he had to do in the whole business."

Who was the officer in actual charge? "Captain Clapp, until Lieutenant Garlington's arrival."

William H. Clapp was stationed in the Far West just then and unavailable as a witness. The spotlight fell upon Louis Caziarc, who had good reason to suspect himself in danger of a scapegoat's role. But conceding his responsibility for the memorandum, he defended it as sound and justified. Landing stores on the way up was his own idea. "It deviated from Lieutenant Greely's plans but only in the direction of greater safety. Those were my views, written for acceptance or rejection."

Caziarc's most uncomfortable moments came when he was under cross-examination by Lieutenant Garlington. Why had he inferred Garlington's approval of the memorandum and indicated as much to the press?

"You read it several times," explained Caziarc. "I was left with the impression you were in favor of the scheme."

"Had you talked with Captain Clapp about it? Did not he consider it a gratuitous piece of work on your part?"

"I don't know. He never said so."

Caziarc had testified that not until Garlington's return on the *Yantic* was he aware that his memorandum had been separated from the sailing instructions. Upon so belatedly learning this, had he taken pains to correct the impression given the Secretary of War and the Secretary of the Navy, thus removing from Garlington the stigma of having disobeyed orders?

"Every effort was made to do so. Captain Mills repeatedly saw the secretary [of war] and it will be found in the *New York Herald* of the sixteenth—"

"I am not asking about the *Herald*."

"Everything was done, but it had to be done guardedly."

Attention next swung to Commander Wildes. Before taking the oath, he wanted a technical point settled. Was he present as a witness or an object of inquiry? The court consulted in private, then told him he was there as a witness. And Wildes had no sooner sat in the witness chair when he displayed his intent to withhold any testimony potentially damaging to his reputation. Major Goodfellow had asked him if, upon learning at Littleton Island of the *Proteus* disaster, he had considered landing stores from the *Yantic* as a depot for the retreating Greely people. Wildes answered yes.

"What was your view of the subject at the time?"

"I decline to answer that, sir."

"Do you decline on the ground of its tending to incriminate you?"

"To incriminate? No, sir."

Goodfellow tried another tack: Had the witness and Garlington ever discussed contributing any of the *Yantic's* stores for either the *Proteus* party or Greely's?

"No, no such discussion."

"But when you found the *Proteus* had failed in her mission, why did you not consider leaving something for Greely?"

Wildes's response was a quote from his correspondence with Secretary Chandler: " 'I considered it my first and paramount duty to pick up the boats. I had no fears for Lieutenant Greely.' " Should Greely's party reach Littleton Island, not only would it find caches in the vicinity but plenty of game, the waters between Littleton and the mainland literally stank with walrus, "the stench from their ordure fouling the air."

Why had Garlington's relief expedition failed? Wildes's answer to that was that the two ships sent north were very unlike each other. "The ship to do all the work was foreign, with a crew picked up anywhere, composed of beach-combers." Wildes recalled that when the Navy Department planned an expedition to find the lost *Jeannette*, it had convened a board of high-ranking officers who "sat for weeks studying and determining questions, down to the minutest detail. In the present case I do not know of anything of the kind having been done."

No one pointed out that all the study had proved of no avail in the case of the *Jeannette*. But Wildes had said enough in the witness chair to stir General Hazen's wrath. As a result, Wildes had to endure the C.S.O.'s cross-examination. How did he know the *Proteus* crew was made up of "beachcombers"?

"It was too late in the season to secure a good crew. Captain Pike said he had to get what he could."

Hazen continued. "You have said that the authors of this expedition hadn't studied the experience of previous Arctic explorers. Was I among those authors?"

"I have nothing to add, can only judge of what everybody can see for themselves."

Smarting from Wildes's answers, Hazen asked the court that Captain Clapp, "who knows more of [study and preparation] than anyone in the world but myself," be summoned to testify. And when Major Goodfellow wondered what material purpose this testimony would serve, Hazen left the hearing room to write a rambling letter insisting that his reputation was at stake, that the testimony describing the *Proteus* as an inferior ship with an incompetent crew "tends to show a radical and almost criminal neglect of duty." Clapp's testimony was vital now because in December 1881, as Hazen wrote, "I placed in his hands the whole subject of Arctic work," an assignment the captain had held until Garlington's arrival on the scene. Hazen stated also, "I propose to show that the *Proteus* was suitable in all respects."

Spurred by Hazen's advice and newspaper reports, Captain Clapp had already taken the initiative toward getting himself heard. Writing from his far-off post of duty, he told Major Goodfellow that he felt his character threatened: "This is in every way unfair to me. I am stationed in a log camp, 2000 miles from Washington, and am being investigated without a chance of being heard in defense or explanation." Clapp was soon on his way. From almost as great a distance in another direction, a similar protest had come from St. John's, where Captain Pike was no less eager to protect his reputation.

In due course, both men were in the hearing room. Clapp proved to be of no help to General Hazen. He was in the Arctic exploration business just temporarily. But from the start he had advised not only that stores be landed on the way up but that they be placed at Cape Sabine or higher up the same west coast of Smith Sound, rather than on the east at Lifeboat Cove and Littleton Island, even though, he asserted, "these suggestions would involve departure from Lieutenant Greely's plan." And he testified that when he had been directed by General Hazen to prepare a "rough" of instructions for Lieutenant Caziarc, at the head of the Signal Corps clerical division, to formalize, "the paper here put in evidence was the result."

Captain Pike told of his disagreement with Garlington over going farther north into Smith Sound: "I did not object, I thought it my duty to defer to his wishes." The *Proteus*, he said, was a strong ship, equal to the task. Admittedly, her people were not of top quality, but neither were they mutinous. Half had served with him on previous voyages. Stoutly, Pike defended his seamanship. Ice was nothing new to him: "I have been at it for over thirty years. I was first into ice at age fourteen."

Recalled to the witness chair, General Hazen conceded that after Congress had legislated against continuance of Greely's work and ruled to bring the party home from Fort Conger, it had made sense to him that Greely's instructions could be modified to the extent of leaving stores at Littleton Island on the way up and of "making the depot on the west side of Smith Sound." It was the subsequent decision to send a tender—"itself a depot"—that made him revert to Greely's original instructions. Of that contrarily worded memorandum, Hazen repeated that he knew next to nothing: "I had no hand in it except to reject it." Almost breezily, he betrayed an ignorance of Arctic conditions. He had never doubted the *Yantic*'s ability to reach Littleton Island and was unaware of Melville Bay's treacherous features. He admitted, "I thought a ship at all seasons could get through by keeping near the west coast of Greenland."

The court asked, "And you were perfectly willing to risk the safety of the expedition upon the *Yantic* reaching Littleton Island?"

"Yes, sir."

When Hazen requested a tender to accompany the *Proteus*, did he expect the two vessels to be within sight of each other from St. John's to Littleton Island? The C.S.O. responded that he was "not sufficiently a navigator to know. I had no absolute certainty of either vessel getting there. But I believed the *Yantic* would reach Littleton Island as much as I believed the *Proteus* would."

Garlington, by this time firmly on record as having felt convinced that the *Yantic* could never safely cross Melville Bay, faced his superior with questions. He asked Hazen if his belief in the *Yantic* reaching Littleton Island had equalled that in the *Proteus* doing likewise. "Is that exactly what you mean?"

"The *Proteus* being an iceboat and the *Yantic* not, perhaps that answer should be modified. But in general, I expected both ships to reach there."

"That was supposing the *Yantic* would meet no ice?"

"No hard ice, but what she could have forced her way through."

"Did you have any idea of what kind of ice that would be?"

"I supposed broken ice, different from the firm pack."

On 17 November in Washington, about a week after the court of inquiry

began its work, Garlington informed General Hazen of a project in cooperation with Lieutenant Colwell of the Navy for bringing the Greely party home.
Garlington would command the expedition, and Colwell would captain the
ship. Clearly the two men were anxious to achieve a success that would erase
memory of the recent failure. The expedition would leave no later than 10 May,
which meant that the relief ship, a stout steam whaler, should be quickly
obtained and fitted out at an American Navy yard. A second vessel would go
along as convoy. Garlington wanted the main effort to remain the Army's, the
escort ship a naval craft with sheathed bows and minimal complement providing all possible space for carrying the main vessel's coal and provisions.

The ships would stay together as far as Cape Sabine, from where, assuming no word of Greely thus far, sledge parties would strike out north.
Garlington added further requirements. Before departure, he and Colwell
would make clear-cut written agreements with each other. Finally, and still more
significant, they insisted that "the commander should not be hampered with
detailed orders but should be directed to act according to his best judgment."

But as the year drew to its close, nothing occurred or was said that could
have comforted Henrietta Greely, burdened with two children and an invalid
father. Her mental distress showed physically. "I am sorry to hear," wrote her
mother-in-law from New England, "that you are losing your beautiful hair."
The elder Mrs. Greely had followed news accounts of the official inquiry. She
wrote, "General Hazen did not do his duty . . . there is blame all around and
they have disgraced themselves." But Henrietta viewed the C.S.O. as her principal hope, and she stressed to him that "the important thing is to bend every
energy toward preparing a fitting plan to rescue the party at the earliest moment
next year." Notwithstanding her domestic concerns, she had found time to contact influential allies, including members of Congress and newspaper editors.
Few of these, however, could do more than commiserate with her, scold the
government for having virtually written off the men it had sent into the Arctic,
and recommend that it move fast to do better the next year.

Efforts were under way, but in desultory bureaucratic fashion, with
General Hazen less of an ally than Henrietta seemed to think. The C.S.O. was
now among those refusing to acknowledge cause for alarm. "I do not view Mr.
Greely's situation as one of jeopardy," he wrote for the *Proteus* court of inquiry.
"The expedition may have reached Eskimo, even Danish, settlements." Or
Greely might have pitched camp in the vicinity of Littleton Island or Lifeboat

Cove, where, Hazen reminded the court, Sir George Nares recorded evidence of abundant game, "reindeer and walrus bones . . . remains of seals, foxes and hares . . . thousands of sterna of little auks." Then again, the party may have turned around and gone back to Lady Franklin Bay. In any case, Greely would be "fairly off for the winter." The only "source of apprehension [was] that the *Proteus* party left promises of succor this season which was not rendered." Thus self-redeemed, Hazen was appointed chairman of a four-man board formed in mid-December to study plans for bringing the Greely party home as early as possible.

The other three members were an Army officer and two from the Navy. That the panel would be represented jointly by the Army and Navy had risen from an exchange between the heads of both services, cabinet ministers sure to have felt by this time that much of the present anxiety, with perhaps greater grief ahead, flowed from their own cardinal indifference or ignorance. It went without saying that this time, preparations would not be bound by Greely's program. Greely had reached Lady Franklin Bay, wrote Robert Lincoln, "with an ease which later experiences show was extraordinary and even unfortunate in causing the difficulty of his return to be underestimated." It was too bad that General Hazen had told Garlington he was not necessarily obliged to heed that memorandum. "I shall never cease to regret," Chandler wrote back to his cabinet colleague, "that the sagacious counsel of the supplemental instructions were unknown to you, were rejected in the Signal Office, and were withheld from myself."

# IV

# CAPE SABINE

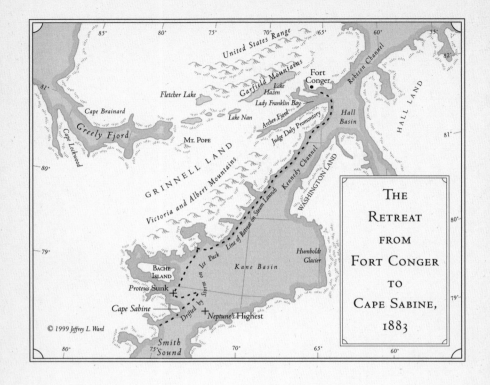

THE
RETREAT
FROM
FORT CONGER
TO
CAPE SABINE,
1883

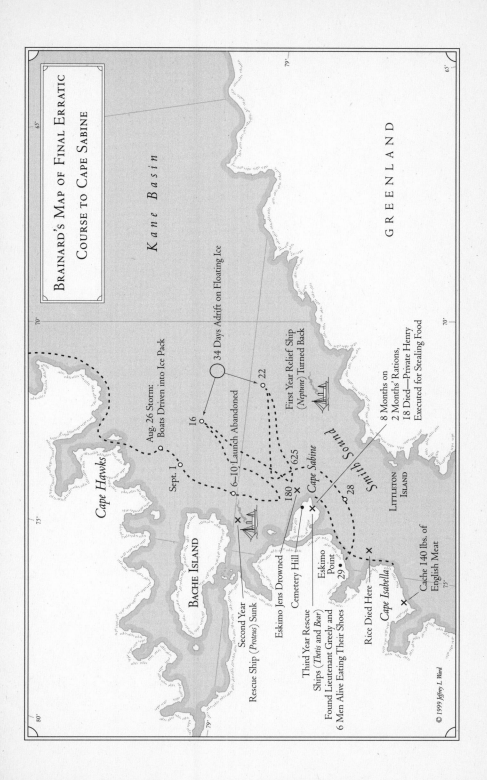

BRAINARD'S MAP OF FINAL ERRATIC
COURSE TO CAPE SABINE

*Kane Basin*

GREENLAND

*Cape Hawks*

Aug. 26 Storm:
Boats Driven into Ice Pack

34 Days Adrift on Floating Ice

16

22

6–10 Launch Abandoned

First Year Relief Ship
(*Neptune*) Turned Back

625

180

*Cape Sabine*

28

29

*Smith Sound*

8 Months on
2 Months' Rations,
18 Died—Private Henry
Executed for Stealing Food

LITTLETON
ISLAND

Sept. 1

BACHE ISLAND

Second Year
Rescue Ship (*Proteus*) Sunk

Eskimo Jens Drowned

Cemetery Hill

Eskimo
Point

Third Year Rescue
Ships (*Thetis* and *Bear*)
Found Lieutenant Greely and
6 Men Alive Eating Their Shoes

Rice Died Here

*Cape Isabella*

Cache 140 lbs. of
English Meat

© 1999 Jeffrey L. Ward

## 20

# CAMP CLAY

WHIPPED BY HEAVY snow squalls, struggling to save what they could of food, sleeping bags, instruments, and records, Greely's party huddled together yet again on scarcely more than a fragment of the turbulent pack. Of what had befallen either of the relief expeditions sent out from their homeland, the men knew nothing. They drifted in Kane Basin, the ice field their present home.

Firm land was often tantalizingly close, unreachable because of "too much slush and brash for boating, the ice too mobile for sledging." And the twenty-five marooned men felt themselves spinning southward at ever-increasing speed. The coasts of Ellesmere Island on one side and Greenland on the other began to recede, chances of landing at Cape Sabine or Littleton Island to dwindle. Those two locations constituted the end of the line of food caches. In the minds of Greely and his people, they had come to represent succor or salvation. Ample supplies and informative records might be waiting at Sabine, and a relief party at Littleton. But now, after the expedition's thirty-two days adrift, strong northwest gales and tidal currents swept the floe past hoped-for destinations, threatening to drive it out of Smith Sound and into the middle of broad Baffin Bay, which would spell sure doom.

The floe cracked yet again. Lockwood wrote, "Rubble piles up on the very edges near the tent." They took the tent down and scrambled upon a larger floe that conveniently approached. This relocation gave some slight comfort, and while Lockwood, on 26 September (one week after Secretary Lincoln's description of Greely's situation as "by no means hopeless") could see "nothing but starvation and death" ahead of them, he wrote admiringly that "the spirits of the party are remarkably high." He did not say how high they remained in the teeth of "the most violent northwesterly gale of the retreat," which fell upon their floe even as he penciled his notes. Nothing could be cooked. Greely issued frozen pemmican for the men to chew in their bags. Snow drifted into the reassembled frail tepee, whose canvas sides shuddered under the wind's pounding, destroying any hopes of sleep. Probably better off than the tepee detachment were the men under bags in the party's boats.

Their new floe crashed against a towering berg. The collision brought relief, for it slowed the party's southerly drift, "a providential intervention," Brainard called it. Prospects for making land revived. The nearest shore was westward, some four miles off, at the entrance to Baird Inlet, twenty miles south of Cape Sabine. Early on the twenty-ninth, Brainard set out to check on travel possibilities. He returned with a favorable report, and the party began the slow, laborious process of ferrying or hauling their gear and supplies across the split and hummocky ice field.

During the operation, Sergeant Cross stole rum and became so drunk he had to be taken off the drag ropes. Greely scarcely bothered to notice. At long last, after more than seven weeks of hardship and sometimes sheer terror, over a distance totalling some 500 miles by sledge, boat, or while helplessly adrift, he expected soon to tread solid ground. The winds had slackened. With buoyed hopes, the party fought on westward, alternately dragging the loaded twelve-man sledge over floes and pulling at the oars of the two remaining boats. It was piecemeal progress. But at 5:00 P.M. on the last day of September, the first boatload touched shore.

Some of the men raised a feeble cheer. Greely joined in but had few illusions concerning their safety. They had continued their southerly drift even while struggling westward, and were now at the mouth of Baird Inlet. A quick inspection of the landing site uncovered traces of native habitation. Otherwise, there was no sign of life, and as Greely christened the area Eskimo Point, he remained deeply frustrated by his inability to foretell what might lie ahead. Assuredly, the party must winter on this Ellesmere side. There was no early prospect of crossing to Littleton Island. Wrote Greely, "We could not average more than two miles daily across a moving pack."

The strong tide rose and fell every six hours, "disrupting and twisting the pack in all directions." The pack itself consisted of "infrequent paleocrystic floes, with much rubble and slush ice." Greely figured his present food rations could last thirty-five days. When they were reduced to ten, "as a forlorn hope an attempt will be made to reach Littleton Island by sledge." He calculated that this day would arrive the following February, in 1884, and in the meantime food stocks might be augmented by game. Along with hope, however forlorn, Greely congratulated himself on the fact that during the long ordeal since leaving Fort Conger, he had lost none of his data-packed journals, instruments, or natural-history specimens.

Following a two-day respite, Greely directed Sergeant George Rice with the Eskimo Jens to make north for Cape Sabine, where they would deposit the expedition's record of events to date and, most important, could ascertain if any American relief vessel had called there the previous two summers and left not only news but food added to what the English were believed to have cached. The pair set off on foot, with a one-man sleeping bag big enough for two at a pinch. During their absence, Greely located a sheltered spot and divided his men into three parties, permitting each to build its own rock house for wintering. They dug out granite boulders with bare hands until knuckles bled and muscles stiffened—all in near zero temperatures. Greely labored alongside his men and so strained his back, he wrote, "I cannot stand erect. The work has taxed to the utmost my physical powers, already worn by mental anxiety and responsibility."

To avoid a fatal weakening among his party, he took Dr. Pavy's advice and increased the daily ration to fourteen ounces of pemmican, eight of hard bread, and a pound and a half of potatoes. The hunters—Kislingbury, Sergeant Francis Long, and Eskimo Fred Christiansen—began their periodic excursions to find game, but at first brought in nothing.

And always Greely worried about a possible collapse of discipline. He sensed that his men's nerves were dangerously on edge. Convinced as he was of his talents for command, it made him heartsick to learn of "reflections on my fairness, especially when I have tried so hard to satisfy all." Lieutenant Lockwood informed him that Corporal Elison, criticizing the commander, had used words "which might easily be construed to be mutinous." Elison had been born in Baden, Germany, and to avoid military service had fled to the United States, where he had soon found himself in an army anyway. He responded to Lockwood's charge of mutinous language by pleading that he had only repeated remarks made by others. This statement did not save him from a stern reprimand.

They had been ashore one week. The winter huts steadily took shape. Edward Israel, at twenty-one the youngest of the expedition, accused Sergeant Brainard of commandeering the best material for the hut he was working on. Greely, extra-solicitous for Israel, "as it was wholly owing to me that he joined the expedition," persuaded him to apologize. Greely felt he knew who fomented the most growling—Sergeant Maurice Connell. He reduced him to private, openly telling the men that Connell had become a demoralizing influence. Connell complained, "You've never treated me like an N.C.O. anyway." He turned his back on the commander, muttering, "I don't care a damn about the matter." That night Greely told Lockwood quietly that when they returned home, he would prefer mutiny charges against three of the party—Octave Pavy and Lieutenant Kislingbury, and now Connell.

None of these events was allowed to completely shatter optimism. The hunters returned from their latest forage with a 150-pound seal. That same day happened to be Antoinette Greely's birthday, so the commander got everyone to drink to her health, he himself downing "half a gill of English rum." And by then, rough habitation was almost completed, walls bolstered by ice, two huts with canvas roofs. The third, housing a party headed by Sergeant Brainard, was more comfortably sheltered by an upturned boat for which lots had been drawn. Moss wrenched from between rocks served as bedding. Lieutenant Lockwood described the party's situation as alarming, yet quite logically outlined "three chances [we have] for our lives. The chance of finding American provisions at Sabine or at [Cape] Isabella; the chance of crossing to Littleton Island when our present rations are gone; the chance to shoot sufficient seal or walrus near here to last us during the winter."

Sergeant Rice and Eskimo Jens, meanwhile, had encountered thick weather crossing Ross Bay. The only safe lead amid rough ice detoured them westerly around tiny Cocked Hat Island before they could reach Payer Harbor just below Sabine. During Rice's reconnaissances, he established the cape as actually an island, fashioned by a narrow channel that connected Ross Bay and Buchanan Strait (and promptly became "Rice Strait"). At Payer Harbor, sight of an upright tripod led Rice to a depot of 240 rations. But then he made other discoveries at Sabine and nearby Brevoort Island. They included caches left by the *Proteus,* so that when he and Jens returned to Eskimo Point at 5:00 P.M. on 9 October, it was with mostly devastating news. Among the papers brought in was Lieutenant Garlington's 24 July report (now eleven weeks old) describing his vessel's loss. Lieutenant Kislingbury read the report aloud, perhaps because of the commander's poor vision. Private Henry noted, with ponderous humor, that "work on the palaces" was suspended, and once the cooks had prepared "our slim evening repast, we all gathered in one of the completed mansions. With bated breath we listened."

What they heard was that ice had turned back the ship expected in 1882 and that the second, their old *Proteus,* was a sunken wreck not twenty miles distant. Garlington's words of the ship standing "enormous pressure nobly," succumbing to "this measureless force," gave a touch of eloquence that Greely's people could have done without. The report stated further, "Few provisions were saved." It was some consolation to learn that Garlington had established a depot, 500 rations of bread, tea, canned goods, with sleeping bags, three miles from Cape Sabine. Greely learned also of the cache of 240 rations (with a boat ruined by bears) left in 1882 by the first relief party, the *Neptune's,* under "Major Beebe of the Signal Service"—a reference which must have raised Greely's eyebrows, for the only Beebe he remembered was a lowly ranker of intemperate habits who served as General Hazen's private secretary.

Besides the small cache on the Sabine side, Beebe had left an equivalent amount of provisions across Smith Sound on Littleton Island. As far as Greely could calculate from Garlington's record, which he did not find altogether clear, most of the *Neptune's* stores had gone back home. The caches in this region, including what the English had left in 1876, provided some 1,300 rations— enough to feed his party for sixty days at most.

With mixed feelings, the men at Eskimo Point continued to listen. After the loss of his ship, Garlington intended to head south in boats with Captain Pike's crew to try to intercept the naval steamer *Yantic,* bound north as escort vessel but with orders not to enter ice. He might also contact a Swedish steamer expected in the neighborhood of Cape York. The message ended with Garlington's "sorrow" at failing to reach Lady Franklin Bay and his vow that "everything within the power of man" would be done to save Greely's expedition. Those final words read at Eskimo Point were greeted with faint cheers. Sergeant David Ralston thought that if stretched enough, the hundreds of rations might see the party safely through the winter. Kislingbury was encouraged by the concentration of relief plans upon Littleton Island. He believed that Garlington must have met the *Yantic* and told her captain to leave all available supplies if he got the ship that far north. Kislingbury's excited vision was of the lieutenant himself on Littleton Island, that "he will remain until we can cross. God bless my friend Garlington! His suffering must have been great indeed. But I firmly believe he is now at Littleton Island."

Greely hoped so, too, but without conviction. He feigned some share in the modest surge of sanguinity, but with that forte for realistic assessment so vital an element of command, he could now foresee hardship, hunger, "and possible death for a few of the weakest. Our fuel is so scanty we are in danger of perishing on that score alone." And disappointments accumulated. Garlington hadn't had time to "classify" the 500 rations he had cached at Sabine. Greely was distressed to find that they included scarcely more than 100 rations of meat. Private Henry wrote, "How we gloated over the harvest, gazed upon the box of Durham tobacco and wished it was meat."

Rice and Eskimo Fred, who had crossed Baird Inlet to Cape Isabella in hopes that their compatriots had left stores for them, found none, not even the boat mentioned in Garlington's report. All they discovered was just 144 pounds of canned beef in the Nares cache. Rice also found his party's old whaleboat—it had drifted down ahead of them and wedged intact between floes in Payer Harbor. Digging in the same vicinity beneath the *Neptune* cache, they unearthed the boat Beebe had left. Greely pondered. Had Garlington's cached messages not told of food depots in the general area of Cape Sabine, and the possibilities of further supplies on Littleton Island across Smith Sound, he would have taken to his boats, "turned my back to Cape Sabine and starvation, to face a possible death on a perilous voyage along the shore to the southward."

But as things stood, he could not ignore Garlington's reported intention of heading down the Greenland coast to meet either the *Yantic* or the Swedish ship. He construed Garlington's message as "conveying to me in the strongest terms his fixed determination to return to Sabine if either steamer was fallen in with, and that I could look to him for relief." So while tempted to "turn faces homeward," continuing south by boats in an effort to reach the Cary Islands, with their known depots and a likely anchorage for relief ships, Greely had to take Garlington at his word. "On the strength of his promise I decided to proceed to Cape Sabine and await the promised help, reluctantly turning my back on a southern trip which, a gamble, might have destroyed my whole party or secured its ultimate safety."

Given the season's limited daylight and heavy falls of snow, the transfer to Cape Sabine took almost a week. It produced some grumbling among the party at having to dismantle their newly built huts at Eskimo Point, haul back-breaking sledge loads across Ross Bay, twelve men at a time in harness, on a twenty-mile journey to Sabine in temperatures low enough to foreshadow winter. On 13 October, Kislingbury and Pavy recommended that some loads be left until later; the men were too exhausted. "I declined to follow their advice," wrote Greely, "unwilling to abandon either records, instruments, or any part of our provisions." All they left behind were the English iceboat and two paddles, for possible later use.

Their newly selected campsite was a neck of lowland conveniently close to the *Proteus* wreck cache and to a glacier-fed lake just four miles west. To the east, a ridge about 100 feet high ran parallel to the shoreline. Westward above the lake sloped ice-capped hills, at whose foot would be the party's new home. They were not on a mainland cape, but as ascertained by Rice during his westward detour, a headland of one of a series of islands, islets, and fragmented peninsulas that curved northeastward along the Ellesmere coast. Four miles wide and eight in length, it would appear on British charts as Bedford Pim Island, after a widely voyaged naval officer and seeker of the Franklin party. The consequences of Greely's decision to halt and wait at its eastern extremity was to implant it more tragically in the annals of Arctic exploration as Cape Sabine.

Once more the men had to build shelter, once more pry loose ice-covered rock with thinly mittened or naked hands. They hauled moraine created by the glacier, and it all went into reinforcing the hut's framework, fashioned from

boat oars lashed together and draped with sailcloth and tarpaulin. The men
bodily lifted and upturned their remaining whaleboat upon the frame, and this
served as the roof, with more oars nailed into place as rafters. The boat had a
hole cut in it to allow for a chimney improvised from empty food cans and set
up at the cooking area, where stood a stove Private Bender had made of a sheet-
iron cylinder. During the building, Greely "suffered a bad blow in the face from
Whisler who too carelessly wielded his axe while helping me loose a rock." The
finished hut measured only twenty-five feet in length, eighteen feet wide, and
its walls scarcely five feet high. A post made from lashed oars supported
the center of the whaleboat, and from it hung a seal-blubber lamp and the
barometer.

For twenty-five men, it was less a hut than a tunnel, with hardly enough
height even to kneel in. Least troubled by this accommodation was Private
Julius Frederick, at five feet two inches nicknamed Shorty. The men's sleeping
bags, so often used on the sledge trips from Fort Conger, were never more vital
than now. The better ones were of well-tanned buffalo hide. A sheepskin variety collected moisture too readily and soon could turn into a mass of ice. Each
bag could hold two, even three, occupants. Men sleeping singly suffered more
from cold than those crammed in one bag, for whom physical comfort was sac-
rificed to body heat. The bags were arranged in two lines opposite each other,
heads to the wall. The entrance to the hut was a gap at one end with a canvas
flap doorway. The space adjoining the hut and walled in by snow blocks was
the commissary storehouse. The seal-blubber lamp supplied dim illumination.
It was a humble enough abode, but on the day of its completion, Christiansen
killed a fox, and this was regarded as a good augury.

And the men had news of a sort from home. An old copy of the *Louisville
Courier-Journal* was found in the *Proteus* cache. Most conspicuous was the letter
from Henry Clay criticizing the government's Greely relief plan as inadequate
and urging that two ships be sent north without delay. "What Beebe on the
*Neptune* had left on Cape Sabine could not keep Greely's people alive indefinitely. The cache of 240 rations, if it can be found, will prolong their misery
for a few days." Then would come the end. As Sergeant Rice read these words,
Greely remembered Clay as a potentially useful member of the expedition who
had left it only because of the essential presence of the doctor he had come to
detest. And though one was wrecked and the whereabouts of the other
unknown, two ships had indeed come north. So as a forlorn gesture of appre-

ciation, Greely named his party's new home Camp Clay. Pavy raised no objections.

Clay's further words made depressingly clear that disaster had overtaken
the American exploring steamer *Jeannette*, some search for which (also delivery
of letters from Emma De Long to her husband) had been statedly a part of
Greely's mission in the Arctic. Should the Lady Franklin Bay Expedition run
out of food, "like poor De Long they will then lie down on the cold ground,
under the quiet stars." Greely refused to dwell on that dire prognosis. He had
to make future plans, which he based only on "such provisions as are actually
within our reach." And unlike some of his more optimistic men, he refused to
count on anything awaiting them even on the other side of Smith Sound. "Since
the Garlington record has misled us regarding the boat at Cape Isabella," Greely
wrote, "it is an open question whether there is a cache on Littleton Island."

On 20 October, Greely wrote that "with strict limitations" their food supply might last until about mid-March, by which time they might be with a relief
expedition or otherwise safe on Littleton Island. "If not, what then?" Three
days later, he sent a party to cache the expedition's records and pendulum on
the islet called Stalnecht at the mouth of Payer Harbor, where any relief crew
would be sure to find them. "I am determined that our work shall not perish
with us," he wrote. Much of the following weeks was spent on bringing in supplies from the Beebe and *Proteus* caches. This task proved more exhausting than
anyone had foreseen, for the sledge kept breaking down. As light dwindled into
the long Arctic night, so faded hopes of much game as a source of food. Greely
ordered strict rationing, over Dr. Pavy's objections. Each man would receive
fourteen ounces of food per day, one-third of which was to be meat. "Whether
we can live on such a driblet of food remains to be seen," wrote Lockwood.
"We are now constantly hungry and the constant thought and talk run on food
we hope to eat on reaching civilization."

Alcohol ran short, and cooking over stearin made everybody cough. As
time passed, fuel consisted of seal blubber, barrel staves, tarred rope. Not all
the food had been gathered in. A cache of English meat was believed to be at
Cape Isabella, left by Nares. On 2 November, accompanied by Corporal Elison
with Private Frederick and the demoted David Linn, Rice set out with a light
sledge and eight days' rations to haul it in. They had forty miles of travel
through deep snow and over pulverized ice. Some of the lengthening nights
brought temperatures of thirty below zero. With open water a mile from the

cape, and no ice foot to bear the weight of the sledge, it was left where it lay, and the four men had to detour up ice-coated bluffs to reach the cache. "We climbed as best as we could," Elison scrawled painfully in a notebook, "got the four boxes of meat, started back to the sledge, took us five hours. Hands froze, couldn't thaw them in sleeping bag. Bag stiff." Both of Elison's feet froze the next day. "Unable to assist any on the sledge, thus making it very hard on the others. Went into camp 4 P.M." On the seventh, he wrote, "Broke camp 9 A.M. I'm still struggling along, legs like stilts."

The diminutive Private Frederick helped Elison stagger forward, Rice and Linn dragging the sledge until they, too, were on the point of collapse. Near Baird Inlet, they cut away Elison's boots and rubbed his feet to restore circulation, but without success—the corporal's legs were frostbitten to his knees. His hands had stiffened as well. It became a question of what should be carried on the sledge—the food or the prostrate Elison. Rice quickly decided. He had the food unloaded, cached, and marked with a Springfield rifle upended in the deep snow. For a further nine hours, they struggled on in darkness, guiding Elison ahead, but he kept staggering off course, his eyelids frozen together as if glued.

The men were along a ridge north of Eskimo Point when Linn sank to his knees. Elison, his sufferings compounded by futile efforts to thaw his frozen feet, howled incessantly. Rice and Frederick unloaded an iron-hard sleeping bag, and together they forced Elison into it. Linn and Frederick then wedged themselves into the same bag, hoping their combined body heat would ease the corporal's agony. Rice pressed on alone, the words he would have to utter before the commander already trembling on his muffled lips: "Corporal Elison dying at Ross Bay."

At the camp had occurred the first alarming sign of a pattern of theft, fear, and mutual distrust. Private Schneider, a particular favorite of Greely's, occasional clerk, and one of the party's two best cooks, was seen acting suspiciously in the storehouse. Sure of his guilt, Greely replaced him as cook with Private Bender (his real name was George Leyerzopf), and for better security arranged a canvas roof and door to the vestibule with lock and key. While these matters were on Greely's mind, along with mounting apprehension over the Rice party's prolonged absence, on 9 November around midnight, Rice stumbled into the hut, alone, with frightening news about his comrades back at Ross Bay.

Sergeant Brainard and the Eskimo Christiansen set out immediately. Trudging over rough and heavy ice, they spent seventeen hours bringing the three men in. So solid were they frozen in the bag that it had to be chopped apart to release them. Dr. Pavy examined Elison's blackened fingers and toes and said they needed amputating—also that lacking proper instruments, he dared not attempt such surgery for fear of killing the man. But even those of the party who had always considered Elison a hardy soul were to be surprised by his powers of endurance. He was unable to leave his sheepskin sleeping bag, had to be assisted while eating or using an improvised bedpan, needed his bandages changed repeatedly by either Pavy or Private Biederbick, yet seldom did he complain. Those who did complained of hunger. Again Greely had to devise a program to shore up morale. He wrote "The ravenous conditions of the entire party cannot but have the effect of making most men morbid and suspicious." Throughout the narrowing hours of daylight, there were duties to perform: menus to prepare, dishes cleaned, a hole cut in the lake ice daily for fresh water, the large urinal tub near the hut's flapping doorway emptied. But the lengthening hours of night told severely upon the men's tempers, and beyond the few books and games remaining with the party, Greely had little in recreational material from which to choose.

He fell back on lecturing. In November his subjects ranged from the state of Maine, "touching on its important cities, its history and famous men," to notable battles of the Civil War. There were readings from Dickens, the Bible, even Army regulations. Often the reading was done by Private Henry, because, wrote Lockwood, "he has the loudest voice." By nightfall, rambling reminiscences would drift from sleeping bags, and mutterings of fancied menus and remembered women.

Dr. Pavy, his contempt for the leader hidden but undiminished, was kept busy seeing to his invalids, which, during Thanksgiving Day week, included Lieutenant Kislingbury, recovering from his rupture; Linn, rheumatism, system weakened by recent exposure, mind wandering; Connell, weak from reduced diet; Cross, frosted foot improving; and, of course, Elison, frozen extremities. But Private Biederbick had shot a five-pound white fox. The national holiday was celebrated with a double ration of coffee for breakfast and a fox stew, raisin pudding, hot rum and lemon punch for dinner. "Good for our cooks," recorded a somewhat mellowed Cross, whose scathing references to Lieutenant Greely had become fewer and fewer, as if hunger tempered spite and hostility.

Yet when December brought heavy storms and thick snow drifting into the hut, old animosities revived. It was whispered behind Greely's back that he dodged work. Neither did the approach of Christmas bring the promise of good fellowship. Lockwood noted that "the doctor, Henry, Whisler, Cross, Bender, Connell, Schneider testify to having seen suspicious things," signs of (Greely's) favoritism toward Brainard, or Frederick (whose turn, with Long, it was to cook) getting more of the stew than his share. One night, Greely heard someone fumbling in the dark in Elison's bread can. "I was awake, plainly heard it done." He immediately suspected Pavy. "I was shocked that the expedition's surgeon should so fail in his duty." But Greely told only Lockwood, his appointed successor, and Sergeant Brainard, who issued the rations. The doctor was still technically under arrest, but, Greely noted, "I had to be conciliatory. Pavy's services are so important."

Christmas, with, as Brainard put it, "stars scintillating in their setting of deepest azure," was celebrated, if feebly. Cross complained that craving food robbed him of sleep. Some of the men had saved scraps for the festive day. Others exchanged hardtack for seal blubber. Lieutenant Lockwood, who three days earlier had felt "an apathy and cloudiness impossible to shake off," declared Christmas Day "a great success." Brainard predicted that "Garlington will visit us some time in January." Carols were sung in English, French, and German, the Eskimos chiming in with native airs. Dinner was seal stew and raisins with condensed milk, and the two cooks had managed also to brew a good rum. Kislingbury opened his cigar box and fashioned a cigarette for each of the party. Greely joined in the fun, forcing himself to suppress pangs of longing for Henrietta and their children.

Thoughts of Christmas at home still lingered when, in the gloom of the cramped hut, Elison was heard to gasp. When his comrades eased him out of his sleeping bag, his right foot presented "a horrible sight. The flesh had sloughed away, leaving the bones entirely devoid of covering." Yet the man was astonishingly calm, thought Greely, and "bears his troubles with manly and heroic fortitude." Elison continued to do so, even as, on New Year's Day, the doctor completely severed his suppurating foot by cutting through the ligaments and shreds of skin that held it to the ankle. Within hours, Pavy also snipped a deadened finger from the corporal's left hand. And throughout this darkest and most frigid phase of the long polar winter, it was impossible to close one's ears to the incessant rumble and grinding of the floes in Smith Sound. Lieutenant Greely opened his journal that first week of 1884 and wrote, "How I wish Lieutenant Garlington would come and relieve us."

# 21

# THE FIRST DEATH

IN WASHINGTON ON 20 December, the board appointed to study plans for the next relief expedition had assembled in Room 88 of the Navy Department. It did so, alert to agitation throughout the land concerning the plight of the Greely party. It lost no time in recommending that two full-powered steam whalers be bought and prepared for service. Correspondence was opened with Consul Molloy at St. John's and the American minister in London to arrange a search for suitable vessels. The witnesses who appeared before the board included Garlington, who, after giving a brief résumé of his own Arctic experiences, expanded on his November proposal. He offered his opinion that Greely would be found on the Greenland coast above Cape York and, without realizing how absolutely wrong he was, went on to affirm that the party had yet to leave Lady Franklin Bay "because we know from all the attempts made last year to get to the Arctic regions that it was a very bad season."

Garlington, then still a witness before the *Proteus* court of inquiry, was the only Army officer summoned by the Army-Navy relief board. The other would-be advisers were of naval or other seafaring background. With the possible exception of General Hazen, the board seemed to favor a relief expedition wholly naval, and it paid Lieutenant John Colwell's observations closest attention. He recommended that an American ship go up to Littleton Island as soon as possible, otherwise, "you will find a Scotch whaler getting there first and bringing the men down. It is only a day's run out of their track when they are bound for the whaling regions. It would pay them to see if those people are there and, if so, bring them back as a business speculation."

Captain Pike, in Washington for the court of inquiry, told the board that steam whalers could reach Littleton Island near the end of July. Pike's veteran ice pilot James Norman, also down from St. John's, talked of "portable boats, you could pack them in your sledges." They were built in Newfoundland and, if damaged, easily repaired. Norman informed them that the Dundee whalers took these "sea punts" because they were easily hauled up on the ice and required only four men to pull them across floes and slip them into the water. Captain Greer of the Navy, a member of the board, doubted their efficiency in deep water: "These sealing punts are not good for sea boats, are they?" Norman replied, "I have seen them in some pretty rough water." He thought they could help in a northerly push along the Ellesmere ice foot, should a sledge party have to journey along the west coast of Smith Sound to meet the retreating Greely party.

John Danenhower, navigator of the lost *Jeannette*, volunteered a surprising alternative to sealers and whalers as ships of choice. Why not the "fruiters that go to the Mediterranean, or West Indies traders"? Such vessels could be more speedily procured at Baltimore or Boston, taken to a Navy yard, and ceiled with four-inch planking. When a board member raised the question of ramming through ice, Danenhower demurred: "The capability of a ship to ram ice is exaggerated. I have seen the *Jeannette* try it and her masts would shake like whip-stocks every time, and she accomplished nothing."

The other conspicuous survivor from the *Jeannette* disaster, Chief Engineer George Melville, read from prepared notes, proposing that a steamer and a schooner make for Upernavik, which would be easily accessible in the spring. The schooner would be there first as a store and escort and await the steamer's arrival. The steamer would thereupon force her way to Lady Franklin Bay, returning south if Fort Conger was found abandoned. "Cairns and records left by Greely should tell of their movements," he said. He implored that lessons from the *Jeannette* experience not be forgotten. Ramming could be effected, but only if the ship's bows were more completely plated by iron bars than was De Long's vessel. Melville asserted, "If you meet ice eight inches thick and the floe extends half a mile, put that ship at full tilt, say seven miles an hour, and strike. The blow would not hurt her. Back her off and try two or three times. The chances are you would split the floe." The testimony from both men of the *Jeannette* came at a period when they were at unpublicized loggerheads. But before the relief board, they agreed on one point: the futility of taking dogs. Danenhower declared that had the *Jeannette* not taken dogs, "it would have been better for us." And Melville calculated that "they eat half as much as a man and do only one-eighth his work."

Meanwhile, the *Proteus* court of inquiry had continued. It was a case more complicated than General Benet and his fellow members might have preferred. But the cause of the trouble was soon recognized as inadequate understanding of the Arctic's hazards and caprices. Planning from the start had proceeded without direct participation by genuinely experienced Arctic explorers. Lieutenant Garlington had sailed away north with only a confused idea of what he might be up against. Private Beebe before him was even less suited to the task. The officers Clapp and Caziarc knew only what they had read from books. These truths were not lost on the *Proteus* court. And neither should the court have been oblivious to the fact that while composing his original relief instructions, concerning which he sternly forbade "latitude of action," Adolphus Greely had labored under serious misconceptions of his own.

With the court of inquiry still in session, there had appeared the Secretary of War's annual report for 1883. It sought to put fears for the explorers' safety at rest. If they had remained at Fort Conger, they were well stocked with food, clothing, and other essentials until summer. In view of prearranged plans and the failure of relief expeditions to reach them, they might be coming southward to the entrance of Smith Sound. The report stated, "Even in this case [Greely's] condition would be by no means desperate," for at this point and farther north, supplies were cached. And should these prove insufficient, "it is thought that it would not be impossible for him to retrace his steps and reach the supplies left at Lady Franklin Bay." These words could have been spoken only by someone without the remotest knowledge of what such a journey in those latitudes at the onset of winter would entail.

The *Proteus* inquiry proceeded spottily through December, and upon its resumption in the new year Garlington's attorney, Linden Kent, presented his argument: The memorandum on the landing of stores on the way up was "the poison which has been infused into all branches of this investigation"; the very day after Garlington had telegraphed his sad news of failure from St. John's, the memorandum came "back into this case to do its cruel work"; and, after the shipwreck, the only way Garlington could have helped Greely was by contacting the *Yantic*, which Garlington had "attempted to do." But the ship and the boat parties failed to meet, ice keeping them apart. Garlington's supplies were "desperately small." His peril was far greater than that of "Greely in his house at Discovery Harbor." To lay blame upon Garlington for what testimony indicated was clerical blundering in the signal office was, "to say the least of it, a cruel, merciless and unwarranted tampering with a soldier's reputation."

General Hazen saw what direction the court would take. Blame for Garlington's failure was to be placed upon not just the Signal Corps but its chief. Without waiting for the court's findings, he asked the Secretary of War to order Lieutenant Garlington court-martialed for disobedience and neglect of duty. Lincoln refused. He said that in "the interests of the military service," no such trial was required. And a week later, on 12 January, the *Proteus* court of inquiry issued its report.

As Hazen expected, Garlington was treated gently. He had erred only in decision making. Under orders that nothing be allowed to retard his ship's progress north, he was justified in parting company with the slower vessel. Once the *Proteus* had sunk, he might have decided more usefully to have waited for the *Yantic*. Lieutenant Colwell and Captain Pike had thought there was at least "a bare chance" that the *Yantic* would get through. Garlington could then have arranged for the Navy ship to leave some of her stores at Lifeboat Cove. A month's supply for the *Yantic*'s crew would have fed Greely's party five times as long. Garlington did not wait, had instead headed south in boats with few enough supplies to sustain his and Pike's men and none at all to leave for Greely. But the most all these events amounted to on the lieutenant's part was misjudgment. And it was traceable to the failure of the Chief Signal Officer to give him clear instructions and advice.

And Wildes? Upon leaving Littleton Island on 3 August he had had four months' worth of rations on board. He'd brought a full three months' supply back to St. John's. The court decided, "It is to be regretted that in [Wildes's] earnest desire to succor the *Proteus* crew and relief party" before they entered the Melville Bay danger zone "he [did not risk] the delay of a few hours, even days, to cache a portion of his surplus provisions and stores [on Littleton Island] to welcome the arrival of Lieutenant Greely and party on that inhospitable shore."

Then the court dealt its harshest with General William Babcock Hazen, that memorandum of Lieutenant Caziarc's its principal weapon. Hazen's own words to Secretary Lincoln in November 1882, regarding the following year's relief effort under Lieutenant Garlington, were that in the planning, "every possible contingency must be provided for." Was not the loss of the *Proteus* a possible contingency? The only pertinent reference to it was in the Caziarc memorandum about leaving stores at Littleton Island on the way up. The court ruled, "The ship went to her destruction without anything having been done in advance for the safety of thirty-seven lives on board, no provision made for the Greely party in case of such disaster." Installing a depot on the way up had been repeatedly urged on General Hazen, and thus "his explanations for not doing so, that it would be a deviation from Lieutenant Greely's orders, and that the convoy *Yantic* would be 'a depot' are untenable and illogical."

Worse yet, Hazen had sent that memorandum back to Caziarc for transmission to Garlington without comment. Caziarc had naturally supposed that it was approved. And he never thought otherwise. Hazen had never bothered to tell Caziarc that Garlington had questioned it in his office on the eve of departure and that he, Hazen, had told him not to regard it as binding. Hence Caziarc's unfortunate presumption that Garlington had disobeyed orders. And hence Caziarc's press release to that effect. So the court decided that it was all General Hazen's fault, his "lax, negligent, defective, mischievous method of conducting business . . . lamentable and incomprehensible blindness to facts."

The damage was done. Greely's original instructions were that if the successive relief expeditions failed to reach Lady Franklin Bay, a winter station of men and stores was to be made at Littleton Island or its nearby Lifeboat Cove. That station should have been established "at all hazard, as upon it may depend the lives of Greely and his party." There were probably sufficient supply caches at intervals along the shores of Kennedy Channel and Smith Sound to sustain the party on its retreat, but only as far south as Cape Sabine, with, at Littleton Island across the sound, the small deposit, 240 rations, left by the since suicidal Beebe.

The court having concluded with references to "lack of sound judgment unattended by any willful neglect or intentional dereliction of duty," there would be no further proceedings, no courts-martial. Only in its mournful summary of the Lady Franklin Bay Expedition's likely plight were the tribunal's words devoid of ambiguity: "The omission to make this [Littleton Island] depot threatens serious danger to the lives of Lieutenant Greely and his command." Overall, from July 1882 to August 1883, no fewer than 50,000 rations were taken north in the *Neptune, Proteus,* and *Yantic.* Only a thousand were left where they could be of much use, "the remainder returned to the United States or sunk with the *Proteus.*" That Lieutenant Greely's party would reach Cape Sabine safely was "highly probable, also that they will cross Smith Sound to Littleton Island, but only to find themselves on a desolate coast, without shelter and with little food." To return to Lady Franklin Bay would be as terrible an undertaking as proceeding south. "The heart-sickness and disappointment at being forgotten renders it impossible to imagine what their future course will be. The veil cannot be lifted until the next summer's sun dispels the darkness of the Arctic night."

General Hazen reacted predictably to the court's explicit pinning of blame upon him. He chastised it for having let Garlington off too lightly. And for the man he once had praised as an ideal choice to lead the relief expedition, Hazen now had biting words. That the retreat south following the shipwreck was undertaken safely was not, as the court seemed to think, because of Garlington, who was nothing but a passenger, "helplessly dependent" on Captain Pike's people to seek rescue southward. Yet to Garlington went the credit. Sneered Hazen in conclusion, "This is the first time in military history that an officer was ever commended for the celerity with which he effected his flight from his post of duty."

AT CAMP CLAY, thievery increased. The day Corporal Elison's right foot came off, someone had knifed through the canvas roof of the commissary storehouse and stolen a quarter pound of bacon. A week later, more bacon vanished and bread was taken. Men suspected one another. "Connell marauding during the night on our rations," Private Henry scratched in his notebook. Fingers were pointed at Private Schneider as the man who had cut into the commissary, and there was muttered talk of throttling him. Still, the party held together. In efforts to get proper sleep, bag occupancy changed constantly. "Lockwood still in my bag, weak," wrote Greely on 12 January. "Cross weak, possible scurvy, Bender complaining, so put Bender in Lockwood's bag, having Jewell take Cross's place with Bender and Henry." On Dr. Pavy's advice, Greely had ordered periods of outdoor exercise. They diminished as winter deepened. What the commander recorded as "the minor office of nature" was performed inside the hut, a tub near the entrance for this purpose, "much frequented as cold appeared to weaken the kidneys," resulting in urinary incontinence. The other natural function became "a problem due to physical efforts to assist the torpid bowels, also exposure from weather." Constipation sometimes lasted as long as fourteen days.

On 9 January, Sergeant Rice had returned from a crude observation post up the hill behind the hut to report dense clouds erupting from colliding floes. The sounds of moving ice swelled louder. Rice's news worried Greely, for the increasing restlessness of the pack was bound to lower their chances of reaching Littleton Island. The twelfth of the month was Elison's birthday—Greely "gave him half a gill of rum to celebrate." He seemed unaware that he had lost a foot and a finger. Then Sergeant Cross fell sick. On the fifteenth, he had worked splitting wood for exercise, but the following day he slipped into a coma. Dr. Pavy diagnosed scurvy and fed him spirits of ammonia and brandy. This concoction seemed to energize Cross, for he kept trying to work himself out of his frigid sleeping bag. Private Biederbick, as the party's nurse, called Pavy, and the two improvised rubber hot-water bottles, which they forced into the bag against the sergeant's shuddering body. Again Cross lapsed into a coma. He died at midnight on the seventeenth, two days short of his fortieth birthday, for which he had saved morsels of bread to celebrate.

Pavy told the commander in private that while symptoms of scurvy were evident, Cross had died of malnutrition. Greely felt compelled to address the men. "So as not to excite depression, I ignored the question of scurvy or starvation. I urged the party to take courage, and pointed out that Cross's constitution had been undermined by his early habits." It was the brand of moralizing that Greely in years long past had preached with self-righteous pleasure. Now his words had the practical purpose of freeing the men's thoughts from their hunger and dread of scurvy.

The group's next question was how to dispose of Cross's body. Some favored sinking it beneath ice in the small lake nearby. A majority favored more formal interment. It was sewn up in coffee sacks, and after Greely read the burial service, he and Kislingbury, Brainard, Rice, Salor, Israel, Connell, and Whisler hauled it on the small sledge up the hill at the southeast end of the lake, "what I call Cross Lake," wrote the commander whom Cross had viciously ridiculed. Brainard's words portrayed Cross's funeral as "a ghostly procession of emaciated men moving slowly and silently away from their wretched ice prison in the uncertain light of the Arctic night." Given weak hands and a lack of tools, they scraped rather than dug into the gravel, leaving a hole hardly fifteen inches deep. To conserve ammunition, no salute was fired over Sergeant Cross's shallow grave.

The men kept mostly to their sleeping bags. Those who managed to leave the hut did so only from physical necessity. Few read. Frost and ice coated the interior walls. In the dim blubber-fueled lamplight, the commander strained weak eyes over psalms and poetry, his voice barely audible above buffeting wind gusts. Lieutenant Lockwood improvised a lecture on the St. Louis riots, and while smoking a blend of tobacco and tea leaves, he dreamed of a restaurant in that city named The Silver Moon, where fifty cents bought a dinner, and a nearby bakery offered "excellent bread and something fine in the way of tapioca and coconut pies." The lieutenant interrupted his soliloquy to hand Sergeant Ralston a piece of tobacco for plugging a painfully hollow tooth. This makeshift filling enabled Ralston to murmur memories of early days as an Iowa farmhand. Then he read from *The Pickwick Papers*. Brainard talked of Indian fighting; Pavy described a bullfight and a walking tour through Switzerland. Such efforts were to sustain morale. For moments now and then, they also produced a comforting sense of comradeship, even intimacy.

These were no defense against bodily decline. Lockwood became so helpless he had to be dragged from his bag to the urine tub. Sergeant Jewell lay in a torpor all but two hours each day. And physical weakness triggered spurts of insubordination. Greely forced harsh words at Private Bender and ordered Private Whisler outdoors until he showed more respect. But the next day the commander strove to entertain with readings from *Spofford's American Almanac*. He asked the men to join him in compiling "a chronological table of all the principal events of the world." Sergeant Israel and Dr. Pavy, "full of information, supplies what we lack in the way of dates."

On the twenty-fifth, Biederbick's birthday, Sergeant Brainard returned from one of his periodic ascents of the ridge to report Smith Sound apparently open. Greely decided at first not to reveal this news. "Better [the men] remain hopeful," he thought, "that soon we will be able to cross to Littleton Island by sledge." The moment seemed to come earlier than expected, and near the close of the month, Greely put Sergeant Rice and Eskimo Jens on double rations for the crossing.

The grinding of ice could no longer be heard, a sign the channel might have totally closed. Most of the party still clung to a belief that some of Garlington's people were wintering on the island with provisions left by the *Yantic*. Greely told them bluntly that he counted on "nothing but a small cache," the 240 rations said to have been left by the *Neptune*. At any rate, Rice and Jens were soon ready to leave. Their attempt to cross Smith Sound offered escape, at least, from the latest outbreak of bickering. Wrote Lockwood, who had regained a little strength, "Many of these disputes start off without anyone fully understanding what anyone means. One of the annoyances of this life is trying to cheat the stomach, and make our dole of food seem more than it really is." But they had faith that the whole situation might change for the better once Rice and Jens reached Littleton Island. Almost visible in clear light, it promised salvation.

It was the largest of a cluster of islands nestling within a curve of Greenland coast, named Lifeboat Cove by earlier American explorers. Though bleak, mostly granite, with a 100-foot-high plateau, it had become a favorite stopping place because of its strategic position at the junction of Smith Sound and Kane Basin and its closeness to the Ellesmere shore. Furthermore, Littleton's neighboring islets were thickly populated by eiderduck and other sea fowl. Rice and Jens set out early in February.

Feeding them extra rations had meant cutting back on the rest of the party. They had begun eating seal blubber formerly used to keep lamps lighted. Candles fashioned from stearin now provided illumination in the hut. The blubber was an unwelcome addition to the party's diet, striking some with nausea. So thick was the soup it made that, as Ralston noted, "a spoon stood alone in it."

Sergeant Brainard had accompanied Rice and Jens some distance. The pack could be heard grinding again, and he didn't think they would get very far. He said nothing of this apprehension on his return to the camp, nor during the gale that fell upon it in the night.

Rice and Jens each carried fifty pounds of gear, with documents including copies of several wills and a list Greely had drawn up of "what we need if Rice finds, as I fear not, a party at Lifeboat Cove." Should Greely's doubts prove correct, Rice was to push along the Greenland shore in search of Etah natives. Rice had left his own will behind, written in the form of a letter addressed, curiously, not to the expedition's leader but its once second in command, "Dear Friend Kislingbury," authorizing him to examine his pocketbook and other documents, and stipulating enigmatically that "all papers, letters, photos, etc., which from their nature or the rights of others should not be seen by my parents or others, shall at once be destroyed."

The two returned after only a week's absence. The temperature had been low enough to freeze mercury, arousing hopes that a week of such weather had firmly cemented Smith Sound's ice. They had succeeded in making ten miles across a solid pack, thus were about halfway to Littleton Island when it broke into floes and confronted them with open water. To lighten the mood following this disappointing news, Greely predicted that within three weeks the sound should close again, enough to permit a crossing. And he calculated from Sergeant Brainard's subsistence report that if each man could get by on four ounces of meat and eight ounces of bread daily, "our remaining stores may prolong our lives until April."

The tone of many a diary entry became that of bracing for the worst. Should fate go against the party, "I do not think," wrote Lockwood, "that we shall disgrace the name of Americans and of soldiers." Ralston wrote on 10 February, "God help us after the tenth of next month if the Channel does not close. If it is ours to perish, may we all preserve our peace of mind and die manfully." Should any of them succeed in a crossing, Greely still did not expect that Garlington would be found on Littleton Island. That lieutenant's record of departures and arrivals, in Greely's opinion, showed that he would not have had enough time for returning to the Lifeboat Cove vicinity. Moreover, Greely felt that Garlington's words could not be relied upon: "I was more than ever unwilling to count on anything not immediately under my hand." In the meantime he had to cope with sagging morale.

Clashes returned. "Jewell openly accused Doctor Pavy of selecting the heaviest dish of those issued," Greely wrote. Private Bender complained of short weight in bread. Greely thought Bender "a constant thorn. He is treated with consideration because of poor health." Early on the nineteenth, Bender and Whisler, while sharing the same sleeping bag, punched at each other. Greely was "soon awake and put a stop to it." A fine stew was made of the last of the seal meat. The last scraps of English beef were gone, too. Boiled bacon and pemmican became the strongest food. "If the channel doesn't freeze," wrote Brainard, "and no help from the other side, and no game, we are all gone."

Kislingbury was keeping a daily record of events as "a duty I owe my darling boys." That he had failed to reach the *Proteus* in time to sail with her on that melancholy August day in 1881 was even more of a pity than he could have realized just then. At home, the twice-widowed lieutenant would have been alongside those beloved sons during a distressing period of which— mercifully, inasmuch as while in the Arctic he had enough to worry over— Fred Kislingbury knew absolutely nothing.

He had left his youngest boy, Wheeler, in the guardianship of Colonel George Wheeler Schofield, the widowed husband of the third Bullock sister. Considered an innovative genius in the ordnance field, Schofield had a still better-known brother, General John A. Schofield, briefly Secretary of War during Andrew Johnson's administration and for five years superintendent of the military academy at West Point. So Kislingbury had left home confident that the infant Wheeler would be well looked after by reliable and influential relatives. However the Schofields shared a family secret: knowledge that the colonel, especially since his assignment to command of a Sixth Cavalry detachment at Fort Apache, Arizona, suffered bouts of insanity.

On Sunday morning, 17 December, 1882, as the bugler sounded reveille outside his window, the colonel had taken up his Smith and Wesson revolver and shot himself. Probably (and fortunately) Kislingbury's child was by then living with Schofield's sister in St. Louis. The colonel had left no will, and in the resultant family confusion over the disbursement of insurance payments and personal monies, uncertainty had arisen as to the future of seven-year-old Wheeler Kislingbury. There was no lack of concern. General Schofield told his sister that "it is desirable that you continue the care of the little boy until his father returns from the Arctic regions. We will see that means are provided." But the situation had become complicated by a clause in the directions Lieutenant Kislingbury had left behind, that in the event of Colonel Schofield's death, the boy would be adopted by Charles Clark, Kislingbury's schoolboy friend and business employer in Detroit.

These arrangements, potentially troublesome, had been decided upon because Kislingbury's own brothers, living in Rochester, New York, were of limited means. Walter Kislingbury, aged thirteen and Clark's ward at the out-set, preferred one of his uncles as guardian and had fled Detroit for Rochester. After Colonel Schofield's suicide, it was Wheeler's turn to enter Clark's custody, and as his uncles later protested, Clark had kept them ignorant regarding the boys' welfare. Meanwhile, Kislingbury's eldest son, Harry, was living with his dead wives' parents in Sandwich, Ontario. The fourth boy, Douglas, aged ten, was with the lieutenant's brother-in-law Seth Bullock, a United States marshal and sheriff busily ridding Deadwood, Dakota Territory, of outlaws. It was, all in all, a depressing situation for the four Kislingbury sons, separated as they were from one another, shuttled to and fro, bereft of a mother, and with a father somewhere north of the Arctic Circle who knew nothing of what befell them and lived only for the hour when he once more held them in his arms.

The weakest of the men at Camp Clay included Lieutenant Lockwood, who once had regarded himself among the sturdiest. Soon after noting in his diary that he "ate two dog biscuits saved from this morning," he complained to Greely about the smallness of the bread ration. The commander thought it unfortunate for an officer at that moment to appear dissatisfied with the size of his rations, but readily forgave him when he, Lockwood, blamed "constant hunger as productive of ill-temper." It also produced fear, especially when 1 March, the date Greely had fixed for crossing Smith Sound, came and went without the formation of any new ice. Mercury still froze, but spring tides kept Smith Sound partly open. At a lookout point on the knoll, Sergeant Brainard, ice crystals forming from each exhaled breath, could hear the crushing of the pack in the sound and to the north in Buchanan Strait. He noted, "Like distant thunder it stirs feelings of unrest and dread."

Had the men strength enough to remove the boat that roofed their squat shelter, they might have attempted a passage alternately by sledge and water. No one now could expect Smith Sound to freeze over solidly in the spring weeks ahead. And whatever young ice did form, over which perhaps half a dozen miles might be made, would move steadily south toward Baffin Bay. Still, Greely prayed that strong fresh ice would materialize, and he set himself a tentative new deadline for departure, 10 March. But lookouts continued to report water clouds blotting out the Greenland shore. Gales sprang up, and while they raged, it was futile to expect the formation of an ice bridge. At last, Greely "publicly abandoned all hope of the Sound freezing over."

Most now felt that even if they crossed to Littleton Island, they would find few supplies awaiting them and no relief party. And only the frailest of hopes were pinned on the chance of game seeing them through. Sergeant Rice, who had "neglected my diary for some time," resumed entries only because "the outlook indicates the possibility, nay probability, of the whole party perishing." With this likelihood looming ever larger, other diarists in the party summoned the strength to pencil thoughts across damp pages in the glow of the stearin candles, which actually gave better light than had the lamp, besides leaving seal blubber for eating. Rice: "We cannot die like rats in a hole after so nearly pulling through." Brainard: "C.O. calculates our present rations will hold till the first week in April. If we cannot cross to Littleton and we get no game, our end will not be far distant on April 15th." Greely: "It would seem the elements have united against us, we must stay on this side and fight it out."

More than one journal testified to the party's spirits as sometimes "excellent" . . . "buoyant." And labor could come to the relief of sanity. Schneider made the stearin candles; Bender fashioned candlesticks. Julius Frederick, promoted sergeant in Cross's place, prepared footgear for walking across to Greenland, although the time for expecting an ice bridge across Smith Sound had passed and everybody knew it. And though a stew made of blubber, breadcrumbs, raisins, and salt water laid Biederbick low with stomach cramps, he was soon back on his feet, working as "hospital nurse."

But moods could change in a split second. The day after Rice, upon the ridge, spotted ptarmigan that fled before the Eskimos could scramble up with guns, Bender and Henry used "blasphemous language" in front of Greely and growled that "we would all be dead in five weeks." Greely knew that even should the sound miraculously close, the men would be unable to move far in their present condition, and he himself admitted to being "so troubled, my temper is not as good perhaps as it should be. I have tried to please all but shall now give it up."

When a drifting snowstorm smothered the hut and prevented any outside exercise, someone accused Dr. Pavy of stealing his patient, Elison's, bacon. Rice wrote without elaboration of "an unpleasant discussion this evening. I much fear the horrors of our last day here." A later entry in Rice's diary told of a conversation on the quiet with Private William Ellis, who had heard talk of cannibalism. "I am much afraid of a demoralization of the party. The conversations and hints show a state of warped imagination which may result in things too bad to contemplate."

Southeast gales blew hard. The last of the lemons, butter, and raisins were gone. Besides seal blubber, the only food left now were some potatoes, a can of beef extract, hardtack, and lard. Greely sent Private Francis Long with the two Eskimos on an extended hunt for game. Born Franz Joseph Lang in Germany and an infantryman in the United States Army, Long was an expert marksman, perhaps the best of the expedition. But he and the Eskimos returned after forty-eight hours empty-handed and thoroughly exhausted. At one point, Long's sleeping bag froze shut and he had to squeeze in with the Eskimos. Brainard shot a single ptarmigan, which provided precious little nourishment but helped cheer the men. Still more welcome were four dovekies downed by Long and Eskimo Fred Christiansen. Private Biederbick, duty cook, did an excellent job; the men were loudly appreciative and Greely a shade more optimistic, although "the only way we will get from here is by ship." Also, with the little extra grub, Sergeant Brainard would have to keep close watch on the makeshift commissary. "Certain of the party cannot be trusted if we come to extremes," wrote Greely. "I have my eye on a gun and will not hesitate to use it if the occasion requires."

Now they had enough rations to last until 15 April, some four weeks off. Brainard rigged a crude net, an iron hoop and cloth, with which he hoped to catch shrimp. The day after a breakfast consisting of, per man, four and a half ounces of meat and dinner of four ounces more, with soup made of salt water and hardtack, Rice took the shrimp net baited with sealskin scraps to a point along the ice foot a mile from the cape, where he could sink it. The net could be set and drawn at ebb tide, when the falling water left open a crack in the ice. Rice was out for four hours in temperatures below zero and snared about a hundred "shrimp"—actually crustacea no lengthier than half an inch and known to whalers as sand fleas or sea lice. They were mostly shell, and it took about 700 of them to make an ounce, seven times the size of Rice's catch. "Only game can save us," wrote Greely, but added that "other than Henry's blasphemous remarks I have heard none speak of our coming fate other than with decency and respect." Greely could not read into the mind of each man nor know what each furtively wrote. He would not have been surprised that Pavy still blamed him "for all our sufferings."

Those with enough energy to stagger outside caught tantalizing glimpses of birds, seals, bear tracks, a fleeting fox. But however hungry or despondent, several of Greely's men were particularly resourceful. Gardiner invented a sledge using burlap and barrel hoops. Bender tried to make a fishhook, a claw on the end of a stick, "to fish up seaweed or kelp." Whisler stitched together rubber strips and bits of gunnysack, improvised scarves and gloves for the shrimpers. The weather continued blustery. Snow fell continually, as did frost within the hut, "wetting and chilling us to the marrow." Both Eskimos had become total invalids, their feet and faces badly swollen—"dropsical effusions," Pavy diagnosed. Clambering around grounded bergs and among ice-coated rocks, Brainard took turns with Rice to haul up shrimp, which, according to Greely's doleful estimate, were only one-third digestible matter. And, noted Brainard, "we can only draw the nets through the crack at low tide, so to take advantage of it, must get up at 3 A.M." That was 22 March. Brainard's diary entry for that day concluded with a grim question: "We can live about twenty days more.—then what?"

## 22

# THETIS AND BEAR

BY THE BEGINNING of 1884, as the men of the Lady Franklin Bay Expedition prayed for relief in their cramped hut at Cape Sabine, the other enterprises inspired by Karl Weyprecht's dream had come to a close or were about to. Some 700 men had participated in the great experiment. As the *London Times* was about to say, "The purposes of Arctic exploration have changed. Less is thought of getting to a high altitude on its own account, and more is thought of making a thorough investigation of whatever the polar regions may prove to contain available for scientific use." Eleven nations sent observers into the Arctic. A German expedition to Baffin Land that had sailed one year after Greely left New York had returned in triumph to Hamburg. The Russian party that had left Archangel for Novaya Zemlya met trouble—a seaman got drunk fraternizing with Eskimos, his legs froze, and he died following amputation. An enmity developed between the expedition's zoologist and its leader. Even so, all scientific objectives were attained, and the Russians were

back in St. Petersburg at about the time Greely's men were retreating into Kane
Basin. A second Russian expedition, said to have been enlivened by music and
laughter, had journeyed by railroad from St. Petersburg into Siberia, thence by
sledge to Yakutsk, and down into the Lena Delta, whose veritable maze, lamen-
tably fatal to the American George De Long, it had surveyed and mapped, and
where it built a scientific station still active well into the next century. These
Russians were back in Yakutsk by the end of 1882.

In the summer of that year, a Dutch party had left Amsterdam, but its ship
became beset in the Arctic and sank. Nobody drowned. An Austro-Hungarian
expedition had completed useful meteorological work on the volcanic Jan
Mayer Island between Norway and Greenland and mapped its every square
mile. A Danish party caught fast in the ice of the Kara Sea had still managed
to fulfill its scientific mission. A British meteorological station was installed
near Great Slave Lake in northeastern Canada; Sweden had set up a station at
Spitzbergen; and the Norwegians an observatory at North Cape, the uppermost tip of the European continent. The American station under Lieutenant
P. Henry Ray at Point Barrow had explored the Alaskan interior before closing down. Its party of a dozen Signal Corpsmen and civilians were safely home.
Only the Greely expedition, assigned to form the northernmost link in the
great international polar chain, had yet to be heard from.

In Washington, the relief board had remained in session until 22 January,
1884. Its recommendation for the purchase of "at least two new vessels
adapted to ice conditions" was sent to Congress, accompanied by a White
House endorsement from President Chester Arthur. And if success was to be
gained, the ships would have to leave no later than 1 May and reach Upernavik
by the middle of that month. This time frame was in accordance with suggestions from two British experts whose comments the board had invited via
transatlantic cable. Sir Clements Markham—the other was Sir George
Nares—thought it clear that Greely would have based his retreat plans "on the
supposition that a large store of supplies would have been cached at or near
Cape Sabine, and that a relief party would winter at Lifeboat Cove." Once at
Sabine, they could gain strength from food. Only an "extraordinary misad-
venture" would deny them some opportunity of crossing to Littleton Island,
where the relief party should be waiting.

The House of Representatives passed the Relief Expedition Bill virtually
without debate. Not so the Senate, where wrangling broke out almost at once.

The opposition came mainly from Secretary Chandler's political foes. Secretary of War Lincoln had gladly receded into the background. That preparations for the earlier relief efforts had been hindered by his lethargy and lack of interest was, he knew, the opinion of others besides his perennially fractious Chief Signal Officer. He was now only too willing to cede the initiative to Chandler, who, for his part, savored the prospect of the Navy coming to the Army's rescue as good publicity for a service whose prestige, never high of late, had further ebbed in the wake of the *Jeannette* affair.

Except for an ice pilot and Eskimo dog drivers who would later join the expedition, this effort was to be an entirely naval show. Offers to volunteer from civilians and other non-naval persons were turned down. William Kislingbury, brother of the Greely expedition's erstwhile second in command, asked to go and was told that the relief party would be confined to officers and men of the Navy, "all subject to ordinary naval discipline."

A conspicuous reject was Lieutenant Garlington. "My reputation as an officer," he wrote the Secretary of War on 27 February, "will be severely injured, I fear, if I am left out of the undertaking." Lincoln informed him that the personnel would be drawn exclusively from the Navy. He added curtly that he failed to see how Garlington's omission would damage his character.

To command this latest relief expedition, Secretary Chandler sent for Winfield Scott Schley, a forty-five-year-old veteran officer from Maryland who had seen action in the Civil War and, in 1870, on the China station, where he had distinguished himself in the capture of Korean forts. As Schley later wrote, Chandler asked "if I had an aspiration for service in the Arctic." Schley was prepared to volunteer or accept orders, even though he "knew it would be a service not ordinarily to one's taste." He asked Chandler, if his appointment be decided upon, that it be kept secret "until the last possible moment, so as to spare my family any anxiety in the meanwhile." Chandler obliged, assigning him to command on 18 February.

Schley might have been ordered earlier had the Senate moved faster to approve the relief bill. The debate had grown hot and heavy. Members recalling the Navy secretary's past brush with financial scandals pressed for details as to cost estimates, which, they complained, so-called urgency had given them scant time to study. On learning that few definite figures were available, Eli Saulsbury, a senator from Delaware, called the proposed relief bill "the most vicious legislation ever before Congress."

Lawmakers routinely scornful of expensive efforts to reach the North Pole railed against yet more excursions into "that mysterious, dangerous and tempting region." Legislators from northeastern coastal states, alert to reported plans for buying British ships, demanded that they be procured domestically. Some wondered what business the Navy had at all in what was originally an Army venture. When Chandler responded from the Navy Department that it was all in the line of routine naval duty, Senator John McPherson of New Jersey called that explanation "supreme audacity and bold impudence."

Impatient with this time-consuming dissension, Senator Eugene Hale of Maine resorted to sarcasm. The relief bill offered the last chance to find Greely's party alive. Hale stated, "If Lieutenant Greely is to be left to perish with his followers, I hope they may die in a parliamentary manner, so that no question may be raised as to their violating any rule." And when the bill finally passed, unaltered, by twenty-nine votes to twenty-two, Hale more soberly declared, "I do not know how I should feel if the expedition should go up there and it learned that those unfortunate men had perished [due to] our delay here."

While the debate dragged on, Chandler wasted no time. He had written to Consul Molloy in St. John's, who, at the secretary's bidding, inquired locally for a suitable ship, with interest as always focused on the iron-plated, Dundee-built whalers and sealers. One such steamer, the ten-year-old *Bear*, a sister ship of the late *Proteus*, was available, and by the end of January the ship's Scots owners had agreed to sell her for $100,000. Following instructions from Washington, the consul in St. John's closed the deal. On 15 February, two days after final passage of the relief bill in Congress, the *Bear* docked at the Brooklyn (New York) Navy Yard for overhaul and outfitting.

A second ship was purchased, the three-masted steam whaler *Thetis*, just two years old and said to be the strongest of the Scots whaling fleet. Formally transferred to the United States and manned by American sailors detached from the European Squadron, the *Thetis* sailed out of Dundee three days later. Yet a third vessel joined the expedition, the *Alert*, originally a Royal Navy five-gun sloop of war, which, converted for Arctic service, had sailed under Captain Nares in 1875. The British Admiralty, in a show of thanks for the American explorer Elisha Kane's help in the quests for the missing Franklin party, offered the ship to the United States as a loan. It was gratefully accepted. The *Alert* was made ready in the River Thames, and on 25 March, flying the Stars and Stripes, turned over to the American minister.

The naval bureaus in Washington were not always noted for mutual cooperation or speedy action. But Secretary Chandler now ordered them to forgo differences and act quickly, in order "to relieve our imperiled countrymen for whose safety our whole people are full of anxiety." At the same time, Schley was told to "investigate Greely's voyage, familiarize yourself with the whole subject of Arctic exploring and relief expeditions," even as he supervised the outfitting of the three ships over which he would have supreme command. This was a tall order, given the fact that the ships were scheduled for departure in ten weeks.

Chandler, with Secretary Lincoln's ready acquiescence, had resolved that the U.S. Navy would have the honor of rescuing the Lady Franklin Bay Expedition. But a move was afoot, with Henrietta Greely most active in San Diego, to heighten rescue prospects through a consummate search effort including the services of experienced commercial whalers. Friends of Henrietta's had joined in, pressuring newspapers, congressmen, and the Navy secretary himself toward the adoption of what was quickly capitalized in their correspondence as the Bounty Plan.

Henrietta's brother Otto, a Boston lawyer, confident that "should all my strings be pulled something should result," further advised her that the president's support should be sought. The wife of a *Journal of Commerce* editor added her voice. She advised Henrietta to "write the president a strong letter," using her womanhood to arouse his sympathies. "Never mind if it is dignified or not! You want to *wake* him to the full sense of the situation." Henrietta heard from a contrary source that both the president and his Secretary of the Navy objected to the Bounty Plan because so many whaling men would sail off in all manner of vessels; lives were bound to be lost and the American government held responsible. Even one of Henrietta's relatives disputed "the pretense that whalers can crush ice, dodge icebergs, easier and faster than our strong ships." Nevertheless, a resolution appeared before Congress offering $25,000 to whalers and any others who might bring about Greely's rescue.

The House of Representatives opposed the bill. It was approved in the Senate. At once, Chandler sensed the possibility that his Navy might be robbed of the glory of getting to Greely first. He privately impressed upon

Commander Schley the desirability of at least one of the official relief ships reaching Upernavik the moment ice conditions permitted. Word of Chandler's reluctance to countenance the Bounty Plan had reached San Diego. Henrietta addressed a letter to President Arthur and sent the appeal to General Lockwood for personal delivery at the executive mansion.

Unable to see the president, Lockwood left the letter with a secretary, who assured him it would be placed in Chester Arthur's hands. In due course, Lockwood got his reply on White House stationery and forwarded it to San Diego. The president "expressed solicitude" but was confident that the Navy's relief expedition the next summer would succeed. And a note personally directed to Henrietta Greely over the president's signature sought to reassure her that "nothing which is considered essential to the success of the expedition will be left undone."

Lockwood also called on Commander Schley, who was "quite as much opposed to the Bounty Plan as the War and Navy secretaries. Nor could I argue him out of his position." Schley thought the plan useless, possibly harmful, and tried to persuade the general that his son and the rest of the party must be in good shape, that the government's relief expedition would bring them all safely home. Lockwood was unconvinced. His previous year's optimism had vanished. He stated, "I must confess that I agree with those that think the party left [Lady Franklin Bay] last summer and hence are now in extreme peril. If so, then our plan is important and should not be abandoned."

And it was not. But argument in the Senate over the Bounty Plan's cost delayed its passage until Good Friday, 11 April. Lockwood sent Henrietta the news. Word of the bill's passage, with its promise of American dollars, would reach St. John's soon enough and shortly thereafter alert the whaling captains assembling at Upernavik. So, whalers might very well reach the Greely party. Lockwood added, "But as I have said before, I fear the condition in which they will be found." If, as Commander Schley professed to believe, they had remained at Lady Franklin Bay for another winter, they would probably be in a satisfactory state. But General Lockwood now tended to agree with those who thought that the expedition had left Fort Conger the past summer.

Hesitating before he put his signature to the Bounty Plan, the president sought last-minute counsel from his Secretary of the Navy. It came at once: "As you know, the Secretary of War and I do not believe in the expediency of a reward." Chandler felt duty bound to add, "But Congress having a different opinion, I advise signing." He was in the midst just then of dealing with measures to sustain the morale of Commander Schley's crews—for instance, authorizing purchase in New York of a dozen backgammon boards, six chess sets, and twelve sets of dominoes for each ship. After fighting a series of Atlantic gales, the *Thetis* had arrived at the Brooklyn Navy Yard in March—at about the date when Lieutenant Greely in the Far North counted on there being four weeks' rations left.

The *Thetis*'s temporary crew were paid off and replaced by the Arctic volunteers, all members of the U.S. Navy. They included Chief Engineer George Melville, formerly of the *Jeannette*, and Lieutenant John Colwell, going north for the second time within a year. Strongly reinforced for ice navigation, the *Thetis* would be Commander Schley's flagship. Schley would carry a letter from General Hazen to Greely defining "the sole purpose of this expedition" as securing his safe return. "Any idea of continuing the observations at Lady Franklin Bay on the plan of the International Polar Expedition has been abandoned by the government . . . All the international polar expeditions but yours and Russians on the Lena Delta returned safely to their homes last year."

Unlike commanders of the previous relief expeditions, Schley would have a completely free hand. "Full confidence," Chandler told him, "is felt that you have both the capacity and the courage, guided by discretion, necessary to do all that is required of you." Other last letters were written before the expedition sailed. Greely's mother told Henrietta that she would always love Queen Victoria for her gift of the *Alert*. Mrs. Greely was preparing for the best. She had cleaned her house and "hung out Adolph's clothes for a good airing and packed them away for the summer. What a hero Adolph will be if he ever gets home. I live in hopes." Schley had a farewell message for Henrietta. He was cutting the "dearest home ties with the sincerest purpose to return to you the noblest of husbands."

The *Bear* was the first to clear port, leaving her moorings on the afternoon of 23 April. New Yorkers lined the wharves and the newly completed Brooklyn Bridge to wave and cheer. The *Thetis* sailed a week later, an ensign named Charles Harlow on board doubting whether any man o' war got a more royal send-off. In addition to the cheering crowds, "the blasts of whistles and dipping of colors of the vessels we passed testified to the widespread interest all had in the enterprise," wrote Harlow. Steam tugs and federal launches carrying the Secretary of the Navy and the Secretary of War, with senators and other dignitaries, followed the *Thetis* for hours before the final Godspeed.

By then, the *Bear* was off St. John's. She spent two days taking on coal, supplies, and dogs, and was away again. Still later, and without fanfare, the *Alert* slid down the East River at New York and took to sea. Schley's plan was that although setting off separately, the *Thetis* and *Bear* would rendezvous at Upernavik near the end of May, then proceed in company to Cape York and on to Littleton Island. The *Alert* would follow, to reach Littleton Island about 1 July, bringing the materials for building winter quarters.

As the *Thetis* steamed northeastward through the murk of early May, some of the idle conversation among the eight officers who made up the wardroom centered on past forays into northern waters. George Melville talked of his experiences on the *Jeannette* under Lieutenant De Long and attributed some of that expedition's troubles to the intractability of its Irish meteorologist. The ice pilot James Norman, soon to prove a too-talkative Newfoundlander, more than hinted at the real cause of the *Jeannette* navigator Lieutenant Danenhower's near blindness (a secreted syphilitic condition) and "made some mysterious remarks about the *Proteus* investigation, that it was not all over yet and that more would be known when Greely returned."

In his private journal, between love letters written home, Ensign Harlow also attested to Commander Schley's determination to let no ship get ahead of the *Thetis*, except the *Bear*, and not even she would be allowed to keep her lead. He wrote, "We will doubtless overtake her before we reach Upernavik or Disko. I am very ambitious to be the first and I have no doubt the captain has very much the same feeling. We will go ahead and remain ahead. We must be the ship to find and bring back Greely."

## 23

# "I SHOULD HAVE KILLED HIM"

AT CAMP CLAY, the sun was returning. Even though the thermometer showed –25 degrees Fahrenheit, there was nearly light enough to read outdoors. But 24 March was a day of misery. The men had fitted a plug up the chimney through the hut's roof, which was withdrawn for ventilation when cooking was under way. The duty cook, who was boiling tea over a lamp fueled by alcohol because all the blubber was gone, forgot to remove it. Fumes shot from the lamp into eyes and nostrils and down throats. Gasping and retching men struggled from sleeping bags and stumbled outside to breathe deeply of the frigid air. Some fainted. Hours passed before all had sufficiently recovered to crawl back inside their cell-sized hovel. And during the commotion, someone had stolen half a pound of bacon that Biederbick had stored up in the boat thwart as a last reserve.

The thief betrayed himself by throwing up into the urine bucket. Private Julius Frederick, whose turn it was to empty the bucket, saw Private Henry

doubled over it, and afterward fragments of undigested bacon among its contents. No one recorded the thoughts that ran through all but Henry's mind
that night, but murder was among them. The next morning, Greely ordered an
informal trial. He named Sergeant Rice prosecutor. "I opened the ball on
Henry," Rice wrote. The Eskimo Jens testified that he had actually seen Henry
steal bacon and stuff it within his shirt. Jens would have had qualms about
bringing, alone, such a serious charge against an American soldier. But he had
safe corroboration. Lieutenant Lockwood remembered smelling bacon when
Henry vomited. Sergeant Long told of seeing Henry gulp down two rations
of rum when his comrades were recovering from those choking fumes.

Past instances of theft sprang to mind. Ellis stated that Henry had thieved
canned goods back at Fort Conger, a charge echoed by the demoted Connell,
who was himself not above suspicion when food disappeared. It was a strange
court, made up of members and jury who were less than alert and most of
whom were trussed tightly in sleeping bags. Greely asked every man's opinion.
Each answer was an unqualified "guilty." Greely wrote that evening, "There was
much talk of violence." Only his party's frailty and his own presence saved
Henry from a probable lynching. Greely reminded the men that they were of
a military command, and as commander he alone would take extreme measures
when needed. For months he had spared the expedition's surgeon from severe
and disciplinary measures, and was "unwilling to do otherwise with a private."
He relieved Henry from duty. "The party being too weak to put him under
confinement, I prohibited him from leaving his sleeping bag except under the
supervision of one of his comrades." Sergeant Rice summed up the thoughts
of the others: "I think we would have been justified in putting him to death."

A heavily built man and crack shot, Private Charles Henry was articulate,
even if "blasphemous." His past was something of a mystery. For one thing,
his real name was Charles Henry Buck, and like others of his comrades, he was
of German birth. A small-town Missouri newspaper for which he had worked
as a youngster suggested that his father may have been president of a Prussian
bank. He had enlisted in the United States Seventh Cavalry in 1876. At Fort
Buford, Montana Territory, he had been court-martialed for victimizing fort
traders with forged checks. He'd served twelve months' hard labor and was dis-
honorably discharged. Roaming the West, he had killed a Chinaman in a
Deadwood barroom brawl. After enlisting in the Fifth Cavalry as Charles B.
Henry, he'd joined the Lady Franklin Bay Expedition without any apparent

blemish on his past character, and with an agreement to furnish newspaper articles on life in the Arctic. One or two eventually published in the *Chicago Times* attested to an effective if florid command of the English language.

Three days after Private Henry's "trial" came the commander's fortieth birthday. Private Long, Corporal Nicholas Salor, and Jens celebrated by returning from a hunting trip with sixteen dovekies. Cheers greeted them. The birds' red legs came in useful as shrimp bait. Rice caught fifty ounces during two fishing sessions. He wrote, "We are finding shrimp and tallow stews fine." Only a disgraced Henry took no part in the rejoicing. He had begged to be allowed to do duty, and when Greely refused, he wept.

April brought brighter weather, but no more game. Shrimping trailed off for lack of bait. The "shrimps" could not sustain life, anyway. "We are all longing for a thick rich stew of flesh and blood of a seal," wrote Brainard. "Like animals, we have little left except the instinct for eating." Those who could stagger outside for exercise turned gaunt faces and hollow eyes toward the southern horizon in hope of succor. Would a ship ever come? On the fourth of the month, the Eskimo Fred Christiansen babbled deliriously. He was dead the next morning.

The doctor examined his body and reported a few signs of scurvy. Greely's verdict was malnutrition. After services were read, the strongest of the party hauled Christiansen's body out of the hut and up to the ridge, where it was half-interred alongside William Cross's crude grave. "Linn, I fear, will soon follow," wrote Israel, who was himself "pretty used up." David Linn died the following day, gasping for water to slake his thirst. There was none to spare. It took eight men to haul Linn's body to the ridge, where, alongside the two graves already there, they scooped gravel to a depth of scarcely more than twelve inches before it became hard as marble. As were the others, Linn's corpse was only sparsely covered. And again, to conserve ammunition, the funeral was held without military salute.

There were provisions close by Baird Inlet, south, toward Cape Isabella. Greely knew so. They were the remnants of the Nares cache, abandoned the previous November by Rice and Frederick in their efforts to save Elison's life. Greely had set aside notions of retrieving this small supply, unwilling to put any of his enfeebled party through the rigors of an arduous thirty or forty miles round trip. Now he regretted not having taken the risk, which time and circumstance had made all the greater. More than once, Rice had pleaded for permission to leave for Baird Inlet and Greely had refused. After reading the burial service over Private Linn, he agreed to let Rice go.

At midnight on the sixth, his own strength ebbing, George Rice set out with Julius Frederick, a two-man sleeping bag, and the party's light sledge. Even had they the strength to haul one, no tent was available. For breakfast before leaving, they each had a cup of shrimp stew, one ounce of bacon, one and three-quarter ounces of hard bread, and a watery tea.

Three days after their departure, events forced Greely to another reconsideration, this one belated because of stubborn pride and a rigid sense of duty. For more than two and a half years, Greely had shown few if any indications of relenting in his disregard of Lieutenant Kislingbury as a member of the expedition, much less his second in command. But now Lieutenant Lockwood had lapsed into a coma. Early on the ninth, Greely beckoned Kislingbury and said that since there was no telling what the future might hold, "in the event of my death the command of the expedition will devolve on you."

Lockwood died at 4:30 P.M. He was interred with the three dead on the ridge. Greely felt "constrained to formally order Lieutenant Kislingbury to duty with the expedition." In so doing, Greely "publicly complimented him on the efficient manner in which he had labored." In Biederbick's notes, Greely expressed regret over the prolonged impasse between the two. Kislingbury wrote of Greely's affirmation that, notwithstanding his separation from the expedition, he had conducted himself in a manner "upright. . . ." Kislingbury thanked him with emotion.

If Greely's testimonial signified a reconciliation, it was fated not to last. And neither were hatchets buried between the commander and Dr. Pavy, who, Biederbick reported, continued to filch the helpless Elison's rations. "I make no open charge yet," Greely noted in his journal, "[Pavy's] medical service being very necessary."

Good luck and bad toyed in turn with the men of Camp Clay. Early on the eleventh, Sergeant Brainard tottered into the hut, "falling through our little door," noted Ralston, "calling for hunters, he had seen a bear." Long and Jens were off at once, followed by Kislingbury with his Remington. Climbing to the burial crest, Kislingbury lost strength and pitched headfirst upon the ridge, but the hunters chased the bear three miles and killed it. Then they had to plod back for additional help and the large sledge because the bear was heavy—"300 pounds," Ralston estimated; "it will probably save the expedition." The prize came too late for Sergeant Winfield Jewell, who died even as the bear was hauled in.

Its capture did little to enhance the strength of the party. Dreaming as many of the men did of the sumptuous meals awaiting them at home should they get there, they were losing whatever taste they had for what they were forced to live on. "Shrimps are proving nauseating," Greely scribbled painfully. "Some can't touch them." Bear meat was certainly welcome, and as a reward for Long's marksmanship, Greely promoted him sergeant in the Signal Corps to succeed Jewell. But for Brainard as commissary sergeant, issuing the fresh meat was no easy task. "Firmly frozen," he wrote, "[the bear] had to be cut up with a handsaw. I often feel like giving up in despair." Greely was also losing strength. Biederbick noticed how his hands shook as if palsied: "I hardly think he knows how weak he is. I see others very low." They did not include Connell, who never seemed to tire, nor the ostracized Henry, about the huskiest of the party, nor even Elison, bereft of a foot and fingers but possessed of such fortitude that Greely had promoted him sergeant (since Greely had no appropriate authority, these promotions and demotions were not to be officially recognized).

Rice and Frederick had reached Ross Bay. That pair's ordeal had begun early. Upon their reaching Ross Bay, just below Sabine, a blizzard forced them into camp, which consisted of unrolling their single heavy sleeping bag on ice, crawling into it, and, huddled together, gnawing on frozen pemmican. For twenty-two hours, whirling snow and powerful wind gusts kept them imprisoned. When the storm let up, early on 8 April, they squirmed out of the bag and pressed on, halting the next evening in the lee of a grounded berg. The next morning they were at their old campsite on Eskimo Point and figured that the meat they were seeking had to be cached within a six-mile span. For faster travel with a lightened sledge, they left the sleeping bag and a portion of rations, and soon they were floundering blindly through drifts, searching for the English beef.

Open pools had turned the area into a frozen maze. At 3:00 P.M., the men presumed themselves to be at the exact location of the abandoned cache, but could see nothing of the rifle they had left as a marker. The explanation had to be shifting ice, moving out into Baird Inlet, taking the provisions with it. Deep dismay compounded the fatigue that struck both men, Rice especially, who became too weak to stand, unable to move forward. Frederick panted at him that they were sure to die unless they reached the sleeping bag for rest and shelter. Reviving him with brandy, Frederick managed to get him a thousand yards to a snow-draped berg. They sank against it. "We remained here," Frederick later wrote, "on this desolate piece of ice, with the wind blowing a hurricane, for two hours or more, after which time my poor heroic companion lost consciousness." Frederick removed his only jacket to keep Rice as warm as possible. He cradled him in his arms on the sledge, and was too weary and benumbed to have known the precise moment when Sergeant George Rice died.

It was about eight in the evening. Frederick's vigil had ended. He stood, "completely exhausted, shivering with cold, unable to bury the remains of poor Rice, hardly able to move. I knew that my chances to reach Eskimo Point, about 7 miles to the north, were very small indeed." But he had a sad duty to perform. Seven hours' hard travel got him to Eskimo Point, where he found the sleeping bag "frozen stiff as cordwood." Strengthening himself with a few drops of rum and ammonia, he forced the bag open and worked his body into it. The next morning he staggered back to bury his comrade. He wrote, "I had no shovel, only an axe, and the loose ice I had to remove with my hands, and it is here, on a paleocrystic floe, that I laid the remains of one who was so dear to me."

Frederick's lonely return to Camp Clay with dread news and no provisions took three days. Sergeant Rice had been popular with most of the party. It was Easter Sunday. Somewhere close, a bird sang. No one saw it, and no one spoke until the sound ceased. That same Sabbath, and within hours of Frederick's return, Greely addressed a letter to General Hazen: "We lived all winter on an incredibly small ration and it seems doubly hard to perish in summer within a month or six weeks of final relief. Doctor Pavy has been systematically plundering his crippled patient from November to April. I state this, that public opinion may curse the man if he, as it seems possible, lives to return. I write this as from my grave, with no personal or bitter feelings."

Greely's words came partly from knowing that his own heart was weakening. He had gotten Dr. Pavy to confirm as much. For a brief period, the outlook brightened. The bear hauled in had allowed Greely to increase meat rations to a pound per man daily. But this ration was cut to ten ounces with no further game sighted. Alcohol had been burned for cooking. Now all that remained of it was in Pavy's charge for medicinal purposes. Cooking took up the last of the stearin. For fuel, "Bender and Henry began tearing out the insides of our boat [creating] a depressing effect since it seemed to foretell the fate of the entire party."

Cheerful remarks grew fewer and feebler. Yet some still arose. Schneider proudly announced that he had made 350 candles. Sergeant Brainard contemplated the officer's commission Greely had promised to help him secure once they got home. Such promise, and the commander's increasing tendency to turn to him for aid or advice, had drained the sergeant's private diary of venom and there was, or so it appeared, a genuine affinity developing between the two. The commander promoted Julius Frederick sergeant on the spot, to replace the friend who had died in his arms. But "we are a hungry mob," noted Sergeant Ralston, at the same time refusing to cook when it fell his turn to do so.

Dr. Pavy, for all his professional value, still provoked Greely to anger and frustration. Greely noted on 18 April that the doctor handed in a satisfactorily measured report on the party's health, then surprised him with profuse offers of friendship. The honeymoon, such as it was, soured almost immediately. Sergeant Long reported seeing Pavy drink some of Private Schneider's rum. Biederbick swore on oath that he had seen the doctor take Elison's bread. Greely had always tried to meet unexpected shifts in Pavy's conduct with a blend of tact and sternness. One had to consider "acuteness of suffering, temptations of the flesh, idiosyncrasies of character, traits of depravity, and perhaps mental tensions." He would never fail to take action when he judged it necessary for the solidarity and safety of the expedition. And it was precisely for that reason that in the case of the party's medical officer, Greely could take little or no action at all.

What particularly tormented the commander was the belief that much of the blame for his party's plight belonged to an Army lieutenant now no doubt seated in comfort and safety back home. Greely poured his feelings in a report dated 20 April to General Hazen: "Had Lieutenant Garlington carried out your orders and replaced the 240 rations of rum and 120 of alcohol in the English cache here, and the 210 pounds of mouldy English bread, spoiled English chocolate and potatoes, melted sugar, and 210 pounds of rotten dog biscuits, we would without doubt be saved."

So passed the declining weeks of the strangest American foray above the Arctic Circle. That twentieth of the month was in fact a comparative feast day.

Breakfast was little more than hard bread and tallow, but dinner, Hampden Gardiner recorded, was "a fine meal of giblet stew, hearts, liver, etc., with two butter cans, each three pounds, full of pure blood." Schneider was ordered back on cooking duty and warned by Sergeant Brainard that if seen stealing food, he would be shot at once. Connell, not always above suspicion himself, called Schneider the biggest thief in the camp.

Two days later, the doctor and Lieutenant Kislingbury recommended that Greely restore the daily meat ration to one pound. The commander figured that to do so would exhaust the party's supply within a fortnight. So at first he said no, then agreed to a ration of twelve ounces. Painful bowel movements had left Greely weak, and, he wrote, "my heart gives me trouble." He tried to impress upon the men "the importance of pluck and unity in case anything should happen to me," and authorized Sergeant Brainard, in that event, to take command, "Kislingbury being unable either mentally or physically to do so." This assertion was curious in view of the coherence of Kislingbury's journal entries and the apparent amiability of a letter he wrote to Greely that same day concerning the size of the daily rations. It ended: "You are, I know, doing everything for the best and I have but one desire to help you all I possibly can in this trying ordeal. Your suffering this morning and weakened condition alarms me."

Kislingbury was just as plainspoken in a tribute to Pavy's services. The doctor was "untiring in his efforts to help us all [although] still in arrest." Yet Fred Kislingbury had to have known that, at least in the opinion of the commander, "no food has reached Elison for all these months which has not in some way paid toll to Doctor Pavy." Hitherto, Pavy had spooned food into Elison's mouth. But the injured sergeant felt strong enough to sit up in his bag for short periods, and his comrades had attached a spoon to his finger stumps. "I presume," wrote Greely, "now that Sergeant Elison can handle his own bread and can watch over his own stew, Doctor P. no longer finds it profitable to do the work."

Following a hunting sortie, Francis Long staggered into camp with terrible news. He and Jens Edward had just crossed a clear lane in the kayak to get at a seal sprawled temptingly on a floe, when a small field of broken ice drifted into their path. They promptly disembarked, and Jens dragged the boat across the splintered pan to open water. He clambered back into the kayak, clutching his Springfield rifle, but knife-sharp ice had ripped a hole in the boat's seal-skin covering. It sank, taking Jens with it.

Eskimos in general had never impressed Lieutenant Greely as valuable to an Arctic expedition. While he acknowledged the utility of native dog drivers, he felt they were "unable to appreciate the objectives of these journeys," and (he would write), "their ability to endure privation and hardships has been greatly overrated." Dr. Pavy disagreed. In his opinion, the history of Arctic exploration had confirmed their essentiality to successful expeditions. At any rate, Eskimo Jens had been much admired, not only as a cheerful member of the Lady Franklin Bay brotherhood but as one of its best hunters. Gone with him, too, were a useful if small boat and the party's only good Springfield rifle.

By the end of the month, the nineteen men alive at Camp Clay subsisted on a daily diet of two ounces of bread and twelve of meat per man, with what shrimps could be netted. Some bacon remained, but every portion of the bear was eaten save hair and bone. Regularly, the hunters returned empty-handed and discouraged. Brainard had become chief shrimper, trudging daily up past scarcely covered bodies on the cemetery ridge and down to the ice-scabbed cove, where he set his nets, baited with sealskin or bird legs, in hopes of a bounty of the puny creatures left by the falling tide. Now and then, Kislingbury ventured outside to hack kindling from what bits of wooden crates and boat timber he could find. "We have a small sheet-iron stove," he wrote, "and chop wood as finely as possible to produce heat as rapidly as possible."

Pavy gave the commander calomel twice a day to ease his constipation. The two continued to differ, mostly over the rations issue. "Regrettable," wrote Greely, "but the man is so double-faced and unreliable." Everyone knew of their mutual antipathy. Kislingbury believed that Greely tried to infect the men with his own distaste for the doctor, but that was unlikely. In truth, the accumulated tension and sense of hopelessness weighed so heavily upon Greely's spirit that he had become more easily aroused to rage, seldom a trait during his frontier days when creating and managing a telegraphic web. Connell remarked aloud that someone would be held responsible before God for the graves on the hill. Greely threatened that such language would bring summary punishment.

That infringement of discipline might compel him to a frightful decision preyed increasingly on Greely's mind. "Any attempt to incite mutiny must meet death," he wrote. He couldn't have failed to sense a dangerous mood among the men, even without knowing that Lieutenant Kislingbury privately referred to him as "the devil we have here," and Sergeant Gardiner called him "a heathen, a brute." Private Henry volunteered to help Biederbick dilute alcohol for medicine. Greely immediately suspected that the blackest sheep of his flock was taking advantage of his "illness . . . constipation" to steal some. The hapless Henry did indeed spit up enough telltale liquid, and mumbled, "Go to hell" at Kislingbury when that officer accused him. Private Schneider noted that "but for Lieutenant Greely he would have died at our hands," and the commander himself wrote, "I suppose I should be justified in killing the man."

May began with a blinding snowstorm and renewed outbreaks of thievery. Private Whisler was caught removing a pound of bacon from the storehouse. His excuse was that somebody, either Bender or Henry, had forced the door himself and left it ajar. Then, as Greely supposed, hunger must have overcome Whisler's principles. Greely wrote, "He expressed willingness to be killed or meet whatever fate the party agreed upon. I believe in his repentance." Such leniency infuriated the still-shunned Henry, especially upon learning that when first informed of the commissary break-in, the commander had exclaimed, "Henry, of course."

Food was on everybody's mind. Sometimes the dark little hut echoed to a hallucinatory babble of men dreaming aloud of the lavish meals they would eat if at home. Pavy had been "preaching an increase of rations," Greely wrote. "If his advice had been followed we would all have been dead long ago. As it is, we have ten days before us yet, after which we will try sea vegetation." Shrimp bait ran low. Resigned to starvation, and perhaps incapable of recalling the wife he had left penniless, David Ralston wrote weakly, "I am content, my mind at rest." Greely confined his strongest admiration for Brainard, his first sergeant, who had submitted regular reports and, as personal distributor of rations, made "safe and careful estimates of unknown weights of bread and meat." And throughout the dreadful winter months, "no ounce of unauthorized food passed his lips."

Greely's patience with the doctor reached breaking point. That his debilitating constipation had eased was thanks to Pavy's treatment. But on an early May day when snow fell heavily, the two quarreled yet again, Greely telling some of the others that "were he not the medical officer I should have killed him." Bloodshed there might have been. At the height of the brawl, Private

Bender tried to intervene on Pavy's side. Greely swung on the soldier. "A mutiny seemed imminent and I would have killed him could I have got to Long's hunting rifle." The snow continued to fall, drifts blocking the tunneled entrance to the house. That night, Private Schneider penciled in his journal, "Most of us are out of our right minds." Lieutenant Greely wrote, "I fear for the future."

## 24

# NOTHING OF A SHIP

THE THETIS ARRIVED at St. John's, Newfoundland, early 9 May. Taking on coal, Commander Schley learned that not only had the *Bear* called there, but ten or twelve whaling ships also had left for the Arctic, their captains anxious to win the American reward. Besides coal, the *Thetis* took on a quantity of sealskin boots and twenty-two Labrador dogs, and within two days had hoisted anchor, her course set for Godhavn and the ice fields. In the wardroom, the ice pilot Norman and Chief Engineer George Melville expressed fears as to Greely's fate. He would be coming down and traveling light in expectations of finding an abundance of stores. The *Thetis* made all speed north. When first given the assignment, Schley had told Secretary Chandler that he thought it "in the nature of a forlorn hope." But now he was caught up in the spirit of a chase.

The *Bear* maintained her lead. She was a three-masted ship, barkentine-rigged, with a gross weight of 690 tons, and sheathed from keel to waterline with greenheart, a wood from the West Indies considered among the world's hardest. Three days out of St. John's, the *Thetis* met heavy seas. Her performance grew sluggish. "Our engines," wrote Ensign Harlow, "are a great disappointment. It seems impossible to get more than 50 pounds of steam and more than 50 revolutions, though she ought to make 75." But progressively lightened through coal consumption, she would do better. And however reinforced the *Bear*, the *Thetis* was still stronger, iron-belted to above the waterline along 100 feet of her hull. Her very name suggested optimism. Thetis was the prescient sea goddess who, forced to marry a mortal, produced the Trojan War hero Achilles.

Well ahead of the *Thetis*, the *Bear* had reached Disko Island and its harbor, Godhavn. The expedition's third ship, *Alert*, was not really in the running. Her primary function was as a support vessel, and she had only just reached St. John's. The *Bear*, after leaving Godhavn, ran into thickening ice and had to turn back. She found that the first of the Scots whalers, *Nova Zemlya* and *Polynia*, had just come up. Still astern of them, the *Thetis* pulled into Godhavn on 22 May, with the *Loch Garry*, a coal ship chartered at St. John's, puffing in her wake.

Schley was recovering from stomach cramps when he got news of the *Bear* and the whalers ahead of him. But Ensign Harlow noted, "Captain says he will stay only two days at Disko. He seems anxious to overtake the *Bear* and he can't catch him too soon to suit me. I know what ambition is, I am too jealous of the glory of finding Greely with my ship."

At Camp Clay, the shamed Private Henry had written a postcard addressed to an officer under whom he had served on the prairies: "Only six more days are left us. Starvation looks us in the face. Seven of our party are dead already and the rest of us are resigned to follow. The expedition has been a success but I unfortunately have not been. Remember me to my old comrades." To his family in Chicago, Henry repeated his boast of the expedition's success. He concluded, "Dear parents, brother and sisters, do not grieve for me as I am not worth it." He signed the letter "Charles H. Buck or Charles B. Henry." Others were also writing last letters. Greely penciled at Sergeant Elison's dictation, "I shall die quiet and content. I lost my feet and hands doing my duty, in a manner of which you need never feel ashamed." Pavy wanted all his papers and records to be seen by only his wife, to whom they would be delivered by Brainard.

Brainard himself had spent little if any time on last messages, instead continuing his journal entries, noting Pavy's impression that once the last rations were gone, the party could live only a short while longer on shrimps and the purple saxifrage growing within clefts of rocks. "Some of the weaker ones will have to go," Brainard wrote, "they cannot possibly survive the reduction in provisions." In the meantime, he would periodically visit the fishery for shrimp, even though the wind at times was so strong it almost blew him off the ridge of the dead.

Snow had fallen for days. On 12 May, the party's doctor wrote of the end in sight, his own perhaps delayed by "a little pork and lard" he expected to last him seventy-two hours; "I walk outside to the ice and different things." The commander and the whole party were in their sleeping bags and "demoralized." Pavy wrote of hiding his morsels of food—"like a miser I place them in a small bag under my head." Once Pavy crept outside, the sun was shining, the coast of Greenland distinctly visible across the sound. He saw nothing of a ship.

The last rations were issued. Twelve ounces of bacon and tallow. "We live now on nothing but a few shrimps and some sea vegetation," wrote Private Henry. "The terrible struggling of death by starvation actually had no horror for us, we looked with stolid indifference upon our coming fate." William Ellis, at forty-four the oldest of the party, drew up his will, leaving all the Army pay due him to his mother and to his son, forgetting (or unaware) that the child had died in the spring of 1881 before the expedition sailed.

Schneider wrote, "It is horrible to see eighteen men dying by inches. Only the bad shrimp stew remains us." Few of the eighteen could walk for long, including Pavy, Sergeant Frederick, and Brainard, who, Schneider thought, was "one in a thousand." Those stronger men hauled the tattered remnants of an old Army tent up to a gravelly spot in the sun's rays southeast of the winter hut. Here, not far from the graveyard ridge, they pitched camp in readiness, according to Brainard, "to shelter the last survivors, who will probably not have enough energy to bury their comrades."

Greely had used some of his sealskin jumper for shrimp bait. What was left he gave to the party to roast and eat. Also, "the oil-tanned covering on my bag was cut off and divided." He tore a blank page from his journal on which to write home, giving directions to his "Darling Ritta" about their daughters' future careers: "Instruct them in useful branches only—including German even if French is neglected." He had cut off a lock of his hair for her, and she would also get a stone brought from "the farthest north" by Lieutenant Lockwood. He wrote, "Our chances are going fast—no game now in twenty-seven days and only three days' food left."

Yet while Private Schneider wrote that the men were facing death "like soldiers," enough strength lingered to renew old animosities. The day he wrote to his wife, Greely astonished Lieutenant Kislingbury with a handshake and semi-coherent regrets. But when Kislingbury, desperately anxious to make his sons at home proud of him, seized the moment to beg for a written statement restoring him to full duty, Greely refused. Kislingbury declared that it had been promised him. "I began reminding him of this," the lieutenant noted that evening, "when he cut me short, flew into a passion, loudly called me a liar. God help me, I had to take this. Too weak to write any more tonight." The entire incident, described by Private Bender as the two officers "on the warpath," took place in full view of their starving subordinates.

Greely's account in shrunken handwriting portrayed Kislingbury as "violent" but forgivable—"I later apologized to him and the men for my intemperate language. The verbal order assigning Lieutenant Kislingbury to duty [is] April 3d 1884." Dr. Pavy demanded a certificate to his good standing, signed by the commander. This, he pleaded, was for his wife's satisfaction. Greely at first refused, then yielded in order to avoid another debilitating confrontation. But he confined the testimonial, for General Hazen's eyes, "rigidly to [Pavy's] professional duties." In his journal, Greely declared it "written under pressure. I said in it all I could conscientiously say that was *good* of Doctor Pavy. It is not to be liberally construed." He had sergeants Brainard and Israel insert copies in their journals "for fear that the narrative be tampered with. Doctor Pavy's record, *except as to medical service*, has been mighty bad. I say all this on the edge of the grave."

A pelting snowstorm prevented outdoor exercise. Greely had kept to his bag four days in a row, and was too weak to prevent William Ellis from being "brutally treated" by his fellow private Jacob Bender. The thirty-six-year-old Ellis, a quietly dutiful soldier, had married many years earlier and then vanished, leaving a widow who understood that he had been killed with Custer at Little Bighorn. Unexpectedly, Ellis had returned, only to find that she had remarried. Again he left, this time as a member of the Lady Franklin Bay Expedition.

Ellis died at noon on 19 May, the first in six months to succumb to starvation. The hardiest of the party hauled his body to the ridge the next day and were able to cover it with only a thin layer of gravel. Greely wrote to Henrietta, "My heart troubles me and grows worse. So my chances are very slim." He had made out his will. But the next day, Long shot a raven, to be used for shrimp bait. In his journal, Greely suddenly turned generous toward his old antagonist, the doctor. He wrote, "He is working wonderfully hard getting ice [from the nearby lake]. His strength and energy lately are quite surprising. I am glad to write something good of him."

Greely's mood, more than ever prone to change, was quite different the next day. Sergeant Israel told him that Pavy had composed a letter of gratitude for his services as the party's physician and circulated it among the men. He had secured thirteen signatures, including those of Lieutenant Kislingbury and Sergeant Brainard. The document praised Pavy's "devoted zeal and professional skill in the discharge of his medical duties." Seldom able to draw himself even halfway out of his sleeping bag, the commander labored over another angry report for Hazen's attention: "Dr. Pavy is our strongest man and will probably survive. Every man is at the point of death, and the greater part utterly helpless, in this condition at his mercy."

Melting snow dripped into their frail dwelling like a steady rainfall. Greely decided to move uphill from "this wretched hut," to the tent near the sepulchral ridge. Before they got started, Ralston died, "an excellent observer" who for days past was too weak to hold a spoon. Greely had helped feed him. The two had shared the same bag with Sergeant Israel, who left the bag when Ralston died, but Greely "remained until driven out, chilled by contact with the dead." After the commander read the burial service during breakfast, he ordered that Ralston be buried in the ice foot northwest of camp if his comrades were unable to haul him up the slope. Two days would pass before the sergeant's body could be borne slowly to the ridge. And in the meantime the move to the tent had begun.

The weakest went first. These included Israel, who had to be half carried, and Elison, bereft of fingers and feet. A few, like Whisler, managed to climb alone. Greely got there with a struggle, "carrying my afghan sleeping bag." The barometer broke on the way up, "a great misfortune. I had hoped to continue observations until the last man died." Eleven finally made it to the tent and a small adjoining lean-to. There wasn't enough canvas to cover everyone, and tent flies were frozen to the ground in the hut. So while taking their meals in the tent with Greely and the others, the strongest of the party—now Dr. Pavy, Sergeant Brainard, Corporal Salor, "Shorty" Frederick, Long, and Henry— continued to sleep in the leaking hut.

On 24 May, Whisler died at noon. The next morning he was dragged to the ridge in a pitiless snowstorm. Hunger grew intolerable. Writing to Henrietta, the commander wondered "how we live on a handful of saxifrage, half an ounce of sealskin, and five to ten ounces of wretched shrimps." The saxifrage was mere shreds; the sealskin sliced from thongs used for sledge lashing. They were blended into a shrimp stew, augmented at times by cut portions of oil-tanned sleeping-bag covers. On the twenty-sixth, Henry Biederbick, a private who had proven himself one of the party's most valuable men, contemplated the succession of command under present circumstances. If Greely died, military seniority dictated that Kislingbury take over.

But that lieutenant was himself sinking, which left Brainard, as senior sergeant, next in charge—a situation almost bound to cause dissension. Biederbick decided that while continuing to act as medical orderly, assisting Pavy and helping to feed the most helpless, his principal task now was to try to keep the commander's strength up. Greely had demonstrated "more force of character" than Biederbick had earlier given him credit for. Biederbick wrote, "Better that he and our records be saved than all of us put together. I am very sorry not to have sooner found out his full worth."

Another valuable member of the expedition, the young astronomer Sergeant Edward Israel, babbled quietly in delirium of home life and his mother's cooking. For long months Greely's bag companion, Israel was a particular favorite. "I learned to love him as a brother," the commander wrote. Israel died early on the twenty-seventh. Reading the burial service over him, Greely carefully edited the ritual so it could "in no way be offensive to the Jewish faith." No sooner were these somber duties performed than Biederbick recorded "another squabble" between Greely and the doctor, Greely charging that Pavy hoarded the party's medicine for himself. Lieutenant Kislingbury defended Pavy "as usual," Greely wrote. "I ordered him to cease. All very disagreeable, especially in our state." Greely penciled these words to his wife, but with a touch of optimism. A whaler just might get through in time: Smith Sound had been ice free for the past two weeks.

Fourteen men still lived. Long shot a dovekie, which the commander divided between him and Brainard, these being the best hunters now, and

Brainard the noncommissioned officer Greely had personally appointed successor to command. The bird was quickly eaten. The doleful wait for death dragged on. Between snowstorms, Brainard trudged to the shrimping ground, each time climbing over the ridge where lay "my departed comrades." Lieutenant Lockwood's "brass buttons, scoured bright by the flying gravel, protrude through the scanty covering of earth which our depleted strength barely enabled us to place over him." Sometimes the sergeant brought back kelp with the shrimps, but seldom in substantial amounts.

Huddled within their sleeping bags, some of the fourteen continued making notes. Those of Private Charles Henry (or Buck) revealed him as of good physical and mental condition, surprising in the circumstances, and as always the *Chicago Times* man: "A sepulchral mound of five hillocks form unconsecrated resting places. But a few [of us] still have a chance at the conclusion of this terrible tragedy to be welcomed with universal acclamation as worthy frontiersmen of Uncle Sam." Greely, on the other hand, had lost faith in survival. "We but await the grave," he wrote Henrietta. "Do not wear mourning for me. How happy we were four years ago at the Aberdeen [hotel] with Antoinette. God bless her and you and Adola." He wrote these words on 30 May, on the night of Decoration Day, when streams of fire blazed from horizon to horizon and the commander listened to his companions in the tent speculate upon what might be going on in the world "from which we are cut off."

# 25

# A PRIVATE'S EXECUTION

ON 25 MAY, five days before Greely at Camp Clay wrote of being "on the edge of the grave," Ensign Charles Harlow on the *Thetis* signaled the collier *Loch Garry* to wait at Godhavn for a favorable wind before proceeding under canvas for Upernavik. The *Thetis* left Godhavn with two more whalers, a flotilla that caught up with the *Bear* at Upernavik two days later. The *Nova Zemlya* and *Polynia*, vanguard of the whalers thus far, were anchored to nearby floes. Schley played host to the whaling masters. Although the tales they told were of terrible winters and narrow escapes among giant icebergs, Schley listened with relish. He had been afraid that the whalers would get to Greely first. Ensign Harlow wrote, "Every whaler is after the reward." But Schley now believed the odds were more in his favor. Listening to the whaling masters, he concluded that "their experiences had made them too cautious." Had he gone through what those seafarers had, "such experiences would no doubt qualify me to catch whales but were not worth a farthing for rescuing Greely. That task, I realized, required me to take unjustified risks."

Neither was Schley discouraged by reports that more steam whalers, the *Aurora, Cornwallis,* and *Narwhal,* were twenty-five miles north, ploughing through young ice. And this time he would snatch the lead from the *Bear,* for that ship had not finished coaling. Quickly, Schley hoisted anchor, bade farewell to a surprised Lieutenant William H. Emory of the *Bear,* and set off on the 700-mile crossing of Melville Bay. It was "a daily struggle with ice." It was also a race with whalers. The *Arctic* and *Wolf* overtook the *Thetis* halfway across the bay, even as the American ship drew abeam the *Aurora.* Her master, Fairweather, after spending thirty-six hours seeking an open water lane, gave up and stood in toward land, trying to work an inshore lead. "She had scarcely left us," wrote Harlow, "when the lead opened and the remaining four ships [*Arctic, Wolf, Cornwallis,* and *Narwhal*] stood on, making a fine run toward Cape York." The *Arctic* was Schley's chief rival. She was the most powerful ship in the whaling fleet, and as the month ended showed no signs of slowing down.

All day on 1 June at Camp Clay, the tent writhed to a raging gale. Although the din of thundering gusts and flapping canvas was loud, it failed to drown the voice of Lieutenant Kislingbury when he wrenched himself upright half out of his bag and sang some bars of an old hymn. Then he fell back. He died at three next morning. In the afternoon Greely read the burial service over his fellow lieutenant—a comrade in arms on the Great Plains, and in the frozen north an officer who had borne a humiliation more prolonged and irreversible than he, Greely, could have contemplated when he'd issued the order that began it. And by virtue of the victim's constant presence, it may have weighed, for all anybody knew, as a secret burden upon the commander's own conscience.

Kislingbury had died in the tent. After the service, his body was left outside in the snow. "Party will try to bury him tomorrow," wrote Greely. He noted nothing further on that event. Just down the hill in the soggy winter hut, Corporal Nicholas Salor breathed his last early 3 June. He had shared the same bag with Brainard, who, "having neither the strength to remove the remains nor the inclination to get up myself, slept until 9 o'clock." Maurice Connell complained of a cold. The doctor prescribed spirits of ammonia, which Biederbick was about to administer when the commander intervened. For one thing, medical supplies had run low. Most important, Greely had come to doubt whether

Pavy was himself fit enough to make proper diagnoses. Sergeant Brainard joined Greely in professing to believe that the doctor was losing his senses.

On 4 June, Brainard wrote in his private journal of "an arrangement between the commanding officer and four others and myself by which our condition be ameliorated." Nothing further showed what he meant by this. "Our condition" might have applied to the party as a whole, but the "four others" were not named, nor was there any explanation for the exclusion of the remaining five in the "arrangement." Still more cryptic was a note that same day, written by Private Henry and, curiously, unfinished: "Brainard prepares cairn this A.M. and shrimp bait. N. Salor to be buried tonight and Eskimo Fred to be"—nothing followed. But Eskimo Fred Christiansen had died two months before; he lay on the burial ridge. So what had Henry intended? The words were the last in his diary, and remain a mystery. As for the party's latest loss, Corporal Salor was not interred that night. No one had the strength to haul him uphill. Greely recorded that he was "put out of sight in the icefoot." Beyond that ice foot, Smith Sound presented "a beautiful sheet of water. No ice in sight. How easily we could be rescued."

For once without animus, the commander and Pavy debated the wisdom of eating tripe de roche, which the doctor had advised against, citing past explorers whose nutritional benefits from the lichen were outweighed by its purgative force. The main food supply, if it deserved that description, was still the minute shrimp, which Henry, Bender, and others were caught stealing. Greely anguished over the possible inevitability of taking some "severe action or the whole party will perish."

The next day in comparatively warm sunshine, he and a few others managed to crawl among the rocks with cans to gather lichens. Afterward, the commander drew Henry aside, warning him that only unity and fair dealing could save any of the party. Unconvinced by the private's promise to stop stealing, Greely wrote an order to sergeants Brainard, Frederick, and Long. The party was "perishing slowly by starvation." Henry, a confessed thief, had so far been pardoned. In the note, Greely said, "It is, however, *imperatively ordered* that if this man be detected either eating food or appropriating any article of provisions, you will at once shoot him." Greely's explanation, in the order, for Henry to be shot on sight if caught stealing again was that "any other course would be a fatal leniency, the man being able to overcome any two of our present force."

The commander's moment of decision came within twenty-four hours. Frederick caught Henry filching shrimp from the general mess pot. "Unarmed," wrote Greely, "[Frederick] could not comply with my orders." But as the day advanced, Henry continued his pilfering. The burly soldier made two trips downhill to the winter hut. Greely struggled from the tent and intercepted him on his return. Greely "asked what he had with him. After a while, he admitted taking sealskin thongs, contrary to positive orders, and further, that he had hidden a bundle of sealskin somewhere." Greely floundered back to the tent and wrote the following.

*Near Cape Sabine, June 4, 1884,*
*Sergeants Brainard, Long and Frederick.*

Notwithstanding promises given by Private C. B. Henry yesterday, he has since, as acknowledged to me, tampered with seal-thongs, if not other food at the old camp. This pertinacity and audacity is the destruction of the party, if not at once ended. Private Henry will be shot to-day, all care being taken to prevent his injuring anyone, as his physical strength is greater than that of any two men. Decide the manner of his death by two ball and one blank cartridge. This order is IMPERATIVE and ABSOLUTELY NECESSARY for ANY CHANCE of life.

A. W. GREELY,
First Lieutenant Fifth Cavalry, U.S.A.,
and Assistant, Commanding L. F. B. Expedition

Private Charles Buck Henry was not court-martialed. Given his comrades' dulled condition, such formality was out of the question. Henry's execution "was considered by Greely simply in the light of self-defense for the remnants of my party and was ordered on my individual responsibility."

Greely did not witness what ensued that afternoon. He remained in his sleeping bag. Upon receiving the order, the three sergeants held a preliminary talk some yards from the tent. The flap being open, Greely could see. He could not hear. And he would never be told precisely what his sergeants had discussed.

Their problem was how to perform the execution. By stealth, the burly soldier denied any chance of escape or resistance? By a bullet in the back? Notified solemnly, face to face, of his death sentence? Permitted a prayer or any other last words? Henry would still be surprised, for he had not been informed in advance of Greely's order (nor had the others of the party, Pavy included). So Greely could but watch. At about 1:30, the sergeants were out of sight. They had gone down the hill to the old winter quarters. Half an hour later, Julius Frederick returned and told Henry he was needed at the hut. Henry left with him. Any references to what followed were brief or missing. Biederbick wrote, "We heard shots at about three o'clock."

How had Henry died? Greely was never told. And two of the firing party left oddly conflicting accounts. One was aired within three months of the deed. "Three guns were loaded, two with balls, the other with a blank cartridge. I can't tell, we didn't know, who loaded the gun with a blank. No one knows except the man who loaded it." The weapons were laid on the ground, to be picked up by the executioners. "We found Henry alone, down on the coast. He did not know that we were about to kill him but he knew he had been warned. We walked to within twenty yards of him." The commander's order was read. The shots were fired. "There was no missing him at that range. Without a word the man dropped dead."

A different picture emerged fifty years later. Greely's order, calling for two balls and one blank, could not be carried out. "The only serviceable rifles were of different calibers. We decided only one gun was really suitable. Straws were produced and the man who took the shortest fired the gun." Then the three sergeants swore they would never tell who fired the fatal shot.

When Brainard came back with his fellow sergeants, only then was the execution order read before the party. Greely had given this task to Private Biederbick. And that was all that records would reveal. Greely received no detailed report of how Henry died, nor did he demand any. Of precisely how Henry died, of any farewell utterance or plea for mercy, of even the exact site where his body had been left, there was, officially, nothing. Greely's only comment at the time was that the body would be interred at the foot of the northern ice field. And had he not been weak and confined to his sleeping bag, "I should myself have killed Henry."

The harrowing day had yet to run its course. At 3:45 P.M., Private Bender died—"very cowardly," wrote Schneider, remembering that he had been suspected of thefts Bender had committed. And at six, Dr. Pavy died, "sooner than I had anticipated," wrote Greely, "his death hastened by narcotics. It would seem he fancied the ergot iron." Biederbick had told the commander of Pavy's taking the ergot extract from the medicine chest and drinking all three ounces of it: "He had dosed himself continually by all accounts."

Brainard had left camp again, shortly after supervising Henry's execution. He was away for seven hours. At 11:00 P.M., he brought back two and a half pounds of shrimp. And the mood of the seven surviving men at Camp Clay had strangely altered. "Although this has been a terrible day," wrote Private Schneider, "everyone is in good spirits this evening." The next morning, Sergeant Brainard told Schneider that he had spent a pleasant, more restful night than he had in many weeks.

Early on the seventh, Greely read the burial service over Dr. Pavy and Bender. After breakfast, Brainard, Long, and Frederick, still among the strongest, tied up the bodies and dragged them some distance from the tent. Greely did not know whether anyone could summon the strength to bury them on the ridge or if they would have to be taken to the ice foot. "Probably the latter." The survivors were still living on such lichen growths as tripe de roche and saxifrage, with driblets of stew made up of shrimp and portions of seal-skin. Schneider joined Brainard on hands and knees, "picking reindeer moss [lichen] for dinner." Still aggrieved from past wrongful accusations, Schneider claimed some redemption from the discovery among Bender's and Pavy's clothing of "burned and unburned sealskin, both showing how dishonest they were." Schneider made sure the world would know the truth. As "a dying man," he asserted his innocence. "I only ate my own boots and part of an old pair of pants I received from Lieutenant Kislingbury."

The departure of comrades one after another obliged a rearrangement of sleeping spaces and drew the survivors physically closer together. Schneider moved from the little canvas lean-to into the tent itself, and Greely moved into Bender's sleeping bag.

On the eighth, while picking tripe de roche for dinner, Biederbick found a stocking containing about a pound of what looked like bear meat, presumed stolen by Henry and hidden. Schneider cooked it the same night. If bear meat, it was eight weeks old, but "relished very much." Still, Schneider wrote the next morning, "we are on the point of starvation." In those same hours, the sergeants Brainard, Long, and Frederick removed Pavy's body to a tidal creek. In Greely's words, "The party succeeded in putting Doctor Pavy and Bender into the ice-crack."

Throughout these days of Camp Clay's approaching end, the expedition was without effective command. Greely lay all but helpless in his sleeping bag, comatose for hours. Ice floes breaking up at the shrimping grounds had carried the shrimp nets and rope beyond reach out to sea. As far as Greely knew, his men were eating thongs, boot soles, scraps of moss. Greely later attested, "If there was cannibalism, the man-eating was done in secrecy, entirely without my knowledge." It may have occurred late in May, but a significant date is that of Kislingbury's death, 2 June. At that time, the surviving men were Greely, Elison, Brainard, Long, Gardiner, Frederick, Biederbick, Connell, Schneider, Bender, Henry, and Pavy. Subsequent medical evidence left no doubt: In the wan light of an unsetting sun during those early Arctic summer weeks, one or more of the desperate men at Cape Sabine had been up on the ridge of the dead, busy with scalpel or hunting knife.

The blade had entered Lieutenant Kislingbury's body repeatedly. From the left shoulder across the breastbone to the lower ribs, "the skin and muscles were gone." Two deep openings gaped below the rib cage, portions of flesh cut away, vertebrae tissue removed, "the pelvic bones were completely denuded." Skin and muscle were sliced from the front and back of the thighs and carved off each leg from knee to ankle bone. Kislingbury's was the last body interred on the ridge. Private Whisler had died a week before the lieutenant, and his torso was stripped of flesh, "bones picked clean." There were other mutilations. Of the corpses occupying the final six of the side-by-side shallow graves, all but one was cut, as if, it would be said, by a practiced hand. The body left intact was that of Sergeant Edward Israel, the single Jewish member of the expedition.

Of the remaining nine men left clinging to life at Camp Clay, three or four suffered from an agonizing inability to perform their natural functions. Muscular weakness prevented normal excretion. Men thrust fingers, even sticks, into the rectum to dislodge hard stools. Sergeant Gardiner was one such afflicted. Biederbick gave him calomel and prepared suppositories for him, but to little avail. Shorty Frederick, an indefatigable cook, cut the last portion of sealskin into small slices and boiled them together with lichens and shrimps. He even possessed the energy to saw wood and do other camp work. Corporal Elison almost gleefully urinated without assistance, holding the pan with what remained of his hands. He was already managing to eat his stew without help, using the spoon tied to the stump of his wrist. "His case is most singular," Greely noted with something like pride. "He is in the best of health."

The weather had warmed, with Fahrenheit temperatures in the thirties. Long shot three dovekies. Two were given to the hunters as extra rations, and to make sure the hunters slumbered properly between hunting trips, Biederbick dosed the birds with tincture of opium. Each night after dinner, Long and Brainard left camp in search of more game or to reset the shrimp nets. But Brainard wrote on the tenth of the month that "my nets are lost and the bait gone." On the twelfth, he mustered enough strength to reach the highest point facing the sea, about 100 feet, and plant a flag made of scraps of sailcloth and old clothing, in hopes of its sighting by a northern whaler. A gale blew it down the next day, but in the teeth of the wind, Brainard doggedly climbed the hill again and set it back up.

That same morning, Hampden Gardiner struggled half out of his sleeping bag, clutching an ambrotype of his mother and another of the wife he had left only two months after they had wed. He talked quietly to the pictures as he had so often in recent days. They were still in his hands when he died at 5:00 P.M. "He will be buried in the icefoot," noted Private Schneider, "as it is seen the rest of the bodies are uncovering with every light wind and are thus laid bare."

Disposal of the dead had become an exhausting task, even for the three sturdiest survivors, Brainard, Long, and Frederick. Two days elapsed before they could haul Gardiner's body a mile across rough terrain and leave it at the ice foot. At the same time, Connell said something about it now being every man for himself. Greely worried. The sergeant he had broken to private declared his intention of abandoning his comrades and living alone on his own resources. Connell still had some strength left, so "the guns were put out of his reach." Sustenance by now had dwindled to almost nothing. Shrimping had ended— the water fleas would not bite on the sealskin scraps Brainard used for bait. The sealskin, cut into thumbnail-size squares, became an ingredient of broth made of moss and lichen, which the men had little strength left to scrape from between rocks. Sergeant Brainard wrote, "We are now so hungry I believe we could eat anything."

On the sixteenth, sergeants Brainard and Long had to drag Schneider from his bag for a bowel movement. Yet the next day, after begging for opium pills to help him die easily, and half paralyzed from the waist down, he recovered strength and "sewed a patch on Brainard's boots." Then he became delirious. Connell seized the opportunity to steal his small portion of charred sealskin.

Others in their bags could do no more than mutter contemptuous curses. Schneider died at six in the evening. "He will be buried if possible tonight in the icefoot," Greely wrote in a tiny scrawl.

Greely now thought his six remaining comrades could cut enough sealskin from the clothing of living and dead to last ten meals, "if eked out with reindeer moss, saxifrage buds, and tripe de roche." He wrote of feeling slightly improved, except for weak knees: "Can walk no distance. I do not know how we live, except on our hopes and expectations of a ship." He drew up a list of deaths so far and their presumed causes. Cross had died of scurvy, Jens drowned, Rice perished from exhaustion. Starvation accounted for others, Dr. Pavy's demise "hastened by narcotic." What Greely wrote alongside Private Henry's name would never be known. Either the commander or someone else later completely blacked it out.

# 26

# SEVEN REMAIN

COMMANDER SCHLEY'S CONTEST with the whalers had ended. The fishing fleet had fallen astern or tacked westward for the whaling zones. Schley breathed easier. On 18 June, conning from the *Thetis's* crow's nest, he had shaped course for Cape York. The *Bear* had left Upernavik, Lieutenant Emory striving unavailingly to narrow the distance separating his vessel from the flagship. For a while, Emory savored the chance of winning the race to Greely through information from Eskimos claiming to have seen white men on land south of Cape York. Emory hoisted an ensign at each masthead, main, and mizzen, colors that might be spotted ashore. Nothing resulted, and by then the *Thetis* lay off Cape York, miles ahead of the *Bear*.

Lieutenant John Colwell went ashore with four men, a sledge, and a dory full of provisions. He searched amid barren rock and snow-filled hollows, talked in sign language with a handful of natives, and returned to the ship, reporting no trace of Greely. The *Thetis* had an injured rudder. A new one was hung in short order, and the *Thetis*, with the *Bear* still trailing, continued up the ice-clad waters whose northern neck, between Cape Isabella on the Ellesmere coast and Cape Alexander on that of Greenland, formed the entrance to Smith Sound. Both ships steamed steadily closer to land now, pushing through masses of soft ice, Schley for hours in the crow's nest, decks astir with preparations for taking passengers on board, and stops made at every cape or inlet to check for cached messages.

Late on 19 June, north of Cape Dudley Digges, two pans of ice, each sixty feet across, blocked the *Thetis* from a promising lead. "Ramming failed to force a passage," wrote Ensign Harlow; "left us with our bows high and dry on the floes so that the engines could not back her off." The crew bored holes through the ice and dropped six torpedoes four feet below the surface. "They were exploded and so eased the nip that by reversing the engines we immediately glided off." Even then the *Thetis* had to do some heavy butting. Her movements slowed, she steamed beyond Saunders Island on the twentieth of the month, passed Cape Parry, and by midnight approached Littleton Island.

That day was Lieutenant Greely's sixth wedding anniversary. The summer solstice had arrived, but freezing temperatures and a snow-laden gale immobilized even those who might have groped outside for exercise. The wind blew harder until the frail tent fell on them. It was now home to survivors locked within stiffened sleeping bags jammed one against another. No one had the strength to set up the tent pole again. Near the seven living had lain Private Schneider's lifeless body. His comrades had managed to work only his head outside the tent flap. It was hours before they tried again to get him to the ice foot, only to collapse themselves halfway. They left him covered by the drifting snow. They had crawled back to the tent, and after it fell in upon them, canvas covered all like a sodden shroud. Pinned within his bag, the commander managed to write, "Connell's legs paralyzed from the knees down. Biederbick suffering terribly from rheumatism. Buchanan Strait open this noon a long way up the coast." That was all Greely could write. The pencil fell from his quivering fingers.

At three next morning in whirling snow, the *Thetis* crept along Littleton Island's north side and moored to a grounded iceberg. The storm eased, affording better visibility. From the *Thetis*, now, there were no signs of the *Bear* or the bounty-hunting whalers. The lull was brief, the weather closed in again, and to the west a gray wall of falling snow blotted out the bleak outline of Cape Sabine.

Commander Schley, his ice pilot, Norman, and Chief Engineer Melville were rowed ashore at Littleton Island. On the southwest side, they found the Nares cache of 1875, its provisions in excellent condition. They also located the records left by Garlington and Beebe before him. It was apparent to Schley that Greely had not reached Littleton Island. But under the 1881 ruling, neither would he have remained at Fort Conger. "Moving south, had he and his comrades lost strength, or boats, or suffered other misfortune and failed to reach Smith Sound," then they certainly couldn't be found in this vicinity.

Schley was also unable to believe that Greely had reached Cape Sabine. Had he got there, he would have the whaleboat Lieutenant Garlington said he had cached at nearby Cape Isabella. Greely would then have crossed the sound to Littleton Island for the *Neptune* stores. When the sound froze, he could have walked across. Since Greely had obviously never reached Littleton Island, the captain of the *Thetis* reasoned that he could not have reached Cape Sabine. Schley feared the worst. As Ensign Harlow wrote, it appeared that "the failure of the *Proteus* to fulfill her mission made Greely's obedience to orders a retreat to death." All that could be hoped for was that Greely had stayed where he was at Fort Conger.

It was midsummer eve, the sun at its zenith north of the equator but unseen by the men of the *Thetis* in the gloom of spray mist and driving snow. Schley considered plans. He needed to satisfy himself as to what, or who, might be discovered across Smith Sound, even though "nobody could have imagined for a moment that, with prospective starvation on one side of the water and a provision depot (albeit a small one) twenty-three miles off on the other, a party supplied with a boat and oars would have preferred the former alternative." While Schley ruminated over lunch, the *Bear* hove in sight and drew alongside. Commander Emory came on board, and the two consulted. Schley remained doubtful of finding anyone in the area.

His most optimistic guess was that Greely and his men were safe and sound at Fort Conger, or, if retreating, had prudently turned back after learning of the *Proteus* fiasco. All the same, Brevoort Island and Cape Sabine were traditional message depots for northern explorers. So the rescue expedition decided to check at least that region before continuing north into Kane Basin. They

would scour that small group of features off the Ellesmere coast made familiar to them through study of the proceedings of the *Proteus* court of inquiry
and of innumerable books on Arctic exploration—Stalnecht Island, Brevoort
Island, Payer Harbor. And Cape Sabine.

Early on the twenty-second, as noted by Ensign Harlow on the flagship,
the sea's ebb and flow "had broken up the floes. Northerly winds had piled up
the ice in all shapes. The whole bay was a network of tidal channels." Closest
at hand on the other side was Brevoort Island, a mass of gleaming black rock
three miles long, and Stalnecht, that islet of low-lying rock connected with the
shore at low tide. Westward sprawled the much larger island, crisscrossed by
glacier-filled ravines and bare-rocked ridges, whose northeastern extremity was
Sabine. The *Thetis* would lead under steam and sail, the *Bear* following. Schley's
searchers could at least check the condition of the meager rations and leave a
new and larger cache. "We were anxious to push on," wrote Harlow. "The
sound was nearly clear of ice, the wind favorable but increasing in force." In
the early afternoon of 22 June, "the fires were spread, the line that held us to
the iceberg was singled. We were ready to start."

After a four-hour crossing of Smith Sound, Schley made fast his ship to
the ice foot beneath the conical mass of Brevoort Island. He detailed shore
parties. One would search the island, another would visit the Stalnecht islet, a
third would comb the shoreline around Payer Harbor. A fourth under
Lieutenant Colwell would take the *Bear's* steam cutter *Cub* and look for the
cairn that, as the lieutenant remembered, Garlington had left three miles north
of the *Proteus* wreck. And it was when Colwell's party was ready to leave, the
*Cub* about to be lowered, that one of the Brevoort Island searchers came running toward the ship, clutching a package and yelling, "Greely is on Cape
Sabine!"

The package was hurried into Schley's hands and quickly unwrapped. It
contained six records outlining the work at Fort Conger, the retreat to Smith
Sound, the discovery of Garlington's lamentable news, and the location of
Greely's camp at Cape Sabine. But Greely's signature on the papers was dated
21 October, 1883. So his party had left Fort Conger and had certainly not
turned back. With only forty days' rations in the caches and little fuel, how
could they have survived eight mostly winter months? The Lady Franklin Bay
Expedition might be at Cape Sabine, but in what condition, dead or alive,
Schley dreaded to imagine.

As Schley studied the papers found on Brevoort Island, a party under Ensign Harlow made fresh discoveries on tiny Stalnecht. First they came upon records left in a bottle by the Nares expedition in 1875, endorsed in turn by Beebe in 1882 and Garlington in 1883. Harlow added his own signature, replaced the papers in a fresh bottle, and wedged it back among the rocks. Then he discovered a cairn: "Removing a few stones I found several tin boxes, their contents scratched on them, two wooden cases, a bundle of flags, and a leather sextant case."

The cairn also contained, set upright in its narrow box, a standard pendulum. Tucked in one side of the sextant case was a leaf from a notebook and, penciled on it, "This cairn contains the original records of the Lady Franklin Bay Expedition, the private journals of Lieutenant Lockwood, and a set of photographic negatives. The party are permanently camped at a point midway between Cape Sabine and Cocked Hat Island. All well." This message also was dated October 1883. Harlow unrolled the flags, lashed one to a pike, and sped to the islet's highest point, from where he excitedly semaphored the news of his discovery.

Lieutenant Colwell was in the steam launch alongside the flagship, all set to locate the *Proteus* wreck cache. Commander Schley gave him fresh instructions, ordered the ship's steam whistle sounded and a signal hoisted recalling his search parties. The *Cub*, with Lieutenant Colwell, headed for land. Schley transferred from his flagship to the *Bear* for closer inshore passage and followed in the launch's wake. Both craft moved cautiously along ice-clad rocky shore familiar to John Colwell. He halted near the *Proteus* wreck cache, scanning the area through his spyglass. He saw nothing of significance and resumed a coastal search jeopardized by worsening weather. The wind rose. Low clouds raced above an increasingly choppy sea. The time was a little after nine on the twenty-second.

AT CAMP CLAY, minutes had gone by since the sound of a ship's whistle made Greely wonder if his dulled mind played him tricks. For the previous forty-four hours, no more than a droplet of water and a few square inches of soaked sealskin had passed his lips. Hoarsely, he bade sergeants Brainard and Long go outside and look at the sea. Long struggled first up the hill commanding the broadest view. Brainard attempted to follow, but had to quit halfway. He watched Long try to set up the distress flag, which had again blown down. That seemed to be all. Brainard stumbled back downhill and reported no help in sight. More minutes passed. And it was Brainard, huddled at the flap of the downed tent, who first heard the approach of firm footsteps crunching in the snow. Greely, inert in his bag and all but smothered by the tent's canvas, heard a strong strange voice calling his name.

When Brainard left him on the hill, Long had set up the flag and turned to follow, but he had then spotted, out in the strait, a black smudge his narrowing eyes identified as a ship. While Long stood there, grasping the flag, Lieutenant Colwell in the *Cub* had rounded the point. He saw the ridge, Long's figure etched against the darkening sky. Running the launch in as close as he dared, Colwell jumped ashore. Long dropped the flag, staggered downhill, and pitched headlong into his rescuer's embrace.

Leaving the sergeant safely in the launch with the *Bear*'s chief engineer, Colwell hurried up the slope with the ice pilot, Norman. They carried bread and pemmican. They reached the crest, and then (except for the instruments and journals already recovered by Ensign Harlow's men on Stalnecht) all that remained of the Lady Franklin Bay Expedition lay spread before them—a collapsed tent covering seven starving men surrounded by empty cans, scattered ammunition, scraps of clothing, and other debris. At the tent, Colwell groped in near darkness amid a tangle of rope and canvas. He found Greely, motionless in his sleeping bag, head resting on his hand. Like his companions, Greely's "hair was long and matted, face and hands caked with dirt, body scantily clad with dirty, wornout garments." Each man held close a little bundle of what personal valuables and papers he wanted saved. "All were in their bags, awaiting the end."

As Colwell and Norman carefully doled out food to the emaciated survivors, Ensign Harlow came with a camera and tripod. Greely had put on his eyeglasses, which was how Harlow recognized him. "I prepared to make the plate I had so often pictured—the meeting with Greely." Taking the photograph was far from easy. Harlow was equipped with only four plates, light fast faded, and "twice the wind overturned my camera despite the spread of its legs." The camera was wet, the plate holder swollen. "Despite all, I got a focus and snapped the shutter. Gave the tent two plates, put one on the winter house and one on the graves."

By forenoon on the twenty-third, the rescue ships' captains were ashore with surgeons, who brought stretchers and medication. The wind blew harder yet, bringing heavy sleet. Swathed in blankets and lashed to stretchers, the last men alive at Camp Clay were borne to the ice foot for conveyance by steam cutter to the waiting vessels. Lieutenant Emory of the *Bear* stayed onshore to supervise a complete search of the camp and its surrounds, gather up what scattered papers might be found—and see to exhumations. Commander Schley had "determined at once to remove all the dead for transfer to the United States."

Little by way of disinterment was required. The dead lay in line on the hill beneath a thin coverlet of gravel. Schley described a row of graves not fifty yards from the tent "with protruding heads and feet of those later buried." One by one they were lifted and wrapped in blankets. In this somber task, performed in deep gloom and squalls of sleet, Ensign Harlow, after gingerly resting his photographic gear on rocks near the flattened tent, assisted the officers Emory and Colwell. "On a piece of canvas cut from the tent," he said, "I drew a diagram of the graves, numbering each one from the right facing their heads. This precaution was necessary to avoid confusion in identifying the remains." Schley's men stitched canvas tags to the blankets, in order of disinterment. On the *Thetis*, Greely had fainted while being carried below to the wardroom. In Surgeon Edward H. Green's words, the commander was a pitiful sight, "skin hanging from his limbs in flaps, face, hands and scalp blackened with a thick crust of soot and dirt." He was bathed and dressed in clean clothing. Stimulants revived him to a point where "he insists on talking, craving news and demanding solid food." As his strength returned, the commander had more to say.

He objected to Schley's decision to gather the bodies for return to the United States, saying that they should stay instead where they fell. Why Schley thought otherwise, he later disclosed, was because families would want their loved ones brought home. As well, the government in Washington had willingly paid for transporting the perished De Long party all the way from Siberia. Schley explained, "It would fail in its duty if it left these explorers in their rude graves at Cape Sabine." According to Greely, Lieutenant Lockwood had expressed a desire "to rest forever in the field of his work. Why disturb them?" But it was too late. Bucking ice-capped waves, two cutters approached the *Thetis* and the *Bear*, containing eleven of Cape Sabine's dead.

The elements reacted with a final burst of fury at being robbed of them.

The wind became so strong and the swirl of shattered floes so encompassing that Ensign Harlow, in one of the boats, feared they would never reach their ships. The *Thetis* and the *Bear* steamed as close to the cutters as safety allowed. Ensign Harlow wrote, "By alternately drifting and struggling to keep the boats head to wind, their bows deeply loaded with dead, shipping gallons of water that smashed with broken icefloes nearly to the thwarts, we finally got along-side." Even then the storm had not finished with them. As one of the cutters slammed against the *Thetis*'s hull, two bodies were flung overboard, to be recovered only seconds before the waves would have swallowed them.

Six of the dead were taken on board the *Bear*, the others on the *Thetis*. At first they were carefully wrapped, stowed in the ships' dories, and covered with ice. Lieutenant Colwell was still onshore at Camp Clay, making certain that nothing significant was left behind. Peering from the winter hut in the direction of the ice foot, he saw a dark object against patchy snow. Ensign Harlow later wrote what Colwell had found: "The mutilated remains afterwards identified from a bullet-hole as Private Henry." These were taken to the *Bear*.

Notwithstanding the efforts of Harlow, Colwell, Chief Engineer Melville, and others to properly identify the dead, records and recollections of those strange hours off Cape Sabine were confusing. Henry's body had been found by accident. The actual site of the bullet hole (or holes) would never appear on record. Greely informed Schley, "officially, referring to his diary as verification, that seventeen men of the Lady Franklin Bay Expedition had perished by starvation and that one had drowned while out sealing. The names and death dates follow." They included Henry's. Greely, on the *Thetis*, said nothing "officially," if at all, of the soldier's death by gunshot. And no special search ensued for the spot near Eskimo Point where Sergeant Frederick had buried, as best he could, his dead comrade Rice, who, it was supposed, had been washed out to sea with the remains of Salor, Bender, Gardiner, and Dr. Pavy. Error obscured detail. Schley quoted Greely as numbering five buried in the ice foot. "They were swept away by winds and tides before my arrival," Schley reported. "No trace of them could be discovered."

Seamen on the *Thetis* hoisted an oil tank out of the engine room and placed it on the forecastle, securely wedged. It was prepared to receive five bodies, numbered 1, 3, 8, 9, and 10, identified as Kislingbury, Whisler, Linn, Eskimo Fred Christiansen, and Cross. Aboard the *Bear*, machinists made watertight a snow-melting tank on either side of the foremast. Like the *Thetis* tank, each was filled with a mixture of salt water and alcohol. When they were exposed for stowage in the tanks, stripped of tattered and filthy clothing, some of the dead were recognized by photographs brought to the Arctic, others identified "by other characteristics." Schley would report, "I am therefore satisfied no mistake was made."

These tasks filled the hours of midnight to dawn on 24 June, as the ships prepared for home. Startling discoveries were reported from the decks of both. When each body was bared, ready to be swathed like mummies in cotton cloth strips, tallied, and put into the tanks, "it was found," wrote Schley, "that six, those of Lieutenant Kislingbury, Sergeants Jewell and Ralston, Privates Whisler, Henry and Ellis, had been cut and the flesh removed." Ensign Harlow was one of the *Thetis* officers detailed to "prepare the dead for immersion for safe carriage to St. John's, where it is the intention of the captain to have iron caskets made that are hermetically sealed, never again to be opened. It was a hideous job but I did not shrink from it. I refrain from details, thinking it best not to be put into writing."

In the dusky forenoon of the twenty-fourth, the *Thetis* signaled the *Bear*. By mid-afternoon, both vessels, with their pathetic cargoes, were under way, the *Bear* in the flagship's wake. The survivors on board steadily regained strength, except Joseph Elison, who awoke screaming the first night at sea and sobbed that he had dreamed of being left behind at Cape Sabine. Fog, snow, and heavy sea ice delayed the passage south.

On the night of the twenty-fifth, the ships lay beset by densely packed icebergs between Northumberland and Haklyut islands. Surgeon Howard Ames of the *Bear* boarded the *Thetis* and helped Surgeon Green subdue a delirious Elison by morphine injection. They examined his injuries. Both feet were gone, the ends of the tibular and fibular protruding and the stumps "suppurating freely." The fingers of Elison's left hand were intact but "broken and dead." Of his right hand, two were gone. Green "removed the remaining fingers and thumb with bone pliers." Ames consulted with the *Thetis* surgeon about amputating half of Elison's leg. Dr. Green said it was best to wait.

North of Upernavik, Schley's ships met the *Alert* and the collier *Loch Garry*. The captains were at once informed, as were the Dundee whalers encountered elsewhere off the Greenland coast. Greely would later deem "the wise act of Congress in offering a bounty to the Scots whalers the turning point in our fortunes." Without the rivalry engendered between the Dundee crews and their

American counterparts, Schley's ships would have reached Cape Sabine to find none of the party alive. As for the whalers' people and those of the *Alert*, it seemed to Ensign Harlow "rather hard [for them] to have to turn back so soon in the race." Their disappointment was all the more marked, in Harlow's view, when contrasted with Commander Schley's boastful manner since the rescue. The ensign was thoroughly disgusted. Over dinner in the wardroom, Schley and the *Bear*'s Emory exchanged compliments to a degree Harlow found "absolutely sickening. Two men sitting before eight others and slobbering over one another. Why not retire to their room and embrace?" Free talk in the wardroom was all very well, but short-lived. By landfall, a gag rule would be imposed.

On the Fourth of July, celebrated with punch made of rum recovered from the *Neptune*'s cache on Littleton Island, the surgeons decided to cut off both Elison's legs. They reasoned, "His blunted mind will prevent mental shock"— this with whisky and ether. Dr. Ames sawed off the left stump, Green the right. The amputations were of no avail, for Elison died three days later. Denuded of hands and legs, weighing just seventy-eight pounds, the soldier who had displayed such miraculous endurance was sewn up in a blanket and put in a tank with his comrades. The four-ship flotilla reached Godhavn. At the insistence of the Danish inspector of Disko Island, the remains of Eskimo Fred Christiansen were taken ashore and uphill for burial.

The ships continued southward. Their crews had much to gossip over, mostly in whispers. And off Labrador on 16 July, following a storm that slowed the *Thetis* and the *Bear* to two knots and left the *Alert* and *Loch Garry* far astern, all hands aboard the foremost ships were summoned on deck and read a special order. The order stated that upon arrival at St. John's, *"there shall not be any communication with the shore or any person outside the expedition until the result of the cruise has been sent to the Secretary of the Navy."*

The ships were off Newfoundland the next morning. As soon as the fog lifted and officers had gone ashore, telegraph wires were set humming. Early tidings reached the Navy Department in Washington at nine o'clock. Telephones rang, a typewriter clacked away, and hectograph copies of every incoming telegram were rushed to other government departments and to the White House. President Chester Arthur reacted more with regret for the loss of life than with gladness over news of polar records won for his country and the naming of a mountain for him. In contrast, Greely's first report was exul-

tant: "For the first time in three centuries England yields the honor of the farthest north. The two years' station duties, observations, explorations, and the
retreat to Cape Sabine were accomplished without loss of life, disease, serious
accident or even severe frostbite." Ensign Harlow cabled the *New York Times* that,
for the time being, he was under orders to keep his mouth shut.

None of these early communications mentioned the shooting of Private
Henry. Schley's first report summarized the information Greely had given him
on the way down. After the successful retreat to Cape Sabine, crossing Smith
Sound was impossible. Winter gales kept the channel from closing. So 240
food rations on Littleton Island could not be secured. Regarding the dead,
Schley's telegram concluded, "I would urgently request that the bodies now on
board be placed in metallic cases here for safer and better transportation. This
seems to me imperative."

At St. John's, the rescue ships were targets for sightseers. Greely was
secreted ashore and allowed the exercise of a two-block stroll. Cables from
American newspaper editors pleaded with Commander Schley or his officers
to "send all you can as soon as possible." The *New York Times* wanted 6,000 words
for its Sunday edition. Finally, Schley told Harlow, "Go ahead, send all you
want to." Harlow hurried to the telegraph office and "sat at the wires until the
office refused to send any more," the operator worn out. Harlow's dispatch to
the *New York Times* contained no reference to the mutilated condition of some
of the dead.

In Washington, the corridors of the State, War, and Navy Building were
astir with excitement. Out of town just then, the Secretary of the Navy sent
the homecomers congratulatory messages and told Schley to "use your discretion about the care and transportation of the bodies. Prepare them according
to your judgment." President Arthur reiterated his opposition to Arctic enterprises, whose gain he considered insignificant when measured against the cost
in coin and human life. Some newspapers were ready to agree. "Arctic exploration has involved an immense waste of money and life," declared the *Chicago
Tribune*. "It is time that it stopped." Antipolar sentiments were all the sharper
because the incoming reports of the Lady Franklin Bay Expedition followed
so soon upon the *Jeannette* disaster, whose aspect of scandal and cover-up were
right then the subject of congressional investigation. "Not even when it is
played under favorable conditions is the game worth the candle," said the *New*

*York Times,* while a Philadelphia paper referred to Arctic exploration as "monstrous and murderous folly."

Notable among those who went public with views pro and con were two Americans with recent experience of the hardships and dangers of northern exploration. Lieutenant John Danenhower, who had returned half blind as one of the two most publicized survivors of the *Jeannette* and who was in a very personal sense among its most tragic victims, reaffirmed a belief that polar expeditions were exercises in futility: "There are much better fields for exploration and scientific work."

Commander Schley wondered why Lieutenant Garlington, after the wreck of the *Proteus,* struck out southeast in his boats instead of southwest toward Cary Islands, "where there was every reason to suppose the *Yantic* would touch." The parties could have met and returned jointly to Littleton Island and established a winter station there as ordered. Instead, the ship and the boats had taken opposite courses. The press excoriated General Hazen for failing to give Garlington clear-cut orders. Hazen's defense was his commitment to the Greely plan. And he could hardly be blamed for events that ensued from the wreck of the *Proteus.* But all the arguments, the excuses, and the public postmortems were about to be overshadowed in the American press by sensationally headlined hearsay to the effect that members of the Lady Franklin Bay Expedition, during the final days at Cape Sabine, had in their extremity resorted to eating one another.

# 27

# FUNERAL FLOTILLA

WITH SECRETARY CHANDLER'S permission to prepare the dead as he judged proper, Commander Schley at St. John's had placed an order for metal caskets. He telegraphed Chandler of his action. As soon as the caskets arrived and the bodies were transferred to them, he would steam for the United States. Thus ensued eight days' delay ordained by the dead. Yet it was an interval enlivened by dinner parties on the *Thetis* and the *Bear,* to which prominent Newfoundlanders were invited. "Society is making quite a demand on the officers," noted Ensign Harlow. "Every evening there is something going on."

This daily display of shipboard hospitality was cut short by the hauling of a dozen caskets on board. Made of boiler iron, each weighed 700 pounds, complete with a lid secured by fifty-two large screw bolts and a coat of black paint. Schley made sure a silver plate with the name and death date of its content was mounted on each casket. Once the lids were firmly bolted in place, the relief ships, escorted out of harbor by crowded whistling tugboats, turned their prows southward.

In the United States, political thought concentrated on the forthcoming presidential election. Foremost among those anxious for a continuing Republican administration was William Chandler, who would thereby remain in the cabinet as Secretary of the Navy. Chandler was determined to revitalize the American Navy, to replace its wooden hulls with warships of steel. Getting the Navy Act of 1881 passed, which set the groundwork for a twentieth-century naval force, he had repeatedly courted trouble. To head off a critical scandal connected with the loss of the *Jeannette,* the secretary already had gone to such lengths as suppressing court-martial charges the ship's late command-er, George De Long, had filed in the Arctic against his navigation officer. And Chandler had to cope with allegations of graft. The success of Schley's expe-dition had come as a political godsend. Intent on making the most of it, he set about organizing a grand welcome home at Portsmouth, New Hampshire, his native state.

He telegraphed Robert Lincoln, "Trust that you will be present." The Secretary of War declined, with good reason: to avoid meeting soldier-explorers likely to hold him accountable for failed relief expeditions. Meanwhile, bereaved families wanted to know of the true fate and the where-abouts of their lost kin. Lilla Mae Pavy was perplexed by "telegrams painfully contradictory." She wrote Henrietta Greely, then preparing for the long rail-road journey east from San Diego to greet her husband, "Rejoice with you while my own heart is broken." A second Mrs. Pavy, also distressed, was far from mourning the doctor's death. Claiming to be his only true widow, Alicia Pavy wrote from France, asking the Secretary of War if Pavy was among the survivors. He had left her destitute in 1871, with a child to care for. She wrote, "If really he has died of cold and hunger, then he has met the punishment he well deserves."

At daybreak on Friday, 1 August, fog rose above the New England coast and the rescue-ships-turned-funeral-flotilla stood on for Portsmouth. *Thetis, Bear,* and *Alert* were first sighted by the naval sloop *Alliance,* stationed well off-shore to lead them into harbor, where eight or ten warships waited, decks thronged with Portsmouth dignitaries, national politicians, and Lieutenant Greely's friends and family. Secretary Chandler and General Hazen had joined naval officers on the quarterdeck of the 5,000-ton *Tennessee*, flagship of the North Atlantic fleet, a vessel that typified the old wooden ships that Chandler hoped to replace with steel battle cruisers.

Chandler had programmed the whole show—this was the Navy's day. Under his strict orders, no one, not even Commander Schley's wife, was permitted on board the *Thetis* until Henrietta Greely, escorted by her twin brothers, Otto and Loring Nesmith, boarded the ship for a private reunion with her husband. And it was only after a discreet interval that other relatives, led by Greely's mother and his two infants, were allowed on the *Thetis* to hug him.

As dusk fell, Greely went ashore in the Navy yard admiral's barge. Later, as arranged by Chandler, he moved into a cottage among the apple trees on nearby Seavy's Island, safely secluded from news-hungry reporters. This cottage would be the Greelys' residence for the next several weeks. The five other survivors were transferred to the Navy yard hospital. Portsmouth, meanwhile, was in a wildly celebrative mood. So many citizens were let on board the *Thetis* to view relics from the Lady Franklin Bay Expedition that guards had to be posted to protect, for instance, Greely's distress flag and sledge, from souvenir hunters who might have chipped them to pieces.

On Saturday, while visitors still swarmed topside, Secretary Chandler and General Hazen met in the *Thetis*'s main cabin with Commander Schley, who told them of the mutilated bodies (back in St. John's, talk of cannibalism was already rife, thanks to the ice pilot, James Norman, loose-tongued in liquor and rancorous after having been ordered off the *Thetis* by Schley for drunkenness). It was also at a private meeting in Portsmouth that Greely gave Hazen and the secretary his first intimation of the "terrible responsibility" which had compelled him to order the execution of one of his own men.

On Monday the fourth, a parade snaked through Portsmouth. The relief ships' captains rode in open carriages. Seated because still weak, Greely reviewed the scene from a grandstand in Market Square. On doctor's orders, he was not at the Portsmouth Music Hall for the climax to the day's events. Chandler was the chief speaker, praising the Navy's relief expedition even to the point of scornfully recalling the Army's failed attempts. Secretary of War Lincoln, conveniently at Gettysburg reviewing militia, was ignored by every orator. Loud applause greeted General Benjamin Butler's declaration that

Americans would not rest until they planted Old Glory at the top of the world: "The North Pole belongs to us!"

The funeral ships were off New York at noon on the eighth, and the bodies borne ashore at Governor's Island by a Navy yard tug. Artillery fired a twenty-one-gun salute. With the caskets on caissons, the cortege rumbled off in bright sunshine to the island's hospital, where, after a religious service, all but two of the caskets were delivered to friends and families of the deceased. The exceptions, Henry's and Schneider's, were returned to the wharf, from where a steamboat carried them to Brooklyn. Private Schneider's remains were placed in a receiving vault pending the arrival of family members from Germany. Private Henry was interred in the Cypress Hills soldiers' plot with full military honors. No friends or family members were present. And measures were already under way to block attempts to have any of the caskets opened.

To this effect, the Secretary of War had sent telegrams to regional quartermasters. The official explanation was that opening any caskets might pose a threat to public health and that, anyway, the bodies would be unrecognizable. This was the response of General Winfield Scott Hancock, division commander, to a lieutenant in Delphi, Indiana, who had telegraphed that Private Whisler's family wished to view the remains. The general added, "The sooner [the dead] are put into the ground the better." Relatives of Sergeant Cross were similarly refused. He was buried in the Congressional Cemetery, Washington, D.C., a huge wreath spelling "Arctic" resting on his grave. Sergeant Israel was laid to rest in the Hebrew Society's lot at Mountain Home Cemetery, Kalamazoo, Michigan. Lieutenant Lockwood's body lay briefly in state at St. Anne's Church, Annapolis, before interment at the Naval Academy Cemetery. Schneider's body was soon on a steamer bound for Bremerhaven.

Rumors about the true cause of Private Henry's death were officially ignored. On 11 August, General Hazen telegraphed Greely from Long Branch, New Jersey, where he had just arrived "after a pleasant journey and suitable disposal of all the dead," which, materially, was more or less true. But the ghost of Private Henry was not so easily exorcised. Hazen told Greely that at a private meeting with Secretary Lincoln in New York, he "went into the matter you and I talked of the evening before I left Portsmouth."

The reference was to Henry's execution. According to Hazen, the Secretary of War viewed Greely's decision in "the highest possible light." The question was what to do publicly about it. Perhaps a court of inquiry? But upon reflection, General Hazen felt the commander should "rest easy, for [Henry's] wrongdoing was in the nature of a mutiny." The War Department would say nothing until Greely was fit enough to draft his formal report. And if anyone asked why Henry was buried with military honors, the answer would be that at the time of burial, official policy had been determined by an "appropriate propriety of silence."

No such reticence prevailed in the office of Queens County, New York, health authorities. When the head of Brooklyn's sanitary department gave permission on request for Henry's body to be conveyed through the streets, he had understood that the soldier had starved to death. Later he heard a different story. He recommended exhumation. So did the county coroner, who wanted an inquest. Although an Army cemetery, Cypress Hills was under his control, not Washington's, and it was he who would certainly order an exhumation if anybody submitted an affidavit based on reasons to believe that Henry had died a violent death. A clerk in Lincoln, Nebraska, named Dora Buck identified herself as the soldier's sister and asked for an autopsy. None followed.

On 12 August, the *New York Times* ran front-page stories of a soldier's execution and rampant cannibalism in the Arctic, under the headline HORRORS OF CAPE SABINE. General Hazen sensed an attack upon himself personally. Since Hazen had years before crossed swords with figures supported by the paper, the *Times* never missed a chance to attack him. It now published, Hazen told Greely, "what it has been after all the while, adding all the lies it sees fit." The C.S.O. had no doubt that Private Henry was "a desperate vagabond," but Greely was told to issue a short statement to this effect. "As to the talk of eating human flesh, say what you are prepared to," Hazen advised.

Much of the *Times* material was patently unbelievable, but the newspaper now could claim justification for its traditional opposition to polar exploration while indulging gleefully in a sensationalism the equal of any which had boosted the circulation of its rival *New York Herald*. The *Times* questioned, had Greely wanted the bodies left in the Arctic because "the men all expressed the wish to be buried on the very edge of the great polar sea"? Highly suspicious, trumpeted the paper. Likewise Commander Schley's official reason for sealing the dead in caskets being the "great change" in temperature between St. John's and New York. What "great change"? As for reports of bodies washed away after burial amid ice floes, "the truth is plain," the *Times* stated. Their flesh had been eaten and the remains left where they lay. Officers of the two relief vessels knew it, the paper accused, but dodged interviews. In the *New York Times*'s view, what all this meant was that officialdom had embarked upon a cover-up of cannibalism.

# 28

# "This Cannibalism Business"

To quash the excitement stirred by its competitor, the *New York Herald* questioned a Navy Department staff officer. His replies were hardly helpful. If cannibalism had occurred, "it was no more than had happened time and again." Newspapers elsewhere spoke up. The *Philadelphia Bulletin* wanted the charges investigated and General Hazen court-martialed. The paper asked, "Why has he escaped so far?" Since it was not Hazen's nature to keep quiet for long, he beckoned newsmen to his handsome home on K Street and conceded that cannibalism might have occurred.

Secretary Chandler kept above the fray. He believed that nothing must impair his Navy's current celebrity. One of his departmental heads warned him of big trouble brewing, that he should separate himself from it in advance. Word had leaked of problems between Greely and his second in command at Fort Conger and of Kislingbury's disbarment from scientific work. The bureau chief explained, "There must be an explosion soon. I hope the [Greely] party will be clear of your guardianship before it happens." Chandler at once telegraphed Secretary Lincoln that Greely's people were fit and anxious for a furlough. Let them have it, Lincoln replied, along with a portion of their accumulated salaries.

In Rochester, the Kislingbury family wished to be left alone. However, egged on by the *Rochester Post Express* editor, who promised to finance an exhumation in return for exclusive rights to its reportage, the late lieutenant's three brothers agreed to it. Early on the morning of 14 August, while Greely was about to be feted by Newburyport townsfolk, an undertaker and five helpers at the Mount Hope Cemetery took up a heavy casket and, in the presence of two Kislingbury brothers and two doctors, unscrewed its fifty-two iron bolts and lifted the lid. The doctors examined its contents for forty-five minutes. After the reinterment, they signed a sworn statement, which said, "In our opinion the flesh was cut away with some sharp instrument." The grisly details followed. All doubts vanished, leaving the Kislingburys benumbed with shock and despair. Not only had their brother suffered prolonged humiliation on the orders of his commander, but in the most unspeakable manner, even in death, dignity had been denied him.

Reports of the Rochester exhumation prompted another, that of Private William Whisler, whose parents lived quietly on the outskirts of Delphi, Indiana. Their son was buried in a small country churchyard. In the pale light of daybreak, his casket was raised and opened. As at Rochester, two doctors viewed the contents. They declined to make a statement unless asked to do so by higher authority. Thus local observers—fourteen persons had attended the exhumation—reported that scarcely more than a skeleton occupied the casket, that "all flesh had been cut from the limbs and shoulders as if by an expert."

Meanwhile, Greely was invited to represent the United States at a meeting of the British Association for the Advancement of Science in Montreal. More than temporary escape from inquisitive American newsmen, this excursion provided an occasion for Greely to address a distinguished body for the first time as an experienced Arctic explorer. However obsessed he once was by the desire to beat the British record for Farthest North—and he had done so—Greely now had good reason to thank the British. London newspapers praised his expedition's achievements, and downplayed the man-eating accusa-

tions, which were, said Clements Markham, head of the Royal Geographical
Society, "a disgrace to American journalism."

On 23 August, Greely wrote Secretary Chandler, "The cannibalism business has all blown over. The common sense of the people react fully from the
first shock. If it did not, that is not your funeral at any rate. The [rescue] is a
feather in your cap which cannot be plucked out." No such kudos were going
to Secretary of War Robert Lincoln, who was not so sure the cannibalism furor
had died down, and he was certainly disturbed by stories of a soldier's execution at Cape Sabine. Aware that some form of public statement was expected
of him, Greely announced that he had kept silent on the shooting "to avoid a
public scandal." The nation would have to await his official report for details.
Greely went so far as to say, "[Had I not ordered Henry shot,] I should have
failed in my duty to the rest of the party."

No more ghoulish copy was expected from the *New York Times.* Had Private
Linn's parents known in advance what was now alleged, they would have had
his casket opened and the contents examined, regardless of the War Department's ban. But now it was too late, and they would not disturb their boy's
grave. Still the story would not go away. Portions of Schley's report leaked,
including his mention of mutilation. When a newsman accosted Brainard, the
sergeant said curtly, "I know nothing of cannibalism." Julius Frederick, reached
at his home in Indianapolis, thought "there might have been some cannibalism. I saw no instance."

Greely felt that he, too, had better say something on the man-eating stories now, rather than wrestle with them later for his official report. He stated
that while press accounts seemed to leave no doubt that cannibalism occurred,
he had known nothing of it. "I can give no stronger denial," he insisted. Calling
on Greely to vouch for their innocence, his fellow survivors might have welcomed something weightier. All they got from their former commander was
"I cannot tell whether they told the truth or not. I can but answer for myself
and for my orders to the expedition."

Had he waited a few days longer, Greely could have continued to say nothing. From the government came an explanation for those mutilations. It evolved
at a confidential meeting between the Secretary of War and the Secretary of
the Navy and was possibly conceived at the White House. Chandler, Robert
Lincoln, and Commander Schley had conferred privately at the Brooklyn Navy
Yard. Once back in Washington, the Secretary of War had cabled Chandler,

then in New England, "I think we should see the President together at earliest convenience." And out of this caucus emerged a novel theory.

It required significant revision of Schley's report, and the addition of certain words. Schley originally had said, "Six [of the dead] had been cut and the fleshly parts removed." The new doctored version stated that the human flesh had been removed "to a greater or lesser extent, with a view no doubt to use as shrimp bait."

Weakened though the report was by the addition of those sixteen words, this published explanation signaled that the cannibalism issue was now closed. Besides, nothing could alter the opinion of those who preferred the more sensational story. This was, after all, the age of Barnum. Show business beckoned from the minute the survivors stepped ashore in New York.

Union Square Theatre was about to stage a dramatization of the English novel *God and Man*, under the more eye-catching title *Storm Beaten*. Since the production featured icebound castaways, the theater managers saw profit in having a genuine example on show.

General Hazen relayed this information to Greely, saying he wouldn't object if any of the men, at liberty in Portsmouth, were willing to go along. All that *Storm Beaten* finally got from the dissolved Lady Franklin Bay Expedition were short appearances by Private Biederbick. But within two weeks, without the knowledge of their superiors, sergeants Brainard and Long and privates Frederick and Connell had themselves a manager named Randolph and were on display at a Cleveland, Ohio, dime museum for a thousand dollars a week. Randolph denied that his clients were degrading the United States Army. He asserted, "Neither Sergeant Brainard nor his comrades are on exhibition as Freaks or Monstrosities." All the same, orders were soon flashed from Washington to Cleveland putting Brainard and company on the earliest train east.

Greely finished his detailed report within seven months. For unexplained reasons, its publication was withheld for three years. Some diaries were returned to survivors and kin of the dead, though Private Schneider's was missing. Greely suggested that it had been thrown overboard accidentally during the passage home, or stolen by one of the *Thetis* crew. And according to Lieutenant Ray, formerly commander at the Point Barrow post and now a Signal Corps staff officer, knife thrusts had desecrated not only Cape Sabine's dead. Pages of diaries had been cut as well, "especially Kislingbury's." Hazen

himself wrote Greely that the Secretary of War was told of "records and journals mutilated for the purpose of covering up certain things."

Charles Clark, the Kislingbury boys' guardian, demanded the immediate
return of their father's diary. Greely retorted that he had never known
Kislingbury to keep one. He added that "unrecorded facts" had been hidden
out of regard for the feelings of the lieutenant's children. With so many stories at large, Greely now was determined to get an unambiguous version of
events before the public even in advance of his official report. Telling Hazen
that publishers were anxious for his personal story, he obtained the C.S.O.'s
consent and went to work on it. But documentation was haphazard, at best.
Diaries that Hazen let him see contained gaps. Greely's own official journal
ended with a late-1883 entry on the eve of the landing at Eskimo Point. The
balance of the commander's records, with a number of dates omitted, occupied notebooks instead of regular letterbooks, and at least one was lost or left
at Camp Clay. Most information thereafter filled missives to Henrietta, written in apprehension that he might never see her again.

The expedition's diaries, from the rescue until arrival in Washington, were
in Sergeant Brainard's custody. They included William Cross's savage aspersions
cast upon the commander. For his own contribution to the expedition's record,
Brainard had composed a narrative in diary format on the *Thetis* coming home.
He had shown it to Commander Schley. It told of routine life at Fort Conger,
the exploratory sledge trips, including his record-breaking journey with
Lieutenant Lockwood and the succession of deaths at Cape Sabine. Brainard
kept his personal notes concealed.

The expedition's photographer, George Rice, had stipulated that in the
event of his death, his personal papers, assembled in a sealed package, were to
be "destroyed unopened." They were brought home and turned over to the
Chief Signal Officer with Rice's other effects and a fine photographic yield.
Portions of Rice's diary were copied at the War Department. Greely said he
was "confident that [the package] contains nothing but very private letters and
papers." He recommended that the late sergeant's wishes be respected. On 1
December, at the War Department, the package was destroyed by burning.

Greely embarked on a lecture that drew crowds. Press coverage described
his sturdy build, long hair parted in the middle, how gracefully the heavily
bearded and bespectacled explorer manned the podium. He was "greatly lionized, surrounded by rapturous women." This publicity was all very well, but the

promotion Greely had missed during his Arctic sojourn was nowhere in sight. Greely suspected "some serious influence against me." His future in the military seemed obscure. "I must regret," William Chandler wrote him, "that you don't get the recognition you are entitled to. But it will come."

What did come was a move by Robert Lincoln that convinced Greely not only of the secretary's opposition to Arctic enterprise but of personal hostility toward himself. About to leave office as the national government changed hands, Lincoln told General Hazen to open the expedition's diaries held by the Signal Corps to anyone on request. Greely had understood that they were to be kept from view until the release of his report.

Scandalmongering resurged. Pencils eagerly poised, newshounds lined up at the G Street office for glimpses of intimate writings. They were not disappointed. Private Henry had described his commander as "a miserable coward." Kislingbury was effectively under arrest until his death. Were Pavy not the party's doctor, Greely, in his own words, "should have killed him." Greely had drawn a rifle on Private Bender. Such were the startling bits and pieces Americans read those wintry February days of 1885.

Rumored to contain references to cannibalism, Private Schneider's diary came to light in a curious fashion. An employee of the Mississippi River Commission discovered notebook leaves scattered along 200 feet of riverbank in Missouri. Examination of a water gauge showed that the river had cast up the pages on or about 22 February, some seven months before their discovery. (The date coincided with Secretary Lincoln's order to make diaries available to newspapers.) The finder turned them over to his employer, one J. A. Ockerson, who gathered from their contents that they were portions of Private Roderick Schneider's journal.

Before reporting the discovery, Ockerson tried a little detective work "to solve the mystery as to how a diary thrown overboard at Cape Sabine," if not stolen, as Lieutenant Greely had suggested, "could have reached the place where it was found." The puzzle remained unsolved. Nothing on the leaves mentioned cannibalism, nor did they criticize Greely, who confirmed the writing as Schneider's. Greely had no comment on the odd coincidence that although the finder of the pages was, said Ockerson, "no relative of the man in your party," his name was Brainard. He was "no longer in our employ."

The Chief Signal Officer and the outgoing Secretary of War battled over the tragedy at Cape Sabine for the last time. The C.S.O.'s annual report for

1884 blamed Frank Wildes for dawdling at Disko and failing to leave stores at Littleton Island. Garlington's cache had fooled the Greely party into a false sense of security due to his "demoralized condition and disobedience of orders." Garlington struck back. From duty in the Far West, he telegraphed, "Is there no protection afforded me from the brutal attack of the Signal Officer?" Secretary Lincoln ordered the offending words struck from Hazen's report. (As for Wildes, just then, he also had to suffer a hinted accusation of cowardice from the Secretary of the Navy: "Nothing but a keen sense of danger could have led you to turn your face homeward.") Hazen aimed his sharpest barbs at Robert Lincoln. Had he sent out a second relief expedition when Hazen urged it, all of Greely's party would have been saved. Time had remained. St. John's sealers had been ready and coaled. A dispatch to Consul Molloy would have sent them at full knots for Cape Sabine.

Lincoln's own report called Hazen's words an intrusion into what was none of his business. Not sending another party out the moment the *Yantic* returned was "a proper decision reached by the Secretary of the Navy and myself." Lincoln had made sure that the decision against a fall 1883 effort was as much Chandler's as his own. Like it or not, the two cabinet officers were linked, and neither wished to leave office dogged by the specter of Cape Sabine. The situation demanded a scapegoat. None other than William Babcock Hazen was so tailored for the role.

He had called for a court of inquiry. "Continued efforts for an investigation would constitute a breach of discipline," wrote the Secretary of War, aware that his C.S.O. was impossible to muzzle. On 1 March at the Ebbitt House, touted as Washington's most elegant hotel, Hazen talked freely with a man from the *Evening Star*. Hazen afterward insisted that their exchange was "not in any sense an interview. I had not the remotest idea he would make public what I said." Perhaps not. But what Hazen said was along the persistent theme of blasting Lincoln for Cape Sabine. Front-paged that evening, it was read by the secretary within forty-eight hours of his quitting office. He at once charged Hazen with "conduct prejudicial to good order and military discipline." On 3 March, packing to leave the White House, President Arthur ordered the general to consider himself under arrest.

The incoming chief executive, Grover Cleveland, was one of Hazen's old friends. But he allowed the trial to proceed. It lasted two weeks. Hazen's defense aimed at a triple target, Lincoln, Garlington, and Wildes, all for neglect of duty.

The court adjourned 20 March, but without an announced verdict. Lincoln had hurried from town, and his successor was on an extended vacation. During the delay, Hazen sought Greely's public support. Hazen entreated Greely, "Both you and I stuck to the plan we best knew how. Why it failed can be more forcefully pointed out by you than any other." But Greely, on friends' advice, would not pull Hazen's chestnuts out of the fire. Henrietta's brothers told him he would be a fool to try. With the verdict still to come, he wrote his chief that "it would be distasteful for me to open up the whole subject. Let the matter rest." The following month, the court ruled, "By indulging in unwarranted and captious criticism of his superior [Hazen] had set a pernicious example," and he was pronounced guilty as charged. The general's punishment was a presidential wrist slap.

Hazen felt humbled enough to quit sparring. The year of his trial saw publication of *A Narrative of Military Service*, his self-serving account of Civil War campaigning. But diabetic, his leg still carrying a Comanche bullet, William Hazen appeared less and less in public. The old soldier was at last fading away.

# 29

# ALWAYS A COMMAND

EARLY IN 1886, Charles Scribner's Sons published *Three Years of Arctic Service*, Greely's memoir, free of the humdrum of technical minutiae with which he had dutifully crammed his still unpublished report. Now he could say whatever he had a mind to. Robert Todd Lincoln had left Washington for the tranquillity of a Chicago law practice. William Chandler, no longer at the Navy Department, remained Greely's trusted friend. General Hazen, ailing and inconspicuous, was still Chief Signal Officer. Greely dedicated his two-volume work to the expedition's members, living and dead, whose "energy accomplished the farthest north." The dedication praised the party's "loyalty and discipline." Karl Weyprecht and scientific objectives were cursorily dealt with in the early chapters. Greely had drawn chiefly from the journals of Lockwood and Brainard, "the only regular diaries, with my own, kept during the retreat and subsequent life at Camp Clay." He especially praised Brainard, who, he wrote, would by this time, in any other country, have received his commission.

He explained that Henry had to die in the interests of justice. Kislingbury? Ordered home at his request, he had missed the ship and remained at Conger doing no duty. Dr. Pavy? Skilled in medicine but unfit for duty in a military environment because of mercurial moods and "habits arising from his previous Bohemian life." And cannibalism? Of this, the less said, the better. "I know of no law, human or divine, broken at Sabine and do not feel called on to dwell longer on such a painful topic."

Greely had harsh words for Garlington: "His action in taking every ounce [of supplies] when turning south cannot be justified, nor his retaining a large dog under such circumstances." Wildes? He knew twenty-five of his countrymen counted on aid that year, but his orders did not require him to assist them. Here Greely watched his words. Wildes was Navy, and too severe a criticism of his conduct might have reflected on Chandler.

Robert Lincoln was the villain. Although the expedition was an Army affair, its "organization and equipment were accomplished under great disadvantage from the open hostility of a cabinet secretary." And had Lincoln sent out a relief expedition within ten days of the *Yantic's* return in the fall of 1883, all of Greely's people would have been saved. Greely avoided acknowledging that the dogmatic tone of his own relief instructions might have played a part in what went wrong. Of his rigid stipulation that relief vessels make no stop on the passage north, he said nothing. He knew that Lieutenant Caziarc's "supplemental memorandum" had been brushed aside to conform with instructions he himself had laid down. But all Greely noted of that controversial item was that "no doubt General Hazen regrets that it was not allowed to stand."

The book did well with the British, who felt Greely had good reason for criticizing his own government. Newspapers compared the "extreme frugality" with which the Lady Franklin Bay Expedition had been fitted out with "the unstinted sums lavished on the expedition of Sir George Nares." The French, too, thought well of Greely. He was feted in Paris, and there chanced to meet the impoverished woman claiming to be Octave Pavy's abandoned wife. Across the Atlantic, the other Mme. Pavy still clamored for details of the doctor's death and the whereabouts of his papers. While not objecting to a court of inquiry into the whole Pavy business, Greely had "no desire for a second *Jeannette* investigation simply to place this woman into notoriety." How had Pavy died? He had become irresponsible, suicidal, perhaps had mistaken the ergot for rum. This theory, the troublesome Lilla Pavy said, contradicted Sergeant Brainard's description of her husband, who on the very day of his death talked of rescue and another expedition. Brainard admitted to Greely that his account may have differed from those of fellow survivors but promised him that he would "remain true and loyal to the cause." Brainard was duly rewarded. Greely's encomiums in his book had not gone unnoticed at the White House, and before the year ended, Sergeant Brainard was commissioned second lieutenant in the United States cavalry. Of the survivors, only Maurice Connell threatened any problem. He could, if he "had the least inclination," give to the world "facts [the Signal Office] seems afraid to produce before the public."

Stationed in San Francisco in the Signal Corps' weather service, Connell was a second-class private who was convinced he should be a sergeant "on the same footing as the others." Unless Greely worked harder to get him promoted, Connell would talk to congressmen. Brainard warned Connell that he was under surveillance. Connell showed no surprise. "As you know," he replied, "the [spy] system was encouraged even on the icefield by *our officer* and it seems the devil haunts me still." Connell wrote "the devil" directly: "If you are aware of the pressure brought upon me to talk on certain subjects, and which I've so far resisted, you would think differently of my conduct." This statement amounted to blackmail. His Army service about to expire, Connell spoke of using his civilian liberty to talk freely, even write a book. Already he was in touch with the Kislingburys. Recognizing the Irishman as a potential source of embarrassment, Greely advised him to reenlist. So did General Hazen, who told the private that he could always count on his, the C.S.O.'s, friendship, "but I hope you will drop the matter." But Connell's silence could be procured only by promotion. So, he was elevated to private first class, then sergeant, and when he wanted a transfer to Eureka, "an easy station and a good climate," he got this, too. "I think," Brainard told Greely, "Connell will never give more trouble."

The other thorn in Greely's side had been Mme. Pavy, the American wife, especially after she had secured a dozen or more pages of the doctor's notes from General Hazen, who had ruled them "indecipherable"—they were written in French. Translated, they appeared in two successive issues of *North American Review*. The magazine's editor, James Redpath, once had run a booking agency for musicians and magicians. He was shrewd, enterprising, a self-styled reformer and crusader for forlorn causes, a scrivener who thought he knew a good story when he saw one. When Brainard objected to the first installment of the Pavy "disclosures," Redpath responded agreeably. If

Brainard indicated which of the passages he thought at fault, Redpath would "see to it that [the writer] sustains or retracts." Even so, the second article, about to be published, "seems to bear her out," wrote Redpath. "I presume Congress is sure to demand a probe and put every survivor under oath."

No retraction followed. But neither was Congress in any mood to stage what would have been a discordant encore to the *Jeannette* investigation. And it was presumed that this latest handful of Arctic survivors would not have welcomed one, either. Congressional palaver over cannibalism, mutinous plots, bureaucratic bungling, and a soldier's execution in some remote corner of the Arctic would have been grist for Redpath's journalistic mill. But there was no probe, and Brainard, once more swearing loyalty to "the cause," advised Greely that he need fear nothing further from the Pavy woman.

General Hazen died early in 1887, two years after his court-martial. Greely's nomination and subsequent confirmation for the post of Chief Signal Officer, automatically promoting him brigadier-general, had its detractors. Jealous young officers resented being passed over. Fred Kislingbury's brothers charged that even now, Greely "would not scruple to blacken Fred's good name." Lilla Mae Pavy protested in person before the Senate military affairs committee, even while she appealed to Greely for financial assistance. But, according to Brainard, she had "lost all her venom."

Greely was now better placed to pressure Congress for monies due Sabine's survivors and the kin of its dead. Brainard was made captain, and with his help (he hired a lobbyist), funds were fairly distributed, including a small pension for Jens Edward's and Frederick Christiansen's children. The Eskimos had been "brave, loyal." Greely endorsed an application for money to help the Kislingbury boys. "I know [Kislingbury's] thoughts were of his children and that he hoped and trusted the government would not let them suffer," he said. And even when Lilla Mae Pavy appealed for federal aid, Greely's official comment was that although Dr. Pavy had been disobedient and under arrest, his contract certified him as at least temporarily a member of the Signal Corps, and "he performed his duty to the end."

None of Greely's people was left in need. He secured Henry Biederbick a rating as hospital steward in the Army's medical department. Biederbick quit the service to become customs inspector in New York, a post he held until his death in March 1916. Matilde Ralston, penniless since the loss of two husbands and "left to die in an almshouse," found work in Washington when

Greely pulled the right strings. For Mary Cross, widow of the sergeant who had so vilified him and who was the first to die at Camp Clay, the C.S.O. found employment at the Treasury Department. And however reluctant to discuss still unanswered questions regarding the expedition, the survivors never wavered in their outspoken pride of having been among its members. When Julius Frederick died in 1904, he left two daughters named Thetis and Sabine. The previous year, Sergeant Long had actually returned to the Arctic on an attempt by a wealthy American to claim the North Pole. Once again, Long spent two winters imprisoned by ice. He had served thirty-two years with the weather bureau when he succumbed to a fatal stroke. Five years later, in June 1921, Sergeant Connell, by that time a model of redemption, died in San Diego.

Greely's official report of the Lady Franklin Bay Expedition finally appeared in 1888. Much of it echoed portions of his *Three Years of Arctic Service* but painted its arguments in softer hues. Why the stay at Cape Sabine? Smith Sound was open all winter, making crossing impossible. Game? Insufficient despite daily hunting. And insubordination? If any, it failed to demoralize the party. "To say we were always a command, never a mob, epitomizes the record," Greely wrote. Noble words, yet challenged by Captain Brainard as incomplete. On 19 January, 1890, at Fort Bidwell, California, he wrote privately of having held his silence until now, "when all the actors in the affair, except Connell, who knew of it but did not participate, are dead." It was an odd introduction, considering that all "the actors" had died in 1884 at Cape Sabine. Brainard continued with "a statement of fact which should be read in connection with my journal." Read by whom? Brainard did not say. The paper was addressed to no one in particular. It detailed Greely's desire to drift southward on ice floes, "trusting to Providence, an act little short of madness." So a conspiracy was hatched in the middle of Kane Basin, and Brainard was invited to lead a mutiny, "for it was nothing less." He had declined. But the idea was sound. Had the mutiny occurred, "it is not improbable that every man would have escaped with his life."

Brainard prefaced his account by writing that at this late date, "no one can be injured" by it. Had he forgotten that Greely was very much alive? Indeed, those last lines of Captain David L. Brainard's "statement of fact" were tantamount to an indictment of Greely as responsible for Sabine's dead. Did he think of publishing or officially reporting it? If so, he had second thoughts. He set the statement aside as something not for anybody else's eyes. Not yet.

That year Greely ridiculed Fridtjof Nansen's theory that all one had to do to reach the North Pole was purposely enter the ice and drift with it across the polar basin. Greely had by this time studied, written, or lectured so extensively on polar matters that he regarded himself as an authority. Of the Norwegian's notion, he wrote, "The history of Arctic expeditions had enough follies without bearing the burden of Doctor Nansen's illogical scheme of self-destruction." Others shared Greely's view. Nansen went ahead anyway. In September 1893, he sailed from Norway on the *Fram*, crossed Kane Basin, and entered the pack off the New Siberian Islands. Then he vanished.

Before the world heard anything more of the Norwegian explorer, the non-explorer so instrumental in launching the Lady Franklin Bay Expedition had reentered Greely's life. Once back from the Arctic and met with the startling news about his old friend, Greely might have tried to contact him. Perhaps he quietly did. But Henry Howgate and his mistress had eluded even the Pinkerton detectives hired by then Secretary of War Lincoln. Howgate still had Washington friends who remembered the jovial ideas broker and the parties he and Nettie Burrill had hosted. They would have agreed with the upstate New York newspaper that attributed General Greely's blossoming reputation as Arctic expert to the Signal Corps captain, who "in spite of moral infirmities was a brainy man who knew what he was about when he selected Greely to command the Lady Franklin Bay Expedition."

In a hideout on Lake Michigan's northern shore, Howgate heard that Greely had been ordered to remove the Howgate name from every Arctic feature he had attached it to—lake, mountain, or glacier. Howgate sadly appreciated the reason for this action, but via his daughter, then schoolteaching in Ohio, he had pleaded with Greely to try to retain at least her name on the map (there was a Mount Ida). Greely owed him that much. "You, better than any living man, know how earnestly, effectively and unselfishly I labored in the cause of Arctic exploration, providing the opportunity for your splendid achievements," Howgate told him. Greely turned over the letter to Secretary Lincoln, who brushed it aside because it provided no clue to Howgate's whereabouts.

Howgate furtively returned east and, calling himself Harvey W. Williams, opened a basement bookshop on 4th Avenue in New York City. Here he dwelled eight years, made regular appearances at book auctions, and even performed jury service. He married Nettie Burrill after his wife died in Florida.

A former Secret Service chief caught up with him and, on 27 September, 1894, intercepted him as he climbed from his bookstore to the street. Howgate admitted his real identity and went quietly.

He was given fifteen years' imprisonment (about as long as he had been at large). Ill health and good behavior reduced the term to five. Then he moved in with Ida in Washington. Her father's days as social lion with Signal Corps autonomy were only memories, as were his Arctic-colonization dreams. But no one could have denied that Henry Howgate had worked harder than any other American to get the Lady Franklin Bay Expedition under way. And Greely might have been forgiven if, while still Chief Signal Officer, he had paid his old friend more than one clandestine visit before Henry Howgate's death in June 1909.

Meanwhile, the world had shrugged off Fridtjof Nansen as lost. Another Scandinavian had come forth with an idea for conquering the North Pole. He was Salomon Andree, a forty-one-year-old Swedish balloonist. At the Sixth International Geographic Congress in London, Greely scoffed at Andree's plan. The balloon was sure to leak gas. Other delegates were equally skeptical. Yet Andree had the last word. Staring down his detractors, he demanded, "When something happens to your ships, how did you go back? I risk three lives. You risked how many? A shipload?" (Greely might have argued that ice was no less an enemy at high altitudes than at sea level. Andree and a two-man crew left Spitzbergen in late July 1897. Ice quickly coated the balloon's double-coated silk envelope, whose wreckage was found, with three skeletons, more than thirty years later.)

Nansen reappeared in 1896, the latest of a long line of voyagers the North Pole had lured, only to mock. The floes had borne the *Fram* to a point not close enough to the Pole for Nansen's liking, so with a single companion he had left the ship and taken to kayak and dog sledge. Forced to retreat, and unable to reach the *Fram*, the pair had struggled south for Spitzbergen, staying alive by eating their dogs. But ice had carried the little *Fram* from Siberia to Spitzbergen, confirming Nansen's theory of a polar drift. Furthermore, the Norwegians' overland journey had taken them to a higher latitude than that reached by Lockwood and Brainard. Greely's reaction was to publicly excoriate Nansen for abandoning his ship. Greely's words appeared in *Harper's Weekly*, as did those of Nansen's defenders in subsequent issues. Nansen himself kept silent until

1897, enraging Greely all the more by publishing his experiences under the proud title *Farthest North*.

That same year came news that the man Greely blamed most for the ordeal at Cape Sabine, along with Robert Lincoln, was awarded the nation's highest honor. Following his failure to relieve Greely's party, Ernest Garlington's Army career had dimmed, and he had been given routine assignments before rejoining his old regiment. For fifteen years, the Seventh Cavalry had hungered for an opportunity to avenge Custer's defeat at Little Bighorn. The chance came at Wounded Knee Creek. Garlington's unit, Troop A, opened fire on "hostile Indians." No less a massacre of Native Americans than other so-called battles of the era, it was characterized by courage and savagery on both sides.

Badly wounded, Garlington had fought on. For his "gallantry in action" he was commissioned captain and awarded the Congressional Medal of Honor. Memory of Garlington's lamentable voyage on the *Proteus* had faded, and in 1901 he was made Inspector General of the Army, a post he held for ten years. Garlington retired from the Army in 1917 and settled in San Diego, where he died, at age eighty-one, in 1934.

On his descent from Sabine to Upernavik after the shipwreck, Garlington's most valuable companion had been John Colwell. The sometime United States naval attaché in London, where he organized a ragtag spy system during the Spanish-American War, Colwell had served thirty-six years in the U.S. Navy when he died in 1936. Neither did Greely-relief misadventures damage Frank Wildes's career. Only a year after his hapless return from the Arctic, he was promoted captain, then rear-admiral, for "conspicuous conduct" during the war with Spain.

Thus was fate's ironic design for three whose specific mission had been to succor the isolated Greely expedition. Each had returned admitting failure: Beebe, soon to take his own life; Wildes, to win high-level promotion; Garlington, in Greely's view the most unworthy, to hold a top staff job while sporting the nation's highest award for valor.

# 30

# THE UNFORGIVING ARCTIC

GREELY SERVED AS head of the Signal Corps for about twenty years. Throughout this period, he was most influential in the modernization of military communication. If the murk clouding the Cape Sabine affair had not left a lasting uneasiness in influential minds, awards galore might have come his way. Between 1899 and 1903, he supervised the construction and operation of 10,000 miles of telegraph lines in the Philippines, Cuba, and Alaska, and invented a secret code for telegraphic transmission during the war with Spain. Advancement still eluded him. In 1903 he asked for a promotion. "In my service of 42 years I have never failed of success in any work entrusted to my military charge," he claimed. The Secretary of War endorsed his application, but it went nowhere. Not long afterward, Greely supported the attempts by Smithsonian Institution secretary Samuel Langley to achieve powered flight. Greely had long foreseen the military potential of manned aircraft and was instrumental in getting Langley a $50,000 federal appropriation to fund his "Aerodrome." Even after the aircraft sank in the Potomac River, Greely contributed money of his own to continue Langley's experiments, soon terminated by the news from Kitty Hawk. So besides lost investments, Greely had to bear some of the ridicule directed at the pioneering aeronaut.

Aware that he would never again venture beyond the Arctic Circle, Greely reinforced his reputation as an authority on polar exploration through extensive reading and writing. Military duty came first. In 1906, he was commander of the Army's Pacific Division when the San Francisco earthquake coincided with an eastbound journey he was making to attend the wedding of his daughter Adola. Stalled halfway across the country, Greely badgered the War Department for permission to turn back west. The War Department finally yielded to Greely's importuning, but as if to show how it felt toward an officer who seemed incapable of taking no for an answer, it gouged him for travel expenses. Greely had to pay his own way back to a still-burning city. After spending three weeks supervising rescue operations—"I am up to my neck," he cabled Henrietta from the Presidio Army base—he had the situation under control. And although denied a request for a personal White House visit to brief President Theodore Roosevelt on affairs out West, Greely was at last promoted to the rank of major general.

Late that same year, the War Department learned that Utes were straying from their South Dakota reservations into Wyoming and harassing cattle ranchers. Greely was sent to make the Utes see reason. He massed an intimidating force of cavalry, and used calm words. The Native American trespassers went home without a shot fired. It was yet a further demonstration of Greely's qualities of command. Management of men, courage in combat, organizational abilities, tact, and imagination all were impressively displayed throughout Adolphus Greely's long life, with one exception. They had proved no match for the Arctic.

Two other Americans had entered the polar race—such "dashes" had reverted to pre-Weyprecht chauvinism. To the best-known of the newcomers, Greely developed an instant dislike. PEARY HAS GONE FARTHER NORTH, ran a *New York Times* headline while Greely was talking with the Utes. Peary had broken the record set by Nansen ten years earlier. Through self-promotion and the backing of a well-heeled group calling itself the Peary Arctic Club, Robert E.

Peary was soon perceived as the American most eager to capture the polar prize. And as the nineteenth century yielded to the twentieth, he was at Fort Conger, the first explorer there since Greely.

Peary arrived home from the north in 1903 to be lauded a hero. Greely was not among the idolaters. He considered Peary an egoist obsessed with the notion that destiny had given him the North Pole, though he had yet to reach within 400 miles of it. Greely's antagonism increased when he learned that Peary had demolished the main hut so painstakingly built by the Lady Franklin Bay Expedition and had three small ones made from its timbers. Peary spoke of finding Fort Conger littered with trash, scraps of clothing, and mislabeled cans of food—all proof, he alleged, of a panicky abandonment by the Greely party. As for "the horrors of Cape Sabine," Peary said, "they were not inevitable but a blot on the records of Arctic exploration." In the controversy over which man reached the Pole first, Peary or his former medical officer Frederick Albert Cook, Greely at first took Cook's side. Fifteen years later, he still tended to support Cook, who was "probably nine-tenths right in his claims." But neither claimant, in Greely's final opinion, had attained his goal.

And neither had either of those two American explorers achieved much that would have furthered the aims of the by-then-forgotten Karl Weyprecht. However, while regretting the loss of life, the Austrian would have been pleased with the results of his International Polar Year. None of the participating nations had failed him, the Americans no less than the others. In spite of ill-preparedness, personal conflicts, travail, and suffering, the Lady Franklin Bay Expedition had accomplished most of its stated aims. General Greely had much to be proud of. Setting out quite lacking in Arctic experience (except for that of Octave Pavy and the Eskimos), and with precious little support from its own government, the expedition had faithfully adhered to Weyprecht's international program.

More than Weyprecht might have wished, scientific objectives were supplanted by eagerness to wrest the Farthest North record from the British. Even so, forming the northernmost link in the circumpolar chain, the Americans had carried out regular observations that furthered man's knowledge in meteorology, terrestrial magnetism, tidal movement, and auroral phenomena. And even throughout the most perilous stages of the retreat from Fort Conger, they had clung to natural history specimens and the most valuable of expedition records, charts, photographs, and instruments.

Of benefit to future explorers, nutritional safeguards were affirmed. That the expedition was spared (with one doubtful exception) the scourge of scurvy could be attributed to Greely's use of fresh musk-ox meat and pemmican combined with lemon juice. Dietary data was part of the rich material packing the second volume of Greely's belatedly published report. Mapping new territory and getting closer than anyone had to the North Pole—the sort of nationalistic venture Weyprecht had frowned upon—was, after all, an approved American goal, thanks to Henry Howgate, who, while on his felonious course, had pestered or seduced politicians into integrating his colonization fantasy with the International Polar Year program. So Greely made sure to emphasize, along with the Farthest North prize, other "firsts," geographical and scientific. His expedition had discovered "a series of polar sites for which limited data, if any, were previously available," and at the same time he had attended with such personal care to the botanical work that "over 60 species [of Arctic plants] were collected, several of which escaped observations of trained naturalists of the British 1875–76 expedition."

Greely resigned from the Army in 1908. He took a round-the-world trip with Henrietta, wrote *A Handbook of Alaska,* and produced the latest edition of his *Handbook of Polar Discoveries.* In 1912 came *True Tales of Arctic Heroism in the New World.* He was not without friends in Congress, one of whom, Henry T. Helgesen of South Dakota, intended to disprove Robert Peary's polar claims. Greely, on the quiet, supplied him with statistical ammunition. But Helgesen died within a year. America was on the brink of war with Germany. Attention focused on more urgent matters than Arctic argument. Without bothering to weigh the pros and cons of Peary's case, Congress officially pronounced his testimony unimpeachable. And when Greely more openly voiced objection, Peary jeered, "I am sure General Greely himself will not claim that he ever led a serious sledge party in Greenland or anywhere else."

Greely's two sons went off to fight in France. They were there when, on 15 March, 1918, their mother died. Henrietta's passing was unexpected. Greely had been told that she was recovering from pleurisy and pneumonia. Henrietta was widely mourned in Washington, especially by those who knew her as a gracious hostess and, progressive for her day, involved in social reforms. Greely was himself an advocate of civic improvement and was particularly active in the founding of the first free library in the nation's capital.

Greely was never free from the shadow of Cape Sabine. In 1923, a naval commander wrote the *New York Times* that Greely's expedition was "one of the greatest tragedies of the past generation." Greely, aged seventy-nine, rebuked him for linking the expedition with relief efforts. "In my expedition," Greely insisted, "field work and scientific observations were unsurpassed. No man died, no man was disabled. The expedition, after a retreating voyage of 500 miles, landed at its assigned rendezvous with every man in health, all records intact, all scientific instruments preserved." The expedition had succeeded. Rescue attempts had blundered.

A prominent twentieth-century explorer, Wilhjalmur Stefansson, believed that Greely's poor eyesight alone should have disqualified him for the expedition's leadership. Moreover, Greely told his men before embarking, "As you are aware, I myself know nothing about ice navigation." (Stefansson got this information from Peary.) As for cannibalism, the "breaking of the severest tabu our culture knows," which had caused Stefansson and others to edge away at Greely's approach, they could not foresee the techniques available three-quarters of a century later, proving that the breaking of such taboos in the far northern latitudes was not a total rarity. As stated by a modern Canadian anthropologist, "The Arctic is perhaps the most unforgiving of environments and we challenge it at our peril."

Greely never again ventured into that icebound unknown. Yet he studied accounts of subsequent expeditions with the keenest interest. As advancing age turned him into a reclusive armchair explorer, he continued writing authoritative articles by the dozen and an occasional book. *Reminiscences of Adventure and Service* in 1927 was followed a year later by *The Polar Regions in the Twentieth Century*. He still had foes, some in politics, who doggedly espoused the cause of Robert Peary as discoverer of the Pole. Greely's relations with the National Geographic Society, of which he was a longtime trustee, soured because the Society stuck to its belief in Peary. As Greely wrote after having four times refused its presidency, "My influence with the National Geographic Society is not potent." But he attended sundry banquets, where he met cordially with the only other survivor of the Lady Franklin Bay Expedition.

Unlike his old commander, David L. Brainard had remarried (after his first wife had admitted misconduct and unavailingly begged his forgiveness). In 1918, he was military attache to the American legation in Portugal, and the following year resigned from the Army as brigadier-general. Journalists seeking yet further sensational stories on the Lady Franklin Bay Expedition pestered him for material giving it a fresh slant. One writer, convinced that Brainard held back dark secrets, wanted more on the mutinous plotting in Kane Basin, and said to Brainard, "I remember you asked me not to print these things, as it would shock Greely to have them appear." Neither did they appear in *Outpost of the Lost*, which Brainard wrote while Greely still lived.

At twilight on Wednesday, 27 March, 1935, the usual serenity of Georgetown, Washington, D.C.'s, most quietly historic quarter, was interrupted by the blare of a military band and the clatter of horses' hooves on cobblestones. Troop F of the Second Cavalry Regiment, United States Army, halted their mounts at a block on O Street. Neighbors had gathered to watch. At first they saw little of interest: khaki-clad soldiers, motionless horses, and bandsmen with instruments at the ready. Four noncommissioned officers were already inside the small brick house numbered 3131, at full attention and gripping regimental colors. On a side table rested a birthday cake. Its candles formed the figure 91. Alongside the cake lay an Army saber, ready for slicing.

Outside, the band played ruffles and flourishes. Automobiles had braked in front of the house, the leading car bearing the square red flag of the office of War Department, and onlookers recognized the frock-coated man who bounded from it and up the wooden steps to the doorway as George H. Dern, Secretary of War. The band played the national anthem. Inside the house, Secretary Dern, surrounded by gold-braided aides, read a citation that included the words "long life of splendid public service." He pinned a blue-ribboned star-shaped medal to the left lapel of Adolphus Greely's neatly tailored jacket. Greely murmured words of acknowledgment. This brief formality over, the party stepped outside onto the elevated front porch. The mounted troops presented sabers in salute.

Applause echoed from both ends of the roped-off block. Local residents knew that their just-bemedaled neighbor was Adolphus Greely, years earlier a general of some distinction. Beyond that, few were familiar with his earlier career. Some had never set eyes on him, for, although he lived eight years in the little old house, he had seldom emerged for a stroll along Georgetown's tree-lined streets. The band struck up a quickstep. Dignitaries clustered on the porch with Greely included the more recognizable William Mitchell, himself a retired general and ten years earlier the subject of a top-level dispute culminating in his court-martial. Then the music stopped. "Billy" Mitchell read aloud a three-page single-spaced survey of Greely's career, emphasizing his valuable contributions to the growth and technical development of America's twentieth-century Army. Flanked by four of his six children and two solemn-faced infant grandchildren, Greely said nothing. Blinking through thick-lensed glasses, he waved farewell to the cavalrymen as they wheeled their horses right-about and moved off. The band, now silent, marched away behind them. The Secretary of War reentered the official limousine, his departure followed by that of other politicians and the military delegation.

It may be conjectured whether Greely savored any irony from the fact that the nation's highest award had come to him almost half a century after its bestowal upon the fellow Army officer who had failed to rescue the Lady Franklin Bay Expedition. Probably, Greely had harbored no grudge. Awarding the medal to a noncombatant required a special act of Congress, traditionally in recognition of a singular peacetime performance, such as Lindbergh's accomplishment over the Atlantic, Byrd's above the North Pole. Greely was only the fourth recipient to be so singled out. And he was the only honoree not selected for any specific act of valor.

All the good that he had done in and out of uniform unquestionably enti-tled Greely to some expression of the nation's thanks. His had come at a unique age (his ninety-second year!) with a broadly ambiguous citation. Not even euphemistically was anything said of his having led his country's first venture in a multinational cause. No doubt Greely had resigned himself to the fact that it was unmentionable.

He died on 20 October, 1935. Among his final correspondence was a birthday greeting from the Soviet embassy, something he may have warmed to more than his belated Congressional Medal of Honor. The Russians congrat-ulated him on celebrating another milestone in a rich and full life: "Our Soviet Arctic scientists who are struggling against the ice to open the Northeast Passage to navigation are constantly heartened and encouraged by the coura-geous and valuable work performed in the Far North by yourself and other Americans." Eulogized as a genuine American hero, Greely was buried in the Arlington National Cemetery with full military honors. A War Department statement praised his "superlative courage" not only in combat but in his "peacetime thrilling adventures in search of scientific truths." That was as close as the statement got to any mention of Greely in the Arctic.

The last survivor wrote another book, *Six Came Back: The Arctic Adventure of David L. Brainard*, published five years after Greely's death. Only then did

Brainard reveal the mutiny talk in Kane Basin. It was an expurgated repeat of his 1890 "Statement of Fact," but it went far enough to disclose that most of the party had regarded Greely's notion to drift with the ice as madness.

Not long before his death on 22 March, 1946, Brainard told a reporter how and why Private Henry had died. But he kept to his "sworn oath" never to name the man who had pulled the trigger. Brainard and Greely were buried in the same honored national cemetery with military honors more or less as sacred as those given to the man whose killing they had enforced sixty-four years before—perhaps less, inasmuch as hundreds had lined Brooklyn streets with hats doffed in respect as Henry's military cortege passed by. Brainard's grave is marked by a prominent headstone. Henry's is in ground as militarily hallowed as that of his executioner. A small flat stone listed as number 3912 in the soldier's plot of Cypress Hills Cemetery bears his name. Nothing denotes the true cause of death. Cemetery records show that Private B. Henry "Died of Starvation."

And the Lady Franklin Bay Expedition's bases? Donald Baxter MacMillan, a youthful member of Peary's controversial 1908–09 Arctic stay, was the only American explorer of note to penetrate the upper latitudes in the immediate years after Peary. MacMillan wrote of what he saw at Fort Conger in words reminiscent of Peary's—scattered debris, scraps of clothing, stuffed birds, and cans of tomatoes labeled potatoes. He had "entered the hut" (actually there were three, Peary having demolished that built by Greely) and discovered a tattered schoolbook on a small table. Written on its flyleaf in a boyish hand was the prayer "To My Dear Father, May God be with you and return you safely to me. Your affectionate son, Harry Kislingbury." MacMillan reported that he wrapped the book in oilcloth and, years later, having traced the orphaned boy to Arizona, returned the book to him.

But MacMillan uncovered something more disturbing at Fort Conger. He wrote, "What I could not understand was the oven of the kitchen stove was filled with Eskimo skulls." A young doctor named John Goodsell, attached to that 1908–09 Peary party, also wrote of skulls at Fort Conger but not in the oven, which held food cans variously labeled, one marked onions containing rhubarb. Goodsell's memoir testified to skulls found at the site, nine in all, one of them "covered with long yellow hair." The skulls may have belonged to Inuits who had eaten contaminated foods at the time of Peary's inadequately documented sojourn at Conger in 1901. The food at that date, left by Greely, would have been twenty years old. Peary died in 1920 without having said or written a word on the MacMillan-Goodsell discovery of skulls at Fort Conger, and, wrote Goodsell, "we were never able to solve the mystery."

At Cape Sabine in 1917, MacMillan stood on the crest of what Brainard, in his books, had christened Cemetery Ridge and surveyed what was left of Camp Clay. "I could plainly see the ring of rocks which held down the tent of the dying men," he wrote. In 1924, MacMillan took a bronze tablet north with him, paid for by the National Geographical Society. His party drilled holes in a large rock near Camp Clay's ruins and bolted the plaque in place. Its inscription reads: "To The Memory of The Dead—Who Here Gave Their Lives To Ensure The Final And Complete Success Of The First Scientific Cooperation Of The United States With Other Nations."

The ships? After the 1884 rescue, the *Thetis* had patrolled western Atlantic waters and the Pacific from Cape Horn to Alaska. Eventually she was converted into a Newfoundland sealer and, in 1950, purposely grounded off St. John's and broken up. Her relief sister ship, *Bear,* served in both world wars. In 1948, under tow from Canada to Philadelphia for sale, her old timbers crumbled, the towline snapped, and the sea finally claimed her.

And Karl Weyprecht's dream? A second International Polar Year was held in 1932–1933. Forty-four nations participated. The Third International Polar Year, in 1952, was renamed the International Geophysical Year. From it has developed a diversity of programs to study Earth's phenomena. Observation posts have been manned on the shores of Lake Hazen, one of the few Arctic features to maintain a name bestowed by Adolphus Greely. There remain Greely Fjord and Rice Strait. Mostly gone is "Eskimo," a term now discarded by the Etah tribes of Greenland and Ellesmere's proud Inuits. A fertile mecca for anthropologists, archaeologists, and students of the polar ecosystem, Ellesmere Island contains the northernmost of Canada's national park preserves.

Following an agreement between the Canadian government and the Inuits in 1993, the indigenous population enjoys a measure of autonomy and respect unknown in Greely's day. The region is in fact a new territory, born in 1999 as Nunavut, a free translation of "Our Land." The Ellesmere National Park Preserve includes Fort Conger but does not extend sufficiently southward to embrace Bedford Pim Island, whose principal visitors are specialists from the Arctic Institute of North America, headquartered at the University of Calgary.

Their purpose is scientific study, not tribute-paying to old Arctic misadventures.

But in 1983, to commemorate the centennial of the Lady Franklin Bay Expedition, a group of students and faculty of Mercersburg Academy, Pennsylvania, flew north and, on foot, crossed a mile-wide ice bridge from Cocked Hat Island to Pim. Worsening weather and uncertainty about the stability of the ice bridge limited a search for Camp Clay's actual site, and the small party attached a brass plaque honoring Greely to a cairn at Wade Point, where he had landed and which he named Eskimo Point.

Jets from the U.S. Air Force base at Thule, on the Greenland side, routinely fly over Ellesmere Island. The Royal Canadian Mounted Police mans an airstrip at Alexandra Fjord for two summer months each year. Ice-breaking cruise ships equipped with helicopters venture, weather permitting, through Smith Sound as far as Kane Basin. If unobscured by fog, the outline of Littleton Island may be discerned to the east, and that of Cape Sabine to the west. Ice-rimmed shores limit sight-seeing except by helicopter. The region attracts researchers from the Arctic Institute. But the actual site of Greely's last camp, seldom visited, is left undisturbed. Boulder configuration identifies the hut; scraps of the tent lie fossilized in patches of ice. Along the burial ridge, if studied at close range, ten shallow indentations may be discerned, a pitiful row petrified in ice-hardened gravel, the imprint of tragedy and likely to remain so forever.

# THE MEMBERS OF THE LADY FRANKLIN BAY EXPEDITION

FIRST LIEUTENANT ADOLPHUS W. GREELY
Fifth Cavalry, Acting Signal Officer

SECOND LIEUTENANT FREDERICK F. KISLINGBURY
Eleventh Infantry, Acting Signal Officer

SECOND LIEUTENANT JAMES B. LOCKWOOD
Twenty-third Infantry, Acting Signal Officer

OCTAVE PAVY
Physician and naturalist

SERGEANT EDWARD ISRAEL
Signal Corps, U.S. Army

SERGEANT WINFIELD S. JEWELL
Signal Corps, U.S. Army

SERGEANT GEORGE W. RICE
Signal Corps, U.S. Army

SERGEANT DAVID C. RALSTON
Signal Corps, U.S. Army

SERGEANT HAMPDEN S. GARDINER
Signal Corps, U.S. Army

SERGEANT WILLIAM H. CROSS
General Service, U.S. Army

SERGEANT DAVID L. BRAINARD
Company L, Second Cavalry

SERGEANT DAVID LINN
Company C, Second Cavalry

CORPORAL NICHOLAS SALOR
Company H, Second Cavalry

CORPORAL JOSEPH ELISON
Company E, Tenth Infantry

PRIVATE CHARLES B. HENRY
Company E, Fifth Cavalry

PRIVATE MAURICE CONNELL
Company B, Third Cavalry

PRIVATE JACOB BENDER
Company F, Ninth Infantry

PRIVATE FRANCIS LONG
Company F, Ninth Infantry

PRIVATE WILLIAM WHISLER
Company F, Ninth Infantry

PRIVATE HENRY BIEDERBICK
Company L, Second Cavalry

PRIVATE JULIUS FREDERICK
Company L, Second Cavalry

PRIVATE WILLIAM A. ELLIS
Company C, Second Cavalry

PRIVATE RODERICK R. SCHNEIDER
First Artillery

JENS EDWARD
Hunter and dog driver, native of Greenland

THORLIP FREDERICK CHRISTIANSEN
Hunter and dog driver, native of Greenland

# ACKNOWLEDGMENTS

WORKING TO COMPLETE an account of the *Jeannette* polar expedition, which steamed out of San Francisco in 1879, I had occasion to mention Adolphus Greely, who led his own little band northward in 1881 from the whaling and seal-fishing port of St. John's, Newfoundland. My references were few and brief, no more than incidental to the main narrative. And when the *Jeannette* story was finished, I felt that the Arctic had held me in its gelid grip long enough. There was no further need to imagine myself as one among men whose flesh sloughed off frozen limbs, whose breath puffed from cracked lips in clusters of ice crystals — and whose empty bellies forced their dulled eyes to study dying comrades as a potential source of life-saving meat. No, I'd had enough of the Arctic.

But it had not done with me. At a social function in New York, members of the Explorers Club directed my attention to the Lady Franklin Bay Expedition, of which, I was assured, the full story had yet to be told. Added encouragement came from the Arctic Institute of North America, University of Calgary, Alberta, Canada. There followed invitations to examine material, much hitherto inaccessible, including private journals not always in harmony with the official record of events. Thus my resistance to another polar plunge was undermined from the start and replaced by dedication to the task of discovering how the Greely expedition came about and what befell it.

Research led to such unexpected finds as telltale documents salvaged from a landfill in the shadow of a prison in Virginia and scraps of a notebook long hidden in a silver vegetable dish that also contained, significantly, two spent rifle bullets. These were relics of an Arctic riddle. Beyond argument, the Greely party made history by representing the very first instance of American participation in any major international enterprise. And its immediate triumph lay in having penetrated closer to the North Pole than had any previous explorers, breaking a record held by the British for 300 years. But following the expedition's course from turbulent birth to bizarre and tragic finale meant having to confront disturbing questions.

Assistance in this direction and in other demands of the work came from persons and organizations to whom I owe deep gratitude. The curator of collections at the Explorers Club, Janet E. Baldwin, was particularly helpful in locating photographs and informative papers. Karen McCullough, editor of *Arctic*, and Peter Schledermann, both of the Arctic Institute of North America, Calgary, generously supplied photos of most recent vintage. Equally helpful, in Washington, D.C., were the ever courteous staff at the National Archives, notably Marjorie Ciarlante, Michael P. Musick, and their colleagues; and, at the Library of Congress, Virginia Steele Wood, specialist in naval and maritime history, and research assistants in the Manuscript Division.

My thanks go to Leo L. Ward of the Historical Society of Schuylkill County, Pottsville, Pennsylvania, and to Susan Lintelmann of the United States Military Academy, West Point, New York; James W. Cheevers, curator of the United States Naval Academy Museum, Annapolis; and James F. Caccamo, archivist at the Hudson Library and Historical Society, Hudson, Ohio. Thanks go to Ted Heckathorne of Woodinville, Washington, for fresh information on Robert Peary; to Thomas F. Schwartz, curator of the Lincoln Collection, Illinois State Historical Library, Springfield, Illinois; and to Philip N. Cronenwett, special collections, Dartmouth College, Hanover, New Hampshire.

Welcome cooperation came from Lyle Dick, historian, Parks Canada, Vancouver. Thanks also to the historian, Royal Canadian Mounted Police, Ottawa. Aerial photograph No. A-16604-1767, (c) 1959 Her Majesty the Queen in Right of Canada, is reproduced from the collection of the National Air Photo Library with permission of Natural Resources Canada.

I am deeply indebted to members of the Kislingbury family who provided unpublished photographs, letters, and diary material. Linda Kislingbury Cain of Novato, California, played the leading role in this contribution to my work, her task inspired by devotion to the memory of her great-grandfather, the ill-fated second in command of the Lady Franklin Bay Expedition.

David G. Colwell of Los Angeles sent me fascinating material relating to his bold and good-humored grandfather. Maps and information were zealously supplied by Tim D. Rockwell, archaeologist and historian, who in 1983, as dean of Mercersburg Academy, Pennsylvania, led a party of students and faculty to Bedford Pim Island for on-the-spot commemoration of the hundredth anniversary of the First Polar Year.

Thanks to Neil S. Nyren, my superb editor and friendly adviser, for whom I have great admiration.

Finally, I want to acknowledge the contributions of Jan Herman, editor and historian, Naval Medical Command, Washington, D.C.; Jack Towers; Morris Questal; Marty Deblinger; John Sherman; and Douglas F. Greer, M.D. I may have omitted the names of others who have helped me along the way, but if so they need have no doubt that their contributions are warmly appreciated.

Three persons dear to my heart — daughter, Vivien Olsen; daughter-in-law, Tamara; and my son, Bruce — have assisted me in various ways at no small inconvenience to themselves. To them, love and heartfelt thanks.

# SOURCE NOTES

THE MATERIAL FOR this book is drawn principally from rich collections located at National Archives and Records Administration (NARA) in Washington, D.C., and in College Park, Maryland; the Library of Congress (LC), Washington, D.C.; Dartmouth College, Hanover, New Hampshire; Explorers Club, New York City; and the United States Army Historical Institute, Carlisle Barracks, Pennsylvania.

At the latter repository, I found a group of Adolphus Greely's self-revealing letters to his niece, Clarissa, many of them detailing his romantic distractions during the period when he organized and expanded telegraphic communication between Army forts on the Great Plains and across southwestern prairies. Indispensable to any study of Greely the man and Greely the Arctic explorer are the 141 boxes of papers donated to the Library of Congress by his daughters and whose themes cover his youth and Civil War service, his leadership of the Lady Franklin Bay Expedition, his command of rescue operations in earthquake-stricken San Francisco, his settlement of a dispute with Native American Utes, and his keen interest in scientific developments as typified by correspondence with inventors Marconi, Alexander Graham Bell, and Thomas Alva Edison.

At NARA, the record groups most rewarding to Greely researchers are RG27, records of the Weather Bureau, Polar Expeditions, College Park, Maryland; and RG94, Letters Received by the Office of the Adjutant General (Main Series) 1881–1889, on microfilm 689, National Archives Building, Washington, D.C. Significant Greely items are in Dartmouth College's Vilhjalmur Stefansson collection.

Instead of a list of separate citations requiring many pages and much tedious itemization, a survey of diaries will better serve the reader. Seldom has any enterprise produced so many as did the Lady Franklin Bay Expedition, some dutifully recording natural phenomena as directed, others furtively penciled for the writer's eyes only, the whole reflecting a mix of emotions: jealousy, contempt, and despair tempered by dauntlessness and loyalty.

The most convenient source for many of the diaries, some in easily readable type, is M689, Rolls 12 to 18, NARA. The Explorers Club holds the photographer George Rice's "sledge journal," with diaries of privates Roderick Schneider and Joseph Elison and, ending 18 April, 1882, Sergeant William Cross. The Historical Society of Schuylkill County, Pottsville, Pennsylvania, has more Elison diary pages. Greely Papers, LC, Container 69, has a copy of Schneider's journal which Greely notes was "stolen by a seaman of the relief expedition." No evidence was found to support this accusation, nor explanation for how its pages were found scattered along a Mississippi riverbank. These Schneider diary fragments, with correspondence relating to their discovery, are in RG27, NARA. An additional Rice journal, 7 July, 1881, to 2 August, 1883, is at Dartmouth College.

Sergeant David Ralston's diary, with dates between 1881 and 1884, is in RG27, NARA, as is Private Henry's, with its puzzling final words "Eskimo Fred to be." Portions were published in the New York Times, 7 February, 1885, and headlined a sad arctic record in the Evening Star, Washington, D.C., 8 February, 1885, with reference to "a curious journal kept by Private Henry." Sergeant Cross's savage aspersions upon his commanding officer are among the diaries in M689, NARA, which also includes the bitter entries of Dr. Octave Pavy.

Of the same vituperative character are the secret jottings of Sergeant Brainard. His diaries take some sorting out. Careful examination of the Brainard Collection, RG200, NARA, provides much for speculation. The material consists of "original diary notes," to quote from an archivist's description, and three volumes based upon them prepared by Brainard after the rescue and turned over to Commander Schley on the voyage home. Of special interest is a letter, 19 January, 1890, inserted in the journal describing a plot to relieve Greely of command on grounds of insanity.

A Brainard collection is housed at Dartmouth College. Its searcher's guide states that Brainard kept a diary throughout the expedition, eventually publishing two books from it, "in both [of which] the portion of the diary included in this collection has been expurgated, omitting details and changing Brainard's language."

In 1954, Brainard's stepdaughter donated documents and memorabilia to the U.S. Army's historical division. A month after the bulk of it was transferred from storage to the military historian, she wrote of having found an additional item: "I came across a small silver vegetable dish, wrapped up. Inside was a long narrow notebook containing the penciled diary entries made in 1884. I am mystified about this—most of it I couldn't read ... there are two bullets, which I have a feeling may be tied up, perhaps, with the execution of the man who stole the food." This letter, dated 13 September, 1954, is among Dartmouth College's Brainard material. The notebook, its pages expressive of scorn for the commander, is in the Brainard Papers, RG200, NARA, Maryland. The location of the two bullets is not known.

The Explorers Club holds diaries of Lieutenant Lockwood. A Lockwood journal dated 17 April, 1882, to 6 January, 1884, is at the U.S. Naval Academy Museum, Annapolis. Lockwood's diary from 3 April, 1883, to 7 April, 1884, appears as an appendix to Greely's published report of the expedition. The journal of Lockwood's Farthest North achievement, 31 April to 1 June, 1882, is reproduced as Microcopy T298 (one roll), NARA.

Brief excerpts from Lieutenant Kislingbury's diary, of whose existence Greely professed himself unaware, appeared in the *New York Times,* 11 February, 1885, and Washington's *Evening Star,* 8 February, 1885. Copies of diary portions are in M689, Roll 17, NARA. Valuable pages are privately owned by Kislingbury's great-grandchildren, who kindly made them available to me for this book.

Besides what can be studied of Octave Pavy's writings in M689, RG27, NARA, Washington, D.C., a manuscript copy of his expedition diary is found in RG27, NARA. Pavy's wife published this in two issues of *North American Review:* March and April 1886, titled "Dr. Pavy and the Polar Expedition" and "An Arctic Odyssey."

Adolphus Greely's journals, original and copied, are so numerous and at such diverse locations as to bewilder the researcher. At National Archives, College Park, in RG27, we find a Greely diary, 17 September, 1883, to 29 April, 1884, with several gaps; galley proofs of his published diaries; a manuscript abstract of "Journal of the Expedition, 1 July, 1881–27 July, 1883," signed by Greely; and an original Greely journal, 1 July, 1881 to 30 April, 1882, containing specimens of Arctic flowers and plants, "badly damaged by salt water."

The Explorers Club holds a large notebook containing "Daily Journal of the Lady Franklin Bay Expedition, 1 July, 1881, to 29 December, 1882"; "Papers from the Journal, 1 January, 1883–1 August, 1883"; "Fort Conger: Greely Expedition Pages from Record Book 15 July, 1882–28 August, 1882"; and two journals of sledge trips the commander made into the Grinnell Land interior.

Dartmouth College's Stefansson collection includes Greely diary extracts July and August 1881. At the same source is a list, drawn up by Brainard for unexplained reasons, of dates on which his commander made no journal entries. The largest accumulation of Greely expedition journals fills containers 69, 70, and 71, Greely Papers, LC. Also see containers 94–97, "Arctic File." In RG27, NARA, a small brown book opening with 15 October, 1883, contains a note by Greely: "Part of my diary recorded in a temporary book was lost in Camp Clay."

So much for the profusion of diaries. Narrative comments follow. An informative, succinct account of the Greely expedition is found in William Barr, *Expeditions of the First International Polar Year, 1882–83* (Calgary, Alberta: Arctic Institute of North America, 1985). Useful contemporary notices are in *Journal of Science* 21; *Nature* 30; and *Saturday Review* 60.

CHAPTER ONE

The departure of the *Proteus* from St. John's is described in Greely to Hazen, 11 July, 1884, Greely Papers, LC; and Greely, *Three Years* (New York: Scribner's, 1886). Last letters from Henrietta and Greely's declaration of "pain and happiness" are in Greely Papers, LC. Lieutenant Kislingbury's emotions at the time of departure are revealed in Kislingbury to Ella M. Morrow, Fort Royal, New Mexico, 20 August, 1884, Kislingbury family papers, the source also for a good account of the voyage north as penned by the lieutenant to his sons.

The Lady Franklin Bay Expedition owed its existence to the independent efforts of Karl Weyprecht and Henry Howgate. Thanks to the military attaché at the Embassy of Austria, Washington, D.C., I obtained detail on Weyprecht and a rare photo of him. Weyprecht's work in founding the International Polar Year (now the International Geophysical Year) is described in William Barr's works.

CHAPTER TWO

Adolphus Greely's youth through his Civil War service and postwar cotton plans can be traced in the Greely Papers, LC, and Greely correspondence in the Special Collections Department, William R. Perkins Library, Duke University, Durham, North Carolina. The Greely Papers at the Military History Institute, Carlisle Barracks, provide glimpses of Greely's early romantic attachments. For a good account of his work on the military telegraph, see *The Line That Talks*, Pioneer Press, Bismarck, South Dakota, 29 October, 1877. That Greely was moved by the Franklin memorial in Westminster Abbey is disclosed in an undated item in Container 53, Greely Papers, LC.

CHAPTER THREE

In the United States it was Henry Howgate who set pivotal events in motion. For his Arctic-colonization plan, see "Polar Colonization and Exploration," *American Geographical*

*Journal* 10, 1878; "Captain Howgate's Polar Colony," *Western Review of Science and Industry* 2, June 1878; "The Howgate Plan," *Kansas Review* 1, 2, and 44; and Albert J. Myer Papers, Box 1878–1892, Military History Institute, Carlisle Barracks. Howgate's lively personal life is described in "The Fugitive Captain," by George Walton, *Washington Post*, "Potomac" section, 16 February, 1969. "The sooner we cease to waste time and lives in Arctic exploration, the better"—so ends the *New York Times* editorial, 29 December, 1876, scoffing at the Howgate plan.

CHAPTER FOUR

The Greely Papers, LC, are the single important source for the love letters that passed east and west across the continent from 1877 to 1878. Greely's faith in Howgate's plan as feasible and his certainty of returning safe and sound "otherwise I should not desire to lead" are in Greely to Henrietta, 27 January, 1878. Howgate's neglect of his wife and Greely's pity for her are noted in Greely to Henrietta, 27 February, 1878, and Henrietta's understanding reply is 10 March, 1878.

CHAPTER FIVE

William Babcock Hazen's turbulent career is summarized in *Dictionary of American Biography*. The court-martial of a fellow officer who accused Hazen of cowardice is detailed in Letters Received by the Office of the Adjutant General (Main Series) 1871–1880, M666, Roll 344, NARA. Also see Marvin E. Kroeker, *Great Plains Command* (Norman, OK: University of Oklahoma Press, 1976), and "William Babcock Hazen," by Paul Scheips, in *Cosmos Club Bulletin* 38, October 1985, Washington, D.C.

A quantity of Hazen's papers were discarded by the granddaughter of Hazen's widow, who married Admiral George Dewey. The papers were found in a refuse dump or landfill at Lorton, Virginia, and purchased by an antique dealer who in turn sold them to the Smithsonian Institution's Armed Forces History Division, where they are catalogued as Collection No. 427, Archives Center, National Museum of American History, Washington, D.C. Further useful Hazen data is found in M1064, Roll 30, NARA.

That Greely was considered Howgate's "right-hand man" is in an undated, unsigned note among the Adolphus Greely Papers, Duke University. The assertion that Greely would "lay before you certain papers" is in Hazen to James H. Blount, House Subcommittee on Appropriations, 4 February, 1881, Greely Papers, LC. The papers were "drafted by me," notes Greely. The Kislingbury family supplied information on the lieutenant's early years. References to his frontier service appear in Letters and Telegrams Received from Headquarters at Fort Custer, June 1880–July 1881, NARA, College Park, Maryland. His emotional report of double widowhood and his desire to join the expedition are in Greely Papers, LC.

CHAPTER SIX

The information is based in part on a manuscript copy of Greely's expedition report, with War Department orders assigning him to command, RG27, NARA. In his manuscript, Greely submits to Secretary of War Lincoln on 8 March, 1881, a general outline of his plan for establishing a polar base, and on the seventeenth asks that the Army surgeon-general provide medical supplies for thirty soldiers. These papers and further evidence of how urgently he pressed the War Department for action are in RG27, NARA. His letter of 17 March, 1881, seeking Lincoln's authority to use the appropriation is in M689, Roll 12, NARA, Washington, D.C.

Correspondence between Greely, Hazen, and the adjutant general of the Army (i.e., Lincoln's War Department) in Letters Sent by the Adjutant General (Main Series), 1880–1890, M565, NARA, highlights Greely's anxiety to expedite outfitting. For brief references to his wife's difficult delivery, see Container 1, Greely Papers, LC, and in the same collection is the 22 May, 1881, letter from a cousin who was, "sad to lose the twin boys."

Hazen to Adjutant General, 23 May, 1881, directing attention to Greely's immediate need for supplies at St. John's, is an exhibit of the *Proteus* court of inquiry, as is Hazen to Lincoln, 20 June, 1881, seeking permission to order gunpowder transferred to the relief ship. For Greely's wrath at St. John's, see Greely to Caziarc, 25 June, 1881, and Greely to Hazen, 30 June, 1881, in containers 13–17, Greely Papers, LC. The expedition's final preparation and departure are described in *New York Herald*, 8 July, 1881.

CHAPTER SEVEN

For a general account of the voyage north, and for a detailed description of the building of Fort Conger, see Greely, *Three Years*. The first signs of disciplinary problems are noted in Brainard's journal, RG200, NARA, and Kislingbury's private diary, in his family's possession. Pavy's background is described in the *Dictionary of American Biography*, this venerable series thus placing him on the same noteworthy footing as Greely and James Lockwood. Also see *St. Louis Courier of Medicine*, February 1886; "Pavy's Expedition to the North Pole," by D. Walker, *Overland Monthly* 8, June 1872; and Pavy diary fragments, M689, Roll 12, NARA. Greely tells of having to reprimand Kislingbury and Lockwood for oversleeping in his journal, Greely Papers, LC.

CHAPTER EIGHT

Greely's report of relieving Kislingbury from duty is in his journal, Greely Papers, LC. Kislingbury's version is in his own private journal. The balance of this chapter, portraying life at Fort Conger, is drawn from Greely's journal, Greely Papers, LC, and RG27, NARA; Pavy notations, M689, Roll 12, NARA; and Brainard's private diary, RG200, NARA, his self-reproach, "made an ass of myself," dated 13 or 17 September, 1881, softened for his *Six Came Back: The Arctic Adventure of David L. Brainard* (New York: Bobbs Merrill, 1940).

CHAPTER NINE

Greely's *Three Years* and his unmailed letters to Henrietta, Greely Papers, LC, provide the elements for this chapter, Greely's journal registering both awe at celestial displays and increasing irritation with his medical officer. That the men's quarters were off-limits to Kislingbury is noted by Brainard, 23 December, 1881, and 3 January, 1882, Brainard Papers, RG200, NARA. Lockwood's record-breaking penetration of northern Greenland is detailed in Charles Lanman, *Farthest North* (New York: D. Appleton & Co., 1889), and in Journal of the Lockwood Expedition, 31 April to 1 June, 1882, microfilm T298 (one roll), NARA. Brainard's dissatisfaction with Greely appears in his 8 January, 1882, reference to the benefit of fresh meat as an antiscorbutic, Brainard Papers, RG200, NARA.

CHAPTER TEN

The Howgate saga is told in the *Washington Post*, 16 February, 1969. Emma De Long's letter to Henrietta Greely, 16 March, 1882, is in Container 13, Greely Papers, LC. William Beebe's Civil War career and correspondence with Hazen on his relief expedition are in an NARA group of files called Appointment, Commission and Personal branch of the adjutant general's office (ACP Files). That Hazen would hire a ship off his own bat and "the secretary is still ignorant" are in Caziarc to Henrietta Greely, 28 May, 1882, Greely Papers, LC. Beebe's report on his hapless voyage appears in the proceedings of the *Proteus* court of inquiry. Also see Beebe's correspondence with Consul Molloy, RG27, NARA. Beebe's "failure of all my efforts" is to Greely, 4 September, 1882, in Greely Relief Expeditions, RG45, NARA.

CHAPTER ELEVEN

For Pavy's continuing antipathy toward Greely, see M689, Roll 12, NARA, and his wife's articles in *North American Review*, March and April 1886. Brainard's "mutiny might have been declared" is his diary entry for 3 January, 1883, Brainard Papers, G200, NARA. For simultaneous events in Washington, see M689, Roll 12, NARA, which contains Hazen to Adjutant General, 10 November, 1882, asking that Lincoln detail "without delay" a commander for the relief expedition. Lincoln declined. Hazen writes again, 18 January, 1883, that "Lieutenant Garlington must reach Lady Franklin Bay as soon as possible." William T. Sherman's "We know enough already of the North Pole" is in 5 February, 1883, M689, Roll 12, NARA. Friendly advice to Hazen—"hold your tongue"—is in George W. Nichols to Hazen, 20 February, 1883, Archives, Museum of American History, Washington, D.C.

Some glimpses of Garlington's character—feisty, stern—I gathered from an interview with his grandson Henry Garlington in Savannah, Georgia, 15 April, 1999. Data on Garlington is in ACP Files, NARA. Telegrams between Hazen and Consul Molloy on renting the *Proteus* and preparing the *Yantic* are in RG27, NARA, as is the letter of instructions to Garlington.

## CHAPTER TWELVE

Greely's disgust with Pavy as naturalist is shown in his journal entries, Container 70, Greely Papers, LC, the same source for the report of Pavy's arrest. Also see Brainard's diary, 17 July, 1883, RG200, and Pavy's diary, M689, Roll 17, NARA. Greely's letter transmitting charges against Pavy is in RG27, NARA, as is Greely's order replacing the doctor with Lockwood as naturalist. For the vanishing plum pudding and Brainard's "general uprising," see Brainard's diary, 4 July, 1883, RG200, NARA.

## CHAPTERS THIRTEEN AND FOURTEEN

The information here is based chiefly on *Report of the Lady Franklin Bay Expedition 1883,* Government Printing Office (GPO), 1883, and *Argument of Linden Kent Before the Proteus Court of Inquiry,* GPO, 1883. Also see Frank Wildes's report from St. John's to Commodore J. G. Walker, 7 September, 1883, appendix to *Proteus* court of inquiry. Garlington's vow to do "all that can be done" is to Chief Signal Officer, June 1883, copy to Henrietta Greely, Greely Papers, LC.

## CHAPTER FIFTEEN

See Greely's journals for a detailed account of preparations for retreat. Pavy's and Sergeant Cross's scathing words are in their diaries, M689, rolls 11 and 12, NARA. Brainard writes that Greely "lost his head and presence of mind," 10 August, 1883, RG200, NARA. An example of Greely's ignoring advice from his former second in command is in Greely's journal, 13 August, 1883, Greely Papers, LC. The journal also portrays Greely as repeatedly frustrated by his engineer Cross's misbehavior. Brainard's note "Declaring the C.O. insane" and the near conspiracy to supplant Greely with Kislingbury are disclosed in Brainard's diary, 15 August, 1883, RG200, NARA. Also, his "statement of fact," 19 January, 1890, was inserted in his sanitized three-volume *Daily Journal 1881–1884.* For Brainard's own contemptuous view of his commander, see his diary entries for 19 and 21 August, 1883, RG200, NARA.

## CHAPTER SIXTEEN

For the *Yantic*'s erratic course, see *Proteus* court of inquiry proceedings and the log of the *Yantic* in the *New York Herald,* 21 September, 1883; Wildes to Chandler, 16 October, 1883, M147, Roll 121, NARA; Chandler to Wildes, 2 November, 1884; *Annual Report of the Chief Signal Officer,* GPO, 1884; and Wildes to Chandler, 21 November, 1884, Hazen Papers, Archives, Museum of American History, Washington, D.C. Lieutenant Colwell's account of the descent from Cape Sabine and the crossing of Melville Bay is in letters to his mother and sister, 29 June, 7 and 12 July, 7 August, and 12 September, 1883, in his grandson's possession. Brainard's remark "Greely seldom gets out of his bag" and an account of the expedition's retreat are in Brainard's diary, 1 September, 1883, RG200, NARA.

## CHAPTER SEVENTEEN

*Evening Mercury* of St. John's, 19 September, 1884, reports that Garlington had "never seen a floe." Caziarc's letters to Henrietta Greely, 15 and 21 September, are in Greely Papers, LC. Lincoln's and Chandler's decision against sending a relief expedition, "Greely's case by no means hopeless," is relayed in Captain Samuel Mills to Henrietta Greely, 20 September, 1883, Greely Papers, LC. Secretary Chandler's scolding letters to Frank Wildes, 2 November and 19 December, 1883, are in Secretary of the Navy, Letters Sent, M209, NARA. That Lincoln considered Garlington's effort "a disastrous failure" is in M6, Roll 88, NARA.

## CHAPTER EIGHTEEN

Greely's journal, and the diaries of Brainard and Kislingbury, form the basis for this chapter, recounting the final stages of the party's drift and with particular relevance to the commander's council on the floe.

## CHAPTER NINETEEN

The raw material for this chapter is mainly the *Proteus* court of inquiry proceedings, in which can be traced the tortuous path of the troublesome "supplemental instructions." The court's working pages are contained in M689, Roll 16, NARA. Beebe's suicide is reported in the *Evening Star*, Washington, D.C., 7 August, 1883. Chandler tells Lincoln, "Shall never cease to regret," on 5 March, 1885, Chandler Papers, LC.

## CHAPTER TWENTY

The principal sources for this chapter are Greely's journal, Greely Papers, LC, and his *Three Years*. Elison's account of his ordeal is at the Schuylkill County Historical Society, Pottsville, Pennsylvania.

## CHAPTER TWENTY-ONE

The relief board's hearings are in Arctic Relief Expedition, RG45, NARA. Also see *Annual Report of the Secretary of War*, GPO, Washington, D.C., 1883. Brainard wrote, "Twenty days more" in his diary on 22 March, 1884, RG200, NARA. Rice's "things too bad to contemplate" is in his diary, March 1884, M689, NARA. On the fate of Kislingbury's youngest boy following the guardian's suicide, see John M. Schofield Papers, boxes 50, 54, and 86, LC.

CHAPTER TWENTY-TWO

The achievements of other nations in the circumpolar plan are reported in William Barr's works. Garlington's "reputation at stake" and Lincoln's "can't see why" are dated, respectively, 27 February and 4 March, ACP Files, NARA. Schley's thoughts upon assumption of command are in his *The Rescue of Greely* (New York: Scribner's, 1885).

Henrietta Greely's efforts to secure help from St. John's whalers are described in her correspondence contained in Greely Papers, LC. The clearest indication of official opposition is found in Chandler to Chester Arthur ("it would not be wise to offer large rewards to private parties"), 17 March, 1884, Letters Sent by the Secretary of the Navy to the President and Executive Agencies, 1821–1886, M472, NARA. Also see G. W. Nesmith to Chandler, 26 March, 1884, Chandler Papers, New Hampshire Historical Society, Concord, New Hampshire, and Lockwood to Henrietta Greely, 9 and 11 April, 1884, Greely Papers, LC. A succinct account of the Schley relief operation is provided in "The Navy and Greely: The Rescue of the 1881–1884 Arctic Expeditions," by Lieutenant David G. Colwell, USNR, in *Naval Institute Proceedings*, January 1958. A most valuable portrayal of Schley and the relief effort is in Ensign Harlow's journal, June 1884, Naval Academy Museum, Annapolis.

CHAPTER TWENTY-THREE

For Private Henry's background, see the *Moberly Monitor*, undated clipping, Moberly, Missouri, and letter to *Army and Navy Register*, 6 September, 1884, from Seventh Cavalry officers, Fort Buford, Montana. Greely's 13 April, 1884, letter blaming Garlington for the party's plight was found by Commander Schley and came to light years later. It appears in an undated clipping from the *National Republican*, Washington, D.C., in Container 1, Greely Papers, LC. Greely's fast-deteriorating relations with Octave Pavy during these last weeks at Camp Clay are inferred from the doctor's letters to Greely, 25 and 27 April, 1884, RG27, NARA, and from Greely's journal entries for this period, Greely Papers, LC.

CHAPTER TWENTY-FOUR

Ensign Harlow's diary is a fascinating source. At Camp Clay, Henry's "starvation looks us in the face" is on a postcard he sent to his former commanding officer, 9 May, 1884, disclosed by Captain George F. Price to Henrietta Greely, 18 August, 1884, Greely Papers, LC. Also note letters dated 27 September to Price from Jay Stone, acting chief clerk, War Department, and Stone to Price, 2 October, 1884, RG27, NARA. The circulated certificate to Pavy's "devoted zeal and professional skill" is in RG27, NARA. Kislingbury's signature heads the list, which also includes Brainard's. Greely's last letter to his wife, written in diary form, 26 to 30 May, 1884, is in Museum of American History, Archives, Washington, D.C.

CHAPTER TWENTY-FIVE

Henry's diary is in RG27, NARA, as is Greely's order to shoot Henry, a copy of which appears, with meager additional detail on the soldier's execution, in M689, Roll 17, NARA. Julius Frederick's account is the most detailed, yet it also is vague. "We did not know who loaded the gun with a blank," was reported in the *New York Times,* 8 September, 1884. Brainard's differing version was published in the *Evening Star,* Washington, D.C., 13 October, 1935. Also see *Army and Navy Register,* 6 September, 1884. The mutilation of Kislingbury's body is described in *Rochester Post Express* and *New York Times,* 15 August, 1884. Greely's list of causes of death, with Henry's blacked out, is in RG27, NARA.

CHAPTER TWENTY-SIX

The first portion of this chapter is based mainly on Schley, *The Rescue,* and Harlow's journal at Annapolis. The ensign's narration is particularly illuminating. Also see Harlow's article "Greely at Cape Sabine: Notes by a member of the Relief Expedition," in *The Century Magazine.* Greely's own account of the rescue is in his official report and in *Three Years.* While silent at St. John's about Henry's execution and exultant over beating the British (recorded in *Army and Navy Register,* 18 July, 1884), Greely fired an immediate barb at Garlington, who had left "only 150 pounds of meat," forcing Greely to send a party to Cape Isabella, "resulting in Elison's frozen limbs."

CHAPTER TWENTY-SEVEN

Schley's telegram to Chandler, 17 July, 1884, "urgently" suggesting metal caskets for the dead, is in Greely Relief Expeditions, RG45, NARA. "Six bodies had been cut" is in Schley, *The Rescue.* Schley is also the source for Greely's "officially" blaming starvation for Henry's death. Preparations for disposal of the dead are detailed in M689, Roll 17, NARA. "Sooner they are in the ground the better" is in Hancock to Captain Louis Trudo, Delphi, Indiana, 11 August, 1884, M689, NARA. For Brooklyn health authorities' complaint of having been kept ignorant of the true cause of Henry's death, see their letter to Commanding Officer, Division of the Atlantic, Governor's Island, M689, Roll 17, NARA. Hazen's charge of a long-standing vendetta against him by the *New York Times* is in a letter to Greely dated 23 August, 1884, Greely Papers, LC.

CHAPTER TWENTY-EIGHT

The warning to Chandler of "trouble brewing" is in Gunnell to Chandler, 17 July, 1884, W. E. Chandler Papers, New Hampshire Historical Society. For Greely's "I should have killed Henry" and "no knowledge of cannibalism," see the interview he granted "in Mrs. Greely's presence," *New Hampshire Traveler,* 13 August, 1884. The assertion that there was no need for a court of inquiry on Henry's execution is in R. C. Drum, Adjutant General, to Greely, 14 November, Greely Papers, LC. For the discovery of Schneider diary fragments along the riverbank, see RG27, NARA. Advice that Greely not champion Hazen's cause is in Nesmith to Henrietta Greely, 2 September, 1884, Greely Papers, LC.

## CHAPTER TWENTY-NINE

Brainard concedes that his version of Pavy's death differs from that of other survivors in Brainard to Greely, 22 October, 1885, Greely Papers, LC. Greely's willingness to ask for an inquiry into Pavy's death is in Greely to Hazen, 16 October, 1885. Greely's belief that Pavy "failed in his duty . . . his end ignoble" is in Container 72, Greely Papers, LC. Mme. Pavy's defense of her husband's memory is in *North American Review,* March and April 1886. For Maurice Connell's vague threats, and tactics to ensure his silence, see Connell to Greely, 27 June and 8 July, 1886, and Hazen to Greely, 31 July 1886, Greely Papers, LC.

That Greely "would not hesitate to blacken Fred's name" is in William H. Kislingbury to Major General John Schofield, 25 February, 1887, Schofield Papers, LC. A typical assessment of Greely's concern for the kin of men he had led and lost is in his 11 December, 1884, letter relating to the Eskimos' families, Greely Papers, LC. Brainard's intriguing 19 January, 1890, "statement of fact" is tucked inside his journal, RG27, NARA. Henry Howgate's "keep Ida's name on the map" is in Howgate to Greely, 9 October, 1884, Greely Papers, LC. His request for a loan from Greely also mentioned a Civil War comrade in arms named Cole, "acting for me through old and present family feelings." Howgate asked Greely what the chances were of recovering government money for Cole, who had invested in the purchase of pemmican for the Lady Franklin Bay Expedition. Little did Howgate know that when visited by Pinkerton detectives hunting him, Cole offered to betray Howgate's whereabouts for $15,000. The agents declined. See Howgate, ACP Files, NARA.

Greely defended his expedition in response to its being called "a tragedy" by Commander Fitzhugh Green, *New York Times,* 30 December, 1923. Stefansson's reference to Greely's poor eyesight and "breaking the severest tabu" is in his introduction to Alden Todd's *Abandoned: The Story of the Greely Arctic Expedition, 1881–1884* (New York: McGraw-Hill, 1961). Greely was instrumental in the naming of Bedford Pim Island as a favor to the veteran British naval officer who had befriended him in London. See Pim to Greely, 19 June, 1888, Greely Papers, LC. For MacMillan's discovery of skulls at a littered Fort Conger, see Miriam MacMillan, *Green Seas and White Ice* (New York: Dodd, Mead, 1948). John Goodsell stated in an unpublished memoir located at the Mercersburg County Historical Society, Mercersburg, Pennsylvania, "We were never able to solve the mystery." The Arctic as "most unforgiving" is stated in "The Last Resort: Cannibalism in the Arctic," by Anne Keenleyside, *Explorers Journal* 72, 1995.

# BIBLIOGRAPHY

Allen, Everett S. *Arctic Odyssey: The Life of Admiral Donald B. MacMillan.* New York: Dodd, Mead, 1962.

*Annual Report of the Secretary of War, 1883.* Washington, D.C.: Government Printing Office.

*Annual Report of the Chief Signal Officer, 1883.* Washington, D.C.: Government Printing Office.

Anonymous (notes from a member of the relief expedition). "Greely at Cape Sabine." *Century Magazine,* May 1885.

Barr, William. "The Expedition of the First International Polar Year, 1882–83." Technical Paper no. 29. Arctic Institute of North America, Calgary, Alberta, Canada, 1985.

———. "Geographical Aspects of the First International Polar Year 1882–1883." *Annals of the Association of American Geographers* 73, no. 4 (1984).

Berton, Pierre. *The Arctic Grail.* Toronto: McClelland and Stuart, 1986.

Bixby, William. *Track of the Bear.* New York: D. McKay, 1965.

Bruno, J. C. D., and T. O. Rockwell. "The Greely Commemorative Expedition." *Explorer's Journal* 62(2): 50–53.

Greely, Adolphus W. *Reminiscences of Adventures and Service.* New York: Scribner's, 1912.

———. *Report of the United States Expedition to Lady Franklin Bay, Grinnell Land.* House Miscellaneous Documents, 1st Session, 49th Congress, 1885–86, vol. 22 (in two parts). Washington, DC: Government Printing Office, 1889.

———. *Three Years of Arctic Service.* New York: Scribner's, 1912.

Guttridge, Leonard F. *Icebound: The* Jeannette *Expedition's Quest for the North Pole.* Annapolis: Naval Institute Press, 1986.

Herbert, Wally. *Noose of Laurels: The Race to the North Pole.* New York: MacMillan, 1989.

James, Bessie Rowland, ed. *Six Came Back: The Arctic Adventure of David L. Brainard.* New York: Bobbs-Merrill, 1940.

Keenleyside, Anne, Ph.D. "The Last Resort: Cannibalism in the Arctic." *The Explorers Journal* 72(4), 1995.

Keenleyside, Anne, Ph.D., Margaret Bertulli, and Henry C. Fricke. "The Final Days of the Franklin Expedition: New Skeletal Evidence." *ARCTIC: Journal of the Arctic Institute of North America* 50, no. 1, March 1997.

Kroeker, Marvin E. *Great Plains Command: William B. Hazen in the Frontier West,* 1st ed. Norman, OK: University of Oklahoma Press, 1976.

Lanman, Charles. *Farthest North; or The Life and Explorations of Lieutenant James B. Lockwood of the Greely Arctic Expedition.* New York: D. Appleton & Co., 1889.

Mackey, Thomas J. *The Hazen Court Martial.* New York: D. Van Nostrum, 1885.

MacMillan, Miriam. *Green Seas and White Ice.* New York: Dodd, Mead, 1948.

*Proceedings of the Proteus Court of Inquiry on the Relief Expedition of 1883.* Washington, DC: Government Printing Office, 1883.

Rockwell, T. "The Ellesmere Island Arctic Expedition," *Fram. Journal of Polar Studies* 1(2): 447–460.

Sargent, John Osborne. *Major-General Hazen, on His Post of Duty in the Great American Desert, 1811–1891.* New York: G. P. Putnam's Sons, 1874.

Schley, Winfield S. *Report of Winfield S. Schley, Commander, Greely Relief Expedition of 1884.* Washington, DC: Government Printing Office, 1887.

Schley, Winfield S., and J. R. Soley. *The Rescue of Greely.* New York: Scribner's, 1885.

Todd, Alden L. *Abandoned: The Story of the Greely Arctic Expedition, 1881–1884.* New York: McGraw-Hill, 1961.

Tyson, George. *Cruise of the* Florence. Edited by Captain Henry Howgate. Washington, DC: J. J. Chapman, 1879.

# INDEX